Beer

A HISTORY OF BREWING
IN CHICAGO

Bob Skilnik

BARRICADE
BOOKS

Published by Barricade Books Inc.
185 Bridge Plaza North
Suite 308-A
Fort Lee, NJ 07024

www.barricadebooks.com

Library of Congress Cataloging-in-Publication Data
A copy of this title's Library of Congress Cataloging-in-Publication
Data is available on request from the Library of Congress.

ISBN 1-56980-312-9

First Printing

Designed by India Amos, Neuwirth & Associates, Inc.
Manufactured in the United States of America

Contents

Acknowledgments

RESEARCH FOR THIS book was facilitated by the staff of many Chicago institutions, including the Chicago Historical Society, the Newberry Library, the John Crerar and Regenstein Libraries at the University of Chicago, and the Harold Washington Library in Chicago. Thanks also goes to Beverly Watkins of the National Archives–Great Lakes Region in Chicago; Glenn E. Humphreys, Special Collections Librarian at the Sulzer Regional Library; Tim Waters, formerly at the Chicago Museum of Science and Industry; Bill Siebel, former chairman and CEO of the Siebel Institute of Technology; and Stan Galloway of the *American Breweriana Association* in Pueblo, Colorado.

George G. Weiss, step-grandson of Gottfried Brewery owner John H. Weiss; William Fox II, son of advertising director Kenneth Fox of Fox DeLuxe; and Edwin A. Seipp Jr., great-grandson of the innovative advertiser, promoter, and brewer Conrad Seipp were all kind enough to answer my written queries. Valerie Turness, a descendant of brewer Michael Diversy, helped solve the mystery of the spelling of "Diversey" versus "Diversy," a little thing perhaps, but useful in clearing up what was an annoying inconsistency.

A number of pictures of local breweries from the early 1950s and used in this book was provided by "Uncle" Ernie Oest for inclusion. Ernie passed away before completion of this book, but his contribution of pictures of Chicago's breweries and my gratitude will live on.

Herman and Jan Berghoff, owners of the now closed Berghoff Restaurant, a Chicago institution on West Adams, were kind enough to provide time from their busy schedules for background information on the family's relationship to beer and brewing in Chicago.

I'm also grateful to Don Bull, coauthor of *American Breweries,* © 1984, Bullworks, P.O. Box 596, Wirtz, VA 24184, for permission to excerpt the list of Chicago's breweries in the appendix of this book. His list of breweries throughout the United States is an invaluable research tool for any brewery historian. Don has a number of books about collectibles and beer-related items for sale and would be happy to hear from you.

Thanks also to members of the Chicago Beer Society whose collective knowledge and experience in the craft beer movement yielded an enormous wealth of information.

I'm honored that August Uihlein Pabst, former executive vice president at the Pabst Brewing Company, could make the time available to round out the chapters that deal with the end of the Jos. Schlitz Brewing Company.

Other contributors are Jack and Jim Glunz; Mac Harvey; Bob Bindley of Louis Glunz Beer, Incorporated, in Lincolnwood, Illinois; and Jerry Glunz. Earle Johnson of Quenchers Saloon has also been a big help and supporter of my never-ending Chicago beer history efforts.

Once again, if I've missed someone, please forgive. Without the help of everybody listed, this book might have been just so many words. All of them have my deep gratitude.

Lastly is my special thanks to my remarkable and understanding wife Daria, who never blinked an eye when I said I was going to write a book about the history of beer and brewing in Chicago. Convincing her, however, that I was *really* working, as I sat starting at a blank screen with a locally brewed beer at my side, took some determined effort. I also have to thank my two boys, Nikolas and Francis, who served as faithful beer runners throughout the editing process of this book. I needed it.

Preface

WHY BREWERIES? WHY bother writing about this long forgotten local industry?

As a kid growing up in the predominately Irish neighborhood of
Bridgeport during the 1950s and early '60s, there were two distinctive
smells I'll always remember, the putrid fumes of the nearby Chicago
Stockyards and the balancing sweet malt aroma from our two neighborhood breweries. Living just blocks away from both industries, the
aroma of the breweries was, understandably, more appealing.

In my youth, little did I know that one neighborhood brewery
had once belonged to gangster Johnny Torrio, later passed on to the
control of Al Capone and, eventually, Frank Nitti. During national
prohibition, the later renamed Canadian Ace Brewery was known
as the Manhattan Brewing Company, supplying much of the thirsty
South Side with illegal brew.

But now they're gone. A few years ago, I tried to find some information about the old Chicago brewing industry, but most books of local
history were useless. It was almost as though the industry had never
existed. That is why this book was written.

This study attempts to present a general history of Chicago breweries
and a number of local events dealing with beer and brewing from 1833,
when William Haas and Konrad Sulzer established a small brewery for
a grateful population of almost two hundred, to contemporary times,
where only one lone Chicago brewery exists. No other work details
the history or influence of the once great Chicago brewing industry
or the effects that the brewery owners, products and policies had on
the inhabitants and events of the city. It is not meant to be an exhaus-
tive study, but does attempt to consolidate much of what is known of
Chicago's breweries into one colorful and easily readable work.

Research for this book was often challenging, limited by the lack of
concise, readily available information for an industry that once was
an important element of the city. That local historians have chosen to

neglect the political, economic, cultural and social importance of the Chicago brewing industry or to document the positive and negative contributions of local brewery owners is what I found most amazing during my research for this book. Upon completion of this work, I'm still baffled by this historical oversight.

For our purposes, I have defined the territorial boundaries of old Chicago as they exist today. In 1889, the townships of Hyde Park, Jefferson, Lake and Lake View were swallowed up by Chicago, tripling the size of the city. This land grab and earlier expansions and annexations makes the argument of what really was the true territory of Chicago, as discussed in *BEER: A History of Brewing in Chicago*, a nagging, but probably valid one. By using the contemporary city borders, I am following the lead of brewing industry researchers, Donald Bull, Manfred Friedrich and Robert Gottschalk, co-authors of *American Breweries*, © Bullworks, 1984. An excerpt from their detailed list of past and present American breweries serves as the appendix of Chicago breweries in this book.

The brewers of Chicago were political figures, entrepreneurs, philanthropists, millionaires, socialites and scoundrels. By the early 1890s, the Americanized second and third generation of brewing families had been absorbed into the elite social strata of the city. The marriage of Adeline Huck, daughter of brewery owner and grain trader Louis Huck, to Marshall Field, Jr., before the turn of the century, was one of social significance. The brewing community was no longer perceived as a rough and tumble group of mostly German immigrants, but one of wealth and power. Early editions of Chicago social registers list the names of brewers Huck, Seipp, Wacker, Bemis and others, included with the more familiar names of renowned Chicago families such as McCormick, Field, Swift and Pullman. However, the turbulent years of World War I, with questions of the allegiance of the brewers to the Stars and Stripes and almost four years of the local brewing fraternity willingly subverting the goals of national prohibition, wiped out much of the prestige and respect the pioneer brewing families had striven so hard to achieve.

Prior to national prohibition, the industry's relationship to Chicago's fiscal well being was unparalleled, with an economic influence that far exceeded that of other, more notable local concerns. Chicago breweries, with their many affiliated saloon outlets, contributed over 25% to the city of Chicago's yearly revenue in the form of brewery permit and saloon licensing fees. For years, most local politicians had understood this fiscal dependency and had acted accordingly, side stepping the festering issue of saloon reform. The loss of this annual windfall during the first years of Prohibition had even prompted a desperate Chicago City Council to petition Congress in 1923 to remove the congressional ban on light beers and wines, noting in the petition that the city had already lost $32,000,000 of anticipated revenue in the first four years of national prohibition. Not only did city revenues suffer as a consequence of the *Noble Experiment*, but so did the many local peripheral trades such as the malt, cooper and architectural firms that had long enjoyed the encompassing success of the brewing industry. It's almost understandable that so many brewery owners and once law-abiding citizens were willing to ignore the restrictions of the Eighteenth Amendment and the Volstead Act; for some, it was a matter of economic survival.

With many of the restrictions of national prohibition lifted on the brewing industry in April 1933, the question remains. Why did the local brewing industry later fail? As we shall see, Chicago was an ideal centralized location for the production and national distribution of beer. Blessed with an abundance of water from Lake Michigan and positioned as the center of the grain industry and railroad commerce, Chicago brewers used only two of these assets to further their industry. The local brewing industry, as a whole, never demonstrated the aggressive initiative of smaller sized Milwaukee and St. Louis in the exportation of their products. Milwaukee brewer Val Blatz had already established a downtown depot in Chicago *before* the Civil War, decades before Chicago's Golden Era of brewing during the 1880s. In the overly saturated, smaller sized markets of Milwaukee and St. Louis, exportation of surplus beer meant continued sales; more importantly, it meant survival. In time, export sales would mean regional and, later, national domination of the beer market.

Content in what had appeared to be a large and ever growing market in Chicago, the belated efforts of a minority of smaller local breweries in shipping to outside markets before the twentieth century were often hampered by the earlier inroads made by the far sighted Schlitz, Miller, Phil Best (later Pabst) and Anheuser-Busch concerns. As the out of town brewers were initially forced to expand their businesses beyond their own small markets, the Chicago brewers stood passively by as the aggressive *shipping brewers* literally poured their products into the huge Chicago market. Weakened by the costs of modernization, ill conceived and poorly managed foreign buyouts by English investors, increased local competition, market saturation and the resultant price wars of the 1890s, Chicago's brewing industry proved no match for the successful shipping brewers whose markets increased with the demise of every short sighted, family operated neighborhood brewery.

National prohibition obviously played a major role in fostering the end of the local industry. With the advent of Repeal, the Chicago brewers found themselves facing many of the same problems they had contended with during the pre-Prohibition era. But with the end of Prohibition, there were additional obstacles which furthered the industry's demise. Brand loyalty had become non existent in Chicago; to the average beer drinker, whether brewed as a non alcoholic near beer and later *needled* with alcohol to bring up its strength or a clandestinely brewed full strength drink, beer had simply become *beer* during national prohibition.

Plants idled for almost fourteen years were deemed too expensive to modernize for many of the families that owned the smaller neighborhood breweries. Of the thirty-seven Chicago breweries that closed with the advent of Prohibition or were forced to close in the succeeding years, only twenty-four went back into production when the manufacture of beer was again legalized in 1933. Of these surviving breweries, most were now controlled by new owners. Those families that had abandoned the industry, soon distanced themselves and succeeding generations from the stigma of brewery ownership. But attempts by local brewers to lower cost, maintain a reasonable profit margin and secure their place in the Chicago market were often met with poorly formulated cost cutting measures and a resultant falling off in product quality. The shipping brewers were slowly winning the generations-long battle for Chicago market supremacy. In the immediate years after World War II, it would become apparent that the Chicago brewing industry was destined to fail.

What's now left behind is a nationwide brewing oligarchy, run by what many believe to be faceless corporations, but that is a simplistic argument. Behind the corporate logos, the saturation advertising and the successes and failures demonstrated at yearly stockholder meetings are real men and women who make the decisions that ultimately influence what brand of beer sits in your refrigerator today.

And in a great beer-drinking city like Chicago, the battle continues.

Prozit!

⚹ PART I ⚹

In the Beginning

Chicago's Pioneer Breweries, 1833–1860

EARLY CHICAGO

Prior to 1833, Chicago's sparse population of little more than two hundred could legally quench their thirst at either Elijah Wentworth's Wolf Point Tavern or Samuel Millers' Fork's Tavern. The two primitive establishments were located in the immediate vicinity of Fort Dearborn at the north/south branch of the Chicago River. The owners held the first liquor licenses issued by the young county of Cook. For their enjoyment of their appreciative customers, the innkeepers brewed their own primitive style of ale on-site to supplement the rare shipment of drinkable beer from the East. It sold for 6¼ cents a pint.[1]

Into this dreary environment in 1833 arrived one Charles Butler, a New York financier and successful Wall Street lawyer. Butler had been in communication for the last year with a General Scott who had recently toured the virgin territory west of Lake Michigan after the Black Hawk War. Scott was impressed with the area and gave the opinion that Chicago would one day be an important town.[2] Butler soon made arrangements to visit the area, often referred to by New Yorkers rather encompassingly as "the West," looking for investment possibilities. After an arduous journey from Buffalo, New York, through Detroit, South Bend, and the dense forests of Michigan City, Indiana, Butler later wrote of his first impressions of Chicago, as he approached the area from the pristine sand dunes of the southeastern region:

> I approached Chicago in the afternoon of a beautiful day, the 2nd of August, (1833); the sun setting in a cloudless sky. On my left lay the prairie, bounded only by the distant horizon like a vast expanse of ocean; on my right, in the summer

stillness, lay Lake Michigan. I had never seen anything more beautiful or captivating in nature. There was an entire absence of animal life, nothing visible in the way of human habitation or to indicate the presence of man, and yet it was a scene full of life. . . . I approached Chicago in these closing hours of day, "So calm, so clear, so bright"—and this was the realization of the objective point of my journey.[3]

But after being momentarily swept up in the emotion of the moment, Butler took a harder view of Chicago as he drew closer: "A small settlement, a few hundred people all told, who had come together mostly within the last year or two. The houses, with one or two exceptions, were of the cheapest and most primitive character for human habitation."[4]

After making several discouraging personal tours of the area around the fork of the Chicago River and to the immediate north, Butler inexplicably decided to plunge $100,000 of his family funds into speculative Chicago real estate. He was especially encouraged by Chicago's location on Lake Michigan and its potential as an eventual trading center. The recent release by Congress of federal funds for the dredging of the city's shallow natural harbor, led by a young engineer named Jefferson Davis, helped enhance Butler's decision. Somewhat comfortable with his investment decision but anxious to return to his financial activities in New York, he contacted his brother-in-law, William B. Ogden, to oversee the results of his purchase, and he left Chicago.

Ogden eventually arrived in Chicago in 1835 to check on Butler's land investments. Unlike Butler, Ogden was immediately appalled at what he saw, since the purchased land consisted mostly of swamp and bog. Butler had chosen Ogden because of his experiences in the investment and money houses back home and his past savvy handling of real estate transactions on the East Coast. After his initial shock at conditions in Chicago, Ogden wrote Butler of his concern for the real estate investment, preparing him for the eventuality of a huge loss. After further consultation with Butler by mail and soliciting his approval, Ogden moved quickly, platting the land into saleable lots and commissioning the sale of all the remaining land he now managed. With only one-third of his holdings auctioned off, he quickly regained the $100,000 purchase price, picked up an additional return of $150,000, and stopped the auction. Chicago, Ogden finally determined, had investment potential.[5]

HAAS AND SULZER

In 1833, soon after Butler had made his fateful land purchase, Germanic immigrants William Haas and Konrad (Andrew) Sulzer arrived in Chicago from Watertown, New York, with $3,000, a load of malt, 150 barrels of ale, and all the necessary equipment for construction of Chicago's first full-scale commercial brewery.[6]

During these early years, living conditions in Chicago were exceedingly primitive; the town was inhabited by soldiers, traders, and adventurers. The land within easy walking distance of Fort Dearborn was surrounded by the wigwams of Indian tribes whose braves still presented a threat to the intruding settlers. Just twenty-one years earlier, most of the garrison at Fort Dearborn had been wiped out by an Indian attack, the massacre taking place in the area known today as 18th Street and Lake Michigan. The fort was eventually rebuilt, and settlers warily arrived to stake their claims on land near the new fort. Why Haas and Sulzer chose Chicago for the site of their endeavor is unknown. Any number of towns or cities in the more civilized eastern portion of the country would certainly have been more attractive, less dangerous, and, quite possibly, more profitable for men of a less adventurous bent. But, like Charles Butler, the brewers decided to invest their time and money in this unknown but growing market.[7]

They soon erected a small brewery on a 100 x 200 foot lot purchased from the land holdings of Butler.[8] The Haas & Sulzer Brewery was an immediate success. First year production was approximately 600 barrels (thirty-one gallons per barrel) of ale shared among the town's population of two hundred. As small as the brewery's output might appear today, it was a determined brewer who could annually produce three to four hundred barrels of beer during the 1830s.

A description of early brewing details the difficult work involved in the process:

> The work required for the production of one brew of beer was exceedingly protracted and difficult. The hauling, dipping, pumping, breaking, stirring and boiling were tiresome work for the laborers, indeed, requiring 15 to 17 working hours every day, and making the brewer's occupation one of hard toil and almost unbearable labor.[9]

Brew kettles of six to eight barrels were common, limiting production. With primitive and nonmechanized equipment, anything could go wrong. There were artesian wells and cellars to be dug and malt to be ground by hand. Fires to boil the sweet wort could often be unpredictable, sometimes destroying the small plants. Even after surmounting these considerable challenges, the fermentation could go bad, leaving the brewer with undrinkable stock. It was no coincidence that most early breweries in Chicago were also manufacturers of malt vinegar, often an indication of a batch of beer having gone bad.

WILLIAM OGDEN, BREWER

For Haas and Sulzer, skill, determination, and a little luck paid off. Three years after start-up, with the business firmly established and operating at peak capacity, Sulzer sold his profitable brewery interest to William Ogden. As a new co-owner with Haas, Ogden helped finance the erection of a larger structure at Pine (now north Michigan Avenue) and Chicago Avenue to house a new brewery capable of keeping up with the increased demand for their ale. Continued importation of ale from the East Coast had become prohibitive in cost, allowing the brewers to enjoy a captive, noncompetitive market for their products. As the only full-scale brewery in Chicago, the Haas & Sulzer Brewery thrived and continued to expand.[10]

After selling his stake in the brewery to Ogden, Sulzer remained in Chicago. He purchased one hundred acres of property in the area now known as Lakeview, in the vicinity of Clark and Montrose (formerly known as Sulzer Road) from the ever-obliging Ogden. The land was considered marsh, but Sulzer was successful here, making a living as a gentleman farmer and renowned local floriculturist.[11]

WILLIAM LILL

In 1839, William Lill, an English immigrant, bought out part of the brewery interest from Haas who later moved to Austin, Texas. Although Ogden had no brewing experience, he did take firm control of the brewery's financial matters. An example can be found in a letter dated October 12, 1839, from Ogden to one Alex Logan:

Sir:

I learn from Mr. Haas that you owe the firm of Wm. Haas & Co., composed of Mr. Haas and myself about $107 + interest for which we hold note in our book . . . must have money . . . otherwise we shall have to send the demand to a lawyer for collection.[12]

During the mid-1830s, the financial position of many small businesses in the Chicago area had changed for the worse. Wild speculation on land made poor men millionaires overnight; unforeseen events weeks later could bring them economic ruin. The financial situation of the renamed brewery firm of Wm. Haas & Company was no different than that of most of the other few small businesses in the area. In an attempt to shore up the financial stability of the brewery, Ogden made a careful study of the company's accounts receivable. Although his correspondence during the time indicates his grudging acceptance of write-offs of many of the firm's delinquent smaller accounts, as he wrote to one of his agents, he did his best to doggedly pursue whatever due funds he could:

By the Bye what has become of Haas & Co. judgment against E. D. Perry left with you, can anything be got upon it.[13]

Ogden also assumed responsibility for procuring supplies for the brewery, including hops for future beer production:

I want none other than a perfectly certain article if after I get them here I should find they are mostly bad from any cause, I could not replenish my stock through the winter my brewery would necessarily stop.[14]

With Ogden's tight control over accounts receivable and the acquisition of quality supplies for production, the brewery successfully weathered the financial storms of its early operation.

LILL & DIVERSEY

Michael Diversey, an immigrant from Alsace-Lorraine who arrived in Chicago in 1832, helped operate a dairy out of the Haas brewery. This arrangement was quite common in these early years, with both operations sharing the use of valuable stored ice for their products. The dairy operation supplemented income for the brewery during the non-brewing summer season, usually April through October. Diversey eventually bought out Ogden's interest in the brewery around 1841. The brewery became known, appropriately, as the Lill & Diversey, Haas having severed all ties to the operation. Ogden, first mayor of Chicago in 1837 and entrepreneurial genius, would go on to lead the building of the Illinois & Michigan Canal, persuade family friend Cyrus McCormick to build his farm machinery plant in Chicago, and organize the construction of a sprawling railroad system in and out of Chicago.[15]

In 1854, after dabbling in the distillation of pure and cologne spirits, another example of spoiled beer being put to good use, Lill and Diversey started advertising as brewers of ale and porter. Sales of their flag-ship brew, Lill's Cream Ale, were so good that by 1857, the partners had reinvested the sizable amount of over $250,000 in their brewery.[16] The Lill & Diversey Brewery, sometimes known as The Chicago Brewery, was now considered the largest brewery west of the Atlantic seaboard. Renovated and enlarged in 1866, their plant was a formidable structure, four stories tall with an imposing tower soaring an additional three stories above the main structure. The brewery now covered two acres and seasonally employed fifty to seventy-five men. Located on the southeast corner of Pine (Michigan Avenue) and Chicago Avenues, it would overshadow the nearby Water Tower and its pumping station, built a year later.[17]

CHARITABLE CONTRIBUTIONS

Michael Diversey took his newly acquired wealth from the brewery's operation and shared much of it with the German community of Chicago. He helped establish a German school in the so-called "Dutch Settlement" on the North Side, the Catholic churches St. Joseph and St. Peter in 1846, St. Michael in 1852, and the German daily newspaper,

Der Nationaldemokrat. With his partner Lill, he donated five acres of land to the McCormick Theological Seminary, a fact that is interestingly ignored in the history of the institution on its Web site. Their land grant would account for one-fourth of the seminary's total twenty acres at the intersections of Halsted, Lincoln, and Fullerton Avenues. In addition to his many charitable works, Diversey also held the office of alderman in the predominately German Ward Six in 1844.[18]

COMPETING CHICAGO BREWERIES

Following the success of Lill and Diversey, numerous smaller breweries were established in Chicago, including the James Carney Brewery on South Water Street in 1840, and Jacob Gauch's Brewery, located on Indiana Street in 1845. Peter Schuettler, son-in-law of brewer Jacob Gauch, perhaps disillusioned with his sputtering career as an apprentice brewer, placed a notice in the *Chicago Democrat* of August 13, 1845, offering his share of the brewery for sale and giving notice of the dissolution of his partnership with Gauch. Schuettler used the proceeds of the sale to become a premier manufacturer of covered wagons for the United States Army, built for the military's later exploration and expansion to the far Western territories. He was also quite successful providing brewers with horse-drawn wagons for local beer deliveries. Chicago folklore talks of his ghost still making occasional appearances at his former home at Aberdeen and Adams. Eyewitnesses claim that Schuettler's spirit seems to make a futile search for something in the rooms and corridors of the still-standing building, indicating perhaps, that in heaven, there really is no beer.[19]

Some breweries, such as the Reiser & Portmann Brewery or the John B. Miller Brewery, shut down within a year or two of start-up. A number of local breweries merged or reorganized, many for the better, such as the rapidly expanding Conrad Seipp Brewery.[20]

Enterprising individuals began to bottle beer during this expansive period, including Michael Keeley, who bottled ale and porter. This was not a common practice as beer was normally served as a draft product. For Keeley, the bottling business would prove profitable. He would go on to become a successful brewer in later years.

The demand for beer in early Chicago proved insatiable. On January 1, 1857, an annual business report in the *Democratic Press* showed a total production of beer and ale in Chicago of 16,270 barrels for 1856. Total value of the breweries was estimated at $130,160, the local industry employing thirty-three workers. A score of smaller, unrecorded breweries surely added to these figures.

LAGER BEER

The most significant new brewery established during this pioneering period of the Chicago brewing industry was the John A. Huck Brewery, the first true *Lager Bier* brewery in Chicago. Founded in 1847 by John Huck and John Schneider, the operation was guided, in part, by William Ogden, who sold the land for the brewery to the partners and who, with his experience as a former brewery owner, operated as a silent partner. For Ogden, whose presence and influence weaves in and out of the early years of the brewing industry in Chicago, it appears that malt was in his blood. Schneider eventually sold out his position to Huck in 1850 and moved on to seek his fortune in California.[21]

Lager beer differed from the more familiar ale. It was brewed from a slower acting, bottom-fermenting yeast rather from the top-fermenting ale yeast. For optimum quality and drinkability, it was necessary to store the beer in cool underground caverns for drinking in the spring and summer. Ale, on the other hand, fermented out in a warmer environment in as little as one week, ready for enjoyment.

Initial reactions by American-born residents to the German-styled lager beer were unenthusiastic. To these so-called "nativists," many with a distrust and suspicion of anything foreign, ale seemed to represent the status quo, reflecting the waning influence of the country's English background. This new lager beer represented the unfamiliar, the foreign—the Germans. The Germans, however, saw lager beer not only as a nostalgic taste of home but also as a social lubricant and a healthful "drink of moderation," to be enjoyed with friends and family. To this end, John Huck established the first beer garden in Chicago. Business was so good that he later expanded his operation in 1855 at the corner of Banks and North State Streets, the area later known as Ogden's Grove.[22] The German-language *Der Westen* would later describe a typical summer day at the picnic area:

"Sunshine, woodland green and woodland shade, the sound of

horns! on a Sunday afternoon, what more could a German heart possibly wish for?!—A good mug of beer!"[23]

CHICAGO'S FIRST BREWPUB

By all indications, the brewing of beer in Chicago during the city's early history was a reasonably profitable venture. Almost anyone who could handle the start-up cost of a small brewery and establish a local distribution network could count on an ever-increasing customer base. In 1858, John Hoerber had his combination saloon and boardinghouse elevated to accommodate new city building and street grade regulations. During the modification of his site, he built a small brewery underneath his establishment, which provided his patrons with freshly brewed beer. In doing so, Hoerber established Chicago's first brewpub, beating the now defunct Sieben's brewpub on West Ontario by about one hundred and thirty years.[24]

MILWAUKEE COMPETITION

In 1856, an additional 25,025 barrels of beer, mostly all from neighboring Milwaukee, were imported to Chicago to keep up with the growing demand of the city's more than 80,000 residents. A mere 1,319 barrels were delivered by Chicago breweries for export.[25] Milwaukee's fledgling breweries began to tentatively expand into the lucrative Chicago market during the early 1850s.

One boost to sales for Milwaukee brewers was the exceptionally hot summer of 1854, when Chicago's supply of lager beer was completely exhausted. Less than ten years after its local introduction by John Huck, lager beer now accounted for most of the beer consumed in the city. With summer being a nonbrewing season, the lager beer drinkers of Chicago, mostly German, were beginning to panic at the thought of no more beer until the resumption of brewing in the fall. Hospitable Milwaukee brewers were there to meet the needs of Chicago beer drinkers, exporting enough surplus beer to satisfy the thirst of thousands.[26]

This opportunity to ship excess beer from Milwaukee to Chicago, however, was more a demonstration of business practicality rather than goodwill. While Chicago's population continued to grow, Milwaukee's population growth was stunted by the recognition that Chicago was rapidly becoming the center of trade and commerce in the Midwest. Without the benefit of contemporary sales projections and a stagnating population growth, Milwaukee's brewers nonetheless continued to brew as much beer as they could and hoped for the best. The result often was surplus and perishable beer that was either processed into vinegar or unceremoniously dumped as a spoiled product. Chicago's beer predicament handed Milwaukee brewers the inspiration to look beyond their crowded market and create a fledgling beer export trade.

A year later, Milwaukee's attempts at exporting beer to the city were further aided by the completion of the Chicago & North Western Railway linking Chicago to Milwaukee. In 1857, Phil Best & Company (later Pabst) took advantage of this new passage and opened a shipping business on Randolph Street to further facilitate local sales of their products. The Val Blatz and Jos. Schlitz brewing companies would soon follow. With direct rail connections to the growing city and its proximity of less than ninety miles, Chicago would soon become the key market for Milwaukee brewers.

By 1860, there were thirty-two breweries in Chicago attempting to keep up with the growing population of almost 110,00 and its demand for fresh beer. In less than thirty years, Chicago was on its way to becoming a brewing Mecca.[27]

The Lager Beer Riot, 1855

Oh, lager beer!
It makes good cheer,
And proves the poor man's wealth;
It cools the body through and through,
And regulates the health.
—*Author unknown*

ECONOMIC DIFFICULTIES

During the early years of Chicago's development, the city's growth was tenuous at best. The Financial Panic of 1837 had ruined many investors who had bought land in the area at wildly inflated prices, only to find the speculative bottom fall out. A lack of hard currency, high inflation, and the introduction of President Jackson's *Specie Circular* had caused such a tightening of the money market that banks throughout the United States suspended business; Illinois was virtually bankrupt.

William B. Ogden, benefactor of early Chicago brewers and the first mayor of Chicago in 1837, used the money of a group of wealthy New York investors and his own calming influence and leadership to allay the fears of Chicago's early business men, many of whom were now saddled with crippling debt. Responding to his leadership, Chicago's business community began to recover, offering jobs to thousands of newly arrived Irish and German immigrants. After much personal lobbying, Ogden persuaded Cyrus McCormick to move his farm implement plant to Chicago in 1847. The Illinois & Michigan Canal, dug chiefly by Irish immigrants and opened in 1848, allowed passage from the Mississippi to Lake Michigan. During this period Congress freed up much needed federal funds for port improvements, greatly increasing Lake Michigan commerce to the city. Construction of the Galena & Chicago Union Railroad and the Illinois Central Railroad, along with a laying of track toward Michigan and Indiana, made Chicago, by the 1850s, the most important railroad hub in the Midwest.

THE RISE OF IMMIGRATION

In response to the abundance of jobs available in the growing city and the economic stability that these positions offered, a steady stream of foreigners was drawn to Chicago. By 1850, more than half of the Chicago population of 28,269 was foreign-born, the Irish comprising about 21 percent, the Germans, 17 percent.[1] The lot of the German immigrants in the New World was, for the most part, less trying than that of the Irish. Some of these new German immigrants were university educated or accomplished tradesmen, many having fled the 1848 Revolution in Germany. A later study of the educational and trade backgrounds of Chicago's early German immigrants confirms that almost 62 percent of these immigrants were either professionals, white-collar workers, or skilled craftsmen. These advantages are evidenced by the quickness in which they were able to establish themselves in the local brewing trade and successfully conduct their business in the English-speaking New World so soon after their arrival. [2]

Some of Chicago's early brewers and future members of brewing peripheral trades were included in this second wave of German immigration. Conrad Seipp had wisely left his homeland after serving as a Hessian guard during the 1848 Revolution. Arriving in Chicago soon thereafter, Seipp established himself as the owner of a successful downtown hotel. With the sale of his profitable business in 1851, he entered the brewing trade, and later became one of the most famous brewers in Chicago history. Robert Schmid, who studied architecture in Berlin, arrived in Chicago and began working with the famous architectural firm of Van Osdel and Olmsted before leaving for an independent position as a designer of breweries. As the malting trade developed in Chicago in response to the growing number of breweries and distilleries in the area, positions were quickly filled with German immigrants who had worked in the trade as malsters back home. The Irish, on the other hand, were less fortunate, forced to flee a feudal land system, crop failures, and near starvation with nothing more than the shirts on their backs.

During this early wave of immigration, the German brewers brought to Chicago the technical knowledge and appreciation for lager beer, the golden colored, highly carbonated, smooth-tasting brew, heightened in taste by the use of bottom-fermenting yeast and a long, cool secondary fermentation. Up until the mid-1840s, when one spoke of beer in the United States, one meant the sometimes dark, heavily hopped, low-carbonated malted liquor called ale which utilized a more primitive top-fermenting yeast. The knowledge and understanding of the secrets of lager brewing, along with the importation of the lager beer yeast to the United States in the early 1840s and the Germans' appreciation of its smooth, familiar taste, helps explain the preponderance of early Chicago breweries owned and operated by Germans for Germans.[3]

This new peculiarity of drink was initially shunned by much of the non-German population. Although ale was the only alternative malted beverage and a familiar drink of native-born Americans, whiskey was the drink of choice. The distillation of whiskey from corn or rye was an economic way of using up a bulky and perishable surplus harvest. In this liquid form, whiskey not only was used as a pleasant diversion but also as a portable trade bartering tool, especially in the rural areas where money, script, or bank notes were often unavailable.

THE RISE OF NATIVISM IN CHICAGO

The enjoyment of lager beer drinking, along with a host of other alien customs, habits, and tastes, eventually brought the Chicago German population into increasingly hostile situations with native-born Yankee Americans. Some of this anti-German sentiment was brought upon the newly arrived immigrants by the Germans themselves and their uncomplimentary criticisms of American customs and institutions. Ironically, after failing to bring about social and political changes during the 1848 German Revolution, these often well-educated expatriates clearly expected to bring about sweeping changes in the United States, a feat that they were unable to achieve in the *Vaterland*. One observer described their attitude in Eugen Seegers's *Chicago: The Wonder City*:

> On Sundays they were in the habit of marching through the streets of the city to the strains of blaring bands, preferring to parade past crowded churches on their way to the picnic

grounds, where they amused themselves to their hearts' content while guzzling enormous quantities of beer. In short, with more "courage and vigor" than diplomatic consideration, the German lifestyle was demonstrated in order to show the Yankees once and for all what it means to be a "free German of backbone" and then they enthusiastically assured each other that it was "just like in Germany." [4]

The Irish were also not immune to the scorn of the American-born citizenry. Looked upon as minions of the Pope, who preached that religious laws were above civil laws, the Irish papists also began to feel the hostile wrath of the American-born, so-called "nativists." Beginning in 1853, the *Chicago Tribune* editorial pages began a jingoistic attack on the Catholic (read: Irish) population of Chicago. Another popular publication, *The Literary Budget*, also allied itself with the views of the nativists. Soon, the xenophobic philosophy of nativism began to come together. In Chicago, the members of the Native American Party, sometimes known as the Know-Nothing Party, began forming a fragile coalition of abolitionists, nativists, and teetotalers, eventually connecting drunkenness with the German and Irish immigrants. [5]

LEVI BOONE

In 1855, the local Know-Nothing Party offered up former city physician Dr. Levi Boone as candidate for mayor of Chicago, along with a host of other politically like-minded candidates for key city offices. Much of Chicago's population, ironically including a goodly number of immigrant Germans, appeared to have found something they liked in Boone's candidacy, ignoring the party's knotholed political planks that sometimes ran contrary to their own interests and beliefs.

The dichotomy of the stormy political situation in Chicago during Boone's mayoral campaign can be seen in the inherent prejudices of many of Boone's supporters among the local population. The Germans, as a rule, were strict abolitionists. German Protestants from the northern states of the fatherland, however, were suspicious of southern Bavarian Catholics and the papist Irish, as were most nativists. The teetotalers were against the consumption of alcohol as practiced by the "whiskey sodden" Irish and "lager beer swilling" Germans. Leading this unbelievable coalition were the American-born nativists, fearful of a further onslaught of foreigners to Chicago. The intertwining philosophies of nativism and prohibition would continue to surface in Chicago politics for the next sixty-five years.

It was an early example of Chicago coalition politics at its worst. With hate and prejudice as the common denominator, the Know-Nothings were swept into office on March 6, 1855, giving Levi Boone the mandate he needed.

A week later, in his inaugural address, Boone unveiled his political program, including his opinion on saloon licensing and Sunday closings of saloons.

> I would therefore recommend the Council to refuse to license the sale of intoxicating liquors after the first day of April. . . . Should the Council differ with me upon the propriety of licensing, I would then advise another alternative, that is, to grant licenses to such persons as desire to take them at the maximum price fixed by the (city) charter, that is $300 per year. . . . I wish to bespeak your active cooperation, in closing, all places where liquor is sold upon the Sabbath day.

Refuting accusations made in the local press that he was a "Know Nothing candidate," he went on, nonetheless, with a theme central to the ideology of nativism: "I cannot be blind to the existence in our midst of a powerful politico-religious organization, all its members owning, and its chief officers bound under an oath of allegiance to the temporal, as well as the spiritual supremacy of a foreign despot."[6]

On March 26, the Committee on Licenses of the City Council set the annual liquor fee at $300, setting off a flood of petitions to the Council from local saloon keepers to reduce the licensing fee, but to no avail. Three weeks later, the Council adopted a resolution by the Grand Jury of the Recorder's Court to prevent the sale of liquor on Sunday, effectively closing down all saloons on the Sabbath.[7] Of the 675 saloons in the city, native-born Americans owned only fifty. The remainder of the watering holes were owned by German and Irish immigrants. The immigrant owners of the city saloons perceived that a large degree of these rulings by Boone and his City Council were directed against their establishments and not the American-owned, indicating to them that the crackdown was not necessarily a sign of reform or temperance.

Few of the affected saloon keepers were willing or able to pay the new high license fee. It should be noted, though, that many of the saloon keepers had been derelict in securing a license, even at the old $50 fee. A neutral observer would have had to admit that some sort of regulation of the saloons—and additional revenue enhancement for the growing city—were necessary. Gambling, prostitution, and public drunkenness were on the rise in the wild young city, especially in the unlicensed "dives." But the mostly foreign-born saloon keepers felt that the liquor license increase was actually part of a concerted campaign by local nativists to exclude them from the benefits of the American free enterprise system.[8]

The truth was probably a blending of the opinions of both sides. As a result of the strict licensing enforcement, some saloon proprietors soon went out of business. Others continued doing business, ignoring the new fee and the Sunday closing law.

Approximately eighty native-born American police officers were sworn in to ensure that all current liquor licenses were in order and that the rarely enforced, state-mandated Sunday closing "blue law" would be observed. In the weeks that followed the license fee increase, two hundred saloon keepers were arrested for nonpayment of the new licensing fee or for staying open on Sundays. The Germans were especially vocal about the arrests and hit hardest by the crackdown. They argued that the blue law was a violation of their "personal rights" and an infringement on the traditional Teutonic practice of enjoying beer on Sundays.

In the meantime, American bartenders at the more respectable establishments such as the Tremont House and the Young America, established watering holes of the Know-Nothing constituency, simply directed patrons to a side door for their familiar Sunday constitutional of American whiskey, shunning the foreign-tasting lager beer and the restrictions of the Sunday blue law.

The Germans were incensed at this double standard of enforcement and began to organize against it. German brewers and their patrons gathered at North Market Hall, pledged $5 each, and formed a society to combat the high liquor license fee. John Huck, owner of the John A. Huck Brewery, took on the leadership of the pro-beer society.[9]

The motives of Huck and the other Chicago brewers were pecuniary as well as of genuine indignation. The enforcement of the Sunday law had closed Huck's beer garden on its busy family day. In addition to the loss of Sunday sales, the brewers were also fearful of losing valuable retail outlets, legal or not, in which to sell their beer.

THE LAGER BEER RIOT

A test trial of thirty-three of the violators was scheduled for April 20, 1855, in the courtroom of Judge Henry Rucker. Shortly before the trial, both sides elected to choose one defendant for trial as a test case, the others to abide to whatever ruling the court chose. On that day, however, Judge Rucker was delayed out of town and sent word to reschedule the trial for the following day. The next morning, fortified with one more day of brooding and the offerings of the numerous lager establishments located up and down Randolph Street, a threatening number of Germans armed themselves and marched upon the Cook County Court House. So many supporters in the crowd accompanied the defendants into the small courtroom that Judge Rucker had to ask them to leave. Those that complied, angrily milled about the outside of the courthouse. Blocking the thoroughfare, some fifty police agents descended upon the unruly crowd. Confused and disorganized, the crowd began to fall back.

While the brewery and saloon interests were marshaling their forces, Mayor Boone swore in an additional force of one hundred fifty policemen. About three o' clock that afternoon, the Germans, accompanied by Irish saloon owners and their patrons, now numbering an unruly mob of six hundred, made their way down Clark Street to the bridge spanning the Chicago River. Swarming across, they met a solid phalanx of police forces. With a shout of "Pick out the stars!" from someone in the mob, shots were fired. One of the rioters discharged a shotgun at Officer George Hunt, hitting him in the left arm. With the perpetrator was Peter Martens, a German cigar maker who concurrently fired a revolver at Hunt. Attempting to flee, Martens was shot in the back by a deputized citizen. Martens died three days later of his wounds in a cell in County Jail. Hunt's injury was so severe that his arm had to be amputated the next day.

A young Alan Pinkerton was in the midst of the fray, dragging the wounded and whatever prisoners he could into the courthouse. With the combination of an Irish military group known as the Montgomery Guards, the All-American Chicago Light Guards, and a battery of two small cannon, the riot was finally suppressed. Sixty of the rioters were arrested.

Although only one death was officially recorded, it was said that a number of mysterious funerals in the German community resulted from the riot. A review of the list of those in custody attested to the fact that a majority of the rioters were indeed German. A lesser number of Irish names could be found as well. Of the sixty arrested, fourteen were brought to trial. Boone would continue the struggle, later vetoing an order by the nervous City Council to dismiss all suits against those violating the liquor license ordinance.

Eventually two perpetrators named Halleman and Farrell were convicted of rioting. Isolating two hapless Irishmen out of hundreds of German protesters indicated, perhaps, a fear by Boone and his administration of further German civil disturbances. The two men were granted new trials, but they were never held and they were eventually released.[10]

But the damage had been done. The intensity of the riot and the clumsy treatment of the brewers and the German and Irish saloon keepers and their patrons affected the fragile coalition of voters that Boone had patched together. The party's alliance with the drys added to its woes. With the voters' rejection of a state prohibition law in June 1855, and a mayoral term of only one short year, Boone's government became a lame duck administration and faded away after the next year's election.

The first assault on the personal rights of imbibers versus teetotalers in Chicago had ended in favor of the wets and the German beer- and Irish whiskey–drinking communities. The nativists' disturbing attitude toward foreigners and the influence of the prohibitionist movement in Chicago would be only temporarily suppressed, the larger questions of slavery and state secession looming on the country's horizon.

❧ 3 ❧

Chicago's Developing Brewery Trade, 1860–1885

It literally exploded.
—*Edward G. Uihlein, describing sales of*
Schlitz beer in Chicago after the Great Fire

CIVIL WAR YEARS

At first glance, the growth of Chicago's beer trade during the Civil War and the immediate post-bellum years appears to have been slow and unremarkable, a reflection, perhaps, of the country's hesitant movements both during and after the nationwide upheaval. The imposition of an excise tax of one dollar per barrel of beer and a federal licensing fee of $50 to $100 per brewery, imposed in 1862 by the recently introduced Internal Revenue System, forced the Chicago brewers to adjust the wholesale price of their product to $7 per barrel. Whiskey was also taxed by the federal agency at a higher rate of twenty cents per proof gallon, or $6.20 for a 31-gallon barrel at 100-proof.[1] With the beer tax proceeds used to help finance the struggling Northern government during the Civil War, the local German-born brewers grudgingly complied, not wanting to rekindle any lingering nativist feelings by being perceived as negligent in their patriotic duty to their new country.

Of the twenty-three new breweries that opened in Chicago during this trying period, a number of them went out of business after only a few years of existence, for example, the Chicago Ale & Malt Company (1861–1867), the N. P. Svenson Brewery (1866–1867), and the John Behringer Brewery (1862–1865).[2] One can only speculate as to why these breweries and others failed while so many more succeeded and even expanded, but a number of ideas come to mind. The substantially sized lager drinking German population of Chicago shied away from the products of most of the ale producers, limiting their market. Americans and other immigrant groups began to take a pronounced liking to lager beer, not coincidentally after the wartime excise tax was also imposed on the once cheap-priced distilled liquors. The significantly higher-based liquor tax drastically changed the drinking habits of the everyday man, turning him from the now higher priced whiskey to the comparatively lower priced lager beer. By 1865, whiskey was being taxed at the gargantuan rate of $62 per barrel. With help from the IRS, German lager was evolving into the affordable drink of the working class.[3] Brewers took note of this shift in the drink preferences of their customers, emphasized the debilitating effects of distilled products, their higher price, and declared beer "the drink of moderation." This distinction between distilled versus fermented products, as promoted by the brewing industry up until the advent of national prohibition, would eventually lead to a schism between the liquor and brewing industry that can still be seen today.

Competition from the more established concerns, undercapitalization, and poor management practices surely added to the financial demise of others. Brewery destruction by fire was also a common occurrence in the early brewing trade, often wiping out not only the brewery but also the funds necessary to rebuild.

GROWTH AND CONSOLIDATION OF EARLY BREWERIES

Continuing consolidations, mergers and outright buyouts of a number of breweries during the post-bellum period strengthened the position of a number of local breweries, readying them for the boom years of the 1880s. A few representative examples are noted here:

Seipp & Lehman

Conrad Seipp, a German immigrant, began his brewing career in Chicago in 1854, after buying the small brewery of Mathias Best. Arriving in Chicago in 1849, he started a small, highly successful hotel at the corner of Washington and Wells. In 1851, he staked a claim on eighty acres of farmland near what is now the area around 79th Street and Jeffery Avenue. Soon after he purchased the Best Brewery, a fire destroyed it. Undaunted, Seipp proceeded to build a new brewery on 27th Street, near the Lake. A man of apparent frugality, he and his family lived on the second floor of the newly constructed brewery. In 1858, Seipp formed a partnership with Frederick Lehman. With the additional capital from Lehman's buy-in, the brewery was greatly enlarged to meet the increasing demand for their popular products.

Lehman died in 1872 following a carriage accident. During their partnership, the brewery grew at an amazing rate, selling 48,437 barrels of beer in 1868, having outpaced production at Lill's Chicago Brewery by 17,505 barrels.[4]

Downer, Bemis & Company

During late 1860 and early 1861, Corydon Downer and H. V. Bemis built a small ale brewery at 16th Street and the Lake. Shortly thereafter, Downer retired from the business. In 1864, Bemis built another brewery on South Park Avenue. One year later, local politician John A. McAvoy bought a position in the brewery. In 1866, the company of Downer & Bemis was formed, retaining the name of Corydon Downer. From 1865 on, the entire output of the new brewery was devoted exclusively to the production of lager beer, reflecting an understanding by the owners of the increasing size of the lager beer market. Critics (mostly German brewers) were sure that the brewery would fail in the endeavor since the general opinion of most of the brewing industry was that only Germans could brew true lager beer. McAvoy, a native of Newry, Ireland, and Bemis, born in Center Almond, New York, proved them wrong; 3,500 barrels of beer were sold in 1865, and production was increased to 28,851 barrels by 1869. Apparently not wishing to tempt fate, Bemis and McAvoy did hire a German-born brewer at a later date.[5]

Jacob Rehm & Company

Jacob Rehm, a native of Alsace, began his long career in brewing in 1859 as an employee of Lill & Diversey. During his tenure at the brewery, he somehow found time to serve as Chicago superintendent of police in 1862 and Cook County treasurer in 1863. Prior to his brewing career, he also served as a police officer in 1851, street commissioner in 1855, and city marshall in 1857 and 1858. In 1865, Rehm left Lill & Diversey and started the Jacob Rehm & Company Brewery on West 12th Street.

In 1866, Rehm took on Frank Bartholomae as partner but sold out his position two years later. The brewery was renamed Bartholomae & Company. This brewery would be merged into the Milwaukee and Chicago Breweries, Co. Ltd. in 1890 and into the conglomerate United States Brewing Company in 1909. Rehm went on to become a partner with Frederick Wacker in the operation of a successful malting business on Elm Street.[6]

These consolidations, with a further strengthening of market position by such giants as Lill & Diversey and the John A. Huck Brewing Company, along with the success of recent start-ups such as Sand's Ale Brewing Company and Busch & Brand, increased beer production in 1869 in Chicago to a recorded output of 246,212 barrels. Numerous smaller and unrecorded breweries probably pushed this figure to well over 300,000 barrels. In less than forty years, Chicago's production of beer had increased over 900 percent, an apparent joy to Chicago's growing population of 298,977.[7]

Not everyone was happy with the success of the local brewers. Chicago's more independently minded saloon keepers began to complain and organize against the perceived high prices the brewers were charging them per barrel. Slight price increases by the brewers were customarily absorbed by the saloon keepers who felt there would be resistance from their customers if the saloon keepers passed on the wholesale increase on a barrel of beer to them. At the time, it was pointless for retailers to shop another local brewery for a better price per barrel. The members of the local brewing association had agreed to fix prices on a barrel of beer. There were also charges by saloon keepers that barrels of beer delivered by local breweries fell short of their full capacity.[8]

Tired of a drain on their profits, some saloon owners fought back and started up the Chicago Union Brewing Company in 1867–1868, with an investment of $250,000. Their two-story brick building was soon producing 100 barrels of beer a day for some of Chicago's more independently minded saloon keepers. But it was hard to question the wisdom of the saloon keepers to become involved in the brewery trade. At an average pull of over five hundred, 7-ounce glasses of nickel beer per 31-gallon barrel, their profits were much more respectable than those of the brewers with their beer priced at around $6 a barrel.[9]

THE CHICAGO FIRE

The Great Chicago Fire of October 1871 radically changed the face of the brewing industry in Chicago. An account of the fire by Edward G. Uihlein, the eventual vice president and manager of the Chicago Branch of the Jos. Schlitz Brewing Company, is described in his memoirs:

> The Chicago fire occurred October 9, 1871. I was located with my little factory on West Chicago Avenue and did not have to suffer but the event was of such magnitude that I can not but say a few words about it.
>
> The fire started about 8:30 Sunday evening and apparently it took in a very short time such dimensions that I and my friend Grundlach concluded to go & see it thinking it was somewhere around Madison Street & Clinton. Walking along it proved to be near Canal & Polk Sts. We crossed the bridge when the Fire in less than ten minutes spread across the river taking its course in a north easterly direction. We hurried along Wabash only to find that Monroe, Adams, Washington were reached by the fire and if we undertook to proceed further north we would absolutely be cut off & would perish. So we turned South again and found our way via 12th Str. bridge and reached home 436 Milwaukee Avenue about two o' clock. Reports came the Courthouse gone the Waterworks on Chicago Avenue [part of the Waterworks were destroyed and the city water supply lost after flames from the Lill & Diversey Brewery spread to the pumping station][10] on fire hundreds perished in the LaSalle Str. Tunnel so that part of the Southside and the whole Northside to Lincoln Park was doomed.
>
> Although all the neighboring towns & Cities including Milwaukee, Joliet, Peoria, Galesburg etc. sent fire apparatus of all kinds nothing could check the elements in their fury. All they could do was to defend the Westside where the river gave a good opportunity to help. On the Southside south of Harrison whole blocks were blown up with Dynamite to check the fire going further south with fairly good

success. On Tuesday a rain set in and the limits of Lincoln Park helped along considerable. Well it is not my intention to give a history of the fire but simply mention that I had witnessed all of it.[11]

Lost in the fire, with estimated damages, were the following breweries:

Lill & Diversey	$500,000
J. A. Huck	$400,000
Sand's Brewing Company	$335,000
Busch & Brand	$250,000
Buffalo Brewery aka Miller & Son	$150,000
Schmidt, Katz & Company	$60,000
Metz & Stege	$80,000
Doyle Bros. & Company	$45,000
Mloeler Bros. (Mueller Bros.?)	$20,000
K. G. Schmidt	$90,000
George Hiller	$35,000
Schmidt & Bender	$25,000
Mitinet & Puoupfel	$12,000
(not listed in brewery appendix)	
John Behringer	$15,000
J. Miller	$8,000
William Bowman	$5,000
George Wagner	$5,000
Haas & Powell	n/a
Joseph Jerusalem	n/a
TOTAL	$ 2,035,000+[12]

Brewer William Lill had just finished his first evening dinner in his new $40,000 home when he was forced to leave as the flames approached his property. Brewer John Huck not only lost his brewery, but also suffered the dubious distinction of losing his house in the fire—the last structure in the city to succumb to the flames.[13] Production at the Downer & Bemis Brewery was temporarily interrupted when the water supply from Lake Michigan was cut off by the destruction of the city waterworks pumping station. Within three days, Bemis and his men laid out a temporary line directly to the Lake. Besides meeting the needs of the brewery, Bemis furnished water to the surrounding community at no charge.[14] The fortunes of Michael Keeley, whose continued success at bottling had made him a wealthy man, were wiped out with the destruction of his bottling plant at Harrison and Canal.

Only brewers Busch and Brand, Jerusalem, and K. G. Schmidt resumed production at a later date; Michael Brand's plant was up and running in less than three months while his partner, Valentin Busch, continued to operate their other plant in nearby Blue Island. The fiery disaster narrowed the playing field, allowing the Seipp & Lehman Brewery to comfortably maintain its position as Chicago's most productive brewery. It also helped to increase the market share of the surviving smaller breweries, something that might have eluded them otherwise. Ironically, without the devastation of the fire and the rebounding of the surviving breweries, the Golden Era of brewing in Chicago during the 1880s might never have taken place.

Neighboring Milwaukee breweries also took advantage of the city's misfortune and increased their efforts to secure an even larger share of the Chicago market. The Jos. Schlitz and Co. Brewery seized the moment in Chicago with exportation of its products to the devastated city, but went one step further, utilizing Chicago's strategic railroad freighting position to open up its business throughout the United States. Their business in Chicago after the fire "literally exploded," wrote Edward G. Uihlein. He noted in his memoirs that "orders came in so quickly that it was impossible to fill them all," but he initially chose to ship beer by barge, a cumbersome method of transportation that did not bode well during the winter months.[15] In time, Schlitz would operate two storage facilities in Chicago, each connected to a railroad spur. Schlitz became "The Beer That Made Milwaukee Famous," but Chicago was the city that made it so. Using the vast railroad hub in Chicago as a springboard, the Milwaukee brewery continued its expansion far beyond Milwaukee and Chicago.

Brewery owner Joseph Schlitz had only a short time to enjoy the brewery's newfound success. In May 1875, he boarded the *Schiller* in New York for a visit to Germany. Of the eight hundred passengers aboard, less than half were rescued when the cruise ship sank at sea. Joseph Schlitz was among those unaccounted for.

TECHNOLOGICAL ADVANCES

Despite early manufacturing and technical limitations, the brewing industry in the early 1870s in Chicago was a viable one, having an annual sales figure of over $2 million. In the thirty-odd years that followed the Great Chicago Fire, the increasing production pace continued as a technological and manufacturing revolution took place in the brewing industry, much of it originating in Chicago. Many of the limitations that had plagued the brewing industry were being overcome by the discoveries and inventions of the Industrial Revolution and the adaptation of a number of these findings specific to the brewing industry. The result would eventually become a tumultuous brew of men, machines, and natural ingredients.

MECHANICAL REFRIGERATION

Ice, transported from the huge facilities of the Knickerbocker Ice Company at Wolf Lake, Indiana, the many lakes of neighboring Wisconsin, or sometimes harvested from local rivers when conditions allowed, was an essential item for the production of lager beer. Carefully hoarded in caverns or weather-proofed buildings and covered with sawdust to slow its eventual melting, ice had made brewing a seasonal practice, limiting production to the cooler months of the year. Used not only to cool the boiling wort to a temperature conducive to the *pitching* of yeast, the ice was also indispensable in keeping the beer at temperatures low enough during the essential *kraeusening* and *lagering* stages. Ice was a rare, but fleeting, commodity.

As noted earlier, a lack of sufficient ice in Chicago during the summer of 1854 and the subsequent inability to brew needed lager beer quickly gave Milwaukee brewers a foothold in the Chicago market that was never relinquished. Prices and availability of ice were quoted in the daily newspapers and various trade publications, the brewing trade being only one of a number of industries dependent on its use as a refrigerant. Ice was a necessary evil, hauled to the brewery by wagon and pushed, dragged, and shoved into position by brewery workers at considerable expense.

As the popularity of their products continued to grow, Lill and Diversey commisioned the building of a second ice house in which to store their beer, dispensing with the need for underground caverns. The buildings were described in 1861 as such:

> The ice is in the middle of the ice house, in two bodies, one measuring sixty by thirty and twenty-five feet high, and the other sixty by sixty, and twenty-five feet high, packed in tanbark, and encased in wood, by which means a temperature of forty degrees is kept up during the year. The absence of cellars has been the greatest drawback to Chicago as a brewing point, but these ice houses overcame all that.[16]

In 1877, H. V. Bemis, co-owner of the Downer & Bemis Brewery, working with Scotch inventor Daniel Boyle, erected an ammonia compression machine in the brewery for mechanical refrigeration. Determined to perfect the adaptation of an ice machine to the process of making beer, Bemis worked upon the monstrous-sized unit, correcting and adjusting it until it became an unparalleled success and an example of the first adaptation of this sort of refrigeration in any brewery. The perfected Boyle Ice Machine weighed over fifty tons and supplied refrigeration for the entire brewery, cooling the lagering cellars and fermenting rooms and making ice water for the b*audelots*, used to cool the boiling wort. One immediate advantage of the use of baudelots was the elimination of floating conical shaped *Schwimmers* to cool the boiling wort. These metal containers, packed with blocks of harvested ice, would occasionally leak water into the sterile wort and change the character and taste of the finished product. More often than not, the often-contaminated leakage would spoil the brew. The acceptance of Boyle's machine by the brewing industry was overwhelming. Boyle shipped twenty-two refrigeration units in a short five-month period to breweries throughout the United States.[17]

In 1880, the Fred. W. Wolf Company of Chicago obtained the patent rights to the Linde Ice Machine, introduced in Europe by Professor C. P. G. Linde of Munich, Germany. Linde's drive in designing a mechanical refrigeration device had been financed by the Spaten Brewery in Munich, beginning in the early 1870s. In 1877, with Linde's compression ammonia finally perfected for brewery use, Spaten became the first brewery in the world to control the fermentation and lagering temperatures of their brewery without ice.

Wolf's business as architect and civil engineer had begun in Chicago in 1867. Although Wolf took on Louis Lehle as a full-time architectural partner in 1889, he began to concentrate his efforts toward mechanical refrigeration, especially after the Wolf & Lehle partnership ended in 1894. The Wacker & Birk Brewing & Malting Company of Chicago was the first brewery to install this type of refrigeration unit in the United States.[18]

These machines now allowed year-round brewing, the brewers no longer dependent on the natural production and harvesting of ice or its fluctuating price levels. Although the initial outlay for the installation of a mechanical refrigeration machine was significant, its savings occurred in many different forms. Dozens of ice cutters and handlers were no longer needed. Exact temperatures could now be maintained in the fermenting and lagering rooms. A typical fermentation room during this period of American brewing needed 20 feet of solid ice above the tanks to cool the room. The need for carefully constructed wood trusses to support the massive load of ice added structural problems. This danger could now be eliminated and would result in a better utilization of space in the brewery. The control of ambient temperature also eliminated the need for underground caverns. With the resultant lagering of beer now aboveground in cold storage facilities, the beer no longer had to be pumped to the surface for kegging.[19]

One initial hesitation, however, that a number of brewery owners had with the total reliance on mechanical refrigeration was dispensing with the supplementation of natural ice in their cooling rooms. The fact that their supply of ice never needed to be replaced eventually won them over to the effectiveness of mechanical refrigeration as the single source of cooling in breweries.

BEER SCHOOLS AND ADVANCES IN BEER STABILITY

The development of an analytical laboratory for the isolation of viable yeast and the detection of wild yeast and putrefying bacteria became a recognized necessity for the production of clean tasting, longer lasting ale or lager. After publication of *Etude sur la Biere*, a revealing study of yeast in beer by Dr. Louis Pasteur in 1877, more Chicago brewers began to farm out samples of beer and yeast for testing and analysis to Dr. John E. Siebel's Zymotechnic Institute, founded in 1872. Siebel nonetheless battled to keep the business afloat by also serving as a city and county gas inspector, a draftsman and designer for the Commission of Public Works, a teacher at a local German high school, and an employee of a German language newspaper.

Siebel's vision seemed to finally come together in 1882 when he and Michael Brand, a well-known Chicago brewer, joined together and opened the first scientific school for practical brewers, using Brand's brewery and malt house on Elston Avenue as an on-the-job training facility. The majority of the local brewing community, however, continued to look at the notion of brewing as a science with open skepticism, contemptuously referring to Siebel and others who followed his analytical musings as "beer doctors." Enrollment in the Siebel/Brand operation eventually fell below a level of profitability and the joint operation collapsed.

Undeterred, Siebel continued on his own to operate his laboratory for brewing studies while also publishing volumes of scientific papers on various aspects of brewing, malting, and mechanical refrigeration. Twenty years later, the science of brewing had finally won over its detractors' Old World perceptions of the making of beer as nothing more than a form of medieval alchemy.

In the late 1890s, Siebel and several of his sons expanded their operation and in 1901 incorporated the business as the Siebel Institute of Technology. Courses were offered for brewers, maltsters, engineers, and bottlers. John E. Siebel's vision of operating an oasis of scientific study and instruction for the brewing industry had come to fruition. The organization still thrives today as Siebel Institute of Technology & World Brewing Academy, now housed in the Goose Island Brewpub on North Clybourn, with hands-on training also taking place at the World Brewing Academy in Grafelfing, Germany. The author is an alumnus of Siebel.

In 1886, the Wahl-Henius Scientific Station was also founded for the clinical testing and analysis of beer.

With organizations such as the Siebel Institute of Technology and the Wahl-Henius Scientific Station proving their worth, once skeptical brewers became convinced of the merits of production and product analysis and the use of clean yeast for consistent quality of beer. Brewing as an art was giving way to the more reliable methodology of science.[20]

EARLY BOTTLING EFFORTS

The practice of bottling pasteurized beer began to gain wider acceptance during the 1880s. Bottling would eventually offer hotels, restaurants, and saloons the opportunity to present a representative choice of brands and styles of beer, bought by the case rather than relying on the more perishable and space-consuming barrels with their accompanying dispensing equipment. The profit potential of the home market was also becoming evident, waiting to be exploited by brewers, independent bottlers, and distributors alike. Some brewers readily embraced this practice, establishing bottling departments near their breweries, but the outlay for bottling equipment was enormous. Counterpressure bottling machines, capable of delivering beer charged with carbonic acid gas for foaming purposes and to prevent contact of beer with outside air, were supplemented with conveyors capable of carrying the bottles to capping or corking machines, sterilizing stations, and, finally, labelers.

A reoccurring expense that all bottlers tried to contend with was the use of the bottles themselves. Early efforts to induce customers to return the empty clear glass bottles to the breweries were initially met with raised letter admonitions on the containers that read THIS BOTTLE NOT TO BE SOLD or PROPERTY OF (brewery name) CHICAGO. The early brewers complained of their ever-shrinking inventory of bottles, but the wasteful practice of simply hoping that beer drinkers would return their empties to the brewery continued uninterrupted until World War I. The implementation of deposits on bottles and wooden cases would come about in the U.S. brewing industry due to the government-mandated wartime practice of material conservation.

There were earlier attempts at bottling beer, but they met with limited success. Bottling in its earliest stages of practice consisted of filling handblown glass bottles or earthenware containers using a rubber hose attached to a keg to siphon the beer into the container. In its most primitive form, a cork was typically driven into the bottle by hand or a pressing machine, then wired down at the bottleneck to hold the cork in place, and sometimes labeled by hand. Carbonation was achieved by the practice of *kraeusening*, the introduction of young, actively fermenting beer to a batch of almost completely fermented beer. This unreliable practice often led to bottles blowing their corks or the containers exploding during transit because of an uncontrollable secondary fermentation. Storage and handling abuse by the retailer or even the customer further aggravated the problems of exploding bottles.

Since the Civil War, beer had been taxed by the barrel. With the advent of large-scale bottling practices, the Internal Revenue Service (IRS) once again stepped into the practice of brewing to ensure a proper taxation of the bottled product. New government procedures for accurately accessing the proper tax on all beer that left the brewery created a further financial drain on those breweries that chose to bottle beer, with bureaucratic standards and regulations that demanded retooling and reconfiguration of their plants. The IRS mandated that brewery bottling departments now had to be separate and distinct from the brewery, separated from the main plant by a public highway. Kegs would be filled with beer, a tax stamp adhered to the keg, the kegs then transported to a seperate bottling facility, and the beer finally emptied into bottles.

Under pressure from the brewing industry, led by Milwaukee's Captain Frederick Pabst, this impractical and restrictive practice was eventually modified by Congress to allow beer to instead be pumped from the brewery by pipelines to the bottling department under strict rules of construction and operation. Even this revised practice was an added expense, necessitating the excavation of a "government tunnel" from the brewery to the bottling plant. The beer was then pumped off into measuring tanks in the bottlery and the tax paid to an on-site revenue agent with tax stamps normally adhered to outgoing barrels.[21]

This tax revenue practice and the large outlay for all the machines and devices needed for bottling led to the existence of separate bottling businesses, independent of the breweries themselves. In this way, small local breweries (or even soda pop manufacturers) could contract out their bottling needs and enter the growing bottled beer market with little or no additional cash outlay. This brewing niche became an important part of the brewing trade in the late 1880s and 1890s, temporarily allowing small and midsized breweries to continue operation without increasing capital expenditures on new bottling equipment. The escalating operating expenses of these independent bottling operations, however, would eventually prove detrimental to the brewers' profits.

For those small breweries willing to utilize the independent bottlers, the result was a wider selection of beer types and brands for retailers and consumers. But the practice of using independent bottling plants would eventually end. Competition and the need to tighten production expenses forced brewers to make the critical choice between reverting to draft beer production, buying an expensive bottling line, or quitting the business of brewing.

MALTING IMPROVEMENTS

By the 1870s, Chicago was the undisputed biggest grain market in the world. With numerous breweries in Chicago and distilleries in nearby Peoria, there was an acute need for malt houses in the immediate area. *Malting* is the controlled germination of barley during which enzymes are formed and the food reserves are sufficiently modified in the grain kernel so that they can be further hydrolyzed with warm water during the *mashing* process. From the mashing of malted barley come the sugars that feed the yeast, the next stage of *fermentation* leaving carbon dioxide and alcohol behind. Initially soaked in steeping tanks until the proper moisture content is reached, the barley is then allowed to germinate under controlled conditions. Finally, the partially germinated barley is *kilned*, dried in a controlled current of hot air, stopping germination. The length of kilning determines the color and flavor intensity of the malt, analogous in practice to the roasting of coffee beans.

By the mid-1880s, there were twenty private malt houses in Chicago in addition to those vertically integrated with local breweries.[22] Malting techniques were now becoming more efficient. In 1882, Louis C. Huck, son of pioneer brewer John Huck, patented a system for air drying malt and ventilating malt houses. Using a huge fan, which ventilated the kiln and growing floors, and adding refrigeration to attemperate the air, he further modified his invention, adding the Saladin pneumatic malting system to his malt house. This system controlled the temperature and moisture necessary for germination and stirred and turned the grain by machine, ensuring a more efficient operation and a resultant quality product. The Saladin method is still widely used in the malting business today.[23]

BREWERY ARCHITECTURE

Chicago's predominance as a center for brewery architecture is well documented in the brewing trade journals of the 1870s and on. Centrally located in the Midwest and with an unfolding architectural school of new building design evident during this period, Chicago enjoyed a geographic advantage over East Coast architects in taking on projects in the Midwest to as far west as California.

From the designs of locals Frederick Wolf, Frederick Baumann, Louis Lehle, August Maritzen, Wilhelm Griesser, and others arose a proliferation of ornate but equally functional breweries built in Chicago and throughout the United States. The architectural team of Wolf & Lehle is best recognized as the most notable Chicago firm in local brewery architecture. Their influence and design, however, were also greatly utilized by Schlitz in neighboring Milwaukee and by other breweries as far away as the Phillipines.

What catches the eye of even the untrained observer of local brewery design is the use by these architects and industrial engineers of the neo-Romanesque *Rundbogenstil* (rounded arch style) that can still be seen on the east wall of the Carl Corper Brewery on South Union. Round arched windows, crenellated rooflines, and corner towers were elements of the massive fortresses used for these late nineteenth-century breweries. The late Victorian-era design by architect Adolph Cudell for the still-standing Schoenhofen brewery administation building stands in contrast to the reconditioned Schoenhofen warehouse and powerhouse, east of the office structure. This building was designed in Prairie style by Hugh M. G. Garden, working for local architect Richard Schmidt in 1902.[24] It stands as testimony to the evolving styles of the succeeding generation of local brewery architects.

Italianate and Greco-Roman design were also used extensively in Chicago brewery construction during the period from 1870 to around 1900, the still-standing Mutual Brewing Company exhibiting an example of the later style. Later built brewery structures are almost devoid of ornate style and maintain a functional industrial look, a reflection of the changing economic conditions of the local brewing industry after 1900 and a change in architectural philosophy. Function now ruled over form.[25] A tour of still-standing Chicago breweries is included in the Epilogue of this book.

What these ornate brick buildings from the late 1870s to the turn of the century had in common was the concept of natural gravity flow in the brewing operation. By placing the raw brewing materials in the top floors of the brew house, usually distinguished from the rest of the plant by vertical towers, the boiling wort would flow down from the copper kettle to the hop-jack, which strained the hot wort of the flavoring hops, and finally, to the cooling chambers of the *baudelots*, preparing the cooled wort for the introduction of the yeast. With each successive step in the brewing process, from lagering, cooling, filtering, and carbonation, the product would continue to flow from floor to floor for a final stop at the kegging or *racking* department.

By the mid-1880s, the enormous brewing kettles would often need to be stabilized with the interlacing support and structural features of the towers themselves. This dependent support technique probably explains why almost all of the brew house towers of the remaining old brewery structures found throughout the city today have been leveled. Without the support afforded by the combination of interlocking kettles, enveloped with the supportive steel framing of the surrounding towers, the existing walls of the towers would have soon collapsed once the kettles were removed.

PROFESSIONAL BREWER'S ORGANIZATIONS

The Chicago brewers realized the importance of organizing a professional association devoted to the growing technical aspects of brewing and the need to further the interest of the local brewing industry. In June 1867, the United States Brewers Association (USBA), invited by the recently formed Brewers Association of Chicago, held a national convention in Chicago, the USBA acknowledging the city's growing importance as a respected brewing center.[26]

BREWER PUBLICATIONS

Various brewery trade publications began operation in Chicago during the 1870s and 1880s, keeping the industry apprised of new technological findings and matters peculiar to the brewing and malting trades.

The most successful and longest running publication was *The Western Brewer*, which began in 1876 and was published by J. M. Wing & Company. This German/English publication settled on an all-English format in 1882 after a questionnaire revealed that the majority of readers preferred the English language version. Originating in Chicago, *The Western Brewer* was a potpourri of scientific findings specific to brewing but regularly laced with an inner look at the social aspects of the brewing community, listing the births, deaths, weddings, and frequent trips to Europe of the brewers and their families. Moving to New York after being purchased by the H. S. Rich & Company in 1887, the publication took on a more national focus on the brewing industry, with reoccurring diatribes on the temperance and prohibition movements. It was published under this title until 1920. From June 20, 1920, until December of 1932, the publication was known as *The Beverage Journal*, reflecting the constraints of Prohibition. From January 1933 to May 1934, it was once again called *The Western Brewer*. In May 1934, until it's demise in 1960, it was renamed as *The Brewer's Journal*.

Other publications of note were the *Brauer und Malzer*, begun in 1881 by Eugene A. Sittig, eventually merging with *The Brewer and Malster and Beveraguer*, which ceased publication in 1937. *Der Braumeister*, started in 1887, was the official organ of The Master Brewers Association. In 1891, the monthly publication was taken over by Doctors Max Henius and Robert Wahl and renamed the *American Brewers Review*. Like the early issues of *The Western Brewer*, it was published in Chicago and was particularly focused on the political scene in Chicago during the pre-Prohibition years. It ceased publication in 1939.[27]

THE ORIGIN OF THE
PROHIBITION PARTY

Since the onset of the Civil War, the temperance movement in Chicago had been dormant, the slavery question and, most important, the very existence of the Union having been tested. With the end of hostilities and a return to normalcy, reform and the more radical Prohibition Movement began to resurface.

For years, the brewers had considered prohibitionists no more than a nuisance. At the Seventh Annual Convention of the United States Brewers' Association, held in 1867 in Chicago, the brewers changed their benign attitude and began to take a more serious stance with prohibitionists. A resolution was passed by national brewing leaders stating that "we will use all means to stay the progress of this fanatical party."[28]

Seemingly in the face of this challenge from the brewers, the Prohibition Party was organized in Chicago, on September 1, 1869. Five hundred delegates from nineteen states were present at the party's ratification at Farwell Hall. The organization of a national Prohibition Party, capable of running a candidate in the upcoming presidential election, gave evidence that it was becoming a force that could organize in a fashion that had eluded earlier dry advocates.

But during the 1880s and 1890s, despite the devastation of the Great Fire and the occasional annoyance of local prohibition and temperance efforts, Chicago's breweries would reach unprecedented levels of production, spurred on by an increasing population growth and an array of technological and manufacturing improvements. The Golden Age of brewing was about to begin in Chicago, but with it would evolve the elements of its decline.

⚜ 4 ⚜

Brewer Influence Grows,
1870–1900

Chicago will soon stand ahead of
her present position in brewing
among the cities of this country.
—*Chicago Tribune, 1880*

New Breweries, Consolidations

An article published in the *Chicago Tribune* on January 1, 1880, gives
a revealing look at the brewing industry in Chicago during the late
1870s. The local breweries during this time were capitalized at a combined value of over $12 million. Close to 340,000 barrels of beer were
brewed in 1879 at a wholesale price of $8 per barrel. With the peripheral
malting trade, valued at $1,500,000, brewing was a huge, important
industrial power in Chicago. The city ranked sixth in national beer
production, employing over one thousand in the numerous breweries
scattered throughout the city.

The sales leader was the Conrad Seipp Brewing Company, located
on 27th Street near Lake Michigan, which brewed 108,347 barrels in
1879. Seipp was noted in the article as being "the only Chicago brewer
who ships beer to any extent outside the city." Most renowned was his
Salvator brand bottled beer which was heartily welcomed as far away as
California. A testimonial from a Seipp customer in Colorado claimed
that Seipp's beer "had done more to reform the mining districts of
the West than all the moral agencies that have ever been sent there,"
replacing the more debilitating whiskies that had been the drink of
choice among the miners. With a cash infusion from the buy-in of his
partner Frederick Lehman in 1858 and having taken quick advantage of
the devastation of the Chicago Fire in 1871, which weeded out nineteen

local competitors, Seipp had the necessary capital to take on the high initial outlay for a bottling and export operation.

Ranked second was the Downer & Bemis Brewing Company at 24th Street and South Park with a total production of 66,878 barrels in the same year.

Providing malted barley for the brewers were a number of malt houses, including the George Bullen & Company, H. L. Huck, Charles L. Epps & Company, Charles Pope, the Northwestern, Binz & Pollock, and Charles Sheer. These Chicago-based malsters had taken advantage of their centrally located position and the city's vast network of railroads which used Chicago as their hub. With these nearby facilities, they were able to provide a savings in transportation costs over the distant East Coast malt houses.[1]

Start-up breweries included the Keeley Brewing Company, established in 1878; the Wacker & Birk Brewing and Malting Company, founded in 1882; the Junk Brewery, 1883; and the Cooke Brewing Company, started in 1885. The Non-Alcoholic Beer Company opened in 1893 on North Clybourn, apparently having tried to establish a niche market for reformers, temperance, and prohibition advocates. The brewery closed the same year, indicating that, at least in Chicago, those who talked the talk didn't necessarily walk the walk.[2]

The enterprising Michael Keeley, whose bottling business had been destroyed in the Great Chicago Fire, was once again in business soon after the disaster. In 1876, he left the liquor firm of Keeley & Kerwin and purchased the old F. Binz Brewery on 28th Street. The plant had a reputation for brewing inferior products. First year's output was six thousand barrels of good quality beer and ale, increasing to ninety thousand by 1888. Keeley also distinguished himself by holding the position of president of the Milwaukee & Chicago Brewers Association in 1887, a rare honor in Chicago's brewing fraternity for a non-German.[3]

In 1882, Frederick Wacker, with his son Charles and Jacob Birk, formed the Wacker & Birk Brewing and Malting Company. Birk, a successful harness maker and former owner of the old Wheeling House on Lake Street, had no experience in the brewing industry but his considerable business skills would help make the firm a success. Birk would go on in later years to form the Birk Brothers Brewing Company with his sons William and Edward.[4]

In a male-dominated industry, the name of Magdalena Junk stands out in the history of Chicago brewing. Married to Joseph Junk, a German immigrant from Salmrohr, she ably took control of her husband's brewery after his death in 1887. Faced with indebtedness from her husband's earlier financial difficulties, she soon cleared the business of all debt and expanded the plant on 37th Street and Halsted in Bridgeport. Modernization of the brewery made it possible to increase production from 14,000 barrels in 1887 to 43,000 in 1900. Assisting Magdalena in the operation of the Junk Brewery were her sons Edward and Joseph, both popular figures in the local brewing fraternity.[5]

One of the few Irishmen to successfully enter the brewing trade in Chicago, John S. Cooke purchased the Chicago Union Brewing Company in 1885, founded earlier by P. O'Neill and an independent group of saloon keepers. Starting with sales of only two barrels a day, Cooke quickly expanded brewery operations. Through hard work and perseverance, his family increased sales to 103,000 barrels in 1900. His sons, George and Charles, assisted him in the daily operations. Both sons took over brewery operations after Cooke's death in 1899.[6]

MILWAUKEE VERSUS CHICAGO

Of the many local breweries in operation during this period, few made any real effort to export their products outside the Chicagoland area, the Conrad Seipp and the smaller K.G. Schmidt brewery being notable exceptions. Both breweries took advantage of the huge developing Western market, the Seipp brewery with its previously mentioned Salvator and the Schmidt brewery being particularly successful with its Budweiser brand.[7] The Chicago brewers' overall provincial view of exporting though is reflected in a comparison of beer production figures for 1879. For the first time ever, Milwaukee, with a population numbering a little over 115,000, surpassed Chicago's beer production, having brewed 411,245 barrels that year, and shipped much of this beer to outside markets. Chicago brewers initially showed no alarm at this creeping trend, content to manufacture only 336,204 barrels for its population of about 503,000 and disposing of most of it in the city.

Milwaukee's export aggressiveness continued through the next few years. By 1884, Milwaukee beer production would more than double to 803,371 barrels, much of it destined to fill the steins and mugs of thirsty Chicagoans. During this same period, Chicago would meekly demonstrate a rise in beer production of less than 35,000 barrels from its 1879 barrelage.[8] This growing trend would soon crowd the Chicago beer market which was beginning to demonstrate a finite capacity for additional growth.

Before the advent of mechanical refrigeration, the abundance of ice and brewing water from nearby Lake Michigan, combined with an experienced labor force—almost exclusively German—and a geographic shipping advantage over Eastern brewers, gave Milwaukee *and* Chicago the enviable opportunity to expand their markets. Milwaukee brewers, however, with a smaller local customer base and numerous local breweries competing for limited dollars, realized early on in their efforts of the need to develop a viable export trade. They therefore pushed shipping of their products with a greater vigor than their Chicago brethren. The initial motive of Milwaukee brewers moving into the huge Chicago market in the mid 1850s was probably more defensive in nature than exploitive. The exportation of surplus beer to neighboring Chicago meant survival and a relief valve for any Milwaukee brewery that had overestimated its home market demand. But as the country expanded to the Pacific, the Milwaukee brewers, now experienced in solving the problems and cost factors associated with shipping beer outside their market, realized the potential of national sales.

The expansion to the desolate West, where breweries were few, was soon accompanied by Milwaukee beer. The Milwaukee brewers were also rolling over much of the local competition in the Southern states where a lack of sufficient ice during the hot summer months limited production. This disadvantage was eagerly exploited by Northern railroad cars packed with fresh beer and cheap ice.

Having suffered through a lack of beer during the oppressive summer of 1854 and been saved by the eager to please Milwaukee brewers, the majority of Chicago breweries nonetheless continued to concede the export market and its huge profit potential to Milwaukee. With extreme shortsightedness, the Chicago breweries used the excuse of high shipping rates to justify their lack of expansion into other markets, "and [they] have left the outside trade to the Milwaukee brewers, who have made a specialty of that branch of the business," noted the *Chicago Tribune* in 1880.[9]

The Phil Best Company of Milwaukee led the invasion of Chicago, selling sixty thousand barrels of beer in Chicago in 1879, which was more than the combined output of mid-sized Chicago breweries Schmidt & Glade, M. Gottfried, and the Fortune Brothers Brewing Company. By 1883, Best Brewing, with two branches and forty-five teams and drivers in Chicago, had a sales staff in Chicago almost as large as in hometown Milwaukee. The Jos. Schlitz Brewing Company also continued to expand its exportation to Chicago, shipping thirty-five thousand barrels of beer to the city in 1879.[10]

While Chicago's brewers retired for the night, surrounded in the opulence of their mansions and fine possessions, perhaps dreaming of expanding potential beer sales to a bloc of new saloons on the other side of town or a close by village, Milwaukee's brewers were supervising the nighttime loading of specially fitted rubber-lined railroad cars packed with beer and ice that would quietly leave Milwaukee for transport to Chicago. Arriving in town early the next morning, the beer was rushed off to strategically located depots and ice houses throughout the city. No longer content with the restrictions of export sales in Chicago, the Wisconsin brewing firms now used Chicago as a jumping off point for deliveries throughout the Midwest, the South, and the rapidly growing West.

Although the beers of these firms were brewed in Milwaukee, the city's breweries still depended on supplies such as barrels, wagons, and copper boiling kettles, which were provided by Chicago's thriving peripheral brewing trades. Even most of the malt used by the Wisconsin firms was purchased from the many malt houses in and about Chicago.

Increased competition from their northern neighbors, however, eventually became a matter of concern for Chicago brewers. Feeling the effects of market saturation and a slowing of beer sales in the city, they petitioned the City Council for relief from the invasion of out-of-town breweries in the form of a proposed substantially high-priced license fee for non-Chicago breweries. The Council ignored their pleas for trade restrictions, not wanting to set off reciprocal movements by Milwaukee, and the invasion continued. Inexplicably, no viable, concerted effort was made by the Chicago breweries to invade the competing Milwaukee market.[11]

THE GOOD LIFE

Despite occasional events that challenged the maturing Chicago brewing industry, times were good for its brewer bosses during the 1870s and 1880s. Ornate residences, membership in exclusive clubs, and diversification into other economic undertakings, especially the malt trade, demonstrated their new wealth and all the advantages acquired through their brewing efforts. The leading brewers and their second-generation families had begun to secure a social status equal to the respected Fields, Armours, Palmers, and McCormicks. A look at the *Chicago Blue Book of Selected Names of Chicago and Suburban Towns* from the early 1890s and beyond reads like a "Who's Who" of Chicago brewers, listing the Hucks, Wackers, Seipps, Brands, and other leading brewers and their families. The marriage of Albertine Huck, granddaughter of pioneer brewer John A. Huck, to Marshall Field Jr. in 1892, was an event of social significance in Chicago. This union of two well-known, wealthy, and powerful families demonstrated the equality, respect, and financial standing the local brewing fraternity had finally achieved in the business and social communities.[12] But today, their parallel stature with easily recognizable names from the local meatpacking and newspaper industries, hoteliers, and retail and mail order store owners of yesteryear have cryptically been discarded from any contemporary mention in Chicago's early history.

The brewing families had acquired their considerable fortunes through hard work, determination, and luck, sometimes by just being in the right place at the right time. Their struggles were really no different than the struggles of other self-made millionaires in Chicago, and like the others, they were determined to enjoy and, on occasion, flaunt the trappings of their new wealth.

THE CARDINAL

Severing his connections with the brewing industry, H. V. Bemis sold his entire interest in the recently constructed Downer & Bemis Brewing Company to his partner and local politician, John H. McAvoy, in April 1884 for the kingly sum of $750,000 cash. In a display of unlimited wealth and extravagance, Bemis used the proceeds of the brewery sale and opened the Hotel Richelieu in 1885 on Michigan Boulevard. A huge structure, much of it done in imported white marble, it rivaled the finest hotels of Europe. Over $500,000 was spent on appointments such as sculptures and elegant place settings. An art gallery was featured in the hotel, exhibiting numerous works collected by Bemis during his frequent trips to Europe. The "Cardinal," as Bemis was referred to by friends and associates, imported a four-star chef with staff from Paris, making the kitchen, accompanied with the offerings from his wine cellar, world famous.[13]

Although Bemis and his shrine to opulence entertained such local luminaries as George Pullman, Marshall Field, Mayor Carter H. Harrison, and the visiting Buffalo Bill Cody, the Hotel Richelieu eventually proved too rich for the tastes and pocketbooks of most Chicagoans. It folded in 1893. The subsequent auction of its contents brought bidders from London, Paris, Vienna, Berlin, and St. Petersburg.[14]

BREWER PHILANTHROPISTS

Brewer families also became known as patrons of the arts and were active in numerous local charitable causes. In 1890, the Conrad Seipp family donated over $135,000 to sixteen charitable organizations. Francis J. Dewes paid for the Alexander von Humboldt monument dedicated in 1892. The Schoenhofen family also contributed to fourteen charitable organizations in 1893, totaling over $60,000. The Wackers and Seipps generously contributed toward the erection of the Schiller monument in Lincoln Park.[15]

POLITICAL INFLUENCE

Chicago brewers used their wealth and influence to secure a number of public offices during this Golden Era as illustrated:

Rudolph Brand	City Treasurer 1881–1883
Michael Brand	Alderman 1872–1873
John A. Huck	Alderman 1859–1860
Louis C. Huck	County Treasurer 1875
Ernst Hummel	Legislator 1885–1887
John H. McAvoy	Alderman 1869–1870

Adam Ortseifen   City Treasurer 1899–c. 1901; Democratic
                 Nominee for Illinois Governor 1900
Hermann Plautz   City Treasurer 1887–1889
Jacob Rehm   Chief of Police 1873–1875
W. C. Seipp   City Treasurer 1879–1881[16]

SUNDAY CLOSINGS, PART II

Having adapted themselves to American democracy and the Chicago political process, on occasion, a mutually exclusive event, the brewers were now more organized and better prepared to protect their interests, especially from the growing reformist and temperance forces of the city.

In 1872, shortly after the Great Fire, a wave of reformation swept through the city, organized by a *Committee of Seventy,* composed of leading and influential citizens and clergymen. Over one hundred thousand Chicagoans were out of work, many without shelter as a result of the recent conflagration. Crime and public drunkenness were on the rise.

Part of the reformers' demands was for a more vigilant regulation of saloons, including the perennial demand since the Boone administration of 1855 for enforcement of the Sunday blue law. Saloon keepers and brewers, having heard the arguments before, protested that they were merely satisfying what the people wanted and that the problems of unemployment and housing, not the regulation of the citizenry's drinking habits, should be the responsibility of elected officials.

Mayor Joseph Medill had attempted to mollify the demands of the committee in a personal meeting, agreeing with their objectives but noting the Herculean task in changing the habits of the drinking public, especially the Germans. The Lager Beer Riot in 1855 had forcefully demonstrated that the German community in Chicago truly believed that drinking on Sunday was not a crime against morality as temperance forces had insisted. The issue, however, of the German community's Sunday enjoyment of beer went much deeper than the philosophical and religious issues of morals; it was seen by the Germans as an issue of the right to exercise the centuries-old drinking traditions of their Germanic culture, mixed with the feelings that government officials were infringing upon their "personal liberties."

But further pressure from Mancel Talcott, president of the Police Board and an avowed advocate of the Sunday law, forced Medill to order the enforcement of section 4, chapter 5 of the city ordinances to close Chicago saloons on Sunday.[17]

The Germans and Irish, recalling the events leading up to the Lager Beer Riot, felt the reform movement was simply another thin veneered layer of nativism, organized by the old Know-Nothing forces in Chicago. Under pressure from the German and Irish bloc, Talcott eventually resigned as president of the Police Board but was replaced by Mayor Medill's appointee, Elmer Washburn. On April 28, Washburn reiterated the order that the Sunday closing law would be enforced. Police Board Commissioner Mark Sheridan entered a protest to the records of the board meeting when the order was issued. "The right of the people to be secure in their persons, homes, papers and effects against unreasonable searches and seizures, shall not be violated," Sheridan proclaimed, expanding the argument far beyond Sunday closings. At one point during the meeting, Washburn and Sheridan almost came to blows, Sheridan once again claiming that the Sunday blue law violated personal rights as advocated by the Constitution. Sheridan had reason to empathize with the views of the local brewers and saloon keepers—his father had been a brewer in his native Ireland.[18]

Mayor Medill, more or less washing his hands of the whole affair, notified the City Council that he would be gone from Chicago for an indefinite time, claiming poor health. He took an extended trip to Europe, hoping that the politically sensitive affair would somehow be rectified before his return. Lester L. Bond, sworn in on August 18, 1873, as acting mayor, continued Medill's policies in his absence. The Germans and Irish, however, were not ready to roll over.

THE PEOPLE'S PARTY

Having experienced the disastrous consequences of Levi Boone's election in 1855 and the riotous results of their earlier political naïveté, a coalition of brewers, distillers, and saloon keepers organized the People's Party, funded in part by Chicago brewers Peter Hand, Jacob Rehm, John McAvoy, F. J. Dewes, Michael Keeley, and Michael Cassius McDonald, a well-known local gambler. The *Chicago Tribune* scoffed at this coalition of gambling and drink interests and began describing the organizers and their meetings as "Advocates of Free Whisky and Free Lager" and "The Beer Guzzlers' Meeting."

The constitutionality of closing saloons on Sunday was once again argued by many Germans as one of personal rights for the individual. "The question is not whether I wish to drink a glass of lager-beer or wine, in company with friends or family, on Sunday, but whether any other man or set of men shall have the power to say I shall not," a sympathizer indignantly wrote the *Tribune*. Some Germans saw the closings as another nativist move directed toward their traditional Continental customs. Could native-born Americans dictate, "You Germans shall not do so and so, and you Germans shall do so and so?" asked a speaker at one of the many political rallies on the North Side.

The new political party reached quick agreement on their political positions and searched for a mayoral candidate. One of the more prominent planks in the new party's platform declared that the Sunday blue law was "obnoxious" to a large portion of the people and should be rescinded. In an attempt to balance any future criticism from reformers, the platform conceded positions on the regulation of liquor licenses and the appointment of beverage inspectors but firmly reiterated the party's position on Sunday closings, declaring that law and order should be preserved, but "not at the expense of personal liberty."[19]

THE ELECTION OF 1873

In the following citywide election of 1873, Harvey Doolittle Colvin, the People's Party candidate for mayor, and his entire ticket, endorsed by the Liberal and Democratic Central and Executive Committee of Cook County, were swept into office. Colvin was no saint, known as a bit of a high-roller and winkingly referred to by Chicago's sporting men as "Harvey." As expected, soon after the swearing in of Colvin and his ticket, the Sunday blue law in Chicago was repealed.

During his inaugural address of December 1, 1873, Colvin reemphasized his feelings on the Sunday closing of saloons in Chicago. "If the Common Council, in its wisdom, and having undoubtedly full power upon the subject, should determine either to repeal or modify the Sunday prohibitions and Sunday clauses in the license law, or to fully secure the religious exercises of a portion of our citizens from all disturbance, without interfering with the harmless enjoyments of other citizens, it will do no more than its duty toward the majority of the people of this city."[20]

Several other attempts were later made to resurrect the Sunday closing law, but were voted down by the City Council.

In 1874, in a spirit of compromise, the City Council did pass a new, seemingly innocuous law requiring saloons to lock their front doors and draw the shades of their establishments on Sundays, leaving both the side and rear doors open to the public. The act placed a resultant premium on corner locations.[21]

The political strength and influence of the brewing community of Chicago had come a long way since the Lager Beer Riot of 1855. Their developing wealth now gave local brewers the prestige and political power that they had lacked during the Lager Beer Riot days. Recent events had ably demonstrated that they were not afraid to use it. Their victory, however, soon set up further abuses by some saloon keepers who interpreted the election's results as free license to ignore municipal regulations on closing times, gambling, and prostitution.

Unconcerned about the compounding problems of the city saloons, Chicago's brewers would soon begin a program of buying or controlling a majority of Chicago's saloons in order to increase beer sales. In doing so, they would become highly visible targets for the growing Prohibition Movement.

Unionization, 1886–1900

We will not allow any interference
with our legitimate rights as
owners of breweries.
—*Chicago brewery owners
to union organizers*

WORKING CONDITIONS
IN CHICAGO BREWERIES

For many students of early American breweries, the idea of the brewing industry as a romantic one prevails. Indeed, the scenario of a struggling foreign-born reaching the shores of a young United States, beating back adversity and eventually establishing a successful brewery, has a certain Horatio Alger ring to it. For the workers who struggled to help the early brewer bosses achieve their dreams, however, the reality was disturbingly different.

The everyday conditions of the brewery workmen in America were arduous. Long hours and poor pay were the norm. Beatings of employees by owners or their foremen were common. Brewery employees were susceptible to respiratory ailments, including tuberculosis. Rheumatic disease was reported as being higher among brewery workers than the general population. Besides industrial diseases, there was always the threat of accidents causing disability and even death.[1]

WAGES AND BENEFITS

Compensation for brewery workers varied during the 1840s from an average of $4 to $12 per month, the lower wage usually for those who boarded free or at a reduced rate either at the brewery or at a nearby saloon. In many instances, the saloon was under the control of the brewery. The average salary increased little by the 1860s. A ruling by the Internal Revenue Office in 1868, favorable to brewers nationwide, allowed the brewer bosses to include beer as part of the workers' wages. In cities where free beer was permitted, wages were paid at the lowest rate. This free beer privilege, or *Sternewirth*, would eventually become a common perk in American breweries, an inducement that not only kept the employees going during the grueling fourteen-hour workdays, but also served as a means of pacification. A numbed worker, wallowing in an alcoholic haze, was less likely to revolt against the harsh conditions surrounding him.

A movement by national brewer organizations to institute a system of issuing daily beer tokens to brewery workers, each token representing one-half liter of beer which could be turned in at the end of the day for cash if not used, was unsuccessful. This token system, known as the Frankfurt system, had been successfully implemented in Germany to combat the destructive problems of drunkenness on the job and chronic health problems related to alcoholism. There is no evidence, however, that this approach was used by any brewery in Chicago or anywhere the United States during this period.[2]

In the early 1880s, the average national wage of brewery workers started to fall, the result of a nationwide recession that had begun during the early to mid-1870s. Because of the local rebuilding efforts after the Great Fire of 1871, the effects of the recession in Chicago were less noticeable and somewhat later in coming, buffering Chicago from the economic downturn until the end of the decade.

LABOR TROUBLES

In July 1877, a series of labor strikes took place in a number of Midwestern cities, including Chicago, emanating from a nationwide railroad strike and the hardships brought on by the recession. In Chicago, the unrest culminated in a bloody confrontation by police and a roving band of demonstrators on the near South Side. As the demonstrators massed at Archer and Halsted, a group of them splintered off and marched east down Archer Avenue, stopped in front of various businesses, and demanded that workers leave their stations and join them in further protests. As they approached the M. Gottfried Brewery and hollered from the street for the brewery employees to join them, the strikers were incensed to find that the employees would not only *not* join them, but also had proceeded to barricade the entrance to the brewery in its defense. As a heated attack on the front side of the brewery took place, a loyal brewery employee slipped through the back entrance of the plant and summoned help at a nearby police station. After clashing with the police, thirteen of the one hundred or so demonstrators were subdued and finally arrested. The brewery was damaged slightly by the attempted siege.[3]

The noncombative attitude of Chicago's brewery workers was similarly demonstrated throughout the city as walkouts and strikes of other trades prevailed. There was no recorded instances of any brewery workers leaving their posts in any of the various breweries throughout Chicago during these days of civil unrest.

BREWERY WORKERS STRIKE

In 1886, Chicago was rocked by another series of strikes that affected a number of trades in the city, this time including the local brewing industry. After watching the disastrous results of an earlier general strike by brewery workers in Milwaukee, and the calling out of the militia by the Wisconsin governor, the Chicago brewers soon made a quick settlement with the newly formed Beer Brewers' and Malsters' Union No. 1 in an effort to avoid any similar occurrences of trouble in Chicago.[4] The agreement was considered liberal for the times, but still, an indicator of the hardworking conditions in Chicago's breweries during the later part of the nineteenth century. Highlights of the agreement were

10 hour work day
4 hours on Sunday
Washhouse wages $60 per month
Cellars, fermentation and malt house $65 per month
Foreman of malt house $10–$15 more
First man in washhouse $5 more.

An interesting part of the labor agreement was the continuation of the *Sternewirth*. Beer was made available in quart-sized schooner glasses fifteen times a day at 6, 9, and 11 A.M. and 2 and 4 P.M., with each break limited to "only" three glasses.[5]

Despite the apparent accord, Chicago brewery workers threatened another strike in the early months of 1888. Buoyed by a membership of 529 and support from national union representatives, the brewers' unions continued their demands for better wages and working conditions. In addition to these demands for improvements in working conditions, the national Central Labor Union also demanded recognition by the local brewers' associations and the right to dictate terms in which men could be employed and discharged throughout breweries in the United States.[6]

The Chicago brewer bosses, tired of dealing with union leaders whom they considered "arrogant, intolerant and un-American," stood firm with a resolution signed on March 23 by thirty-four defiant local brewery owners. The harsh tone of the signed resolution infuriated the union leaders. The brewery owners had noted that the union was "organized by Oscar W. Neebe, one of the condemned anarchists [from the Haymarket Square incident], now serving time in Joliet." Still smarting over the one-day suspension of local brewing operations on the day the Haymarket Square "anarchists" had been executed, the brewery owners felt the socialist leanings of the unions placed a stigma on an industry that had tried so hard to achieve respectability in Chicago. In a final warning, the coalition of brewers stated, "We will not allow any interference with our legitimate rights as owners of breweries or as citizens of the United States."[7]

Caught in the socialistic fervor of the times, the workers walked out on the 1886 agreement on April 12, 1888, followed two days later by the malsters. The brewery owners, in turn, declared a lockout. The ill-conceived and poorly organized strike was an obvious failure by the second day of the walkout. Many *Braumeisters,* occupying a quasi-managerial role and treated in many instances by brewery owners and workers alike as something akin to gods, refused to leave their positions. Hoping that the workers would come back, the master brewers were placed in an uncomfortable position, willing to do little or nothing in support of the workers while leaving their own options open.

THE STRIKE COLLAPSES

Prepared for the possibility of a walkout, the owners had made earlier contingency arrangements with pensioned brewers and workers in Milwaukee to fill positions left by the *Streikers.* Cots and meals were provided at the Tosetti, Seipp, Keeley, Fortune, and Schoenhofen breweries for these scab workers as production continued in most of the breweries. Although a few breweries had been forced to shut down on the first day of the walkout, beer production was back online in all the local breweries by the second day of the strike. The *Chicago Tribune* lambasted the "Socialistic working brewers," questioning why the "beer-swilling anarchistic disciples have struck." The editorial went on to predict a short strike since their "wide parched throats will begin to long for lager and these big stomachs [will] yearn for their favorite fluid."[8]

Reports during the next few days confirmed that every brewery in the city was still running at full capacity, ably managed by the scab workers. A feeble attempt at bravado occurred when the desperate strikers announced that they were now going to boycott beer made by breweries associated with the local brewers' association since the association had assisted in the hiring of scabs to operate the breweries where needed. Since many of the saloons in the city were either controlled or owned by these breweries, the threat was virtually meaningless, seemingly confirming the *Tribune*'s editorial comments.

In the ensuing weeks, those strikers who had walked out meekly returned to their jobs. The workers' union was exposed as nothing more than a paper tiger that haplessly stood by when the brewer bosses went back on a number of previously agreed upon concessions. On June 8, 1888, the strike was officially declared over.

A special conference of national union delegates was held in Chicago from July 15 through July 18 to discuss not only the state of the Chicago brewers union but also that of twenty other brewery workers' unions throughout the country. Weakened by brewery owners' resistance, intimidation, and lockouts, the delegates reverted to petty bickering and accusations of incompetence at the national level.[9]

One important lesson that was learned at the Chicago conference was the need to organize all the labor organizations involved in the brewing trade. As demonstrated in Chicago and in other labor strongholds, unskilled hands, combined with scab workers and the cooperation of auxiliary beer manufacturing companies, could perform the daily functions of a brewery. Only through the coordinated efforts of the malsters, coopers, drivers, brewers, and other related brewery-affiliated unions could the workers achieve their goals.

The struggle for better pay and working conditions would continue for years to come as the brewery owners returned to the former oppressive conditions that had been so common prior to the initial agreements. Devastated by the lockout in 1888 and the subsequent collapse of the brewery workers' strike, the Chicago brewers' union wasn't reorganized until September 13, 1891. It was not until the early 1900s that the Chicago brewery owners, wounded by the beer price wars of the 1890s and increased local and outside competition, realized the economic necessity of making peace with all the brewery-related unions.[10]

AN EYEWITNESS ACCOUNT

An eyewitness account by Alfred Kolb, a young freelance writer who posed as a brewery worker and later returned to Germany to write about his experiences, described the dangerous conditions and numbness of mind and body that engulfed the average Chicago brewery employee sometime between the collapse of the 1888 agreement and the turn of the century. As was the custom in breweries throughout the United States, most of the workers were German immigrants:

> The T. brewery [probably Tosetti's] is located on the South Side . . . next to the entrance in a low wing was the bottling department. . . . The beer is forced out of the vats by compressed air into the filling machines which do the bottling by themselves. Filled like this and then corked, the bottles are sterilized in a steam bath, and the better brands are then decorated with labels, wires, and tinfoil caps. The washing, brushing, rinsing, bottling, corking, wiring, and labeling was done by machines which were operated by young male or female workers.

But while the bottling operation appeared an easy task, other jobs were more physically intensive, including the stacking and arranging of cumbersome kegs and wooden beer cases.

> I still remember handling wet barrels and heavy beer cases. Amongst the cases were many old ones riddled with glass splinters, splints, and nails. Within eight days my hands

were covered with bloody cuts and cracks. My back had become stiff, my walk and posture clumsy and heavy. . . . Once, right before quitting time, a heavy case full of empty bottles that I was supposed to bring into the basement slipped out of my tired arms . . . a small office penpusher with a four-inch stand-up collar passed by, turned up his nose and said: "That guy's probably loaded!"

The *Sternewirth,* the daily ration of free beer, was, rather amazingly, a perk that this worker felt was not abused.

Beer was handed out at 9 and at 3 o'clock. Of course, everyone drank at other times also, whenever we got thirsty. As long as you didn't put your hands on stout or other good brands, the foreman looked in the other direction . . . this privilege was not at all abused. . . . I hardly ever saw anyone tipsy: except maybe during overtime, when the men restored their dwindling strength with alcohol.

Overtime was also a regular routine that every worker had to endure.

Overtime night work was almost routine; usually until 9, sometimes to 10 in the evening. In that case a half-hour break was taken at 6 o'clock, which would have been all right if the lunch break had not been shortened accordingly. The total length of work was from 14 to 15 hours. We also worked on Sunday mornings from 6 to 12 o'clock.

But the long hours and forced overtime, mixed with a lack of safety equipment, could have its toll on any worker who let down his guard. Death or disability was an everyday occurrence. But what was more frightening was the callousness Kolb saw of his coworkers that accompanied any disaster.

One day the machine operator was caught in the driving belt of a big steam engine and torn to pieces—no wonder, by the way, given the lack of any safety equipment. . . ."Too bad for him," someone said, "he was a good guy! Now he's had it!"

Then someone else said: "Eat and drink, guys; because soon we'll all have had it, and that's that." The others remained quiet; they seemed to agree.

After the poorly executed brewery strike of 1888, wages continued to hold steady in the Chicago breweries, with no chance of a raise in the forseable future, a punishment by the brewery owners for the strike. Child labor was common in the breweries of the era, with young boys receiving 50 cents per day, women paid 75 cents, and young men, one dollar. Overtime was paid seperately, but at the same wage as regular pay. Brewers and malsters, the backbone of the breweries, started at $17 and up, Kolb noted further.

As a freelance writer, Albert Kolb's experiences were tempered with the knowledge that he could return to his room, change his dirty work clothes and leave, an option that hundreds of brewery workers throughout Chicago could never envision.[11]

⚛ 6 ⚛

The Syndicates, 1889–1900

They do not feel like taking part in the
war at Chicago if it can be avoided.
—*Newspaper reporting on Milwaukee
brewers' reaction to a price war
in Chicago during the 1890s*

THE BRITISH ARE COMING

During the late 1880s, with a widespread industrial depression limiting investment opportunities in Great Britain, English investors began to eye the profitable American beer industry. An unprecedented growth in beer sales in the United States during this period, buoyed by record levels of German immigration and enthusiastic acceptance by Americans of lager beer, appeared to make American breweries ripe for English acquisition.

Initial takeover attempts by English investors of Midwest breweries began in 1889 with the offer of $16,500,000 for the combined Schlitz, Pabst, and Blatz breweries in Milwaukee. Schlitz and Pabst were experiencing unprecedented growth—much of this because of the Chicago market—and turned down the proposal. In St. Louis, eighteen breweries were purchased by English investors but brewing giants Lemp and Busch also spurned all takeover offers.

In the same year, however, the McAvoy Brewing Company and the Wacker & Birk Brewing and Malting Company were the first Chicago breweries to be acquired by an English-owned investment syndicate, the Chicago Breweries, Limited. Authorized capital was £600,000, of which £400,000 had been issued in shares of £10 each. The combined barrelage of this merger was 315,000 per year with total sales in 1890 at 206,000 barrels, indicating an underuse of brewing capacity of more than 100,000 barrels. Chicago's brewers saw this consolidation as an answer to a developing industry problem that would eventually have to be faced by both local owners and brewers nationwide.[1]

The established American brewery owners were beginning to realize that new advances in the malting of barley, the means of bottling and pasteurization of beer, and the inevitable installation of electricity and mechanized refrigeration in the breweries would require an enormous capital undertaking; the problem was money for modernization was tight. In Chicago and other large brewing cities, competition was now limiting sales. As a result, most of the local breweries were producing beer well under capacity. By selling out to foreign investors, former owners would have the easy choices of pocketing a huge profit and perhaps staying on as consultants or managers, or simply taking their return on equity and leaving the impending problems of moderniza-tion and increasing competition to the new owners.

THE SELLING CONTINUES

In July 1889, the City Contract Company of London took stock in the Peter Schoenhofen Brewing Company, Limited, with an authorized capital of £400,000. In June 1890, the English-owned City of Chicago Brewing and Malting Company, Limited, captured about one-third of the existing shares of the Conrad Seipp Brewery and its subsidiary, the West Side Brewery, along with the F. J. Dewes Brewing Company (aka City Brewery Company, Chicago), the L. C. Huck Malting Company, and the George Bullen Malting Company. The reported price of this new consolidation was $9,500,000 with $3,106,000 worth of bonds issued to mature in 1910.[2]

In 1891, the Milwaukee and Chicago Breweries, Limited, another English conglomerate, merged with the previously formed American-owned syndicate, the United States Brewing Company. This merger included the Bartholomae & Leicht Brewing Company, the Ernst Brothers Brewing Company, the Bartholomae & Roesing Brewing and Malting Company, the K. G. Schmidt Brewing Company, and the Val Blatz Brewing Company, the Milwaukee company having finally succumbed to the English advances begun in 1889.

As noted in a prospectus in the *Chicago Tribune*, one advantage of combining these breweries was to increase the shipping and distri-bution efficiency of these Chicago breweries using Val Blatz Brewing

Company's well-established distribution network.[3] The K. G. Schmidt Brewing Company had already dabbled in exporting their Budweiser brand to the western states and territories with success, but their foresightedness was the exception.[4] After years of neglecting the export market, it took an English syndicate, working through a Milwaukee brewery, to develop a serious plan for the export of Chicago beer. Later results would prove that, for the most part, this plan was too little, too late.

Swept up by the wave of consolidations that was taking place around them, a group of American investors organized the American Malting and Elevator Company, buying a handful of local, independent malt houses that were providing malted barley and other cereal grains to nearby breweries.

The combined authorized capital of these mergers and consolidations was $11,716,000, an extraordinary sum for the times, and the total brewing capacity was estimated at 1,631,000 barrels annually, little more than half of the barrelage of all the breweries in Chicago.[5]

Investors Build More Breweries

American capitalists, some with little or no experience in the brewing trade, took note of the generous outlay of cash and securities used by the English investors to acquire these breweries and began to construct an additional eighteen breweries in Chicago during the period of the syndicates' greatest acquisition frenzy from 1889 to 1900.[6] Some of these risk takers, with little or no experience in the brewing industry, hoped that English investors might acquire their breweries soon after construction, leaving them with a quick and generous profit. Other American brewery owners-to-be noted the high capitalization of the syndicated breweries and attempted to bypass the problem of huge start-up costs by establishing themselves with a minimal amount of leverage, if any at all. By 1894, Chicago had a total of fifty-three breweries and ranked third in the nation in total number of brewing firms. Philadelphia and New York ranked number one and two, respectively.[7]

The local brewers soon realized that Chicago, having ignored and now denied the export market, and facing a stabilization in demand, could no longer support such a competitive environment.

TROUBLES FOR THE SYNDICATES

The English taste for American breweries began to waiver as investors realized that the properties were often overvalued. Blatz's dilapidated brewery in Milwaukee had been purchased for the kingly sum of $2,500,000. Within a year, it was necessary to pour an additional $400,000 into the plant for needed repairs. Coupled with the burden of overcapitalization, the syndicate's stock quotes began to fall. Dividends were less rewarding than anticipated. English investment brokers offered one excuse after another—bad weather, poor barley harvest, weak economic conditions—but stiff competition from the numerous independent breweries and the other syndicates, mixed with the financial drain of nagging stock and bond dividends, were the real reasons for the syndicates' dismal performances.[8] Robbing Peter to pay Paul, they worked with little operating capital, trying desperately to meet preferred stock and bond dividends. To make matters worse, Irish American saloon keepers threatened to boycott any English-controlled breweries and turned to the independent Irish-owned breweries for product.

Disturbed by the onslaught of foreign capital buying up local breweries, the Independent Brewing Association, composed of several wealthy and influential Chicago citizens, established a brewery in 1891. The organization's objectives were to operate a local brewery maintained "by home capital and conducted on free principles, independent of any and all syndicates and pools." A similar effort by whiskey interests in 1892 formed the Monarch Brewery. In 1903, a group of wealthy saloon owners inspired the formation of the independent Pilsen Brewing Company.[9]

Despite vigorous attempts by the syndicates and independents alike to boost sales, beer consumption in Chicago inexplicably started to taper off. Belated efforts by the local syndicates to increase the export trade offered no real chance in which to increase sales. Schlitz and Pabst in Milwaukee and Anheuser-Busch Brewing in St. Louis, well on their way to securing a national market, had already gained dominant positions, not only in the surrounding Midwest and South, but also in the developing western states. Ironically, they used the vast railway shipping yards of Chicago as the hub of their expansion.

THE BEER WARS IN CHICAGO

With hopes of securing a larger market share and, if need be, squeezing the remaining independents out, the English-controlled breweries abruptly started to bring down the wholesale price of their beer.[10] Having anticipated such a move, the Chicago & Milwaukee Brewers' Association had joined together in 1890 to stabilize the now-sinking barrel price at $6, a $2 decrease.[11] Up until this cutthroat move by the English syndicates, any rivalry between brewers taking over each other's retail accounts had been quite civilized. If an aggressive brewer took a saloon keeper from the account of a rival brewery, he was "obliged" to pay the rival brewery $3 per barrel for each barrel purchased by the retailer for a predetermined period of time as compensation.[12]

This informal gentlemen's agreement, along with a number of more detailed pacts, soon fell apart as the syndicates brought the barrel price down to $4, with a 50 cent rebate, if necessary, to effect a sale. The Manhattan Brewery was the first independent brewery to pull out of the fragile coalition of breweries hoping to stabilize the price per barrel. At this low retail level, there was now less than $1 profit per barrel. Adding to the local problems of price, smaller out-of-town breweries began to import beer to Chicago. Even at a price as low as $3 per barrel, some of these breweries found that their production and shipping costs were still low enough to make a profit in the competitive Chicago market. There was talk in the Chicago brewing community that prices would eventually fall to the inconceivable price of $2 a barrel.[13]

AMERICAN-STYLED LAGER BEER

In an attempt to maintain some sort of profit on their beer, a number of brewers began to introduce larger amounts of the cheaper cereal grains of rice and corn to the brewing mash. This cost-cutting move ran contrary to the old German purity law, the *Reinheitsgebot*, which stated that beer was to be made only with water, hops, and malted barley. But with an eye as much on survivability as profit, the local breweries started to change the Old World character of Chicago's beer. The adulteration of the centuries-old purity standard was the beginning of the a new local beer, the American-styled lager, lighter in taste and character than its all-malt predecessor. The addition of cereal grains, however, not only maintained the bottom line but also helped to hinder the formation of chill haze, an unsightly coagulation of protein from American six-row malted barley that can form when beer is cooled. With the growing acceptance of chilled bottled beer in clear glass, the customer would have no reason to question its drinkability.

Fears of the Milwaukee Brewers

The Milwaukee brewers, who had shipped 325,000 barrels of beer to Chicago in 1890, were forced to participate in this beer war, selling their products as low as $4 per barrel, $4 less than the going rate in Milwaukee.[14] Unwilling participants as they were, the Milwaukee brewers could not afford to pull out of this one-time profitable market while the price war continued. Their biggest fear, however, whispered throughout the Milwaukee brewing community, was of a possible assault on their home grounds by the English-controlled Chicago breweries, possibly importing beer priced as low as $3.50 a barrel and bringing havoc to a previously unchallenged market. "They do not feel like taking part in the war at Chicago if it can be avoided," the *Milwaukee Daily News* reported.[15] Their fears were unfounded as the Chicago brewers failed to take this aggressive sales initiative.

Tied Houses

Price cutting was only part of the syndicates' plans to increase sales. In 1892, both the Chicago Brewing & Malting Company, Limited, and the Milwaukee & Chicago Breweries, Limited, through their representatives, the City of Chicago Investment Company, pooled over $6 million for the purchase of saloons through which to exclusively funnel their products.[16] By adopting this English practice of "tied-houses," it was hoped that profits would rise as the syndicates seized control not only of the lagging beer market but also of the retailers themselves.

Even Milwaukee tried this approach in Chicago. From 1897 until 1905, Edward G. Uihlein, buoyed by the takeover of the Jos. Schlitz Brewing Company by members of his family after the drowning of the brewery's namesake, oversaw the building of fifty-seven Schlitz saloons in Chicago, often using the services of architect Emil Frommann. Concrete reliefs of the Schlitz logo can still be found on the former tied-houses built by Schlitz at 94th and Ewing and 35th and Western on the South Side. Found on the North Side intersection of Damen and Belmont and at two locations on Southport Avenue are similarly designed structures.[17]

One Schlitz tied-house, however, was noted more for its owner than its beer. Across the street from the entrance to the Chicago Union Stockyards, just south of the intersection of Root and Halsted, stood "Big Jim" O'Leary's Horn Palace. O'Leary was the son of the Great Chicago Fire's Mrs. O'Leary. With a white buffed-stone facade and huge sign over the entrance that advertised that its taps were ready to satisfy customers with Schlitz beer, the establishment housed an ornate bar room, billiard parlor, and concert hall that could seat one thousand. It also featured baths and barbershops for stockyard workers with pockets full of wages, who might want to cleanup before entering the saloon's most famous feature—a clandestine and fortified faro and roulette area.[18]

THE WORLD'S FAIR OF 1893

There remained one slim hope for Chicago breweries, one possible surge in beer sales, that might give a needed respite that the local brewers, especially the syndicated firms, could use to stabilize the depressing conditions of the home market. The opportunity was the World's Columbian Exposition of 1893. For Chicago politicians and business leaders, this was a chance to feature a new city that had literally risen from the ashes of the Great Fire of 1871. But Chicago's syndicate brewers envisioned the millions of visitors to the city as a market to exploit. The sales results, though, would be fleeting, an artificial stimulus that would only delay the increasing effects of competition. The wholesale price for a barrel of beer was now hovering around $4, leaving little more than $1 per barrel in profit.[19]

The syndicated breweries, now concentrating more on survival than show, bypassed any participation in the exhibits of national and international breweries that were featured in the Agriculture Building on the Midway. Only two independent Chicago breweries, the Cooke

Brewing Company and the North Western, used the fair as a chance to demonstrate their brewing skills and the quality of their products, both breweries winning awards for their beer in wood and bottles.[20]

The local peripheral brewing trades, with their expanding nation-wide market and relative independence of the struggling sales of the Chicago breweries, were better represented in the exposition hall of the Agriculture Building. The Geo. A. Weiss Malting & Elevator Company; Chicago Automatic Scale Company; Liquid Carbonic; the American Copper, Brass and Ironworks Company; and the Chas. Kaestner & Company all displayed their wares. But the most impressive Chicago participant in the event was the Fred Wolf Company and its Linde mechanical refrigeration exhibit. The Linde machines had already shown their worth to the national brewing industry, but Wolf was now moving away from the faltering brewing industry market.

In a joint effort with The Waukesha Hygeia Mineral Springs Company of Wisconsin, a pipeline was laid from Wisconsin, carrying spring water to pressurized cooling tanks on the fairgrounds. Chilled to a temperature of 38° Fahrenheit by two 50-ton Linde refrigeration units, the spring water was pumped to 300 water fountains on the Midway, providing over 60,000 gallons of spring water daily to the thousands of fair goers. It was the first industrial demonstration of cooling water while in transit.

An analysis of beer sales, comparing the years from 1892 through the surge of sales from the World's Fair of 1893 to the returning normalcy of 1894, dramatically demonstrated the effects of local competition in Chicago. Overall consumption of beer in Chicago had leveled off. Of the market that remained, a larger portion of the market was now being seized by the out-of-town brewers. There was, however, a slim hope for Chicago brewers. A second look at the production figures for 1894 showed an expected drop in sales from the inflated figure of 1893, but the barrelage in 1894 still showed an advance from 1892, that is, sales of almost four hundred thousand barrels. A more aggressive strategy of expanding the number of saloons in Chicago would be the only continued recourse for local brewers to survive.

CHICAGO BEER SALES IN BARRELS, 1892–1894

1892	1893	1894	Decrease 1893–1894
2,275,525	2,761,714	2,656,994	104,720

THE BEER WARS CONTINUE

One more attempt to end the beer wars took place during the fall of 1895. There was industry talk of forming a loose confederation of Chicago breweries to end the undercutting of the price of a barrel of beer. It was proposed that the brewers would form a pool of over $1 million by turning in $2 per barrel sold for a determined period of time. This money would then be supplemented by an additional stipend of 10 cents on the barrel. With a combined barrelage of over 4 million per year, the ever-increasing fund would be deposited in the Illinois Trust and Savings Bank and managed by a board of directors, elected by the brewers. From this fund, dividends would be issued to those breweries that cooperated in regulating the price of beer to a non-competitive level. Any brewery that broke ranks would lose access to the previously invested money and any future dividends. Like previous attempts at cooperation, this compromise never took effect as the brewers maintained a maverick attitude on pricing.[21]

LOCAL INVESTORS CONSOLIDATE

In 1898, one more consolidation of breweries took place in Chicago with the formation of the United Breweries Company, Chicago. With the support of the Chicago Brewers Association, a group of local liquor interests instituted the new syndicate, hoping to stabilize and even raise the price of a barrel of beer to presyndicate days. Involved in this merger were thirteen breweries, twelve in Chicago including the Chicago Brewing Company, Citizens Brewing Company, Carl Corper Brewing & Malting Company, Fecker Brewing Company, Henn & Gabler Brewing Company, Monarch Brewing Company, North Western Brewing Company, Phoenix Brewing Company, William Ruehl Brewing Company, M. Sieben, South Chicago Brewing Company, Star Brewing Company of Chicago, and the Blue Island Brewing Company in neighboring Blue Island, Illinois. Contrary to the syndicate's original business plan, which called for the quick consolidation and closing of some of the breweries, administrators of plants targeted for closing managed to temporarily delay the inevitable, causing fiscal and prolonged legal nightmares for the syndicate's investors.[22]

TROUBLES CONTINUE FOR THE
SYNDICATED BREWERIES

The troubles of the syndicated breweries seemed to go on and on, dissent even coming from within their own ranks. In 1892, during the early days of the syndication craze, William C. Seipp and Louis C. Huck, sons of pioneer brewers Conrad Seipp and John A. Huck, along with T. J. Lefens, abruptly resigned their positions as managers of the Chicago Brewing and Malting Company. The official reason given for the mass resignation was that they had simply agreed to stay on only for a short time to aid in the smooth transfer of the newly formed syndicate to English control. Rumors abounded in the Chicago brewing community, though, that they had been forced out because of dissatisfaction in London with their management of the floundering syndicate. The discharged brewers offered no explanation for the resignations, allowing the rumors to continue.[23]

In 1894, Leo Ernst, vice president and general manager of the Chicago & Milwaukee Breweries, announced that he too was leaving syndicate control and starting up his own independent brewery, which was perceived as an affront to the English owners whom he had served.[24]

Ernst Fecker Jr., an independent brewer, held a realistic view of the brewing situation for the syndicates in Chicago. In an interview with a Chicago newspaper, he said

> I venture the prediction that the English brewing companies will never again earn a dividend on the their common stocks. The trouble is that old time prices cannot now be obtained and it is not likely that they can be obtained in the future. The price of beer is now $5 per barrel and the reduction from $6 a barrel, the price in effect last year, is enough to remove the possibility of dividends being earned on the common shares of the overcapitalized English companies and to make even the preferred shares uncertain.[25]

The independent breweries were also having a difficult time during the price wars, even with the fiscal advantage of being unencumbered with the crippling debt of the syndicates. "I know what I am talking about " Fecker confessed, "because I have a brewery of my own. I am in no combination, have no stock to pay dividends on or bonds requiring a certain amount of interest money to be set aside and I find it difficult to earn a moderate return on the cold cash invested."

With local breweries producing well below capacity, Fecker understood the problems of competition, the demands of anxious investors, and the sudden drop-off in cash flow that the syndicates were now facing. The problems of falling output had been reported by the local press, the *Herald American* newspaper calling the situation "appalling."

Fecker predicted that the drop in production, coupled with the demands by investors for dividend returns, would soon be disastrous for the syndicates. "There is no chance nowadays for brewery combinations to earn money on watered securities. Only the other day I heard that one of these English breweries, which paid 7 per cent on its common stock last fall, was trying to borrow money for the purpose of paying interest on its bonds."

The independent brewer continued with his inside analysis of the syndicates' problems of production. "I have talked with several big brewers, and they tell me that their output is falling 30 to 35 per cent as compared to last year [1893]. The original *Herald [American]* statement that the falling off was 55 per cent was more nearly correct than the compilation of the syndicate stock manipulators."

With continued local competition and no hope in sight for his independent brewing operation, Fecker gave in to the overtures of the locally organized, American-owned United Breweries Company, Chicago, in 1898. He sold out just in time; his former brewery was subsequently closed in 1901 as part of a cost-cutting measure by the American syndicate. Two years later, the American brewery syndicate filed for bankruptcy protection.[26]

With beer prices already lowered during the local beer wars to unprecedented levels, the U.S. government slapped an additional $2 per barrel tax on beer to help finance the Spanish-American War, cutting deeply into what was left of brewing profits.[27] Finally, in 1899, English courts ruled that English firms operating in foreign lands were to be taxed at the same rate as those operating on English soil, erasing a tax advantage the English syndicates had enjoyed for years.[28]

No further attempts were made by English investors to purchase breweries in Chicago, but the damage was done. The beer wars, syndication, the cost of modernization, and the Spanish-American war tax had crippled the Chicago brewing industry.

⚞ 7 ⚟

The Saloons, 1875–1910

We could set our own prices.
—*Edward G. Uihlein, Schlitz*
sales representative in Chicago

PLACING THE BEER

For years, brewers had followed a policy of *placing* beer with retailers. More than 90 percent of beer sales during the early 1880s was draft. Because of the high cost of draft equipment and the availability of only one or two taps in any given saloon, it was necessary for brewery representatives to aggressively convince retailers to take on their product rather than that of their competitors. Any slow moving, bad tasting, or contaminated product or one priced too high could be replaced by a vigilant competitor with the thrifty consent of a saloon keeper looking at the bottom line. Competition was intense with savvy retailers pitting one brewery salesman against another for the best possible deal. Bar displays, coasters, matches, and other promotional items would sometimes be thrown in to sweeten a deal. Money, though, was the key inducement. Beer sales reps would often be obliged to use an allocated sales expense called *spendings* to treat a prospective client's customers at the bar, even if the customers were drinking a rival product. After buying a beer or two, the beer *drummer* might convince the saloon crowd to give his product a try, pressuring the saloon keeper to switch brands to keep his customers happy. This actually wasn't too difficult of a sales pitch to successfully accomplish. Brand loyalty was in an embryonic stage; for most customers, beer was beer. It merely had to be fresh and affordable. This same practice of buying rounds for the house would even apply to established accounts, plus an additional obligation on the drummer that might also include discounts or rebates to the saloon keeper on the barrel price, coupled with favorable credit terms for continued purchases.[1]

THE HARPER HIGH LICENSE ACT

A more dependent relationship between brewers and saloon keepers started to take place after the Illinois General Assembly passed the Harper High License Act in 1883, effective on January 1, 1884. In a bow to one more wave of temperance and reform, state legislators raised the price of a liquor license in Illinois, hoping that a high liquor license fee would force out the lower class dives and slow any further growth of saloons throughout the state. With a license fee of $150 for beer and $500 for a beer and liquor license (later changed to one flat fee of $500 for all), some saloon keepers turned to the breweries for financial assistance in securing a liquor license. In return, the brewers demanded that the retailers exclusively purchase and serve their beer, adding a service charge to each barrel in compensation for the license fee. Of course, if a competing brewer came along and was willing to buy the license and give an even better deal on their products, the saloon keeper might consider replacing the original beer supplier. This dog-eat-dog practice was a constant source of frustration for brewery representatives and owners alike, but it fostered a competitive environment.[2]

SALOONS INCREASE IN NUMBER IN CHICAGO

The English syndicates and their tied-house concept raised the level of retailer dependency to the extreme. The sales and marketing campaigns of syndicate breweries in the early 1890s consisted of a concerted program to increase the consumption of beer by three methods: (1) by organizing holding companies to purchase saloon sites and properties, corner locations with their front and side entrances being the most favored, (2) by establishing cheaply furnished saloons and placing agents in them to sell their beer, the furnishings secured by chattel mortgages, and (3) by signing the saloon keepers' surety bonds and advancing money for liquor licensing and any other permit fees.[3]

Many of the independently owned local breweries had already utilized the signing of surety bonds for saloon keepers as a way to gain some control over retail outlets. A look at the saloon license register for the area of Lake View from the period of 1883 through 1886 shows the names of local brewers Virgil M. Brand, William C. Seipp, and Otto Ernst listed as sureties on a number of saloons.[4]

With this syndicate program of expansion, which would be copied by many of the remaining independent breweries, any would-be entrepreneur with only $50 to $75 could open up a saloon at a brewery-owned or leased site, have it furnished with brewery-owned stock and equipment, be licensed with brewery money, and then obligated to purchase beer at whatever price the brewery demanded; thus the apt term for such a saloon was "tied-house."

Brewery-owned bar equipment, leased to the enterprising businessman, could be extensive. An agreement and lease made between Southwest Side saloon keeper Piotr Adamezyk and the Manhattan Brewery, an independent brewery located northeast of the Chicago Stock Yards, detailed the necessary equipment for a typical midsized neighborhood saloon start-up:

> 40' Bar 24' Bbar (backbar) . . . Footrail, 24' Mirror, IceBox, Office partition with door, 6 Tables, 4 doz Chairs, Ice-Box, Basement, stove w pipes . . . Urinal Closet, one cash register.

In return for the use of this brewery chattel, Adamezyk agreed to "purchase all beer in his saloon from said first party (Manhattan)." The benefit of a small start-up cost for a saloon was negated by a total dependency on the terms and pricing structure of the controlling brewery.[5]

Saloons would often forgo the use of tables and chairs in their establishments. But in many of the neighborhood bars, such as Adamezyk's Back-of-the-Yards business, wives would sometimes accompany their husbands to the traditionally male-dominated saloon for a Sunday drink or two, a practice that was accepted in the ethnic enclaves; women could not, however, stand at the bar. Thus there had to be tables and chairs for female customers.

Despite the restricting arrangements of choosing only one beer purveyor for product, almost anyone could now have the opportunity to run a saloon. The signed exclusivity agreement, however, constrained the practice of saloon keepers pitting one brewery against the other for liquor license fees, surety bonds, or favorable credit terms as had been the earlier practice. With this ease of entry into saloon ownership, the number of saloons proliferated. In 1877, before the tied-house practice was widely in effect in Chicago, only 1,017 saloon licenses had been issued by the city. By 1895, there were 6,522 legally licensed saloons operating in Chicago. The 1884 increase in the liquor license fee and the subsequent assistance in securing licenses by the breweries for saloon keepers, later coupled with the tied-house practice, had the overall effect of increasing, rather than decreasing, the number of saloons in the city.[6]

The sharp increase in the number of city saloons appeared to give the sales results that local brewers had anticipated. The *Brewers' Journal*, using figures provided by the syndicates, reported that sales of beer from the beginning of the syndicates' reign in 1889 through 1894 had more than doubled, totaling 2,656,994 barrels in 1894. These figures would later become questionable as industry insiders began claiming that the syndicates' production figures were being inflated in order to mollify nervous investors.[7]

SALOON FAILURES

The mortality rate of the tied-house saloons, though, was high. If the saloon keeper failed to make payments on his rent or product, his bar would be promptly seized by the brewery, including all chattels such as saloon fixtures, glasses, and stock. "It is understood that said second party has no interest in said property," was a typical clause in a brewery/saloon lease agreement. If business soured for the hapless saloon keeper, someone else might be behind the bar the next day, hoping to achieve better results than his luckless predecessor.[8] "Independent" saloon ownership was quickly seen as an illusion, but there was no lack of willing applicants for saloon positions.

This harsh business practice, with the occasional annoyance of an interrupted cash flow to the breweries from the openings and closings of their poorest performing bars, was balanced with the Darwinian effect of survival. Only the most productive saloon keepers survived and sometimes even prospered. The majority of the breweries hoped that by continuing this practice of replacing poor performing retailers with those with more business acumen, the situation would eventually achieve stability, placing retailers with superior business skills in the poorer performing outlets.

SCHLITZ'S TIED-HOUSE POLICY

In his memoirs, Edward G. Uihlein of Schlitz shows a different interpretation of tied-house policy and their Chicagoland saloon outlets:

> For our own purposes we often invested funds by financing
> our customers. In this manner we not only reached higher
> sale figures, but we also insured our clients against the
> competition. We could set our own prices, but of course
> we never took unfair advantage of this situation. When we
> rented to a merchant who handled our products exclusively
> we were very sure of his reputation and his compliance with
> all laws and ordinances. A respectable merchant need not
> fear an increase in his rent unless an increase in taxes or
> cost of maintenance made it necessary. Needless to say,
> our policies were not highly regarded by the competition.
> However, after some time, when we had achieved a reputa-
> tion for keeping our contracts and the most inconsequential
> of promises we had no problem renting all available space.
> The final result was the respect of the whole business sec-
> tor in Chicago.

Uihlein makes no reference to the Schlitz tied-house policy if a
saloon keeper failed to satisfactorily perform.[9]

THE FREE LUNCH

In an effort to increase their chances of survival, the saloon keepers
looked for endless ways to increase their patronage, the free lunch
being the most popular. Beginning with the simple but effective
practice of giving one heated oyster with every nickel beer, a Chicago
phenomenon, the free lunch blossomed to a dinner of meats, beans,
boiled potatoes, pigs feet, sauerkraut, and bread. This spread might
run the average saloon owner $2 to $3 daily. In the downtown area,
some of the more opulent saloons could spend $30 to $40 with a food
bill consisting of 150–200 pounds of meat, 1 1/2–2 bushels of potatoes,
50 loaves of bread, 35 pounds of beans, 45 dozen eggs, 10 dozen ears
of corn, and $1.50 to $2 worth of vegetables. Up to five men would be

employed at the lunch counter, serving hundreds of businessmen and City Hall politicians as they took advantage of this daily spread.[10]

In the poorer neighborhoods, the free lunch held a higher significance. "I believe it is true that all the charity organizations in Chicago combined are feeding fewer people than the saloons," Royal Melendy, a researcher of the Chicago Commons settlement house determined after a study of the practice.[11]

The whole idea of the free lunch, however, was to encourage the customers to buy beer, not provide social services. By charging a nickel for a seven-ounce glass, sometimes inscribed with the brewery's logo or name, a saloon keeper could realize a profit of over $20 per barrel of beer. The more successful saloons could run through three or more thirty-one-gallon barrels during lunch.

DANCE HALLS

Other saloon owners resorted to less honorable undertakings, including prostitution and gambling. In the immediate area of City Hall were so-called "family resorts" where men could meet women of loose character, to drink and party, often past the legal closing time. The West Side of the city was noted for their concert saloons which would offer a stage performance for free. After performing, the women "artistes" would leave the stage and circulate throughout the hall, persuading the men to buy them drinks. Prostitution was not uncommon.[12]

Reformist Samuel P. Wilson appears to have had an intimate knowledge of Chicago's dance halls and concert saloons. In his 1910 expose, *"Chicago" and its Cess-pools of Infamy*, the author described the goings-on in a typical concert saloon, calling it, "the worst feature of the social evil (saloons)."

> The dance halls are often handsome places, but were simply rendezvous of street walkers, and men who came to seek their company. We enter through a lobby into a bar-room, back of which is the dance hall. The place was furnished with tables, and chairs are scattered about the sides of the first floor, but the central space is kept clear for dancing. At the back is a dimly lighted space, fitted up like a garden, where

those who desire may sit and drink. The place was always well filled. The women present were the inmates of the neighboring house of ill-fame and street walkers. Each one is a prostitute, and each one is intent upon luring some man into her chamber. Men meet abandoned women here, and accompany them to their houses, risking disease, robbery, and even death, with a recklessness that is appalling.[13]

SLOT MACHINES

During the mid-1890s, nickel-in-the-slot machines started showing up in Chicago saloons. Originally developed in Germany to dispense postage stamps, gum, and cigarettes, Yankee ingenuity modified a number of them to pay out money, a precursor to today's video-poker machines. By dropping a nickel in the slot located at the top of the machine, and allowing the coin to negotiate a maze of nail heads, a successful player could receive a payout if the nickel landed in the right slot at the bottom of the machine. Saloon keepers could make up to $15 per day on these devices. These machines could still be found in some Chicago taverns up through the late 1950s. During the turn-of-the-century period, pool tables would also become a fixture in local saloons, adding additional profit to the saloon owner's bottom line.[14]

German *Bier Gartens*, where families often enjoyed oompah bands, sandwiches, and lager beer, were still popular. Two of the more famous beer gardens were located at Ogden's Grove on Clybourn Avenue and Schuetzen-Park, which developed into Riverview Park in 1905–1906, at Western and Belmont.[15]

BEER DELIVERIES

Independent businessmen, bypassing the need for a liquor license and the subsequent dependency on the brewers for a license fee loan or grant, took to the streets. Using horse-drawn carriages, they loaded their saloons-on-wheels with bottled beer, cigars, and sandwiches, arriving at construction sites and work areas to peddle their wares. This practice was openly endorsed by the brewers who didn't have to pay for liquor licenses nor for the added distribution costs of their products and were quite happy for any additional outlets through which to further beer sales.[16]

SALOON AND BREWERY REVENUES

Although only a small percentage of these watering holes dabbled in unsavory and illegal practices, the reformers and prohibitionists looked upon all saloons as dens of inequity, with brewers as catalysts in the downfall of humanity. With pressure once again upon the city politicians to clean up the saloons, local officials were caught in the horns of a dilemma. As noted earlier, the 1883 increase in liquor license fees had the startling effect of increasing rather than decreasing the number of saloons in the city as brewers started to pick up the license expense. From the beginning of the new license requirements in 1883 to 1884 alone, the annual city revenues from liquor licenses rose from $385,964 to over $1 million, much of the money paid out by the brewers. The increased revenues from the surge in new licenses surely had an addicting effect on Chicago's politicians; from mid-1894 to mid-1895, one-tenth of all receipts to the city was now coming from saloon licenses, totaling $3,335,359 in 1894.

Mayor Carter H. Harrison was aware of the political dilemma of balancing the demands of reform groups and nurturing this huge source of revenue. In a meeting between himself and a group of leading Chicago brewers (among them Rudolph Brand, Charles H. Wacker, one of the Seipps, Adam Ortseifen, Theodore Oehne, Otto Tostti, Virgil Brand, and representatives of Schlitz, Lemp, and Anheuser-Busch) during his first term as mayor, Harrison admonished them, asking the brewers to help curb the disreputable conditions that were being reported in the city saloons. His pleas were met with icy stares. Carter saw the cleaning up of the saloon industry as essential. If not, reformers using legal maneuvering might successfully force prohibition or a restriction of the drink trade in Chicago. The brewers, with millions invested in saloon property and the continuing need to further sales, had much more to lose than the small businessmen who ran the saloons. Realistically, if the brewers lost, so would the city, and Harrison knew it.

As they left the mayor's office, however, with Harrison's criticisms of their neglect in establishing control over their retail outlets still ringing in their ears, local brewer Theodore Oehne, seemingly oblivious to the cascading problems of Chicago's saloons, was heard to remark to the group "So, he's turning *Temperenz!*"

Harrison was wise enough to understand that he had to balance pressure on the local brewing community with political reality. He estimated that the powerful coalition of Chicago brewers, saloon keepers, and distillers was capable of controlling over fifty thousand votes, a political fact that could not be ignored.[17]

The economic effect of licensed drinking establishments on the entire city was becoming enormous. Total sales for city saloons in 1894 were around $70 million, beer accounting for $34 million of the total. Expenditures by the saloons, excluding distilled liquors, were $9,750,000. Of the revenues to the city from the liquor licensing fees, 2 percent was allocated for the police pension fund, and a maximum of $20,000 to the Washingtonian House, a hospital for alcoholics.[18]

CORRUPTION

With the semiannual licensing fee windfall swelling city coffers, tempered by the growing demands of reformers that lawmakers do something about the conditions of saloons in Chicago, it became increasingly obvious to city officials that there was a need to gently regulate, or at least give the appearance of regulating and policing, the overwhelming number of saloons now operating in the city. In an effort to add seeming control over a wide-open industry and still keep a steady flow of revenues pouring into the city treasury, the City Council passed a number of ordinances to appease reformers, including the regulation and enforcement of opening and closing hours of city saloons.

Abuse of these laws, not only by saloon keepers but also by neighborhood policemen assigned to keep tabs on the saloons, would occasionally come to public notice. The April 11, 1895, edition of the *Evening Post* reported on the operation of "blind pigs," or unlicensed saloons, near Jackson Park during the World's Fair in 1893. "Probably the most sensational statement in the hands of reform organizations concerning the blackmailing practice of police, is made by a man who during the World's Fair conducted a saloon within the prohibited districts near Jackson Park. This person declared that he was assessed $1,200 a month for the privilege of continuing the illicit traffic . . . it was contribute so much or close up." At the time, there were about twenty-three blind pigs operating in the area, part of the recently annexed township of Hyde Park. The number halved when the gouging prices to operate steadily rose. But the free-wheeling practices of Chicago's saloons would continue with only sporadic enforcement by local politicians and the police department.

The crippling beer wars of the 1890s, increased competition from local and outside breweries, and the imposition of an additional $1 tax on barreled beer for the financing of the Spanish-American War would force the brewery owners to assume a see no evil, hear no evil attitude concerning the growing problems of the local saloons. Increased sales at any cost were necessary for the continued existence of the local brewing industry. Saloons, with all their problems, were the only hope for the Chicago brewers to maintain sales.

But by the turn of the century, the problems of Chicago's saloons would start to rest uncomfortably in the laps of the brewers. It would take at least another decade before they would acknowledge their part in having helped to create the problem. By then, the tail would be wagging the dog.

PART II

Pre-Prohibition

⊰ 8 ⊱

Rebirth, 1900–1905

A brewer love fest.
—*Brewer John H. Weiss describing*
a reconciliation dinner of leading
Chicago brewers in 1901

THE INDUSTRY REGROUPS

The stirrings of a rebirth in the Chicago brewing industry were unmistakable in the early 1900s. For the syndicate-owned and independent
breweries alike, the beer price wars of the 1890s, coupled with the added
$1 Spanish-American War tax increase on a barrel of beer, had had a
crippling effect on Chicagoland breweries. Demands by local unions,
along with the economic necessity of meeting the challenges of new
technologies in the brewing field, had left many of the breweries in a
precarious financial position. With survival as their chief objective,
Chicago brewers began a campaign to reenergize the local industry.
The obstacles to stabilization and possible growth were many, but
surmountable.

In the early summer of 1900, the price of a barrel of beer in Chicago
was once again up to $6.[1] Even with the price increase and the meager
added profit it afforded the local brewers, the continuation of the war
tax and sluggish sales problems started to take their toll on the City of
Chicago Brewing and Malting Company, Limited. In July the company
failed to pay its midsummer dividend, citing the added burden of the
war tax.[2] The investors of the City Contract Company of London, who
had earlier taken stock in the Peter Schoenhofen Brewing Company,
Limited, had had enough of poor returns and the unsettling financial
situation of their investments in Chicago. The Schoenhofen family,
recognizing the desperation of the English investors, offered to buy
the common shares of the minority stockholders at $2.40 per each $10

share and dissolve the English company. The investors were livid with the low offer but soon reached terms with the family.[3]

During this time the United States Brewing Company was having a protracted legal nightmare with one of their brewery managers. After paying $450,000 cash and stock for the Star Brewery on North Rockwell, Patrick Rice, who had been appointed as manager for a term of two years, refused to leave his post when his contract was not renewed. Realizing his dismissal was a prelude to the cost-cutting measure of closing the brewery, Rice, along with his loyal employees, actually barricaded the brewery entrance and retained physical control over the plant. After a series of suits and countersuits, the embattled Rice was finally evicted, allowing management to return to their initial plan of closing the brewery and further consolidating the assets of the syndicate. Not surprisingly, the siege and subsequent court battle drained the syndicate of much needed working capital.[4]

THE WAR TAX

In April 1900, a delegation of the United States Brewers Association, led by their president, Chicago brewer Rudolph Brand of Brand Brewing, appeared before the House Committee on Ways and Means to appeal for a reduction of the war tax, imposed on the brewing industry in June 1898 to help finance the Spanish-American War. They argued that an extraction by the federal government of such a large portion of the selling price of an article (beer) was oppressive, unfair, and un-American.[5] In the face of unfavorable public opinion for rescinding the tax, the tax was reduced a disappointing 40 cents a barrel. The cost of goods at the time for a medium-sized brewery with a capacity of about seventy-five thousand barrels was still around $4.86 per barrel. With wholesale prices hovering around $6 a barrel, brewing was no longer a business of high profits and low overhead.[6]

HARMONY IN THE INDUSTRY

There was a growing realization among local brewery owners that cooperation with competitors, union leaders, creditors, and regulatory agencies was vital for continued existence. As a first step, truces among brewers were becoming the norm in the Chicago brewing community. Modern, reliable equipment; a solid capitalization of assets; a quality product; and a strong management team were the tools to continuing, albeit moderate, profits. Those who ignored the signs of the times and continued with the old ways might soon be run out of business or absorbed by a leaner, more aggressive competitor. Recent experiences had proven so.[7]

Most of the brewery owners, though, had seen the writing on the wall; cooperation was the operative word, especially among competing breweries. A banquet for Chicago's leading brewery owners in 1901 at the home of Edward G. Uihlein, still operating as an officer of the Jos. Schlitz Brewing Company in Chicago, was described by owner John H. Weiss of the Gottfried Brewery as a "brewer love feast." [8]

PREPARING FOR THE FUTURE

In 1902, the war tax was finally eliminated after considerale lobbying efforts in Washington, reducing the tax on a barrel of beer to the old $1 rate. Coupled with a slow but steady increase in beer sales, the resultant rise in the average profit per barrel brought about a flurry of renewed activity in the battered Chicago brewing industry. The Chicago & Milwaukee Breweries, Limited; the United Breweries Company, Chicago; and the Chicago Brewing & Malting Company, Limited, took steps to reorganize, calling in old bonds, raising additional working capital, and consolidating outstanding shares where necessary. Dividends were sharply curtailed, and, in some instances, temporarily eliminated, as the syndicates took a tough stand with nervous investors. In 1903, the Chicago Brewing & Malting Company authorized payment of its first dividend since 1897, proving the effectiveness of its reorganization plans.[9]

The nonsyndicated breweries, led by the Peter Schoenhofen Brewing Company and the Independent Brewing Association, unburdened with the restrictive debt of the syndicates, began a campaign of expansion and modernization. The Schoenhofen Brewery installed the world's largest hop-jack in 1905 to filter their beers of the flavoring herb after leaving the copper. The huge device had a capacity of eight hundred barrels. The Carl Coerper Brewing Company began expansion of their plant in 1903, in Bridgeport at Forty-First and Union. The new structure showed little outward signs of ornamentation or pretension as did the older breweries, reflecting the industry's new philosophy of efficiency and practicality and saving the bulk of the construction expenditures for the latest in modern brewing equipment.[10]

This period of belt tightening and a refocusing of business goals by almost all the Chicago breweries began a revitalization of the local industry. Trade publications noted this new growth, citing an increase of capital stock in many of the breweries that had successfully weathered the beer wars of the 1890s and the war tax. Anheuser-Busch, Schlitz, Blatz, and Pabst also watched the pick up in business and vigorously renewed their endless invasion of the Chicago market, building new depots and storage facilities throughout the city.

EFFECTS ON RELATED TRADES

As the brewing industry in Chicago continued its growth, the auxiliary trades flourished as well. The Liquid Carbonic Company, A. Magnus Sons Company, the Saladin Pneumatic Malting Construction Company, and the brewery architectural firm of Louis Lehle, along with scores of other companies integrated with the local brewing community, continued to meet the needs of breweries not only in Chicago but also throughout the country as well.

The Albert Schwill & Company began construction of the world's largest malting plant in South Chicago, a distinction formally held by another Chicago business, the Northwestern Malt & Grain Company. A twenty-four tank behemoth, with an annual capacity of 2,500,000 bushels of grain, the new plant was poised to supply the needs of the revitalized Chicago brewing community.[11]

PEACE WITH THE LOCAL UNIONS

In 1904, in a further sign of industry harmony and cooperation, the Chicago Brewers' Association entered into contract negotiations with Brewers' & Malsters' Union #18 and Brewery Laborers' Union #337 for a two-year contract. After some posturing by both sides, the brewer bosses offered an extension of the previous contract for one year. In a decidedly different tone than in earlier years, they stressed their willingness to take up the matter of a new contract once business improved. After a quick counteroffer by the unions, noting the obvious improvement of the brewers' financial situations, the Chicago Brewers' Association quickly made a contract with the Brewers and Malsters' Union and the Brewery Laborers' Union. Both agreements were decidedly liberal in pay and benefits. A further concession established a seven-man arbitration board consisting of three management and three union representatives, with an impartial seventh member chosen by the two groups.[12]

The Weiss Beer Brewers of Chicago also made their peace with their brewery workers, giving them practically the same terms as those offered to the lager brewers. The threat of another wasteful and potentially disastrous labor confrontation while the local brewing industry was reemerging from the rough financial times of the 1890s had been averted.

The beginning of the new century for Chicago's breweries was a keystone, bridging the incredible growth of the 1870s, 1880s, and 1890s with the moderate but sustainable growth of the twentieth century. It certainly wasn't like the good old days but the local brewery owners had learned to adapt to a new set of circumstances that had never challenged their fathers and grandfathers. Not only were they adapting, but also it appeared that business for Chicago brewery owners was once again thriving.

⚓ 9 ⚓

Early Prohibition Efforts, 1900–1917

The saloons with their attractions,
and the bartenders, with their
effusive smiles, lure men to drink.
—*The Saloon Problem and Reform, 1905*

The sum of the matter is, the people
drink because they wish to drink.
—*Rudolph Brand, Chicago brewer*

THE ANTI-SALOON LEAGUE

The undeniable connection between city saloons and Chicago's breweries went under attack by local reformers and prohibitionists during the early 1900s. Leading the broadsided assault was the Anti-Saloon League, founded by the Reverend Howard Hyde Russell of Ohio. Russell was a lawyer turned minister. After spending time at the Armour Mission in Chicago and noting the conditions in Chicago's many saloons, he returned to Ohio in 1893 and founded the Ohio Anti-Saloon League. The League's initial efforts in the late 1890s consisted of temperance pledge drives but were soon supplemented with sophisticated political and legislative efforts. Fueled by the financial support of rural Methodists, Bible Belt Baptists, Presbyterians, Congregationalists, and several smaller fundamentalist sects, the Anti-Saloon League, now spearheaded by the efforts of Wayne Wheeler, the League's national lawyer, led forces to defeat the reelection of Governor M. T. Herrick of Ohio. Herrick had taken a strong stand against a local option campaign in the state, making him an easy target for the new, well-financed aggressiveness of the League. Local option allowed petitioners in any precinct, ward, city, or county to place a prohibition referendum on any ballot, a powerful tool for early prohibitionists. The League's efforts defeated Herrick by almost forty-three thousand votes.[1]

Flushed with their first important political victory, Wheeler's forces moved on to larger cities, including Chicago. Their efforts began to exhibit a class and philosophical struggle between puritanical ruralists and the wicked inhabitants of the big city. Chicago was, to the small town mentality of League followers, a center of depravity close to the League's strongholds. It was a city of alien inhabitants who spoke little or no English, where political graft, gambling, and prostitution were common. The League's members felt these foreigners also brought their dangerous religious institutions with them, including the seditious teachings of the papist Roman Catholic Church and the equally menacing philosophy of the Germanic Lutheran Churches. A rural, small-minded perception took hold of the Anti-Saloon League which clearly reflected the xenophobic leanings shared by its membership.

Their central focus of attack upon arriving in Chicago was the brewery-controlled and independent saloons. Prohibitionists narrowed their aims and targeted Sunday saloon closings as their first objective in imposing their puritanical views on the big city heathens. Despite a long-standing state law ruling otherwise, saloons in Chicago traditionally remained open on Sundays. The Know-Nothing character of the prohibitionists' initial efforts was not lost on the German American brewers, many still with strong ties to Europe and a familiarity with the old stories of Chicago's Lager Beer Riot of 1855 and the rebuffed 1873 efforts of Mayor Medill to close local saloons on Sundays.

Chicago city authorities initially resisted the growing pressures of the Anti-Saloon League and others like the Evanston, Illinois, based Women's Christian Temperance Union to do something about the social problems associated with the saloons and their brewery providers. Then Mayor Carter Harrison Jr.'s relationship with the Chicago brewing community had become extremely amiable, as had been his father's, despite a frothy beginning. Having mimicked the political savvy of his father during his five-term mayoral reign, the younger Harrison would initially be accused by local reformist groups of catering to the drink industry. In a sign of solidarity with Chicago's brewers, Harrison led the Grand March of the local brewmasters' association annual ball in 1903, attuned to the political strength of the brewers, and distanced himself from reformers.[2] The mayor, often referred to by the German brewery owners as *"Unser* [our] *Carter,"* knew that there was no political practicality in upsetting the considerable flow of tax revenue that poured into the city coffers from the activities of the breweries and their tied-houses, and most important, to the city's growing budgetary needs.

THE BREWERS AND THEIR SALOON CONNECTION

Nonetheless, political and community opportunists increased pressure on the brewers and city aldermen to clean up the local saloon industry. A special report by the Chicago City Council in 1904 detailed some of the violations that had led to revocations of liquor licenses in 1903:

> Allowing or conducting a gambling business on the saloon premises or as an annex to the saloon; permitting the saloon to be a resort and refuge for dissolute women, thieves, pickpockets, gamblers and confidence men; allowing men to be lured to the saloon, drugged, robbed and assaulted; conducting depraving "vaudeville" exhibitions in connection with saloon and allowing girls under age to appear; . . . being implicated in the collection of police "protection" money from women in the street and being the landlord or renting agent of rooms used for immoral purposes."[3]

Though damning in many ways, the report did go out of its way to acknowledge some of the important functions that many neighborhood saloons provided for working-class Chicagoans.

Feeling the public pressure to start a public relations campaign to disassociate themselves from the more disorderly saloons, the brewery owners' early efforts lacked focus, often taking one step forward and two steps back. In 1904, Mayor Harrison refused a liquor license for a saloon to be opened next to Lyman Trumbull School on Division Street. An appellate court ruling, soon after Harrison's license refusal, decided, however, that the mayor of Chicago, in spite of his recent action, did not have the discretionary power to refuse a license for a saloon wanting to open next to a church or school. A number of local brewers soon made it known that they were ready to take advantage of this appellate ruling and establish saloons in the vicinity of local schools, prompting even the *American Brewers' Review* to question the sanity of such a move:

> No matter what may be the letter of the law, it is quite well understood that the people as a general thing are opposed to saloons near schools, as for fifteen years Chicago's mayors have acted upon that public sentiment. . . . Will the brewers stir up a hornets nest when there is no call for any more saloons to dispose of their product in a profitable manner?[4]

To make matters worse, yellow press charges of saloons and their owners involved with murder, white slavery, prostitution, gambling, and underage drinking became everyday fare in the local papers, further strengthening the resolve of reformers and prohibitionists and creating an increasingly uncomfortable position for Chicago's brewers.

COMFORT STATIONS

For better or for worse, the everyday operations of many of the city saloons were inexplicably tied with the daily activities of the average Chicago citizen. Taking advantage of the new transit system, saloons started to spring up along major arterial routes, offering a brief respite between trolley or train transfers for increasingly mobile Chicagoans. The placement of saloons at busy intersections was a source of irritation to the dry forces but the corner saloons often were the only place where a traveler could find a toilet, warm up when cold, or get a cool drink during the summer months. As far as brewers and saloon keepers had asserted, if the weary traveler also stopped for a beer, so much the better.

In a public relations coup for city brewers, the owners of the Schoenhofen Brewery opened a public comfort station in 1909 at Schoenhofen Park in conjunction with the city. The idea of a public toilet and drinking fountain at trolley transfer points was one originally suggested by reformers, an idea that would allow commuters the option of using a comfort station rather than entering a saloon for relief and succumbing to the temptations of a cool draft beer. Built in a small triangular area located in front of the brewery, the brewery-maintained comfort station was conceived by Joseph Theurer, the president and son-in-law of Schoenhofen.

The original construction plan called for a fountain to be erected as the centerpiece of the park. When the fountain, which represented a stork family in repose, arrived for setup and display, the Municipal Art Commission rejected it, noting that the stork was "a foreign bird," common in the northern parts of Germany. Mayor Busse dismissed the commission's objection and gave the go ahead for the fountain's erection. Total cost for the comfort station was $5,000, with the land, the disputed fountain, and comfort facilities, and $2,000 donated by the neighborhood brewery. At any other time, the objection by the commission of Schoenhofen's fountain might have seemed merely an annoying bureaucratic occurrence, perhaps even a legitimate difference in aesthetic taste, but there was an anti-German sentiment behind the commission's move, a sentiment that would soon become an effective weapon in the burgeoning arsenal of local prohibitionist forces.[5]

SALOONS AND THE WORKING CLASS

The saloons were more than just comfort stations. For the working class and the newly arrived immigrants, saloons often acted as informal employment agencies, providing information of possible open positions in the nearby factories, often gaining obliging new customers as a result. In the many brewery-controlled or owned saloons, the brewers customarily supplied the necessary funds to cash the checks of appreciative workers who would respond with the purchase of a round or two of beer. Perry Duis, in his book, *The Saloon: Public Drinking in Boston and Chicago: 1880–1920*, reports of one saloon at 43rd Street and Ashland, directly west of the Stockyards, that cashed over $40,000 worth of paychecks each month for workers. The backroom of the neighborhood saloon in the ethnic enclaves was often used by local residents as a gathering place for weddings and after burial ceremonies, especially in the predominately Irish Back-of-the-Yards and

Bridgeport communities. For the average workingman, often abused in an industrial non-union environment of debilitating twelve-hour workdays, it could be a place of respite and solitude. "He don't want to go home," observed political satirist Finley Peter Dunne and his all-wise and knowing Mr. Dooley. "There ought to be wan place where th' poor wurrukin'-man can escape bein' patted on th' back," Dunne's mythical Irish barkeeper observed. For all the acknowledged bad that evolved from a minority of Chicago saloons, many of the others now served a multipurpose function in the outlying neighborhoods and had become important fixtures in the lives of the average Chicago citizen.[6]

In the minds of reformers though, the evils of the saloon far outweighed any perceived benefits to the local population. Efforts in 1906 by Anti-Saloon League forces, joined by some opportunistic local civic and religious leaders, to pressure Mayor Edward F. Dunne to close saloons on Sundays, once again proved fruitless. The mayor duly noted that the people of Chicago had decided that question by vote years ago. Surprisingly the normally conservative *Chicago Tribune* commented favorably on the wisdom of Dunne's position. In the years that followed, the newspaper would continue to assume a wet attitude in its editorials.[7]

In December of the same year, the *American Brewers' Review* wrote of the Anti-Saloon League's increasing efforts to support local option bills, recognizing the League's ultimate goal. It warned, "By taking a little at a time they expect to accomplish . . . prohibition." The editorial labeled the League "the most dangerous enemy the brewing trade ever had."[8] A later unmasking of the true nature of the League's intent would prove the editorial prophetic, for it would soon be demonstrated in Chicago and the rest of the country that the intent of the Anti-Saloon League was much more than the mere implementation of saloon closings on Sundays.

The Western Brewer reported that Adam Ortseifen, president of the Chicago Breweries, Ltd., had begun a letter writing campaign to refute mounting arguments sent to city newspapers by prohibitionist organizations advocating saloon closings; these were arguments that had previously gone unchallenged. In the face of the growing strength of local prohibitionist forces, this sporadic and uncoordinated effort by a few brewers would prove ineffectual.

LIQUOR LICENSE FEE INCREASED

By January 1906, the efforts of reformists to shut down or limit the number of saloons in Chicago had finally stirred the political sensitivities of some local politicians. Following this reform trend, the Chicago newspapers began a series of articles suggesting the doubling of the current $500 liquor license fee. The *Chicago Record-Herald* on February 3, 1906, headlined the "huge array of sentiment for saloon permits at $1000" and suggested that the increase in revenue could be used to hire additional policemen. Any alderman who voted against the increase was warned that he would be "condemned at the polls."

Initially it seemed that brewers would naturally suffer from any sort of license fee increase. Their ownership of citywide saloons was strong, and any license increase would directly affect them. The whole campaign though was a highly orchestrated one by wet Chicago aldermen and the local brewery and liquor interests to avoid the more conservative Illinois General Assembly from possibly stepping in and increasing the liquor license fee much more than the proposed $1,000. Illusions of saloon reform in Chicago did have a price, and the local brewers were willing to pay it. The fee increase also served the additional purpose of temporarily appeasing the prohibitionist forces who had become more vocal and efficient in their latest round of antidrink efforts.[9]

The $1,000 liquor license fee passed the City Council and went into effect on May 1, 1906. Soon thereafter, 1,354 of Chicago's 7,600 saloons closed—mostly in the poorer neighborhoods. Things looked worse for the brewers and their retail outlets a few months later when Alderman Daniel Harkin, representing one of the more affluent wards, introduced an ordinance freezing the number of liquor licenses to a ratio of five hundred citizens per permit. When the ordinance took effect, license number 7,353 would be the last license issued under the new ratio limit. The next license could not be issued until the city's population had doubled.[10]

As with the Harper High License Act of 1883, the poorly conceived Harkin Law had a much different effect on the number of liquor licenses than the lawmakers had intended. Because of the now finite number of licenses available, and the speculation of future demand for them, a Chicago liquor license now had a premium value of around $150 over cost. The Chicago brewers took advantage of this unintended phenomenon and quickly applied for additional licenses before the law went into effect on July 31, 1906. This temporary loophole pushed the number of outstanding licenses to 8,097, or one for every 239 men, women, and children in the city.[11] The local brewers also purchased many of the nine hundred or so licenses now available in the premium market, transferred to them by independent saloon owners unable or unwilling to pay the $1,000 fee.

Brewery control over Chicago's saloons was now overwhelming. There could be no mistake or denial; any problems associated with Chicago's saloons would clearly be the responsibility of the city brewers.

The uncomfortable issue of saloon reform was brought up in an Illinois State Brewers' Association meeting in early 1906. Rather than paint the situation in a pessimistic light, the brewers concurred that some practical measures certainly were needed to resolve the situation. A moment after the initial discussion had begun, however, Charles Vopicka of Atlas Brewing motioned to continue the ineffectual committee on saloon regulations and control for another year and quickly moved on to other business. The swiftness of the affirmed motion by the gathering proved to be nothing more than lip service from the brewers to a problem that was becoming increasingly unmanageable. The problem, however, must have gnawed on the consciences of some of the more enlightened participants of the ISBA meeting. A representative of the Conrad Seipp Brewery later conceded that 10 percent of the saloons in Chicago, almost eight hundred, were "objectionable."[12]

For the growing financial needs of the city of Chicago, the implementation of the liquor license fee increase and the brewers' frenzy to purchase additional licenses resulted in a revenue windfall. In just one day, the receipts of the license office reached $478,500. Final receipts for the semiannual liquor license fee of $500 eventually totaled over $3,500,000.[13]

BOTTLED BEER CONSUMPTION INCREASES

As the overall number of saloons initially diminished, then surged again in Chicago after the institution of the $1,000 license fee, a new pattern of beer drinking began to unfold behind the closed doors of Chicago's homes and tenements. Beer sales dramatically increased, bolstered by the convenience of bottled beer, allowing men *and* women to now drink in the privacy of their homes. Heretofore, the practice of women drinking in saloons was frowned upon. If properly escorted by a husband or male family member, a respectable woman could make use of the discreet "family entrance" located on the side of select corner saloons, and take her refreshments at a table with her escort, but this was the exception rather than the rule.

With the availability of bottled beer, it now became practical for the man of the house to pick up a case or two of beer from his local saloon or, in most instances, purchase beer directly from the neighborhood brewery, rather than the corner saloon. The brewers used this steady increase in bottled beer consumption and the corresponding decrease in liquor sales as proof of their perennial argument that beer was a recognized temperance drink, a "drink of moderation."[14] Their argument of beer as a benign, healthful refreshment, unlike the stronger, debilitating liquor, would eventually drive a wedge between the distillers and the brewers during a time when drink trade unity against prohibitionists should have been paramount.

The rising consumption of bottled beer was also alarmingly noted by reform groups. In an attempt to stir up public opinion against the city government's blind acceptance of its segregated areas of vice, such as the near South Side's notorious Levee District, a number of startling claims were made by reformers that managed to bring the embarrassment of the vice districts to the front pages of the local newspapers and the attention of the average Chicagoan. The reformers' investigation suggested a link between the brewers and prostitution in the Levee District, fueled by an embarrassing estimate that over 27 million bottles of beer had been served by the madams of the Levee's numerous whorehouses during the preceding year.[15]

DRY REFERENDUM

Enraged by the unexpected outcome of the new high license fee and the Harkin ordinance, the Illinois chapter of the Anti-Saloon League pushed through a bill in the state legislature to establish home rule in Chicago in 1907. This measure, it was hoped by prohibitionists, would be the instrument to further the cause of local option and, ultimately, citywide prohibition. In the meantime, Mayor Busse rebuked another delegation from the Sunday Closing League, declaring "if the saloons of Chicago are closed on Sunday, it must be without my aid."[16]

Eventual passing of home rule and the implementation of local option did dry up neighborhood saloons in some wards as aldermen bowed to the wishes of their constituents. As a further demonstration of their resolve, antidrink forces organized a prohibition march in Chicago on September 26, 1908. Newspapers estimated that six to ten thousand participants marched; prohibition supporters, naturally, claimed a higher figure. Whatever the number, local politicians were once again forced to take notice of the increasing strength of the prohibitionist bloc.[17]

In March 1909, in an address before the Chicago Section of the Society of Brewing Technology, Henry E. O. Heinemann, editor of the *American Brewers' Review*, spoke of the very real threat of prohibition and the drink question. "I cannot bring myself to look upon it [Prohibition Movement] as a mere passing wave." He reiterated an earlier warning from the editorial pages of the *ABR* that the true purpose of the Anti-Saloon League was not simply to shut down the saloons on Sundays or limit their number, but to ultimately achieve "suppression of the entire drink traffic."

Chicago brewers now had a real reason to worry. Bending to the wishes of their constituencies, two-thirds of Chicago's precincts were now dry, a result of local option. Fortunately for brewers and some saloon keepers, the City Council allowed saloons in dry precincts to remain open along major commercial streets, still sparing the residential areas from the saloons. But if one wanted to get a drink in Chicago, one still could. In the working-class community of Bridgeport, traveling south down Halsted Street from the northern border of the neighborhood, starting near the south branch of the Chicago River to the southern end of the 4600 block, skirting the eastern edges of the Chicago Stockyards, sixty-two legally licensed saloons were open for business with no dearth of customers. The restrictions of local option banned the sale and consumption of alcohol in saloons; it did not, however, prohibit the act of drinking, as evidenced by Chicago crime statistics for 1908. Of the 68,220 total arrests for the year, 40,875 were for drunkenness-related occurrences.[18]

The warnings of the *ABR* almost became a sobering reality in Chicago when a petition with 74,805 signatures was presented to the city election board in 1910 for a citywide referendum on the prohibition question. But a careful examination of the signatures led to an estimate of at least twenty-five thousand fraudulent entries on the petition. As a result, the election board decided to omit the question from the ballot.[19]

In spite of the celebratory posturing of the local brewers in blunting this latest attack by prohibitionists, a poem by Charles Frederic in the March 1910 issue of the *Western Brewer* seemed to indicate a sense of resigned fatalism by some members of the local brewing community:

> When Chicago goes dry,
> As they say that it will,
> When no more you and I
> By our fire when it's chill
> Our glasses may fill
> And the winter defy,
> What joy shall instill
> When Chicago goes dry?
>
> When Chicago goes dry,
> And the summertime heat
> Turns to brass in the sky
> And to fire in the street,
> When a-weary we meet
> And for comfort we sigh
> Then what solace shall greet
> When Chicago goes dry?
>
> When Chicago goes dry,
> And the neighbors come in
> Then a stein foaming high
> Will, alas, be a sin.
> We their friendship to win
> With cold water must try,
> But 'twill seem awful thin
> When Chicago goes dry.
>
> When Chicago goes dry
> What a horrible thirst

Then will spread far and nigh
From the 'Steenth to the First!
Why, I think I will burst
And I know I will die—
Oh, I fear for the worst
When Chicago goes dry!

When Chicago goes dry,
As at present the scheme,
Then old State Street so spry,
Like Sahara will seem.
We will slumber and dream
While the business goes by—
For New York gets the cream
When Chicago goes dry.

When Chicago goes dry,
And no glasses may clink,
When we give a black eye
To the demon of drink,
We'll be longing, I think,
Something wetter to try—
For our business will shrink
When Chicago goes dry.

When Chicago goes dry,
What will other folks do?
Well, the world will not cry
And the world will not stew,
We will sink out of view
While the world hurries by
To some market that's new
When Chicago goes dry.

When Chicago goes dry,
Then the man with the grip
He will gives us a sigh
And will give us the slip
And, on railroad or ship,

To some haven will fly
Where his Beer he may sip
When Chicago goes dry.

When Chicago goes dry—
But a secret I've heard
That was told on the sly
By a wise little bird;
And he says it's absurd,
That the tricks folks will try
That have elsewhere occurred,
When Chicago goes dry.

When Chicago goes dry,
And the cupboard is bare
Folks will drink on the sly
What is now on the square.
And it's better, I swear,
In the open to buy
Than a mask thus to wear
When Chicago goes dry.

When Chicago goes *dry*
We shall owe such a debt
To those people who try
All our courses to set!
Yet I know we will sigh,
We who wanted it wet,
When Chicago goes *dry*—
But it hasn't—NOT YET![20]

Additional citywide prohibition referendums were attempted in early 1911 and 1914, but these efforts also fell through.

CONTROVERSIAL VISITS

Chicago wets had thus far shown stiff resistance to the increasing assaults by local prohibitionists. Arthur Burrage Farwell, leading the Chicago forces of the Anti-Saloon League, was looking for an influential figure to help further the local dry cause and strengthen their political position at home. Inexplicably, Farwell approached the visiting Samuel Gompers, president of the American Federation of Labor, and solicited his support of the "cause," suggesting he address a local meeting of the Anti-Saloon League.

Targeting Gompers for help was a naïve choice by Farwell. Unionism was sweeping the nation, buoyed by the millions of newly arrived ethnics, especially the hordes of lager-loving Germans. Prohibitionists had already displayed xenophobic tendencies, not lost on the newly arrived foreign element. For the hundreds of thousands of foreign-born Chicagoans, prohibition equaled nativism.

Gompers knew where his support came from and brusquely refused Farwell's overture. The union leader noted that his travels throughout the country had demonstrated to him that prohibition was a failure. "I told Mr. Farwell that I could not consent to endorse local option and appear at the meeting because I am not in sympathy with the movement," he told Chicago reporters. Following the standard wet argument, he went on. "Proper regulation of the liquor traffic is much more effective than the abolishment of saloons under the local option or prohibition laws."

Speaking of his observations in the state of Maine, dry since 1851, Gompers pointed out the hypocrisy and futility of prohibition as he saw it. "There is not a city in Maine where you cannot go openly and get all the whisky you want and all the beer you want. I have seen some drunken people in my life, but I have never seen drunks so drunkenly drunk as those in Maine."[21]

Rebuffed by Gompers and needing to make a show of strength in Chicago, the national forces of the Anti-Saloon League stepped into temporary control of the local league chapter. They used the planned attendance of secretary of agriculture, James Wilson, in October 1911 at the Second International Brewers' Congress in Chicago as a platform to dissuade President Taft from seemingly lending any sort of approval to the brewing industry. Taft received a written protest from Homer C. Stunts, first assistant corresponding secretary of the Board of Foreign Missions of the New York Methodist Episcopal Church in early September. "I hope you will find it in your power to induce him [Wilson] to refrain from relating his name, in any official relationship, to that liquor organization. . . . As I see it, such a step would be giving an entirely needless amount of comfort to the brewing interests."[22] The Department of Agriculture nervously reported to the president that it was receiving fifty to sixty letters a day in protest of Secretary Wilson's scheduled appearance at the brewing convention. Despite the pressure from the League, Taft ignored the campaign, and Wilson participated as the honorary president of the Brewers' Congress. Secretary of Agriculture Wilson later reported to Taft that "my judgement is that the best has been done that could be done, and there where a friend to you may have been lost I am well satisfied one, if not more, has been gained." As to threats by the Anti-Saloon League to retaliate against Taft's stand at the polling place, Wilson was of the opinion that they "do not vote the Republican ticket anyway, and some do not vote the Democratic ticket. They vote the Prohibition ticket. These people are the noisiest."[23] Taft was defeated in the next presidential election.

BOTTLED VERSUS DRAFT

Rebuffed in their persistent attempts to close city saloons on Sundays, local prohibitionists did manage to score a small victory in 1913 when the *Chicago American* and the *Record-Herald* newspapers refused to accept further advertising from beer and liquor interests.[24] Newspaper advertising had become an important vehicle for the local brewers since the turn of the century. Milwaukee's aggressive Pabst had led the way in utilizing the local press to push their products. The brewers made an end run around this move by stepping up an ad campaign of outdoor billboard signs and ads in the smaller ethnic newspapers.

The Peter Schoenhofen Brewing Company began running a series of light-hearted, one panel cartoons in the Chicago *Abendpost* newspaper, with the implied message that things went better with their flagship brand Edelweiss Beer. Milwaukee's Jos. Schlitz Brewing Company took a more serious approach in their German newspaper ads, hammering out the message that their beer, bottled since 1911 in amber bottles, was far superior in taste and more healthful than rival brands still using clear bottles. But it was Anheuser-Busch (A-B) that took the sophisticated approach of catering to the different ethnic groups that lived in Chicago. In their *"National Hero Series,"* A-B's ads featured glowing tributes to William Wallace, "Scotland's Great Patriot," and his struggles against "England's tyrannous rule," and days later praised

Leif Ericsson, "The Discoverer of America," and the "liberty-loving sons and daughters of Sweden, Norway and Denmark." After A-B's demographically niched appeals to these various Chicago tribes, the brewery ads would all end with a nod to the sensibilities of "these great lovers of Personal Liberty" and harshly criticize any attempts by anyone to enforce "Prohibitory Laws." While many rival breweries seemed to skirt the prohibition issue, the Busch family wasn't afraid to take a strong public stand on prohibition.

The local and out-of-town breweries also increased the delivery of bottled beer from their breweries or depots, direct to the customer's front door, even to city precincts that had voted themselves dry. In these wards, delivery from the local brewery to a home in a dry precinct was perfectly legal. Those moralists who publicly decried the dangers of saloons in their own neighborhoods could still settle back at the end of the day with a cool brewery-delivered beer at home, all the while digressing on the "saloon problem." All it took was a telephone call to the local brewery for a case or two of bottled beer. The result was a further weakening of citywide saloon sales as the majority of sales of bottled beer in Chicago now came directly from the local breweries.

Despite the fact that business in the local saloon industry was slowing down, overall consumption of beer in Chicago continued to increase.[25] The saloon keepers stood helplessly by as the brewers siphoned off their declining profits with increased off-premise sales. As retail saloon sales continued to tumble, so did the liquor license premium, dropping from a high of $2,800 to zero in 1915.[26]

Saloons were not the only business suffering from the effects of bottled beer sales. Smaller breweries that failed or could not afford to establish bottling lines could only watch as bottled beer gained in popularity while their draft sales further declined. The slim profit margins of brewing now dissuaded the use of independent bottling outfits. Between 1910 and 1918, most likely unable to afford the high cost of a bottling line, twelve small to midsized breweries closed in Chicago as bottled beer continued to gain greater acceptance.[27]

The entrance of the United States into the world war brought about a vast overhauling of the method used to return bottles to the breweries. Conservation of raw materials became paramount, and with charges by flag-waving politicians that German American brewers were aiding the kaiser and his troops, the brewers were quick to follow federally mandated material conservation practices. The United

States Brewers Association contacted its members in August 1917 and strongly advised brewers of the need to implement a deposit system on empty bottles and wooden cases and to assess the effects of such a system on the brewing industry. Breweries soon adopted an organized system of bottle and case deposits. In Chicago, numbers for July 1917 showed a savings of 84,154 dozen bottles used versus 252,376 dozen bottles used in the same month in 1916.

THOMPSON'S BETRAYAL

Throughout the years of continuing assault by the Anti-Saloon League and other local prohibitionist forces on the local drink trade, the United Societies for Local Self-Government, led by local politician Anton Cermak, had spearheaded the drive to beat back their efforts. The United Societies had helped defeat earlier citywide referendums advocating prohibition by demanding a close inspection of signatures on submitted petitions by prohibitionists. The organization also claimed responsibility for the election of a wet Cook County state's attorney and had fought off any efforts to impose the Sunday closing law. The organization was a buttress against Anti-Saloon League efforts and was considered a powerful political force in Chicago politics.

In 1915, Republican mayoral candidate William Hale Thompson had agreed to sign a United Societies' pledge not to close saloons on Sundays in return for Cermak's and the United Societies' much needed support. Thompson's move infuriated local prohibitionists. After Thompson won the election, however, he began to have second thoughts about the pledge, especially after rumors prevailed that a grand jury was about to investigate his nonenforcement of the state-mandated Sunday closing of saloons. States Attorney Hoyne, a Cermak loyalist, had gone so far as to publicly admit that an indictment and possible impeachment of Thompson had been discussed by a reformist-led grand jury.

On October 4, 1915, Thompson and his entourage were headed by rail to an exposition in San Francisco when the city collector read a startling mayoral proclamation to the City Council. By mayoral decree, beginning on October 9, 1915, all 7,152 Chicago saloons would be closed on Sundays. Any attempt to ignore the order to close would be met with a fine not to exceed $200. More important, violators could also have their liquor license rescinded by Thompson. Cermak and his supporters were stunned. "I wish there were an election for mayor tomorrow and I were running against Thompson," said a seething Cermak.[28]

THOMPSON'S REASONS
FOR THE CLOSINGS

En route to San Francisco, Thompson initially explained to reporters that he was simply following the advice of the City Corporation Counsel. "When the Corporation Counsel told me it was the law, why, then, I made the decision."[29] When former Mayor Carter Harrison was asked of his view of Thompson's order, he cited home rule, presuming that the people of Chicago wanted the saloons to stay open on Sunday. Edgar Tolman, who had served as corporation counsel under Harrison, was later asked by a reporter why he had not similarly advised Harrison in the matter of Sunday closings, Tolman declared that he had never given the issue any study while in office; no one had ever asked him to do so. F. Scott McBride, state superintendent of the Anti-Saloon League, naturally characterized the order as a great victory and added, "Chicago, I believe, will soon be totally dry."[30]

SUNDAY CLOSINGS, PART III

Cermak forwarded a copy of Thompson's signed pledge to keep the Chicago saloons open on Sunday to the *Chicago Tribune* for publication, hoping to discredit the mayor. Thompson admitted that he had indeed signed the pledge but stated, once again, that he had to enforce the law. The state law banning the Sunday opening of saloons throughout the state, though, had been passed in 1851. Aside from rebuked attempts to close local saloons in 1855 and 1873, Chicago mayors had followed a benign policy of non-enforcement. In the last few years, however, the burgeoning efforts to close saloons on Sunday had become a festering political irritant, culminating with Thompson's order.

The validity of the mayor's action in 1915 had been legally established years earlier, but no Chicago mayor had acted upon it. In 1906, Reverend William A. Bartlett, pastor of the old First Congregational

Church, initiated a lawsuit against then Mayor Dunne to enforce the state-mandated Sunday blue law and specifically attacked Alderman Michael "Hinky Dink" Kenna's saloon in his suit. The suit went to the state Supreme Court in 1909 where it was ruled that the Sunday closing law was indeed in effect in Chicago as throughout the entire state. The court also opined that enforcement of the law was the duty of the mayor of Chicago.

Coinciding with Barlett's Sunday-closing campaign at the time was one by the Chicago Law and Order League which had attacked the state charters of the Great Northern and Congress Hotels for violating the Sunday blue law. These suits were eventually dismissed but caused the voluntary closings of the bars of the Windemer, Palmer, Blackstone, Grand Pacific, and Virginia Hotels on Sundays. Mayor Dunne had continued to ignore the implications of the court ruling, but not Thompson.[31]

When questioned further about his motives for the Sunday closings, Thompson finally admitted that he had heard the rumors of his possible indictment for failure to uphold the state law on Sunday saloon closings, but insisted that that was not why he acted. Aides of the mayor suggested that the move was a shrewd political move, an attempt to win over the reform forces that had previously criticized him and his administration, a move that might ultimately lead to the presidency.[32]

On the first dry Sunday in Chicago since the days of Mayor Medill and the reformist efforts of the Committee of Seventy, the city appeared relatively quiet. Of the 7,152 dram shops in Chicago, only twenty-eight violations of the blue law were reported. Scores of saloon keepers, though, bemoaned the Sunday closing. For many of them, Sunday was their biggest day.

Alderman "Hinky Dink" Kenna warned that the closings would leave thousands of people without comfort stations on Sundays. "The city has one comfort station [at Schoenhofen Park]," Kenna observed. "Sunday is the only day in the week on which many people can visit friends. If they live at a distance, street cars are used for transportation." Transfer points were usually located on corners as were many of the saloons. Kenna estimated that at least one hundred thousand people used saloons daily during their commute for purposes other than drinking. "Some of them make use of the place as a comfort station and don't spend a nickel."[33]

HABEAS CORPUS ANDERSON

Twenty-two saloon owners tried to get a temporary court injunction against Thompson's order, using the services of William G. "Habeas Corpus" Anderson. Anderson had gained local fame years earlier by defending Captain George Streeter, a defiant squatter who had claimed a parcel of land on the shores of Lake Michigan, formed from the rubble of the Great Fire. In an argument that spoke of the realities of city saloons and their relationship with Chicago's ethnically dominated citizenry, the African American lawyer eloquently pointed out to the court the diversity of customs that many of Chicago's foreign-born citizens embraced and the importance to them of the neighborhood saloon.

"Take the stockyards district for instance. There are hundreds of thousands of persons of foreign birth in that district, taxpayers and voters who have customs peculiar to their nationality such as the holding of weddings on Sunday in the rear of the saloons. I dare say there are 500,000 persons in Chicago who believe in that custom," Anderson argued. Without libations, many of these celebrations would be without their customary toasts to the celebrants. The court, however, refused his moving appeal for an injunction against the Sunday closing law.[34]

Caught in the middle of Thompson's closing order and its effect on Chicago's many ethnic groups was City Clerk John Siman. City law required that permit applications for festivities running from Saturday night through Sundays until 3 A.M. be submitted at a minimum of two weeks before the event took place. City Collector Charles Forsberg had recently approved over one hundred applications for such permits for upcoming events, signed by the heads of local Polish, Bohemian, German, and Italian social clubs. With Thompson's order, Siman expected trouble. "The enforcement of the Sunday closing will certainly stir up a rumpus in my office. These applications have been approved," admitted Siman, "but since their approval, the mayor has directed that the Sunday closing law be enforced beginning at 12 o'clock midnight next Saturday."

Collector Forsberg was also feeling the heat. A manager of the North Side Turner Hall demanded to speak with the city collector to personally plead his case. "We have sold hundreds of tickets for a dance next Sunday," he lamented. "The people who bought those tickets expect that we will run a bar. If we cannot have a bar permit between midnight Saturday and midnight Sunday, closed tight for twenty-four hours, then there will be nothing for us to do but close up."[35]

THE BREWERS REACT

Throughout the initial uproar of the Sunday closings, surprisingly little was heard from the ranks of the Chicago brewing community. After Thompson had ordered the closings, deputy commissioner of public works, Billy Burkhardt, told reporters of a conversation he had had with Tom Chamales, owner of the Green Mill restaurant and bar, about the closings. Chamales had casually remarked that "it would be a big boost for the sale of bottle beer." Some brewers had also appreciated that fact. Within days after the closing order, Milwaukee's Blatz began aggressively advertising in some local papers, promising same day delivery of bottled beer from their Chicago branch. With a telephone call, one could order a case or two of the premium-priced Private Stock. The ads noted that "it will be appreciated SUNDAY by your family and friends." Local breweries soon followed the out-of-town brewery's lead. Would-be entrepreneurs made ready with their own Sunday delivery services from local breweries in case the breweries were unable to ensure prompt deliveries. It was another sales blow for the saloons but a windfall for brewers as a sense of urgency gripped customers. Picking up a case of beer for the weekend started to become an unbreakable Chicago habit.[36]

THE WET PARADE

Anton Cermak and his United Societies finally responded to Thompson's actions on November 7, 1915, with a parade of 50,000 to 70,000 marchers, viewed by over 750,000, some of them wearing lapel buttons declaring "Personal Liberty!" With thousands of participants carrying banners and placards declaring "Why pick on Sunday, the workingman's holiday?" and "Don't take the Sun out of Sunday," reporters noted that this wet parade was at least five times larger than the dry parade organized by Thompson's forces after the mayor's return from California.

The huge prodrink crowd had a definite ethnic flavor to it, described as "one of the most remarkable demonstrations of Chicago's 'melting pot' product in the city's whole history." German Turner societies, Luxemburger societies, Schwabian Vereins, Saxonian Vereins, Austrian-Hungarian societies, the Deutsche Wacht, the German Mutual Aid Society, the Deutscher Unterstuetzunge Bund, the Rheinische Verein, United Swiss Societies, the Militaere und Deutscher Krieger Vereins, the Twenty-Second Ward Liberty League, the Business Men's Liberty League, the Romanian societies, and the Twenty-Fourth Ward Personal Liberty League led contingents of the parade. The North Side Division elicited the most approval from the enthusiastic crowds. As the German American organization passed by the Michigan Avenue reviewing stand, the crowd started to chant "The Goose step! The Goose step!" The members of the reviewing stand, including representatives of the United Societies' executive committee and various wet advocates of the Chicago City Council, leapt merrily to their feet as the contingent obligingly snapped to the distinctive Germanic style of march. In this time of protest and beery celebration, the *Chicago Tribune* breathlessly described the goose-stepping demonstration as "a spectacle, it was one of the biggest things ever seen in Chicago's streets."

Beer drinking Chicagoans of all nationalities had forcefully demonstrated that they wanted their Sunday beer, but the city saloons remained closed on the Sabbath. Cook County towns just outside the city of Chicago reported land office business in their local saloons following the wet parade as participants made for the less restrictive Sunday environment of such wide-open towns as Cicero and Burnham. The issue of Sunday closings would slowly fade away as police continued to enforce the blue law.[37]

Concessions from the Brewers

Responding to the persistent efforts of prohibitionists to close Chicago's saloons, the brewing community made a conciliatory gesture that seemed to indicate a now enlightened sense of awareness by the brewers for the need to implement saloon reform. The Chicago Brewers' Association belatedly announced in mid-1917 that Chicago brewers were elevating the standards surrounding the retail sale of their products, a move that former Mayor Carter H. Harrison had proposed to a delegation of local brewery leaders two decades earlier. William Legner, head of the association, noted that the brewers' goal was "to place the licensed places where their product is sold on such a basis of respectable conduct that the community will have no cause to complain of their existence." As the revenue from local beer sales increasingly came from bottled beer and direct brewery sales, the brewers could afford to assume such a magnanimous stance at the expense of the battered local saloon industry. Economically and politically saloons now were simply more trouble than they were worth to Chicago's brewers.[38]

The efforts of the Anti-Saloon League and other dry elements wouldn't stop with Sunday closings. With every victory, prohibitionists demanded more. The entrance of the United States in 1917 into the hostilities in Europe and the growing resentment toward German Americans had fostered a persistent question of the brewing community's loyalty to the United States. The question had been successfully nurtured by the world war, a resurrection of nativists' sentiments, and the antidrink efforts of the Anti-Saloon League. In Washington, where congressmen were succumbing to the political intimidation and lobbying efforts of the League, there was talk of a food control bill, perhaps limiting or stopping the use of grain for the production of alcoholic beverages during wartime conditions.

The issues of local option, Sunday closings and saloon reform, were beginning to take a backseat to the more frightful possibility of the end of the drink trade, not only in Chicago but also the entire United States.

⽷ 10 ⽵

Wartime Prohibition, 1917–1919

I Swill

—Suggested change in the city of Chicago's
motto as Chicagoans enjoyed their last
legal drinks on the night of June 30, 1919

CONGRESSIONAL ACTIONS

While the brewers and their allies in Chicago battled against the almost fanatical strength and determination of local prohibitionists, national and international events were occurring that would take the matter of prohibition to Washington and out of the hands of local officials.

By the end of 1916, there were twenty-three dry states with prohibition laws on their books. With the well-financed congressional lobbying efforts of the Anti-Saloon League and the American declaration of war with Germany on April 6, 1917, the campaign for national prohibition became interwoven with President Woodrow Wilson's institution of a wartime food control bill.

In 1917, Wayne Wheeler and the Anti-Saloon League lobbied to attach a provision to Wilson's food bill that would make it illegal to use any food material in the manufacture of alcoholic beverages, except for scientific, medicinal, or sacramental purposes. Wet senators promptly threatened to filibuster the bill. A compromise was eventually reached that took beer and wine out of the prohibition clause of the food control bill but gave the president the discretion to later limit or stop the manufacture of beer or wine as he saw fit. The compromise bill was passed on August 10, 1917. As mandated by a rider attached to the compromised food bill, the production of distilled alcohol ceased on September 8, although sales of the remaining stock of ardent spirits could legally continue.[1]

Most threatening to the nation's brewers was a Senate resolution for a constitutional prohibition amendment that had passed weeks earlier on August 1. With the passage of this resolution, the necessary time for state legislators to ratify the constitutional amendment, which had been originally limited to five years, was compromised to six, avoiding a threatened wet filibuster but giving the League more time to marshal their forces. If ratified by Congress, the liquor industry would be given one year to close and dispose of its bonded stock. In exchange for this one-year grace period, the House of Representatives pushed through the Webb Resolution on December 17, which further extended the time for ratification of the constitutional prohibition amendment to seven years, allowing considerable time for the Anti-Saloon League to influence the decisions of the legislative representatives of the remaining wet states.[2]

On December 11, 1917, Wilson exercised his authority to further reduce the amount of permissible food materials used for the manufacture of beer by 30 percent and limited its legal alcoholic content to a paltry 2.75 percent by weight.[3]

On November 21, 1918, ten days after the Armistice, Congress passed a wartime prohibition bill as a rider to the Food Stimulation Act. This bill was to take effect the following year, but the Federal Food Administration used its authority to order the cessation of brewing nine days after the wartime prohibition bill was passed. Preparing for the cessation of brewing in Chicago, local breweries began to produce all the beer they possibly could before the cutoff date of December 1, 1918. A scarcity of grains and the resultant closing of some plants in order to economize made the challenge of this new postwar measure difficult for the industry to respond to in such a short period of time.

Beginning on December 1, Chicago brewers used the downtime after the imposed brewing stoppage to continue to bottle, keg, and sell whatever stock was still on hand. There was also a rotated layoff of the seven thousand five hundred employed by the local industry. In this manner, the local brewers hoped that they would be able to quickly recommence the brewing of beer if given the president's approval. With the brewing moratorium in effect and no hope for a quick resumption of production, Chicago Brewers' Association President William Legner estimated that the country's dwindling supply of beer would run out by May 1, 1919.[4]

THE GERMAN BREWERS
AND WORLD WAR I

The German and German American brewers were not prepared to challenge the dictates of Washington after the declaration of war against Germany. Anti-German hysteria had already gripped Chicago, not only with the nodding approval of the local Anti-Saloon League, but also because of the questionable actions of some German American organizations. When hostilities in Europe commenced in 1914, the United States Brewers' Association began funneling money to the National German-American Alliance, headquartered in Chicago. But as the United States moved from a neutral to a more proactive stance, the USBA continued to maintain their fraternal ties with pro-German organizations. The Alliance used the funds, in part, to send out press releases that were pro-German in tone.

The Anti-Saloon League used the connection between the predominately German-owned breweries and their affiliated saloons as further evidence of the brewers' un-American sentiments. "Pro-Germanism is only the froth from the German beer-saloon," declared an Anti-Saloon League superintendent. "Our German Socialist party and the German-American Alliance are the spawn of the saloon. Kaiser kultur was raised on beer. Prohibition is the infallible submarine chaser we must launch by thousands."[5]

As public opinion turned against "hyphenated Americans," including the highly visible German American brewers, Mayor Thompson, at the time courting the favor of Chicago's German American voters, caused additional problems for the local German community. His refusal to support the early national Liberty Loan efforts or to assume the role of local draft chairman infuriated many patriotic Chicagoans and earned him the name of "Kaiser Bill." In an effort to calm down some of the local anti-German bias and prove their loyalty to the United States, Chicago brewers and members of affiliated brewing trades and businesses later subscribed about $1,400,000 to the Fourth Liberty Loan campaign. Through the efforts of the Manufacturers and Dealers Association of Chicago, brewers distributed several hundred thousand copies of the *Appeal by American Brewers to the American People,* which attempted to repudiate charges that the brewers were pro-German. These efforts proved ineffectual as wartime Chicago developed a siege mentality.[6]

In just one of many instances of German American business owners distancing themselves from rising anti-German sentiments occurring in Chicago, the Bismarck Garden was renamed Marigold Gardens in 1915. Located on the southwest corner of Grace and Halsted Streets in Chicago's Lakeview neighborhood, the Bismarck Garden opened in 1895. Brothers Emil and Karl Eitel had founded the business to serve the sizable number of German Americans living on Chicago's North Side. Bismarck Garden quickly became one of the city's most popular summertime beer gardens. It featured ample shade trees, electric lamps, an outdoor stage and dance floor, a miniature zoo, a huge restaurant with outside seating, and a beer hall that featured European bands, all accompanied with plenty of German lager beer.

In late 1918, A. Mitchell Palmer, who held the federal position of custodian of alien property, began an investigation of the Schoenhofen Brewery and its owners because of the family's close ties to friends and relatives in Germany. The World War I Office of Alien Property Custodian had been created by an Executive Order on October 12, 1917. The Trading with the Enemy Act of October 6, 1917, had already authorized Palmer to assume control and dispose of enemy-owned property in the United States. Instigated by the Anti-Saloon League's Wayne Wheeler, federal agents seized the corporate and trust files of the brewery. Title to the brewery property was then placed in the control of the federal government in order to prevent the possible use of the company assets by enemy aliens against the United States. German owners of breweries throughout the United States suffered similar federal actions. Palmer eventually controlled $506 million of German-owned trusts, including that of the fifteen-building Schoenhofen complex. Ironically, Graf Schenk von Stauffenberg, whose failed attempt to kill Hitler at his Wolf's Lair in Eastern Prussia in 1944 would lead to his own death, was purported to have been a descendant of Peter Schoenhofen, founder of the Chicago brewery.[7]

President Wilson finally ruled in December 1918 that Palmer had no legal right to continue holding the assets of the brewer families. The Schoenhofen Brewery continued to operate during the early years of national prohibition. Among other nonbeer products, it manufactured Green River Soda, a sweet bright green soda pop popularized at the time by Eddie Cantor. The vaudevillian penned the song "Green River: The Snappy Fox Trot" to launch the product, his image black-faced on the original cover of the sheet music. Although the paid-endorsed song was meant to launch the nonalcoholic drink, it was, in every sense, an ironic lament to the dry times ahead: "Since the country turned Prohibition, I've been in a bad condition. Every soft drink I try, just wants to make me cry . . . for a drink that's fine without a kick, Green River is the only drink that does the trick."[8]

RATIFICATION OF THE EIGHTEENTH AMENDMENT

After appeals to the beer drinking public and failed legislative efforts by the brewers to resume brewing, the fate of the drink industry was sealed on January 16, 1919, with the shockingly quick ratification of the Eighteenth Amendment by the constitutionally required thirty-sixth state. One year later, the entire country would fall under national prohibition. The Illinois Legislature in downstate Springfield had already followed twenty-eight other dry states and ratified the National Prohibition Amendment—the Senate on January 8, with a vote of 30 to 15, the House by a vote of 84 to 66 on January 14.[9]

But Springfield was not Chicago. Provisions of the wartime prohibition bill, passed in 1918, had actually pushed the last date for the legal retail sale of beer and liquor to June 30, 1919. Brewers, distillers, and saloon keepers still held out hope that President Wilson would revoke the wartime prohibition bill and give them until January 1920 to put their affairs in order, as agreed upon in the Eighteenth Amendment. The Armistice had been signed on November 11, 1918; as far as the brewers were concerned, the wartime prohibition bill was void. Prohibitionists countered that the war could not be considered over until demobilization of the European Expeditionary Forces was complete, a process that could last six months or more.

In Chicago, Deputy City Collector George F. Lohman estimated that the abrupt loss in city revenue from brewery and saloon licensing and permit fees would exceed $8 million per year should the saloons be forced to close. He also took note of the additional loss to real estate owners of useless saloon sites after the closings, speculating that the financial blow to them would be ten times greater than the loss to the city from liquor license fees. It was a loss that would heavily impact local brewers since they owned a significant portion of the Chicago saloons.

A local Anti-Saloon official naively suggested that raising taxes to cover the $8 million revenue deficit could easily be avoided by simply reducing expenses in all city departments. A *Chicago Tribune* editorial, however, demanded a quick revision of taxes to make up the huge deficit. Acknowledging the cost of politics in Chicago and a need for municipal belt tightening, the paper also suggested that a realistic percentage of the needed money be allocated for the waste of funds that flowed through Mayor Thompson's executive departments.[10]

1919 REFERENDUM

While brewers' and distillers' representatives continued to challenge the wartime prohibition bill and the National Prohibition Amendment in Washington, stocks of beer in Chicago were becoming scarce. By February of 1919, barrel prices had risen to $17, reflecting the dwindling supply.[11]

With prohibition fever sweeping the nation, Anti-Saloon and Chicago Dry Federation forces successfully managed to include the issue of making Chicago a possible dry territory on the April mayoral ticket, months before national prohibition would take effect. It had been an uphill battle for dry forces to include such a symbolic issue for a citywide vote, culminating with a ruling by the Illinois Supreme Court that the question had to be included in the April 1919 election. The results of the referendum clearly demonstrated the present and future attitude of a majority of Chicagoans and their insistence on the right to drink. Wets won the issue by a majority of 247,228 votes, 266,529 men and 124,731 women voting against Chicago prohibition. Had there been a dry victory, local saloons would have been compelled to close their doors on May 1, in compliance with Illinois state law, fostered by local option.

CHICAGO WET AND DRY VOTE BY WARDS FOR 1919

Ward	Dry Votes	Wet Votes	Wet Majority
1	1,024	7,792	6,768
2	3,188	12,826	9,638
3	6,087	11,980	5,893
4	873	13,907	2,806

Ward	Dry Votes	Wet Votes	Wet Majority
5	2,203	9,637	7,434
6	9,791	12,597	2,806
7	10,693	13,004	2,311
8	3,738	8,329	4,591
9	4,836	7,784	2,948
10	405	7,104	6,699
11	857	8,858	8,001
12	1,105	10,488	9,383
13	10,472	13,730	3,258
14	3,043	10,448	7,405
15	2,486	11,221	8,735
16	509	6,966	6,457
17	568	4,490	3,922
18	2,949	9,496	6,547
19	588	5,247	4,689
20	624	4,685	4,061
21	4,104	9,784	5,680
22	728	6,771	6,043
23	5,131	12,370	7,239
24	2,111	11,811	9,700
25	12,563	16,576	4,013
26	6,826	16,288	9,462
27	8,714	19,865	11,151
28	3,531	10,651	7,120
29	3,026	13,350	10,324
30	2,094	9,033	6,939
31	4,979	12,228	7,249
32	10,145	15,160	5,015
33	9,578	17,011	7,433
34	2,280	17,141	14,679
35	6,943	18,622	11,679
TOTALS	114,032	391,260	247,228[12]

"There will be no let up until fanaticism has been completely overthrown," vowed William Fisher, secretary of the Wet Trades Union Liberty League, as he reviewed the overwhelming election results. "This is the message Chicago sends to Congress."[13]

Congress, however, had its own agenda, something that brewers' attorney Levy Mayer ruefully pointed out. Although the referendum had deflected the local option move to make Chicago a dry territory months before national prohibition, its results could not stop its inevitability. Passage of the Eighteenth Amendment had been through legislative action, not by a popular mandate. "Members of the legislature and congress . . . have without a direct vote of the people, undertaken to amend the constitution and say to more than 100,000,000 people that they shall not drink malt, vinous or spirituous beverages of any kind, and that possession of such beverages makes their possessors felons." Mayer then threw down this challenge to the electorate. "I can stand it if the rest of the American people can."[14]

Buoyed by the results of the referendum vote and on the advice of legal counsel, Chicago brewers defiantly restarted the brewing of 2.75 percent beer on May 1, following the lead of New York brewers. At this point, low-alcohol "small" beer was better than no beer.[15]

Hoping to influence President Wilson's decision on extending the wartime prohibition bill's effective date of July 1, 1919, the Chicago City Council adopted the following resolution and left no doubt as to its stance on national prohibition:

> Whereas, In the present day of democracy the majority rules, and the city has by a vote of 300,000 at the last general election declared against a dry Chicago; and
>
> Whereas, If demobilization is not complete before July 1 the country will go dry by presidential decree, which will, when effective, mean a property damage in Chicago of about $15,000,000, a loss of business of $25,000,000 and inability of the administration to meet the pay-roll of the police and firemen; therefore
>
> Be it resolved by the City Council that we petition the United States Senate, Congress and President Wilson to declare the army of the United States demobilized by July 1, 1919.[16]

Hopefully, if Wilson acceded to the City Council's petition and to similar demands from other municipalities that feared that a reliable cash cow was prematurely drying up, it would give local governments six more months to draw additional revenues from the local breweries and their affiliated saloons and give them a little more time to get

their financial houses in order. The absoluteness of national prohibition would still be six months away, not scheduled to take effect until
January 16, 1920, but time was running short. Wilson, however, let
the wartime prohibition bill and the last date for the retail sale of
alcoholic beverages come into law on July 1, 1919. He offered one ray
of hope to the drink interests when he stated that when "demobilization is terminated, my power to act without congressional action will
be exercised."

With this ambiguous statement by Wilson of a possible short
reprieve, there were predictions that saloons in states that were still
wet might be back in operation by the end of August. Local brewer
association president William G. Legner was wary, however, of unwarranted enthusiasm concerning the possible reopening of saloons.[17]

CHICAGO REACTS TO THE
WARTIME PROHIBITION BILL

In Chicago, attitudes toward the upcoming closing date of city saloons
proved defiant, not surprising after the results of the April election.
Over the back bars of many of the saloons were signs declaring, THIS
SALOON WILL BE OPEN FOR BUSINESS AFTER JULY 1. Rumors
abounded that some local brewers were so confident that the ban would
be lifted before July 1, that they were not only brewing beer, despite the
restrictions, but also were once again brewing full-strength brew.[18]

When informed that there were strong indications that some Chicago saloons would remain open after July 1, U.S. District Attorney
Charles F. Clyne countered that he would be forced to prosecute any
violators. It was pointedly noted that Police Chief Garrity had five
thousand policemen at his disposal for enforcement of the closings.
As the deadline date approached, however, Garrity was away in New
York. Acting as chief in Garrity's absence, First Deputy General Superintendent of Police John M. Alcock startled everyone by declaring
that "after midnight it is a federal question [the enforcement of saloon
closings]," and indicated a reluctance to act.[19]

In the seedier areas around Chicago's barrel houses, the crowds
of bums and hoboes grew unusually large as saloon keepers tried to
unload their stock. Huge schooners of beer dropped back to a nickel,
shots of whisky from ten to twenty cents, depending on the quality.

Authorities predicted a marked increase in the number of drunks who would probably apply for the cure at the healing Bridewell, Washingtonian, and Keeley Institutes when the wartime prohibition law took effect.

A last minute price war took place in saloons throughout the city as retailers dumped stock. "Only two days more to shop—do your shopping now!" was a common theme of advertisement seen in many of the saloon windows as the deadline approached. A majority of dealers were staying open well past the 1 A.M. closing time, hoping to squeeze out the last bit of change from thirsty Chicagoans. Traveling salesmen, their satchels loaded with booze, scurried through the neighborhoods making house-to-house calls, trying to entice potential customers of the necessity of buying their products now.[20]

For the would-be home brewer, small cans of *Hopfen und Malz Extrakt* were popping up for sale in delis and food stores. By adding water and a packet of yeast to the malted extract, the beer drinker was promised a stimulating malt beverage of at least 5 percent alcohol in five to seven days.[21]

First Ward Alderman Michael Kenna's Workingmen's Exchange mockingly announced a series of recitations and songs on June 30 to mark the passing of John Barleycorn, including "The Old Man's Drunk Again" and "Father, Dear Father, Come Home with Me Now." At the Hamilton Club, a dinner dance was to be held until midnight when the body of the late John Barleycorn would be brought in by pallbearers for a solemn, but tongue-in-cheek wake. Preparations in hotels, cafés, and saloons throughout the city were being made, proprietors predicting record business. When some establishments still threatened to stay open after midnight, July 1, Alderman Anton J. Cermak of the United Societies warned that those who defied the law would endanger any chance of reopening if President Wilson finally declared the Army demobilized and allowed the bars to reopen.[22]

GOOD-BYE TO BEER

On June 30, 1919, Chicagoans celebrated like never before. Whiskey and some of the more exotic mixed drinks seemed to be the drinks of choice. The reason for this was simple: Cermak declared that

Chicago saloons had run out of real beer before June 30. "Two days before June 30, the last available barrel of real beer had gone from the breweries. There wasn't a beer jag in town, unless some youngster had a make believe."[23]

If Cermak was correct in his sobering assessment, it would have been the second time, since the hot summer of 1854, that Chicago had run out of beer. The Green Mill Garden, the Marigold Room, the Sheridan Inn, and the Rainbow enjoyed record business. On the South Side, the De Luxe, the Entertainers, and the Elite were reported to be open well past midnight. An estimate that over $1,500,000 had been spent on beer and booze caused one observer of Chicago's greatest wassailing occasion to suggest that the city motto be changed from "I Will" to "I Swill."[24]

THE ILLINOIS SEARCH AND SEIZURE ACT

With a collective hangover of tens of thousands, the city slowly awoke the next day to learn that U.S. Attorney General A. Mitchell Palmer had announced the night before that the manufacture and sale of beer with 2.75 percent alcohol could continue until the federal courts ruled on whether such beer was legally intoxicating. Recent test cases in New York had resulted in a decision to question what amount of alcohol in beer could be legally considered intoxicating. "We will proceed in an orderly fashion to establish whether intoxicating beverages proscribed by the law include those having less than 2 3/4% alcohol," advised Palmer. Until the Supreme Court could rule on a legal definition of "intoxicating," or until January 16, 1920, 2.75 percent beer could continue to be sold in those states that did not have dry laws on their books. Impulsively acting on Palmer's ruling, Illinois Attorney General Edward J. Brundage initially issued a statement that the sale of beer and wine with 2.75 percent alcohol could continue in Illinois until national prohibition took effect on January 16, 1920. In accordance with these opinions, the Chicago City Council quickly passed an ordinance authorizing the issuance of temporary sixty-day liquor licenses, a move introduced by Alderman Cermak. The licenses now sold for $50 a month instead of the old cost of $83, which would have also allowed the sale of hard alcohol.[25]

Later that day City Corporation Counsel Samuel A. Ettelson conferred with Attorney General Brundage on Palmer's ruling. As a result of their meeting, despite no federal court rulings on the definition of what amount of alcohol in beer was legally considered intoxicating, Police Chief Garrity was instructed to arrest anyone who attempted to sell any beverage that contained more than .5 percent of alcohol. Brundage now ruled that "the search and seizure act of the state of Illinois, in force and effect after July 1, 1919, defines intoxicating liquor or liquids as including all distilled spirituous, vinous, fermented, or malt liquors which contain more than one-half of 1 percent by volume of alcohol, and all alcoholic liquids, compounds, and preparations, whether proprietary, patented, or not, which are portable and are capable of or suitable for being used as a beverage."

When reporters questioned Brundage on his reversed decision, he claimed that he had been earlier misinformed, stating that:

> I was called on the telephone at my home and informed that the government had modified its provisions of the wartime prohibition act to permit sale of light beverages containing no more than 2 3/4 per cent of alcohol. I said that if this were true, it would be permissible under the Illinois law to sell such beverages here. When the full details of the federal government's action were shown to me I immediately issued the new statement regarding the search and seizure law, which effectually prohibits the sale of anything containing more than one half of one percent of alcohol.

With the enforcement of state law versus a yet established federal opinion, the death knoll for beer in Chicago was sounded at 6:30 P.M. July 1, 1919.[26]

Some saloons and clubs openly defied the closing mandate. It was later reported that fanatical prohibitionist Reverend Arthur Burrage Farwell of the Chicago Law and Order League and his team of vigilant investigators had found violations of the twelve o'clock closing law on June 30. Farwell also disclosed that whiskey was seen purchased at the Dorchester at 67th Street and Dorchester and at the Tavern, located at 58th Street and State. The reverend stayed long enough at these locations to additionally note in his report that women in all stages of undress were seen in both places.

Local Brewers Go on the Offensive

After the closings, the Chicago Brewers' Association passed a resolution to continue to challenge not only the wartime prohibition bill but also to challenge the National Prohibition Act by hastening any test cases through the courts. What they needed was a brewer willing to act as a "victim" for a test case on the legality of manufacturing 2.75 percent beer.

The procedural events leading up to a ruling had already been mapped out by the local brewers and their attorneys. Industry leaders anticipated that an expected federal suit would charge a consenting brewer with a violation of the food conservation act and the selling of an intoxicating beverage. After arrest, the association's plan called for the brewer to plead guilty and pay the fine.

On July 14, a suit was filed by District Attorney Clyne against the Stenson Brewing Company. It was charged that the brewery "did use grains and cereals in the manufacture and production of beer for beverage purposes containing as much as one-half of one percent alcoholic content by both weight and volume" and sold the beer on July 2 to Timothy King, a saloon keeper at 3153 Archer Avenue. Six counts were included in the suit: three for the sale of the beer and three concerning the manufacture of the beer. The Stenson brothers abruptly changed their original strategy of pleading guilty and instead argued that they were innocent of the charges, stating that the November 21, 1918, wartime prohibition bill "relates only to beer which is in fact intoxicating" and that the information used in the charges "fails to allege that the beer made or sold was in fact intoxicating."

They also argued that the wartime prohibition bill should be construed as unconstitutional and void since it was a wartime measure and that at the time of the manufacture and sale of their beer "no war affecting the United States was in progress."

Attorney Clyne confirmed that a dozen more suits would soon be filed against the North American Brewing Company, the Hoffman Brewing Company, and the Primalt Products Company, the old Independent Brewing Association. The Stenson case was the first suit of its kind in the United States since a criminal statute was brought into question. Both Levy Mayer, special counsel of the Chicago Brewers' Association, and Attorney Clyne worked together on bringing the test case to the District Court and eventually to the Supreme Court, hoping to force the federal court to arrive at a definitive ruling of what percentage of alcohol was to be considered intoxicating. A demurrer filed on July 21 by attorneys for the brewers once again argued that the wartime prohibition bill was void since it was passed as a war measure, the war was now over, and that the law did not fix the alcoholic content that beer might contain.[27]

All arguments and legal challenges by brewery industry and legal representatives were ended with the passage of the Volstead Act on October 27, 1919. The act clarified prohibition enforcement procedures and mandated a limit of .5 percent alcohol of any and all drink as the baseline standard for intoxicating beverages. In doing so, the Volstead Act quashed the final question of legality for national prohibition.

Early Effects of No Beer in Chicago

Of the forty-three city breweries operating before July 1, only sixteen had renewed their brewing licenses. It had been expected that most of the remaining twenty-seven breweries would have applied for license extensions to produce 2.75 percent beer. But now, just days into the end of the drink trade in Chicago, saloon keepers were serving near beer, pop, or numerous other nonalcoholic drinks such as Old Crowe Flavor. Of the 120 bars in the Loop, all but 16 remained open, waiting hopefully for President Wilson to declare the Army demobilized and allow a return to a whiskey and real beer business. As the saloon keepers and brewers waited for a sign from Washington, the early effects of the state-mandated search and seizure law began to cascade throughout the restaurant and hotel industry. Waiters at the downtown hotels and clubs started to bemoan their now sober customers. "I got a $1.50 in tips today," complained one frustrated waiter at Vogelsang's Restaurant. "Before July 1, it was a poor day when I didn't clean up $8 to $10 in tips." A Hotel Sherman waiter echoed his comrade's sentiment. "The firewater sure did lubricate a man's pocketbook. How's a man gonna get tips on lemonade?" he asked.

Others realized the futility of it all; whether beer and booze came back briefly next week or next month, national prohibition was just around the corner. At the famous De Jonghe's, a soda fountain was soon installed. Workers at the Palmer House bar were following suit, converting the watering hole into a soda fountain emporium.[28]

In less than a week after the state search and seizure law had taken effect in Chicago, saloon owners started to complain of poor business. One drink or two of near beer or some nonalcoholic concoction was the limit for regulars who continued to visit their old drinking haunts simply out of habit. But the habit was starting to fade. John Dunne, a saloon keeper near the Criminal Courts building, gave all his bartenders the day off for the Fourth of July. By noon, manning the bar by himself, he sold one bottle of soda on a day that business customarily boomed. At 12:10, Dunne had enough and closed for the day. Bartenders throughout the city complained that customers didn't loiter like they did before. After the usual rush at lunch and after work, the once busy bars were quickly deserted as near beer and soda pop failed to satisfy the cravings of patrons for something more stimulating. Once thriving saloons lay deserted save for the empty beer kegs piled next to the bar. Wooden cases still holding bottles drained of their contents and now stacked for disposal beckoned their old customers through dirty saloon windows to enjoy the merits of Schoenhofen's Edelweiss beer, "A Case of Good Judgement," but to no avail.[29]

Chicagoans had given the state imposed Search and Seizure Act less than one week before turning in their verdicts; prohibition, in a state or federal form, was not for them. There were those who quietly observed the reactions of thirsty Chicagoans with marked interest and heard their grumblings of "no whiskey" and "near beer" and watched the frustration and disappointment of desperate saloon owners as their livelihoods slowly collapsed. They realized that the prohibition of beer and strong drink would never satisfy the needs of a population accustomed to serious libations.

One such observer was local pimp and racketeer, Johnny Torrio.

❧ PART III ❧

National Prohibition

The Torrio Era, 1919–1925

It is almost impossible to get a drink
of real beer in Chicago now!
—*Police Chief Morgan A. Collins as
mobster Johnny Torrio's beer-laden trucks
rolled through the streets of Chicago*

THE MILWAUKEE INVASION

In Chicago, as throughout the United States, the enactment of national prohibition on January 16, 1920, would soon become a parched reality. Scores of local breweries continued to operate, de-alcoholizing real beer and turning out insipid tasting brands of near beer, referred to in the brewing industry as "cereal beverages." Initial sales were encouraging but soon fell flat as Chicagoans began searching for something more stimulating. To add to the frustration of local brewers as their near beer sales stumbled, a steady supply of 2.75 percent beer, still legal in Wisconsin, was discovered coming across the northern border from Milwaukee breweries into Chicago saloons. Representatives of the Chicago Brewers' Protective Association met with city, state, and federal officials to complain of the smuggling and the effect it was having on their already insipid near beer sales. As a result of the complaints from the Chicago brewers, a total of nineteen Milwaukee beer trucks were soon seized by federal officials at Zion City as they surreptitiously attempted to make their way to Chicago. Representatives of the Jos. Schlitz Brewing Company, the Pabst Brewing Company, and the Val. Blatz and Fred. Miller Brewing Companies, were ordered to appear before Federal Judge Kenesaw Mountain Landis to explain their beer running activities into the now dry city of Chicago.[1]

Not all of Chicago's breweries were willing to compromise their product and sit back while Milwaukee saturated their home market with real beer. In just a few short months of unfavorable test cases and continued beer smuggling, a number of Chicago brewers had had enough of government-mandated prohibition and interference with their traditional means of livelihood. Their futile argument that any form of prohibition was an infringement on their "personal liberties" had fallen on deaf ears. The brewers' only course of action was now obvious, but illegal. The catalyst they needed was for someone willing to step forward and protect them from possible arrest and prosecution if they returned to the illegal manufacture of real beer.

TORRIO AND JOHN STENSON

In the spring of 1919, brewery owner Charles Schaffner sold his Manhattan Brewing Company, located in Bridgeport at 3901 South Emerald Avenue, to Johnny Torrio and brewer Joseph Stenson with the later addition of bootleggers/investors Dion O'Banion, Hymie Weiss, and Maxie Eisner as co-owners.[2] Torrio, a pimp and racketeer, had arrived from New York somewhere between 1910 and 1912 and soon made a name for himself in Chicago's underworld as he had done earlier in New York. Having interviewed for a position in James "Big Jim" Colisimo's organization, Torrio was offered the role in Chicago as Colisimo's right hand man. "Big Jim" had risen in power through his vice and racketeering activities in and around the infamous Levee District, south of the Loop, under the political protection of First Ward Alderman Michael Kenna.

Torrio became an atypical example of a Chicago gangster. He was a quiet individual who seldom carried a gun or displayed a life of excess, in spite of the huge sums of illegal money he acquired. Although his early career in Chicago was as a pimp for Colisimo's stable of whores, he made it a point never to sleep with them, nor did he smoke or drink. He faithfully arrived at his Michigan Avenue apartment every night at six o'clock to be with his wife, Ann. Torrio soon displayed a knack for business savvy, outstanding organizational skills, and the delicate art of compromise, traits demanded by any successful business organization. The early prohibition purchase of the Manhattan Brewery was a prime example of his intuitiveness and understanding of the frailties of human nature and the profits these weaknesses could bring him.

While some of the local brewers switched to legal enterprises or mothballed their plants, hoping that national prohibition would one day be repealed, Torrio understood that Chicagoans would want their beer during national prohibition, illegal or not. But as sophisticated as his organizational skills and understanding of human nature might have been, he still needed someone who understood the practical aspects of the local brewing industry; that man was brewer Joseph Stenson. In 1919, when the Chicago brewing industry needed a sacrificial lamb to challenge the legality of Illinois Attorney General Brundage's ruling on the wartime prohibition bill, the Stenson Brewing Company had taken up the cause. This willingness by Stenson management to challenge the law had caught Torrio's eye. Shortly before national prohibition took effect, Torrio had secretly begun working with John Stenson, the youngest of the four brothers who owned the Stenson Brewery, to buy outright, lease, or front for the original owners of a growing number of cooperative Chicagoland breweries.

Their plan was simple. Using money from Torrio, Stenson would gain control of the breweries and typically install well-paid flunkies as brewery presidents and plant managers. These Stenson-appointed brewery personnel were to take the fall if the breweries were raided, leaving the real principals unmolested. In short time, Torrio, with the help of Stenson, owned or controlled through fellow bootleggers Terry Druggan, Frankie Lake, and others, the Manhattan, Stege, Pfeiffer, Standard, Gambrinus, and the Hoffman breweries in Chicago. Torrio's control was reputed to have eventually covered around sixty-five breweries in and around the Chicagoland area. In the early years of national prohibition in Chicago, as Stenson helped nurture Torrio's brewing empire, he accumulated a sizable fortune for his efforts. In 1924, newspaper estimates for the cost of John Stenson's expertise was pegged at $12 million a year, earned from a going price of about $50 to $55 for a syndicate barrel of beer.[3]

Persuading frustrated brewery owners to sell or lease their operations for the resumption of brewing and to maintain a steady flow of cash back to them was probably an easy sell for Torrio and Stenson. Many of the city breweries had initially switched, or had made plans to switch, to the production of near beer, soda pop and other products that they were unfamiliar with. With a new venue foisted upon them and the uncertainties of an unknown market, failure or the loss of the business and even the family fortune were distinct possibilities. A short list of city breweries with their planned product lines follows.

Atlas Beverage Co., aka Atlas Brewing Co.—Cereal beverages, ginger ale, cider

Birk Brothers Brewing Company—Cereal beverages, root beer

Fortune Bros.—Macaroni and spaghetti

Primalt Products Co., aka Independent Brewing Assn.—Cereal beverages, soft drinks, ginger ale, root beer, malt syrups and extracts

McAvoy Co., aka McAvoy Brewing Co.—Cereal beverages, distilled alcohol

Best Brewing Co.—Cereal beverages, root beer, ice

The Geo. J. Cooke Co.—Cold storage

Producers Brewing Co.—Cereal beverages, root beer

Ruehl Brewing Co.—Cereal beverages, ice

White Eagle Products Co.—Cereal beverages

The Conrad Seipp Co., aka Conrad Seipp Brewing Co.—Cereal beverages

Sieben's Brewery Co.—Closed

North American Brewing Co.—Cereal beverages

Stenson Brewing Co.—Cereal beverages, root beer, ice

United Breweries Co. (Monarch and Northwestern)—Cereal beverages[4]

Within months of starting up these new operations, many of the Chicago breweries were forced to take a long, hard look at their bottom line. Years of grain shortages, brewing moratoriums, and reformers' assaults had taken their toll on the local industry. Encouraged by the guaranteed sales of Torrio and other up-and-coming bootleggers, the local brewery owners were now promised more money than they had seen in years. With the help and protection of the Torrio cabal, some of them dropped their unprofitable new venues and quickly reverted to the production of real beer. Their often-used rallying cry of "personal rights" merged with the more practical issue of profitability. With a barrel of beer now selling for up to $55, the breweries could easily afford the weekly payoffs to city officials, aldermen, district commanders, and the beat cops who patrolled the neighborhoods, and still make a fortune. National prohibition or not, it was once again becoming the business of beer as usual in Chicago.

DEVER ELECTED

During the latter part of the administration of Mayor Thompson, brewery raids in Chicago had become as uncommon as snow in July. Not only did local saloons continue to operate openly, but thousand of licenses were now being issued by the city for so-called "soda parlors." These establishments were licensed to serve nonalcoholic refreshments; almost all of them served real beer, produced by the accommodating local breweries. Virtually every cop and politician in Chicago knew it, ignored it, and profited from it.

Charges of political corruption, a deficit in the city budget, caused in large part from the cessation of revenue from liquor license fees, and a total lack of control by Thompson of the Chicago Police Department finally led to his ouster in April 1923; he was replaced by reform candidate William E. Dever. Although the city electorate wanted political and judicial reform, they were convinced that the benign neglect that had allowed the breweries to continue to operate since the early years of prohibition would go on. After all, these breweries had been illegally providing beer for thirsty Chicagoans for almost four years. During the first few months of Dever's administration, beer continued to flow in Chicago, as it appeared that Dever would maintain the status quo.

Johnny Torrio continued in his quest for a consolidation of all the gangs in the city that were in the expanding and profitable bootlegging business. The North Side was controlled by Dion O'Banion. Parts of the West Side were run by bootleggers Terry Druggan and Frankie Lake. Torrio held most of the South Side but was having problems with three brothers from the South Side O'Donnell gang.

THE O'CONNOR SHOOTING

Since the earliest days of Prohibition, Ed "Spike" O'Donnell had been serving time in Joliet for a daring daytime holdup of the Stockyards Trust and Savings Bank. Eventually paroled, Spike and his enterprising brothers made up for lost time and hijacked several truckloads of Torrio's beer, soon after his release. When Torrio failed to retaliate, they continued their predatory ways and muscled into the South Side territory of Joe Saltis and Frank McErlane, allies of Torrio. Using beatings and intimidation, they quickly built up a clientele of Torrio's former saloon accounts. In many instances, the beatings were unnecessary; most South Side beer drinkers agreed that the O'Donnells provided a better quality beer from their small cartel of illegal breweries. Torrio turned his cheek, held his street enforcers at bay, and diplomatically retaliated by lowering the price on his beer by $10 a barrel.

The territorial dispute culminated, however, in the shooting of Jerry O'Connor, a beer runner and member of the O'Donnell gang. One of those accused in the shooting was Daniel McFall, a deputy sheriff and known Torrio ally.[5]

DEVER'S BEER WAR

Dever used the shooting to implement an attack on the scores of Chicago breweries that had been operating for years with impunity. On September 12, Mayor Dever met with the press and announced his plan to shut down Chicago's illegally operating breweries. With Police Chief Morgan A. Collins at his side, Dever declared that every brewery in Chicago would be placed under police guard and that every shipment of beer leaving the breweries would be seized for analysis of its alcoholic content. With persistent rumors of police officials protecting the illicit beer trade, Dever pledged that "Beer runners and crooked policemen will get the same treatment." He also discounted as false the all too obvious indications that politicians close to him were getting $10 per barrel for beer delivered by beer runners. Collins echoed Dever's comments about the consequences of police corruption. He insisted though, that with the implementation of their plan, "It is almost impossible to get a drink of real beer in Chicago now." Almost mocking the chief's naive declarations, local newspapers reported that trucks from the breweries that supplied the O'Donnell gang and from Torrio's Manhattan Brewery were rolling through the streets, continuing to supply their customers.[6]

On the evening of Dever's challenge to the bootleggers and the local beer industry, things began to rapidly change for Chicago's breweries and Torrio's fortunes. During the evening, a total of five trucks of beer were seized as they left from the Manhattan, Keeley, and the Conrad Seipp Brewery on the South Side.

The next morning, Mayor Dever met with city officials and a representative of the federal government to coordinate a battle plan for the suppression of the illegal beer trade in Chicago. His office announced that no more soft drink licenses would be issued until the applicants had been subject to "the severest scrutiny." Chief Collins began to rotate the police guards stationed at the various breweries on a daily basis, hoping to stop any chance of beer runners corrupting his beer patrols. He also expanded the patrols to include all highways leading into the city from suburban towns where there were known breweries still operating. It was the first real attempt by local officials since the beginning of national prohibition to try to stop the flow of beer in Chicago.[7]

THE BOOTLEGGERS' COUNTEROFFENSIVE

With the initial enthusiasm and success of the beer patrols by Collins's men, the breweries began to develop their own counteroffensive to thwart local officials. Brewers started to send out trucks from the front entrances of the breweries loaded with near beer, holding the attention of the police, while trucks packed with real beer slipped out the back exits unchallenged. After all, insiders pointed out, the money from the illegal beer trade was simply too good *not* to put up a fight. Before Dever announced his beer war, it was estimated that Chicago's breweries had been producing eighteen thousand barrels of real beer a week. At a fluctuating price of $30 per barrel, often going as high as $55, the business of beer in Chicago was generating well over a minimum of $28 million to more than $51 million a year in illegal sales. From those figure, insiders claimed that $10 per barrel was earmarked for a slush fund for "fixing."[8]

As the pressure to stop the illegal beer trade continued and listings of saloon closings became a daily feature in the local press, another wave of murders took place as beer runners jockeyed for new accounts to replace those that had been lost due to closings, often stepping into the territory of a rival for the additional business. Police Chief Collins admitted there would probably be more killings, commenting that his department was up against "a powerful foe." He continued to pressure his force for results, suspending a police captain from the South Side suspected of acting as a Torrio ally as a warning to other potentially corrupt police officials.

BREWERY RAIDS

On a tip from an informant, police staked out the Pfeiffer Brewery on North Leavitt, a brewery controlled by mobster Terry Druggan and under the protection of Torrio, and seized three trucks loaded with beer and an additional twenty-three hundred barrels of real beer. Druggan's men had planned to break the police blockade surrounding the brewery by rushing the police with the loaded trucks and quickly delivering the beer to their saloon accounts. The plan fell through when police arrested Martin O'Leary, a member of Terry Druggan's Valley Gang, who was to have led the mad dash from the brewery. In an embarrassing counteroffensive by local bootleggers, a member of Torrio's gang brazenly stole a confiscated truckload of beer from the front of a police station on Irving Park as the driver was being grilled inside. "Someone will be out of a job before tomorrow morning," vowed an embarrassed Chief Collins to the press.[9]

Dever's crusade continued with the revocation of the licenses of saloons caught selling real beer or whisky. In addition, Dever pulled the operating licenses of 355 soda parlors in just a few short days. Drug stores, coffee shops, and even local groceries started to receive the attention of the beer patrols. In one week, 549 people had been charged with violations of the Prohibition Act. The Hoffman Brewing Company was the first brewery casualty of Dever's beer war when it lost its license after the city health commissioner reported that his men had been refused samples of the brewery's products for analysis.[10]

DECENT DEVER

In an address to four hundred Methodist ministers meeting in Chicago, Mayor Dever admitted that his recent crackdown on prohibition violators was probably political suicide but stated his continued belief in his actions. "Even if I were interested only in politics, doesn't everything point to an enforcement of this law?" Buoyed by the positive reception from the ministers, Dever vowed that there would be no end to his campaign to dry up Chicago until every business that had been selling alcohol "hung out the calamity sign." The mayor's one-man public relations campaign against bootlegged beer continued with an address to over ten thousand skeptical lager-loving participants on German Day at Municipal Pier. Dever's speech would reflect a common refrain through his mayoralty; he insisted that he was not a prohibitionist but merely an advocate of law and order and the protectorate of the public's health. "I could never excuse myself as long as 7,000 so-called soft drink places are selling poison," declared the mayor. The theme of poisoned beer prevailed throughout Dever's term with encouragement by the health commissioner of Chicago. "The bootleggers' 'real beer' is either adulterated with certain drugs or is beer recently made, known as 'green beer,'" a somber Doctor Herman N. Bundesen declared.[11]

Beer runners continued their resourcefulness in providing beer to thirsty Chicagoans. With road checks of trucks becoming more common on the streets of the city, newspaper reports were circulating that beer was now being smuggled down the Chicago River concealed under cargoes of fruits and vegetables.[12]

Saloon and Soda Parlor Shutdowns

Police Chief Collins boasted triumphantly that the recent successes of his daily raids would leave Chicago bone dry by early October. He comically observed that a recent tour of the city revealed no signs of liquor, "but I did see the finest collection of padlocks in town, hanging on the front doors of these so-called soft drink parlors." Either shut down by the raids or simply closed because of fear of arrest, the six thousand soda parlor owners who had openly operated in Chicago selling beer were now shocked by their sudden loss of immunity. Everyone knew they sold beer. As long as they kept away from liquor, the police had always left them alone. "There was an unwritten law under which the government sanctioned the sale of beer," complained Anton Cermak.[13] In two months, Dever had revoked the operating licenses of over sixteen hundred businesses for prohibition-related offenses. In addition, 4,031 saloons had also been shut down. The crusading mayor seemingly had the upper hand.[14]

WETS COUNTERATTACK

Politicians sympathetic to the wet cause or under the influence of local bootleggers started a move in the City Council to place a referendum on the ballot of the upcoming judicial election. Chicagoans were to be polled by a yes or no vote, "Do you approve of the city administration's present policy in the enforcement of the liquor laws?"

Alderman "Bathhouse" John Coughlin presented a resolution in the City Council requesting an amendment of the prohibition laws to permit the sale of beer and light wines. Suspending the normal council procedure of sending proposed resolutions to committee, the City Council of Chicago quickly adopted the following:

> Whereas, Since the enforcement of Article XVIII (the amendment to the Constitution of the United States of America prohibiting the manufacture, sale and transportation of intoxicating liquors for beverage purposes); and
>
> Whereas, The City of Chicago has lost through license revenue the sum of eight million dollars annually; and
>
> Whereas, During the so-called "dry period," which has been over four years, the City of Chicago alone has lost a total revenue of over thirty-two millions of dollars; and
>
> Whereas, On account of such tremendous loss to the taxpayers, the burdens of the taxpayers have increased two-fold, and as a consequence thereof taxes on real and personal property have doubled; therefore, be it
>
> Resolved, That we, the City Council of the City of Chicago assembled, hereby petition the Congress of the United States to amend the Act commonly called the Volstead Act, so that the sale, manufacture and transportation of light wines and beers for beverage purposes will be permissible; and, be it further
>
> Resolved, That a copy of this petition be forwarded to Congress and the Senate as a body and to each and every member thereof.[15]

Dever countered these moves by his own city council by once again going to the people, defending the legality of his beer war. "I believe in good, wholesome beer at moderate prices for those who like it if it can be sold legally, but as long as it is banned by a law of the nation, ratified by the States, and strengthened by auxiliary legislation of the States, we cannot have it. And if the people of Chicago cannot have good beer, wines and liquors legally, they are not going to have poisonous green beer, deadly hooch or moonshine so long as I can stop it, and I believe I have." With Dever's persuasive argument against the dangers of poisoned beer being so strong, the proposal to place the wet versus dry issue on the judicial ballot soon faded away.[16]

EVENTS LEADING TO THE SIEBEN BREWERY RAID

One of the most famous Prohibition-era brewery raids in Chicago had begun with a routine inspection back on August 29, 1923, of the George Frank Brewery (the old Sieben Brewery) on North Larrabee Street, weeks before the start of Dever's beer war. Prohibition agents entered the brewery and were shown about by one of the Sieben family members. The Sieben family had leased the property to George Frank, the neighborhood brewery now licensed for the manufacture of near beer. As the group neared the racking room, the agents could hear employees frantically knocking off bungs from barrels of beer. Sieben refused to let the agents enter the locked room as the beer drained from the containers, heightening their suspicions that real beer was being bottled. Frank soon arrived and allowed the agents access to the racking room. When they entered, they saw that the floor of the room was wet and covered with foam, indicating to them that an attempt had been made to dispose of the contents of the barrels in the room. In their haste the employees neglected to empty all the barrels, and samples were taken for testing. As a result of the raid and the subsequent lab results, the permit of the Frank Brewery to brew real beer, dealcoholize it, and create near beer was revoked. The criminal case against Frank was later dropped, however, on a technicality.[17] Although in violation of federal law, the brewery defiantly continued to operate.

DION O'BANION

North Side gangster Dion O'Banion had made quite a name for himself in the early years of Prohibition. O'Banion, described by the local press as a "florist and brewer," was a volatile member of Torrio's fragile coalition of mobsters that ran the city beer rackets in the early twenties. O'Banion's business style was quite different than that of Torrio's. Where Torrio would customarily smooth over objections between rival gangs over territorial boundaries and mediate disputes that arose in everyday bootlegging operations, Dion was combative in his approach to rival gangs. The contrasting example of the difference in Torrio's and O'Banion's business demeanors was apparent when two enterprising Chicago policemen held up a Torrio beer truck one night. "You can have the beer," the crooked cops told the drivers after taking $250 from them, "if you come across with $300 more. Go get the money and we'll hold the beer." The men called O'Banion on a line that police headquarters had earlier tapped and explained their predicament. "Three hundred dollars to them bums?" O'Banion screamed over the phone. "Why say, I can get em knocked off for half that much."

Sensing they might be in over their heads, the beer runners gave Torrio a call and reported their conversation with O'Banion. "I just been talking to Johnny," one of the drivers later called back to O'Banion, "and he says to let them cops have the three hundred. He says he don't want no trouble." When word of the incident was later picked up by the local press, the *Chicago Daily News* rightfully opinioned that "it was the difference in temper that made Torrio all-powerful and O'Banion just a superior sort of plug."[18]

Chafing under Torrio's influence, O'Banion became furious when members of the Genna family began to sell cheap homemade alcohol in his territory. O'Banion demanded that Torrio send the Gennas back to the Taylor Street area where they had initially done business and enjoyed success. Before Torrio could reach a deal with the Gennas, O'Banion's men hijacked a truckload of the Gennas' cheaply made alcohol in retaliation. Torrio's compromising skills somehow managed to stop the Genna family from striking back at O'Banion and his crew but the animosity between Torrio and O'Banion festered.[19]

O'Banion's Betrayal

Shortly after the Genna incident, O'Banion met with Torrio and his protégé, Al Capone, and shocked them by announcing that he was getting out of the bootlegging business and retiring to Colorado. He offered to sell his share of the Sieben Brewery (aka The Frank Brewery), which the three of them jointly owned, for $500,000. Torrio and Capone jumped at the offer, happy to hear that the troublesome Irishman was leaving town. As a gesture of goodwill, O'Banion offered to make a final, symbolic shipment of real beer from the illegally operating brewery with his partners, and asked that Torrio and Capone accompany him in the transaction. What Torrio and Capone didn't know was that O'Banion had been tipped to a federal raid on the brewery for the early morning of May 19, 1924, the same day that they were to meet at the brewery for the final sale. Because Torrio had a prior conviction for violating Prohibition laws, O'Banion hoped that his Machiavellian plot would lead to their arrests, including his own—a chance he was willing to take. With Torrio having to contend with a second federal conviction for bootlegging, a possible fine of up to $10,000, and a jail term of three years, there could be time enough for O'Banion to wrest away control of all Chicago operations from Torrio and the up-and-coming Capone.[20]

THE RAID

On the early morning of May 19, 1924, the raid was conducted on the brewery with Torrio and O'Banion present, but interestingly Capone never showed. After arresting a number of armed lookouts outside the brewery, the police and federal agents entered the property and discovered five trucks loaded with 150 barrels of real beer. Inside the brewery, agents also found wet mash and a number of barrels of beer in the racking room. Outside on the loading dock, O'Banion was seen by one of the raiding party as he threw a book underneath the dock. Scribbled inside the seized book were recent delivery dates of beer from the brewery and a listing of Chicago police officers and a prohibition agent who had been taking bribes for protection of the illegally operating brewery.

Throughout the raid, O'Banion seemed quite amused with the whole affair, joking to one of the members of the raiding party, "You ought to get a raise!" At the Federal Building, O'Banion slipped out of the police bullpen behind two detectives and almost managed to escape, getting as far as the marshal's office before he was pinched and escorted back. Unfazed by his recapture, he slipped a janitor $20 and had him get breakfast for himself and his fellow prisoners.

But Torrio knew something was wrong. He had expected to be brought to the district police station, not the Federal Building. When it came time to make bail, Torrio peeled off $7,500 from a wad of bills he carried but left O'Banion to wait until his bail bondsman showed up with the required $5,000 for his release.[21]

The seizure of real beer from the Sieben Brewery and its crippling effect on Torrio's organization was reflected in the fluctuating price per barrel of beer which immediately skyrocketed from about $50 per barrel to $100 after the raid. O'Banion's captured notebook, which detailed payments to police officials and a crooked prohibition agent, caused a further tightening of security around those legally operating breweries that were still licensed to make near beer. Chief Collins ordered that three police guards now be stationed around the breweries, not only to monitor possible criminal activity at the brewing sites, but also more important, to watch each other.[22]

NEEDLE BEER

Five legally operating breweries, the National, Ruehl Brothers, Monarch, Atlas, and Primalt, were now operating in Chicago making near beer.[23] The high-priced real stuff started giving away to the stronger "needle" beer, near beer injected with alcohol through the bung-hole of the barrel. The near beer, labeled with a legal federal revenue stamp, left the breweries unmolested by police squads. Cooperating beer joints carried a bottlegged supply of alcohol on-site for final processing. Many of the owners of Chicago's more than ten thousand speakeasies favored needle beer over real beer simply because of the price; near beer was selling for the low price of $35 a barrel.[24] Another, more flavorful method of adding alcohol used a mixture of ginger ale and alcohol to replace an equal amount of near beer which was drawn from the barrel. With this method, the beer took on a much-enjoyed sweeter profile, a taste difference that some brewers would take into account upon the repeal of Prohibition.[25]

Torrio's Revenge

Months after the Sieben raid, O'Banion continued his bootlegging operations on the North Side. His actions indicated no preparation for a Colorado retirement as he had confided to Torrio and Capone in early May. If Torrio had lingering doubts as to whether O'Banion had set him up for a second federal conviction, they were now gone.

On November 10, 1924, three men entered the flower shop that O'Banion owned on North State Street. As O'Banion greeted the men, they fired six shots into him, the last shot to his head. It was the final act of revenge for Torrio who had abandoned his compromising demeanor and finally allowed one of the Genna brothers and two accomplices to end the life of the double-crossing O'Banion.[26]

Assassination Attempt on Torrio

O'Banion's influence, however, would reach from beyond the grave. Still under indictment for the Sieben raid, Torrio and his wife returned home from a day of shopping downtown. As Torrio followed his wife into their apartment building, gangsters Hymie "Earl the Polack" Weiss and "Bugs" Moran, friends of the departed O'Banion, pulled up in a blue Cadillac and jumped out of the car. Thinking that the chauffeur still sitting in the car was Torrio, they opened fire, wounding him. Realizing their mistake, they spotted Torrio nearby and fired wildly, hitting him in the chest and neck. One of the assassins stood over Torrio as he writhed in pain on the street and fired one shot into his arm, another to his groin. Moran finally reached down to put a final bullet into Torrio's head and squeezed the trigger, but the chamber was empty. Both men panicked and fled, leaving Torrio critically injured, but not dead.

At Jackson Park Hospital, Al Capone slept on a cot in his mentor's room, offering protection in case another assassination attempt might take place. Capone was lucky to be there himself. Less than two weeks before Torrio's shooting, Capone had narrowly escaped an attempt on his life at 55th and State by Weiss, Moran, and "Schemer" Drucci.[27]

Torrio Relinquishes Control to Capone

While mulling over his own mortality as he lay in the hospital, Torrio must have realized that his fragile coalition of pimps, racketeers, bootleggers, and murderers had fallen apart. In less than one month, Johnny Torrio left the hospital to recuperate at home. On February 9, 1925, he showed up in federal court to answer to the charges from the Sieben Brewery raid. Still weak and wearing bandages from his wounds, he pleaded guilty and was sentenced to a fine of $5,000 and a prison term of nine months in the Lake County Jail in Waukegan, Illinois. While still in prison, Torrio sent for Capone. Sure that he was still a marked man and that a third federal conviction would probably mean life imprisonment, Torrio told Capone that he was handing over the remnants of the organization to him and his brothers, beginning a new, more dangerous era in Chicago.

After serving his jail sentence, Torrio spent a few years overseas and eventually returned to New York where he led a quiet life as a bootlegger. After Repeal, he secretly held an interest in a liquor distributorship in New York. His genteel solitude was broken in late 1938 when the Internal Revenue Service began investigating his ownership in the firm. Fearing that Torrio would flee the country, federal agents arrested him on charges of evading almost $87,000 in taxes as he attempted to pick up a passport at a local post office. An older Torrio, with much of the fight knocked out of him, threw himself on the mercy of the federal court and received a two-and-a-half-year prison term at Leavenworth. He lived out the rest of his life in White Plains, New York.[28]

⊰ 12 ⊱

The Capone Era, 1926–1931

There's plenty of beer business for
everybody. Why kill each other over it?
—*Al Capone, peacemaker*

CAPONE'S WILDCAT BREWERIES

Capone now completely controlled what was left of Torrio's crumbling empire. Although the output of near beer from the federally licensed breweries continued to provide a base for needle beer, output could not keep up with demand. In addition to the problems of meeting supply, the federal government had finally started to pick up the enforcement pace of the national prohibition laws, working with local police officials when necessary. With police attention regularly paid to the former illegally operating breweries, now shut down as a result of Mayor Dever's campaign, Capone was forced to start a number of clandestinely located "wildcat" breweries throughout the city and suburbs to supplement the insatiable Chicagoland demand for beer. These makeshift breweries, usually tucked away in deserted industrial areas, produced real beer but often experienced trouble in securing the raw materials needed for the brewing process.

Unexpected help for Capone's supply dilemma came from brewing giant August A. Busch who somehow discovered that Capone had recently directed some of his men to steal golden gates, devices used to tap barrels, from his St. Louis brewery. Busch sent his young son Gussie down to Miami to talk to Capone where the mobster was relaxing on an extended vacation. During the meeting, the two ultimately reached a deal that provided Capone's breweries not only with over two hundred and fifty thousand of the tapping devices, but also with yeast, sugar, and malt extract (syrup) for their makeshift brewing operations. Malt extract was a critical ingredient for these small, unsophisticated brewing operations. Bypassing the lengthy operation of mashing the bulky malted barley to extract the sugars needed for fermentation, a process that could take hours, the bootleggers and their brewers could now dilute the syrupy malt extract with boiling water, add hops, and in a short time, have the wort chilled down and ready for the addition of yeast. In a week or two, they would have real beer available for their customers.

Momentarily forgetting with whom he was dealing during their discussions, young ambassador Gussie asked for Capone's signature to seal the deal. Capone shrugged off the naïve demand, and Busch wisely backed down. At a cost of $2 per golden gate plus additional income from surreptitiously accepting unknown amounts of brewing supplies, Capone made a small fortune for the Anheuser-Busch Brewing Company during the lean years of Prohibition.

As a young man, Gussie would often tell friends of the golden gate episode and his meeting with Capone, but as he grew older (and wiser), he avoided the subject. The story was corroborated by Gussie's daughter Lotsie in her family history.[1]

A CHICAGO WORT BUST

One way around the problem of trying to keep a wildcat brewery in operation was to go directly to the source, the legally operating breweries themselves. Aside from the manufacture of the usual near beer, soda pop, ice, and other benign products, the extraction of condensed malt extract from fermentable wort and the sale of the bulkier wort itself had become a profitable operation for local breweries.

Since the first days of Prohibition, homebrew shops had popped up throughout the area, offering everything needed, including tins of sweet malt extract, to make a couple of gallons of beer in the privacy of one's basement. In wort, the combination of water and extract contains no alcohol, but by following the small print instructions for the beverage's preparation, "let ferment for 48 hours, then bottle and let PRESTO do the rest!" the result became a potion that the cans claimed would be "invigorating" and "thirst-quenching."

Bakery operations supposedly used wort as a sweetener, while some "independent bottlers" purchased it to make near beer. South Side bootleggers, however, had rightly concluded that if they purchased bulk containers of wort, they could bypass the mashing cycle, eliminate the problems of removing spent grains from their clandestine plants, and temper other excess brewing activities that might catch the eye of local officials. As a result, some breweries began providing local bootlegging operations with bulk containers of wort, the fermentable precursor to real beer.

On July 19, 1926, prohibition officers, on direct instructions from Washington, raided the Archer Products Company at 2762 Archer Avenue (Archer and Throop Streets) and took possession of the plant. Formerly known as the Citizens Brewery, the old turn-of-the-century plant was licensed to continue operations during the mid-1920s as a manufacturer of malt syrups and wort. The feds arrested eighty-five employees, however, for the manufacturing and selling of legal, non-alcoholic wort. Benign wort became illegal, however, when it was sold to nonbaking or legal brewing operations—or when yeast was set to it.

The plant was described in the malt syrup trade publication, *Malt Age*, as being run by individuals of "rather unsavory reputation," who had been in trouble with the government before and whose sales methods were "exceedingly raw," in other words, local bootleggers—most likely the Capone organization since it was a South Side operation.

There was little concealment of the intent of the sales of the wort. The government agents were able to follow the recent sales of the fermentable liquid and establish connections with known wildcat brewers and enterprising saloon owners who operated their own small basement breweries. At the time of the seizure, Assistant District Attorney Jacob I. Grossman, in charge of the prosecution, gave out a statement relative to the status of the case, in which he said that wort was illegal because it could be used for practically nothing except the manufacture of real beer. Wort, as far as the government had determined, had no other regular commercial use such as found with grape juice, malt syrup, sweet cider, or corn sugar, all of which could be used in the legitimate manufacture of foods (as well as for outlaw beverages, a fact ignored by the feds).

On Tuesday, January 4, 1927, the case was called before Federal Judge James H. Wilkerson in Chicago and an injunction was obtained, closing the plant for one year. The brewery was eventually permitted to reopen at the end of eight months, having been closed since July of 1926.[2]

HOMEBREWING GETS TOUGHER

The idea that Prohibition era malt extract was only utilized by mom and pop, working feverishly down in the basement to make a small batch of homebrew while little Johnny watched for the police is an endearing one, even romanticized by a number of poems from those supposed dry times. Through the first five years or so of Prohibition, thousands of so-called "Malt-and-Hop" stores had sprung up throughout the nation to satisfy what everyone knew was really the growing trade of homebrewing supply stores.

Although these stores were small and often unsophisticated, owned by enterprising individuals who also wanted to take advantage of a beer-free nation, they were often supplied by the biggest names of the pre-Prohibition brewing industry.

The National Malt Products Manufacturers' Association, an umbrella trade group of former brewers that controlled and self-regulated the malt extract industry, was headed by representatives from Ballantine & Sons, La Crosse Refining Company (Heileman), Anheuser-Busch, Pabst, Premier Malt (eventually purchased by Pabst), and others.

By early 1927, however, the malt syrup industry found itself under increasing pressure from Assistant Secretary of the Treasury Lincoln C. Andrews, who decided to take on the industry and what he believed were abuses that were being practiced by the thousands of Malt-and-Hop shops throughout the country. Andrews took particular umbrage with "Malt-and-Hops shops who display in their show windows together with Malt Syrup, complete paraphernalia for making a home beverage."

In moves that were very reminiscent of the brewing industry's earlier reaction to problems associated with saloons before Prohibition, the brewery-dominated malt trade union took the same see, speak, and hear no evil stance with the independent homebrew shops—sell the product, and if the heat was on, blame the retailers for the problems associated with the product, all the while hoping that the feds would eventually get distracted or go away. Similar to their self-imposed "solution" for the problems associated with saloons, the malt syrup trade association set up eight self-governing regulations to police the sale of their products and passed these on to the Prohibition Department for its approval.

A summary of the National Trade Associations' suggested regulations on the sale of malt syrup follows.

(a) The possession or distribution of any formula, direction or recipe for the manufacture of intoxicating liquor is prohibited.

(b) The sale of any substance, advertised, designed or intended for use in the manufacture of intoxicating liquor is prohibited.

The assembling and sale of malt syrup, hops and gelatin in one package . . . must be stopped immediately . . . [also] the advertising, sale or gift of yeast, corn sugar or gelatin in connection with the sale of malt syrup.

We make the following recommendations in regard to the labels and advertising used in connection with the sale of malt syrup:

1st: Labels and advertising should contain no language that in any manner refers to beverages or that the product may be used in the manufacture of a prohibited beverage;

2nd: Labels and advertising should contain no cuts, figures or designs that by inference or otherwise convey the idea that the product is intended for or may be used in the manufacture of a prohibited beverage;

3rd: All names formerly used in connection with the sale of intoxicating beverages, such as "Bock" "Stout" "Porter" must be eliminated from labels and advertising;

4th: All names which embrace or include the word "brew" (whether in the English, German or any other language) or which convey the idea, either directly or indirectly, that the product is intended for brewing purposes must be eliminated from labels and advertising;

6th: Any and all language, which either directly or indirectly conveys the idea that the product may be used in the manufacture or both: All cuts of stems, mugs, breweries, or brewery equipment, must be eliminated from all labels and advertising of a prohibited beverage must be stricken from labels and advertising;

7th: All such expressions as "no boil" "no fuss" "no muss's" "no odor" "ready for use" must be eliminated from all labels and advertising.

8th: All warnings appearing on labels or in advertising wherein the purchaser is warned against the use of the product in the manufacture of an intoxicating beverage must be stricken therefrom.[3]

The hypocrisy of the trade union's deal with the feds was a transparent subterfuge. Although the squeeze was on the small retail homebrew shops that sold innocuous 2.5 pound cans of malt syrup, the biggest abuses continued to take place within the brewing industry and its illicit workings with bootleggers.

In 1979, the use, labeling, and advertising of malt extracts as a brewing ingredient was once again legally allowed by the federal government. Brewing enthusiasts can now make up to two hundred gallons of homebrew per household.

CAPONE'S PEACE CONFERENCE

While makeshift arrangements for the production of real beer took some of the pressure off Capone's recently acquired organization, the problems of dealing with O'Banion's old gang continued to plague Capone. "Hymie" Weiss had recently spurned Capone's attempt to form a business alliance, a successfully proven technique that Capone had learned from his mentor, Torrio. Capone had reasonably offered Weiss all the beer concessions in Chicago north of Madison Street, leaving the rest of Chicago for himself. Weiss, however, would only agree to Capone's peace overture if Al agreed to turn over the two remaining murderers of Dion O'Banion. Capone refused and realized he had to have Weiss killed before Weiss killed him. Assassins soon took care of Weiss on October 5, 1926, ironically, just across the street from O'Banion's old flower shop.

With Weiss out of the way, Capone arranged a citywide peace conference on October 20 with the remaining rival gang leaders. It was a highly publicized meeting that took place at the downtown Sherman House. At the mobster summit, Capone made his pitch for unity, offering to share the lucrative beer market with his former adversaries. "There's plenty of beer business for everybody," he reportedly said. "Why kill each other over it?" As a result of the conference, a pact was made with his rivals, Capone acquiring all of the territory south of Madison Street to neighboring Chicago Heights and territory to the west of Chicago, including Cicero.[4]

Securing New Accounts

Capone's beer drummers methodically went to work in their agreed-upon business territory, securing every and all accounts. Their approach to securing new and wayward accounts was straightforward and absolute, with intimidation and physical violence proving to be effective motivators.

If initial attempts to persuade a saloon keeper to take on their bootlegged beer proved fruitless, a well-placed pipe bomb would usually close the deal. The next morning the owner would show up and the whole front of his place would be blown out. Soon after the bombing, Capone's drummers would show up again. "Gee, if you'd had Ace Beer I don't think that would've happened to ya," they'd suggest. Unable to file an insurance claim and having taken a financial loss, the hapless owner now had one last choice if he wanted to get back into the saloon business, that is, "he goes back to the Capone group to get the money. From there on, he only does what they tell him." It was Al Capone's extreme version of the old tied-house concept.[5]

But some saloon owners resisted these drastic measures. One former Pilsen resident recalls how a neighborhood saloon keeper defiantly handled the aftermath of a pipe bombing.

> When beer drummers came around telling the owner he was going to buy beer from them, he said no. He was a tough Bohemian. That night they threw a pipe bomb at the front of his saloon. It blew out the windows and damaged part of the bar. The next morning he boarded up the front of the saloon but let everyone in the neighborhood know that he was going to open up later that day for business.
>
> Down in the basement of the saloon was a small brewery. That's where he got his beer, but he was no different than most of the families on the block. Almost everybody made their own beer—he just made more of it.
>
> When he finally opened up, there was a line of customers waiting to get into the side door of the saloon. I was a kid then but I can still remember how funny it looked to me, you know, the old timers all lined-up and waiting patiently for their beer.[6]

THE END OF THE DEVER
ADMINISTRATION

Local politics, as usual, were the center stage of attention in late 1926 in Chicago. "Decent" Dever, as critics referred to the crusading mayor, and his campaign to dry out Chicago with brewery raids and wholesale closings of saloons and soda parlors, had even begun to target little ethnically owned ma and pa corner grocery stores. As a result of the fanatical tempo of the closings and Dever's unwavering adherence to an unpopular law, he began to unintentionally alienate a sizable portion of Chicago's ethnic electorate and flame the violence between rival bootleg gangs as they continued to fight over territory.

While his beer war outwardly showed results, organized crime continued to flourish. Corruption still permeated local government, in spite of the personal integrity of both Mayor Dever and Police Chief Collins. National prohibition, and all its confusing moral baggage, was slowly bringing Dever's administration down.[7]

Hoping to pacify some of his more vocal opponents, Dever once again brought his dry campaign to the people, continuing his familiar argument that he was really a wet, forced to enforce an unpopular law. Chicago, though, was ripe for a change. National prohibition was a dismal failure in Chicago. Its blanketing of "personal liberty" still projected the perception of nativism to thousands of Germans, Irish, Italians, Poles, and other ethnics who controlled the vote. The same Chicagoans who had voted Dever into office were now ready to abandon him.

After considerable soul searching, mixed with the newspaper pronouncements of murders brought on by open gang warfare in the streets of Chicago, and an illegal drink trade that continued to flourish, Dever too began to realize that Prohibition did not nor could not work. The notion that strict enforcement of a law of which the majority of law-abiding citizens found offensive, was being proven flawed throughout the city. But it was too late for Dever to change course. The well-meaning mayor had lost touch with the very people who had put him into office.

BIG BILL, PART II

After the typical primary dance of local candidates, William Hale Thompson's name once again oozed to the top for the Republican choice of mayor of Chicago in 1927. With promises to reopen every speakeasy in Chicago that Dever had closed and declaring himself "wetter than the middle of the Atlantic Ocean," Thompson's campaign pledges caught the attention of not only the disfranchised electorate but also of "Schemer" Drucci and Jack Zuta of the "Bugs" Moran gang, who readily contributed $50,000 to Thompson's campaign. Not one to be outdone by a rival gang, Capone secretly contributed a $260,000 pay-off to Big Bill's campaign. The *Chicago Tribune* later reported that the money was "ladled out to Thompson workers from a bathtub in the Hotel Sherman, filled with packages of $5 bills." In return for the payoff, an agreement was reached with Thompson forces that Capone would be granted immunity to operate whorehouses and gambling dens and retain control of all beer and booze joints south of Madison Street. It was his old territory, but now the heat would be off. It was the real beginning of the "Roaring Twenties" in Chicago.[8]

A few weeks before the mayoral election, the United States Circuit Court of Appeals upheld the decision of Federal Judge Adam C. Cliffe that the mere smelling of liquor in a restaurant or cabaret was grounds to close the business. As a result of the decision, "smell raids" incredibly closed some of the more famous nightclubs in Chicago, including the Moulin Rouge, the Friar's Club, and Al Tearney's Town Club. Prohibition agents who conducted the raids at these establishments admitted that they had not actually attempted to purchase any liquor at the clubs nor had they even seen any alcohol served—they simply claimed they smelled it. Dever's campaign to rid the city of alcohol was now bordering on questions of constitutionality and just plain lunacy.

THOMPSON'S WIN

Thompson easily won the mayoral election with a total of 515,716 votes to Dever's 432,678 and was sworn in on April 13, 1927. Later analysis of ethnic voting patterns showed a dramatic drop in support for Dever and the Democratic Party in the 1927 election versus the winning results they had enjoyed in 1923. The heavy handedness of his beer war, the feeling by much of Dever's core constituency that national prohibition had an underlying nativist tone to it, and the later assertion that Dever was secretly dumped by the local Democratic Party chieftains, including wet advocate Anton Cermak, all contributed to the inevitability of his political demise. For those appalled at the strength of Thompson's victory, it was suggested that the real mystery was not how Thompson had won, but how Dever had found so many people to vote for him.[9]

For Chicagoans, it was a full and complete repudiation of national prohibition. In disgust, Dever had Thompson privately sworn in before his term actually ended, allowing him time to slip out of town and avoid Thompson's scheduled public inauguration. It was the first time in the history of Chicago that an outgoing mayor had ever skipped his successor's swearing in ceremony.[10]

ELIOT NESS

Soon after Dever's defeat, Capone swung into action, reaping the benefits of his political contribution to Thompson. Later findings by the Chicago Crime Commission showed that Capone had quickly taken over the lucrative beer territories of the Saltis and O'Donnell gangs after the election, increasing the size of his crime empire.[11]

In 1928, with a staff of three hundred agents, the Chicago unit of the Prohibition Bureau was joined by a young agent named Eliot Ness. Hired by U.S. Attorney George E. Q. Johnson, Ness's first forays into the bootlegging operations of the Capone organization took place in nearby Chicago Heights. On the strength of his success in busting a number of the suburban gambling and bootleg operations in "The Heights," Ness was ordered to move his efforts to Cicero and Chicago.

An analysis of Chicago Prohibition Bureau records revealed to Ness that prisoners had never been taken inside a Capone brewery. These breweries were "wildcat" breweries, usually operating in warehouses in secluded industrial areas. Past experiences had indicated that these raided breweries were normally occupied for only forty minutes in a twenty-four hour period. In order to locate new clandestine brewing sites with their personnel, Ness sent two-man teams to trace the movement of empty beer barrels hauled by trucks from the thousands of speakeasies in Chicago as they headed back to the wildcat breweries.

BREWERY RAIDS

From the back of Jim Colisimo's former restaurant, two agents anxiously watched as workers loaded empty beer barrels onto a truck. After stopping at a number of other South Side joints, the fully laden truck made its way back to an old factory at 38th street and Shields, just a foul ball away from Comisky Park. After a few days of observation, it was determined by prohibition agents that the site was merely used to clean empty barrels. It was not a brewery. Disappointed, Ness and his men continued the strategy of following trucks loaded with empty barrels, but with no results.

A few days later, the agents got lucky. Ness's men found an operating brewery in the Singer Storage Company at 2271 South Lumber Street by tracing the route of the cleaned barrels back to the secret brewery. They were confident that this new target was a brewery and not another barrel-cleaning operation by the way the trucks were weighted down as they left the site. Equipped with sawed-off shotguns, crowbars, and axes, the agents watched as a number of trucks entered the premises. Armed with an ax, Ness rushed the entrance and frantically hacked away at the wooden double doors of the suspected brewery as another agent attempted to jimmy it open with a crowbar. Behind the wooden door, however, stood a second, steel door. Having lost the element of surprise, Ness desperately fired two shots through the lock. The door finally opened, revealing nineteen 1,500 gallon vats, two new trucks, and 140 barrels of real beer; but no one was in sight. It was later estimated that the plant was capable of producing one hundred barrels of beer a day. There were no personnel to arrest, but for Ness and his men, it was a triumphant beginning.

Frustrated by the clumsiness of the raid, Ness drew up a design for a heavy-duty steel bumper attached to a ten-ton truck for ramming any door, reinforced or otherwise. The target this time was a brewery at 1632 South Cicero Avenue. Once again watching the goings on at the suspected brewery, they determined that it was indeed another wildcat brewery. As the battering ram of the truck crashed through the doors, Ness was initially disappointed to find that the warehouse was seemingly empty. But as their eyes adjusted to the darkness of the warehouse, Ness and his men realized that the apparent emptiness of the brewery was really another false wall, painted black for deception. Ness ordered the driver of the truck to ram it. This time they found another brewery behind the wall with seven 320-gallon fermentation vats with five men on-site, including Steve Svoboda, a master brewer for Capone's organization.

THOMPSON CAMPAIGNS AGAINST FEDERAL INTERVENTION

In early 1928, the stepped-up presence of prohibition agents in Chicago was beginning to show its effect on the corrupt administration of Mayor Thompson and his City Hall cronies. Around the time of E. Q. Johnson's appointment as U.S. attorney in Chicago, a squad of federal agents had raided a saloon on the South Side of the city, shooting a municipal court bailiff in the back during the struggle. The bailiff, William Beatty, claimed that he thought the federal agents, waving weapons when they entered, were hold-up men and that he had merely attempted to flee from harm's way. Myron C. Caffey, the agent who had shot Beatty, later testified that Beatty had pulled a gun on him during the raid. As a result of Agent Caffey's testimony, Beatty was indicted by a federal grand jury for resisting a federal officer.

Thompson's chief of police, Michael Hughes, demanded that Agent Caffey be instead turned over to his authority to answer charges of shooting Beatty. When George E. Golding, head of the federal squad involved in the raid refused, Chief Hughes took out a warrant for the arrest of Caffey and assembled a squad of Chicago police ready to storm the Federal Building and seize Caffey. The assault on the Federal Building, however, did not take place. Federal Judge H. Wilkerson ruled that Caffey would be turned over to the police after the April primary, defusing the awkward and embarrassing struggle between Thompson's police and federal officials.

Thompson spent the next few weeks preaching of his attempts to save the local citizenry from the dangers of federal intervention in Chicago law enforcement, and incredibly claimed, "We took out a warrant and we'll throw every damn dry agent in jail." But federal agents ignored

Thompson's bluster and continued their drive to solve the Prohibition problems that the city had woefully failed to do.[12]

THE UNTOUCHABLES
CONTINUE THEIR RAIDS

One of Ness's biggest brewery busts was his raid on The Old Reliable Trucking Company at 3136 South Wabash. The agents destroyed 40,324 gallons of unbarreled beer and 115 barrels of racked beer. Brewer Svoboda was once again caught in the raid along with four accomplices. This time, Ness and his men cagily left most of the equipment in place, setting a trap for anyone who might return to reclaim it. The next day, four men dutifully returned for the equipment, including Bert Delaney, another Capone brewer; they were captured.

Soon after the success of the Wabash raid, Ness and his men also seized a smaller brewery at 1712 North Kilbourn, operated by mobster George "Red" Barker, and one more Capone brewery at 2024 South State. The Barker brewery raid was the result of a telephone tip that would cause a wave of paranoia to ripple throughout the illicit brewing trade. One telephone call to the feds could wipe out another rival gangs' brewery; it was much easier and less costly than sending out a bunch of goons to shut it down.

Probably the most publicized brewery raid was the result of a tap on the phone of Ralph Capone. A reference during a tapped phone conversation about reopening a spot on South Wabash Avenue alerted federal agents to watch a previously raided and closed Capone brewery at 2108 South Wabash. On June 12, 1930, federal prohibition agents, led by Special Agent Alexander Jamie, seized the brewery. Fifty thousand gallons of beer, one hundred and fifty thousand gallons of mash, two trucks, and six men were seized in the raid. Interestingly, the *Chicago Tribune* never mentions Ness in their article about the raid the following morning, crediting Agent Jamie for the raid. Ness's account of the raid reads quite differently in his later autobiography. Alexander Jamie was Ness's brother-in-law and had recommended Ness for the position of prohibition agent back in 1928. In describing the Wabash Street raid in his book, *The Untouchables*, Ness takes total credit for the raid, never mentioning Jamie.[13]

AGENT NESS BEATS HIS DRUM

Apparently Ness's heroics made better press in New York than in Chicago. In often gushing prose, a 1931 article in the *New York Times* talked of Agent Ness, his youth, integrity, and intelligence. But Chicago newsmen viewed Ness quite differently. Tony Berardi, a *Chicago Tribune* photographer, recalled that "Ness was considered [by Chicago newsmen] not quite a phony but strictly small time."[14] Ness seems to have had a habit of tooting his own horn; years later, he claimed to have raided twenty-five breweries and seized forty-five delivery trucks, but a report by Ness to U.S. attorney George E. Q. Johnson indicates otherwise:

> Six breweries with total equipment valued at $140,000 were seized . . . total income based upon the wholesale [price] of beer manufactured would have totaled $9,154,200 annually. Five large beer-distributing plants were seized in addition to the breweries. The total amount seized . . . was approximately 200,000 gallons having a wholesale value to the Capone organization of $343,750. Twenty-five trucks and two cars were seized, the value of which totaled approximately $30,950.[15]

In his book Ness described an unusual parade he claims to have organized to infuriate Capone, though no other evidence corroborates this event. Supposedly assembling trucks that he and his men had seized from Capone's breweries—a collection of pickups, ten-ton vans, and glass-lined tank trucks for transporting beer—he and his men brazenly drove them by Capone's headquarters at the Lexington Hotel on Michigan Avenue. Before they got underway, Ness wrote, he had telephoned Capone and told him to look out the front windows of the hotel at exactly eleven o'clock that morning. Right on time, the ragtag collection of the mobster's seized trucks slowly drove by the hotel. From the windows of the Lexington, heads bobbed and arms pointed at the show on South Michigan. The next morning, Ness continued, a snitch met Ness and told him of Capone's reaction to the parade. "I'll kill im! I'll kill im with my own bare hands!" the enraged hoodlum screamed as he busted a couple of chairs over a table.[16]

CAPONE INDICTED

On June 5, 1931, the U.S. government finally indicted Capone on charges of tax evasion. A week later Capone was once again indicted, this time for national prohibition violations. It was the culmination of all the efforts of Ness, his men, and other federal agents who had worked on bringing Capone and his empire down. The indictment listed Alphonse Capone with all his known aliases (Al Brown, A. Costa, Albert Costa, Frank Rose, John Brown, Snorky Capone, Frank Hart, and Louis Hart) and charged him with five thousand offenses against the United States, 547 dealing with the manufacturing of beer with more than one-half of 1 percent of alcohol, without first obtaining a permit from the commissioner of Internal Revenue, the commissioner of Prohibition, the commissioner of Industrial Alcohol and the director of Prohibition, and committing four thousand offenses by transporting the illegally brewed beer. By linking Capone's name to the purchase of a number of trucks seized during the brewery raids by Ness and others, the government had conclusive evidence that Capone was guilty of Prohibition violations.[17]

However, the violations described in the tax evasion indictment were the ones used by George E. Q. Johnson to eventually convict and sentence Capone. Although the work of Ness and his agents caused considerable damage to Capone's bootlegging operations, the dry crusade was little more than a distraction used to tie up Capone's organization while the federal government delved further into Capone's murky tax situation. But even with Capone's arrest and later imprisonment, beer continued to flow in Chicago.

THOMPSON DEFEATED

A few months before Capone's arrest, the results of the mayoral election of 1931 once again forced William Hale Thompson and his cronies out of City Hall, replaced by wet advocate Anton Cermak. Chicago had been chosen to be the site of the 1933 World's Fair, to be called *A Century of Progress Exposition*. With the election of wet advocate Cermak and the potential of millions of cash-laden tourists coming to Chicago to visit the World's Fair, both the new city administration and the remnants of Capone's organization prepared for the prosperity that 1933 might offer.

New Beer's Eve, April 7, 1933

I recommend . . . the passage
of legislation . . . to legalize the
manufacture and sale of beer.
—*President Franklin D. Roosevelt*

THE BEGINNING OF THE END

By 1932, national prohibition was dying. Its dry policy and enforcement had caused a generation of Americans to be raised with a
casual disregard for the law. Probably no issue had done so much to
divide the country since the Civil War. After some political maneuvering, Democratic presidential candidate Franklin D. Roosevelt
had finally declared himself an advocate for Repeal. Incumbent
President Hoover, however, continued to state his belief in national
prohibition, effectively becoming a lame duck even before the final-
ity of the upcoming presidential election in November.

The economic logic of repeal was eloquently expressed by August
A. Busch of the Anheuser-Busch Brewery in St. Louis. In 1931,
Busch had issued a pamphlet titled *An Open Letter to the American People*, sending a copy to every U.S. senator and congressman
and taking out ads in leading national magazines explaining his
position on legalizing the production and sale of beer. With the
country suffering from the throes of the Great Depression, Busch
proclaimed that the legalization of beer would put over one million people back to work, including farmers, railroad employees,
and even coal miners. In addition, the St. Louis brewer argued
that the government would save the $50 million a year it was now
wasting through its failing efforts to enforce Prohibition. Taxation of beer would also help the federal government recoup the

estimated $500 million in revenues it had lost since the beginning of Prohibition.

Attending a meeting in February 1933 of the National Malt Products' Manufacturing Association at the Hotel Sherman in Chicago, and knowing that the tide had turned, Busch declared himself "100 per cent for beer" and boasted that his St. Louis brewery was ready to restart the production of beer as soon as the law would permit. The Siebel Institute of Technology in Chicago was so sure of the relegalization of beer that the faculty announced the resumption of their regular five-month training course for brewers in January 1933. The sweet smell of malt was in the air.[1]

Support in Washington for the reintroduction of 3.2 percent beer began with an opinion by Representative Beck of Pennsylvania that Congress already had the power to legalize beer and that the Supreme Court would more than likely uphold any favorable congressional action. After some political foot dragging, President-elect Roosevelt finally added his opinion to the debate, saying that he favored the 3.2 percent beer bill that now was pending in the Senate. The Senate continued negotiations on a bill to legalize beer and made no change to a proposal to tax a barrel of beer at the rate of $5, effectively acknowledging the eventual reinstitution of the legal brewing industry. On February 15, 1933, the Senate took the debate even further when it voted fifty-eight to twenty-three to begin formal consideration of a resolution proposing repeal of the Eighteenth Amendment. Later that same day, the Senate passed its approval of the Blaine resolution, proposing repeal of the Eighteenth Amendment. The issue was then passed on to the House of Representatives. When Speaker of the House Garner heard of the quickness of the Senate's actions, he commented surprisingly, "The vote was better than most of us anticipated. We will pass the amendment here Monday—I should say, consider it." With a slip of the Speaker's tongue, there was little doubt on what the outcome of the vote in the House would be.[2]

The same day, the Illinois State Senate also voted its approval of repeal of the Illinois dry laws and the state Search and Seizure Act which had been invoked by State Attorney General Edward Brundage back in July 1919. Brundage's narrow interpretation of the law had shut down the sale of beer and booze in Chicago six months before national prohibition actually took effect.[3]

3.2 PERCENT BEER

On February 20, 1933, Congress passed the repeal of the National Prohibition Amendment and submitted its final approval to the states for ratification. In Springfield, Governor Horner presided at a meeting of state senators and representatives and agreed to a June 5 election for a state convention to decide if Illinois delegates would vote for repeal of the Eighteenth Amendment. With the anticipated results of the state convention being in favor of repeal, the resumption of the manufacturing, transportation, and sale of beer in Illinois was imminent. Horner confirmed this when he indicated his readiness to sign the necessary bills invoking revocation of the Search and Seizure Act and the state prohibition laws as soon as they came to his desk.

On March 13, President Roosevelt used the bully pulpit of his office to formally recommend to Congress a looser interpretation of the Volstead Act, which limited alcohol in beer to .5 percent. "I recommend to the Congress the passage of legislation for the immediate modification of the Volstead Act, in order to legalize the manufacture and sale of beer." Upon hearing Roosevelt's recommendation, Governor Horner signed the bill repealing the two State of Illinois dry enforcement laws, now leaving the enforcement of national prohibition solely to the federal government.

Finally, on March 21, 1933, the U.S. House of Representatives completed action on the Cullen-Harrison bill, permitting the resumption of the manufacture and sale of 3.2 percent beer and light wines in those states that were now legally considered wet. The next morning President Roosevelt was scheduled to sign the bill, but a bureaucratic mix-up postponed his signing until March 23.

In the meantime Roosevelt talked of a possible amnesty for violators imprisoned for the manufacturing and sale of beer up to an alcoholic content of 3.2 percent by weight. In Illinois there were 3,380 incarcerated federal Prohibition offenders. Roosevelt's sentiments were perhaps more economic in scope than benevolent. The release of Illinois Prohibition violators, along with the release of similar offenders throughout the United States, would save the federal government millions of badly needed dollars. The president's amnesty proposal was held by Congress for consideration. With a fifteen-day wait required after Roosevelt's signature, 3.2 percent beer would again be available on April 7 in nineteen states that had removed their dry laws. Wet advocates cheerfully anticipated that an additional fifteen states would soon join these wet states.

One day after Roosevelt signed the Cullen-Harrison bill, the Justice Department quietly announced that it was dropping its national prohibition exhibit at Chicago's *A Century of Progress*. No reason was given; for thirsty Chicagoans, no reason was needed.[4]

NEW RETAIL OUTLETS FOR BEER

As Chicago prepared for the resumption of legal brewing, local issues of home rule, licensing, taxation, and dispensing unfolded, especially after the wording of the congressional beer bill declared 3.2 percent beer as nonintoxicating, a legal technicality needed to nullify the alcoholic restrictions of the Volstead Act. With this ruling by Congress, and concurrence of federal opinion by Illinois Attorney General Otto Kerner, Chicago's saloons would no longer hold domain over the retail sale of beer as they had done before Prohibition. As a nonintoxicant, beer could now be available in such places as grocery stores and drug stores, even ma and pa corner stores. In a meeting of city officials, lawyers advised acting Mayor Corr and key city alderman that simply the repeal of the Illinois prohibition law did not revive the old liquor laws. As a result the sale of this 3.2 percent, nonintoxicating beer, now having fallen into the same category as soda water or ginger ale, would be unregulated in off-premise sites unless the Chicago City Council and Springfield acted quickly to correct this unexpected legal quirk.[5]

THE CITY GETS READY FOR
3.2 PERCENT BEER

Unfazed by the political logistics of the resumption of beer, local old-time beer establishments made ready. At the Berghoff on West Adams, eighty-year-old Herman J. Berghoff proudly displayed Beer Retail License Number 1 for newspaper cameramen, the license issued by the City Collector's Office for the serving of beer at his famous bar. Installed in 1897, the Berghoff's wood inlaid bar from Amsterdam, which still serves as the focal point of this Chicago landmark, was made ready for business. In pre-Prohibition days, Berghoff had estimated that he sold as high as forty-two barrels of beer a day. Anticipated demand for the golden nectar now seemed just as positive. At the Righeimer bar on North Clark, Acting Mayor Corr and a host of local politicos rededicated the establishment's famous one-hundred-foot bar. Corr had been thrust into this position after Mayor Cermak had been shot by a crazed assassin while meeting with President Roosevelt in Miami, Florida. Sadly the man who represented the local wet interests for so long died just weeks before he could see the return of beer to the city and nation.

Clerks at the City Collector's office worked overtime to take care of the rush of new applicants for beer licenses. Unexplainably, the City Council had already passed the required ordinance providing for the $150 licensing fee for saloon keepers in December 1932, four months before legal beer would flow again in Chicago. Seven hundred and forty-one saloon keepers had actually paid the fee for the first half of the year even though they were technically in violation of state and federal dry laws. The Chicago City Council had tried unsuccessfully to pull off a similar revenue-enhancing stunt back in 1929. At the time there was a movement afoot in the council to license the five thousand bartenders who regularly poured illegal drink for thirsty Chicagoans. With a $10 annual fee, it would have meant an additional $50,000 income to the financially desperate city. Referred to committee for further study, the idea was abruptly dropped from the council agenda when someone mentioned that national prohibition was still in effect. It would be hard to license bartenders when, in theory, there were no bars. By April 7, more than twenty-six hundred bars were legally licensed to sell beer, a dramatic drop from the over seven thousand licensed bars of pre-Prohibition days.

City breweries began a hiring spree of several hundred with promises of an additional hiring of one thousand more men and women by April 7, as the bottling of beer in Chicago began on March 25. At the Schoenhofen Company, the first brewery granted a federal permit to resume the the brewing of beer in the Northern District, including Milwaukee, two 8-hour shifts of employees began a daily regime of filling 14,000 cases of beer a day. The politically connected Atlas Brewing Company set the ambitious goal of producing and bottling 20 to 25,000 cases a day. Realizing that they'd probably never fill all their outstanding orders by April 7, even with a planned hiring of 200 to 300 more employees, Atlas President Charles Vopicka ordered outdoor posters to be printed for distribution throughout the city during the early morning hours of New Beer's Eve. Under a picture of a smiling Uncle Sam hoisting a beer, the posters asked for the indulgence of any customers who had not yet received their promised beer delivery. At the Prima Company, management estimated that they would soon begin the bottling of over 3 million bottles of beer a day. The brewery had recently been expanded to a 500,000 barrel capacity in anticipation of repeal. Employees of the United States Brewing Company on North Elston decorated the exterior of the plant with flags and bunting. A picture of Franklin Roosevelt hung above the entrance of the brewery, celebrating the man who represented repeal to the grateful brewing industry. Coopers readied thousands of new wooden barrels, as did bottle makers their containers, for delivery to breweries. Fifteen hundred beer delivery trucks were prepped for the big night, supplemented by moving vans, milk wagons, and even coal trucks. Federal inspectors started to make the rounds of Chicago's seven licensed breweries, measuring the aging tanks, which were also used for the computation of federal tax due. A final industry estimate, made days before the resumption of beer in Chicago, figured that approximately 15,000 men and women had found work in breweries and related industries in Chicago. A heady sense of festivity was settling over Chicago.[6]

There was, however, a sobering note to all the gaiety at the breweries. District police captains quietly placed guards at all the breweries to discourage any possible attempts at hijacking when the trucks finally rolled out for deliveries.[7]

WHEN'S THE PARTY BEGIN?

In an amusing misunderstanding prior to the big event, E. C. Yellowley, head of the Prohibition Department in Chicago, ruled that the local delivery of beer could begin at 11:01 P.M. on April 6, which would correspond to 12:01 A.M., April 7 in Washington, D.C. Yellowley's interpretation of the commencement time though was clarified by U.S. Attorney General Cummings who ruled that legal beer deliveries would begin at 12:01 A.M. in each respective time zone.

Illinois House Representative Fred A. Britten thought he had a better idea on when beer deliveries should begin in Chicago. In a telephone conversation to the attorney general, Britten suggested that the commencement time for the serving of legal beer would better serve Chicago's interests if it began as early as 10:00 P.M., April 6. When Cummings reminded the imploring state representative that federal law distinctly stated that beer deliveries could only begin at 12:01 A.M., April 7, Britten, in an amazing display of political chutzpah, suggested a solution to that little time problem. "Chicago will set all the clocks ahead two hours at 10:00 P.M.," he explained to the skeptical attorney general. "The City Council will pass the ordinance," he assured Cummings. To emphasize the seriousness of his request and the careful planning he was ready to carry through to get fresh beer to thirsty Chicagoans, Britten added this assurance to his request. "The trucks will leave the breweries at 10 with all streets cleared and motorcycle squads as escorts." The U.S. attorney general could not be persuaded to allow Britten to implement his bizarre plan.[8]

12:01 A.M.?

As New Beer's Eve moved closer to reality in Chicago, the Chicago Hotel Association started to put pressure on the brewers and the local hotels, urging the hotel owners and managers not to take delivery of beer until seven o'clock Friday morning, hours after beer could legally be sold in the city. John Burke, president of the association and manager of the Congress Hotel, expressed his concerns that a wild night of revelry in Chicago might endanger future repeal of the Eighteenth Amendment, which still needed to be ratified by a two-thirds vote of all the states. "We feel that we should be careful not to kill the goose that laid the golden egg," he emphasized, and added that the anticipated celebration "might give a black eye to things at the very beginning," a very real concern.[9]

Hilmar Ernst, president of the Prima Company and the Illinois Brewers' Association, brushed off Burke's criticism. The problem—if there was one—he noted, was a problem for the hotel men, not the brewers. "Even if the hotels want to begin selling at 9 or 10 in the morning, we'll have to start delivering at midnight to get them supplied. Our brewery alone now has orders calling for the immediate delivery of between 200,000 and 300,000 cases and there will be a lot more by the 7th." Ernst failed to mention that local breweries had also collected over $2 million in deposits and had guaranteed delivery. The IBA president pointed out that the hotels were placing the biggest orders. Worried that delaying the sale of beer until the morning would cut hotel owners out of the huge volume of beer sales that was anticipated, Burke and his concerns were pushed aside by hotel owners and managers. Even a *Chicago Tribune* suggestion in favor of later day deliveries was ignored by the brewers. "The public demands it [beer] at once," sighed Anton Laadt, general manager of the Atlas Brewing Company.[10]

W-G-N radio, anticipating the wild night ahead and the historic significance of it all, scheduled special programming throughout Thursday evening and Friday morning to broadcast from the Atlas Brewing Company at 21st street and Blue Island. Radio personality Quinn Ryan was scheduled to give an on-site description of the beer manufacturing process straight through to the loading of the beer on to the waiting trucks ready for delivery. The brewery was preparing for delivery of two thousand barrels and one hundred thousand cases of beer to retailers on the first night. Additional offsite radio pickups from the Palmer House and the Blackhawk Restaurant would allow at-home celebrants to join in Chicago's New Beer's Eve festivities. CBS Radio Network arranged a radio hookup to broadcast the festivities in the Midwest's most important brewing centers of Chicago, Milwaukee, and St. Louis.[11]

A WARNING FROM THE CITY

Because of the quickness of the reinstitution of 3.2 percent beer and the time-consuming efforts needed to debate, write, and implement new legislation, the City of Chicago and the State of Illinois discovered that they currently had no regulations on their books to legislate the sale of the soon-to-be legal beer. The City Council urged Chicagoans to behave themselves during the celebration and warned hoteliers and would-be beer retailers that the Council's course of action on the eventual regulation of beer would be determined by how well the retailers conducted themselves in the first few weeks of beer sales. In some Loop hotels, cards and table tents were prepared for placement in their dining rooms, informing patrons that hotel management was forbidden by federal statue to provide ice, glasses, or ginger ale while the customers awaited the serving of beer at 12:01 A.M. It was a little white lie, but hotels feared that celebrants, using hotel provided setups, might mix them with bootleg liquor, causing their establishments to be shut down by snooping police or federal agents. Particular attention was to be paid by Chicago police to the more famous Prohibition-era night spots. Clubs like the Frolics, the Chez Paree, Follies Bergere, Vanity Fair, and the Green Mill, along with the College Inn and the Terrace Garden, were warned to be on their best behavior.[12]

Throughout the mix of confusion and anticipation, there seemed to be a sense of serenity coupled with the festivity of the upcoming big event. No one really anticipated any trouble. "Why shouldn't there be a little celebration?" a night club manager was quoted as saying. "Doesn't the country need to add a little gaiety to its gloom, and is there a better time than right after the legal restriction is first lifted to see whether 3.2 beer can be trusted to add to it?" State's Attorney Courtney added to the beery mellowness of the moment by saying that he expected no trouble. Jacob Rupert, New York brewer and president of the United States Brewers' Association, wasn't so sure and recommended that Chicago's breweries delay their shipments until the late morning. The local brewers cried that they would be swamped by back orders if they waited until morning and continued with their plans for a 12:01 A.M. delivery time.[13]

Beer and Food

Absent from the local papers for years, ads for the Berghoff Brewing Company of Ft. Wayne, Indiana, reappeared in the *Chicago Tribune*. In a back-handed reference to Milwaukee's Jos. Schlitz Brewing Company, the Berghoff advertised its beer as "The Beer that made itself Famous." Long-forgotten ads for Schoenhofen's "Good Old Edelweiss" and Pabst Blue Ribbon Beer, "The Old Favorite," started running again in Chicago papers. In a matter of days, beer began a metamorphosis in the city papers, changing from an Old World German concoction, an intoxicating product of the "brewery interests" as it was sinisterly portrayed in years past, into a refreshing family staple that Mom could now add to her weekly grocery list.

"Profitable beer merchandising will take into account the successful adaptation of food sales strategy" advised *Modern Brewery Age*, an industry trade publication. Local stores took heed. As if overnight, beer joined hands with food and, as a result of this marriage of retail convenience, finally became *the* drink of moderation. The Great Atlantic & Pacific Tea Company (A&P) heralded the arrival of real beer to their local stores. To accompany the customer's supply of beer for the weekend, the A&P ads listed Grandmother's Rye Bread, liver sausage, butter pretzels, kippered herring, and Spanish salted peanuts. It was everything a Chicago family needed to "make it a gala weekend—right in your own home." Hillman's reminded shoppers that they too would be carrying beer, "And Don't Forget the Accessories!" which included Limburger cheese and frankfurters. The Loblaw-Jewel chain proclaimed that they had "BEER at its best!" The Mandel Brothers department store on State Street rushed to open a new shop called "The Tavern," equipped to sell beer steins, six favorite brands of beer, and all the foods that go with them. The store's "Men's Grill Room" quickly converted half of the shop to replicate a German beer garden. The Walgreen drug store chain announced that it had also made arrangements with local breweries for a limited supply of bottled beer to be placed on shelves for sale at their outlets. On April 7, their featured daily luncheon special was a roast beef sandwich and a bottle of beer for a quarter, beer now available at their soda fountain counter. Sales later that day were reported as "phenomenal."

On the North Side, a new pretzel company opened to meet expected demand. Pretzels were becoming big business in the city. One snack food plant manager described the industry's reaction to legal beer. "We are ready to turn out pretzels by the billion." Even the local press got in on the food and beer relationship. Mary Meade's food column in the *Chicago Tribune* suggested making a Rye Bread Torte with dark bread leftover from "your beer party," and discussed how pretzels were now back in style. Chicago families were getting ready for beer and a new classification of food—beer snacks.[14]

NEW BEER'S EVE

At 12:01 A.M., Friday morning, April 7, 1933, the drinking light was turned on in Chicago, and legal "democratic beer" was reintroduced to the public. With cheers for President Roosevelt ringing through the air, prohibition agents and city police, supplemented with Brink's bank guards, allowed the brewery trucks to leave the plants and make their deliveries. Things got off to an embarrassing start near the Atlas Brewing Company. Acting Mayor Frank Corr, Atlas President Charles Vopika, Coroner Frank Walsh, and a host of other Democratic Party hacks and functionaries had gathered at the Iroquois Club at 11 P.M. where the guests had been assured that beer would be served an hour before the official deadline. They were forced, however, to wait with the rest of Chicago's eager beer drinkers until beer was finally delivered to the Iroquois and tapped for serving at 12:15 A.M. To their delight, and to the delight of thousands in the city, the beer was conveniently delivered cold from the brewery, saving the valuable time the pre-Prohibition retailer usually needed to ice it down. After a beer or two, acting Mayor Corr stepped before the W-G-N Radio microphone and hailed beer as a hope for prosperity. Atlas Brewing Company President Charles Vopika next came forward and proudly announced that the first case of bottled beer from his brewery was on its way by airplane to President Roosevelt in Washington, DC.[15]

Delays were worse at the Schoenhofen Company. Soon after midnight, trucks and cars were stretched over a mile as crews loaded the beer as quickly as possible. At the Prima Company, management had scrambled to hire an additional three hundred extra trucks for city and county deliveries and had charted an entire train to get some deliveries into Milwaukee and Minnesota that weekend. Escorted by motorcycle policemen, the delivery truck caravan slowly moved from the front gates of the Prima Company and through the celebrating crowd as it cautiously headed eastward toward Halsted Street. The police escorts had been requested of Police Commissioner Allman by the owners of all the city breweries. They feared the real possibility of hijacking during the early morning hours.

Milwaukee brewers were also ready for the Chicago market. At the Brevoort Hotel, forty cases of Miller High Life beer arrived at 1:30 A.M. after being flown in from the Cream City. The Premier Pabst Corporation, now consisting of the Pabst Brewing Company and the Premier Malting Company of Peoria, had a fleet of one hundred trucks being readied at their docks in Milwaukee for eventual delivery of their beer to Chicago.[16]

Three of Chicago's licensed breweries were left in the lurch, unable to take full advantage of New Beer's Eve. The Bosworth Products Company was in the process of a $75,000 plant renovation and company reorganization, soon to be known as the Atlantic Brewing Company. The Frank McDermott Brewing Company had a comparatively small inventory of its Senate Extra Pale on hand and shipped fifteen thousand cases and eight hundred barrels on the first night. Two thousand Bridgeport residents patiently waited outside the brewery hoping to make case purchases. The Monarch Brewing Company showed similar small numbers for available inventory.[17]

IN THE LOOP

Downtown, things were festive but controlled. On North Clark, crowds from Manny Goodman's spilled out on to the street as other beer lovers fought their way inside. In the alley behind the Bismarck Hotel, a throng of one thousand made it difficult for a beer delivery truck to make its first drop-off of twenty barrels. When the truck finally backed into the loading dock, attendants quickly grabbed six barrels and rolled them in to the hotel for the thirsty celebrants. At the Brevoort Hotel, revelers still crowded the famous round bar at 5 A.M. State Street, on the other hand, was comparatively quiet. Malachy N. Harney, Prohibition administrator, thought he knew why. "Experienced beer drinkers will wait until tonight [Friday] or Saturday night to try the new product. They know that beer just freshly delivered is 'angry' from the bouncing it gets. They'll wait until it has had a day or two to cool and settle before sampling."

Agent Harney was obviously an out-of-towner who didn't understand thirsty Chicagoans.

One of the most noticeable features of the Loop crowd was the large number of young females who were joining in the celebration. Operators of the Hotel Sherman, the Brevoort Hotel and other MEN ONLY watering holes had prepared themselves for this intrusion. "What can we do about it?" bemoaned James Galbaugh of the Brevoort. "If the ladies insist on coming in—and I suppose they will—we can't put them out." Waving beer bottles or hoisting heavy steins, their appearances in bars and clubs were a far cry from the restrictive traditions of the pre-Prohibition era. At that time, women were seldom seen in saloons. If so, they were always accompanied by their husbands and routinely hustled in through the family entrance, usually located on the side of the saloon. An unescorted women in a drinking establishment was normally considered a "working girl," whether she was one or not, trying to drum up some needed business.

But national prohibition and twenty thousand speakeasies had, in many ways, liberated Chicago's women. The next day, an older lady, accompanied by her daughter, was overheard describing her feelings toward women and public drinking. As the two generations of women sat at a drug store counter, the younger girl brazenly ordered a beer and goaded her mother to order one, but the older woman refused. "I can't get used to women drinking in public. In my day, a lady averted her eyes if she had to pass a saloon." Her next comment was revealing. "I remember how I longed to look inside those swinging doors," she admitted. And now, in the midst of New Beer's Eve, women in Chicago not only were looking in, but also they were pushing their way to the bar, ordering beer alongside the men.

But at the Berghoff Restaurant, the bar would remain an all-male enclave that night and would continue to enforce this policy of female exclusion until 1969 when the National Organization for Women finally forced the integration of the sexes at the bar. But on this night, Herman Berghoff's vow that "ladies will not be seated at the bar" held firm for the night—and for another thirty-six years.[18]

AT THE SPEAKEASIES

Despite pressure from mob beer drummers, many of the speakeasies curtailed further ordering of bootlegged draft beer and, as a result, ran out by April 5. Those speaks that still held a small draft supply continued to sell at the inflated price of 25 cents a stein even though the barrel price had dropped significantly. At 12:01 A.M., however, the stein price quickly dropped to 10 to 15 cents, the competition of the lower-priced legal beer having its effect. Canadian bottled beer was also plentiful and dropped in price from $1 per bottle to 50 cents as owners hurried to unload their illegal inventory.

With the return of legal beer, some speakeasy owners began to cautiously remove the iron bars from their doors and windows; other owners brazenly displayed bottles of whiskey and gin on the back bar to anyone who now freely entered their premises. Even with its open availability, most owners reported little call for the harder stuff.

Anticipating late deliveries of legal beer as the breweries serviced the licensed, legitimate establishments first, most speakeasy owners placed duplicate orders with three and four breweries, hoping to get at least one beer shipment in before the last of the wildcat and needled brew ran out. But as one delivery quickly followed another, a number of the speakeasies actually had more beer on hand than they could use. The situation would rectify itself by the next day.[19]

Back at the Breweries

The principal areas of confusion and celebration were around the breweries themselves. In the streets adjacent to the breweries, cars were lined up, waiting to get to the loading docks for cases, half barrels, or even the unwieldy thirty-one-gallon barrels of beer. Some local breweries reported that delivery trucks were still waiting in line to be loaded with beer as late as five o'clock in the morning. Police later confirmed that they spent most of their time just trying to untangle the traffic jams around the breweries which began around 9 P.M., having few other problems throughout the rest of the city.[20]

Supplies Start Running Short

In the early morning of April 7, as the sun broke over Lake Michigan, Chicago was still *en fête*. The local breweries were now operating on a twenty-four-hour basis, exhausting workers who were putting in double and triple shifts, trying to keep up with mounting back orders. Between two and five o'clock in the afternoon, frantic requests for beer tied up local phone lines, making it impossible to reach any of the breweries with additional orders.

In Mandel's new Tavern Room, a lack of sufficient waitresses caused a minor ruckus when they couldn't keep up with the initial round of orders. Store detectives were quickly called in to retain order. The Tavern Room manager wisely placed the first round on the house and pulled store personnel from other departments to handle the demanding crowd. Those satisfied beer drinkers who eventually wandered outside were treated to the sight of 6, one-ton champion Clydesdales from Anheuser-Busch pulling a bright red beer wagon through the Loop. A-B owner, August Busch, had big plans for Chicago.

Joe Durbin, editor of *Brewery Age*, had earlier estimated that there would be enough beer on hand for the initial celebration to provide every Chicagoan with thiry-five steins of beer. But unrelenting demand for legal beer soon outstripped supply. The shelves at A&P, National Tea, and Kroger-Consumer stores were stripped of beer before noon. Ecstatic store representatives added that sales of food now referred to as "beer snacks" were the biggest of any day in the history of their chain grocery stores, with the greatest demand being for rye bread, pretzels, cheese, and sausage. Hillman's and other grocery stores reported similar sales. A local cheese wholesaler later noted that citywide demand for Swiss, Brie, and American cheese had been record breaking.

At the Bismarck Hotel, 20 barrels of fresh beer were emptied between 12:30 A.M. and 2 A.M. Perhaps overreacting to the initial rush, Bismarck Hotel officials announced later that morning that 50 barrels of beer would now be part of their normal inventory. The Berghoff took stock of that night's business to find that they had rolled out an unbelievable 81 barrels of beer since 12:01 A.M.[21]

WHERE DID ALL THE BEER COME FROM?

Even with the overwhelming demand, prices for beer remained stable. An eight-ounce glass was selling for 10 cents, a twelve-ounce stein for 10 to 15 cents. Cases ran between $2.30 to $2.90. But by the end of the second day of sales, questions were arising as to the quality of the legal brew. After years of drinking needle beer with an alcoholic strength of around 7 percent, some neighborhood beer *connoisseurs* complained that the new beer didn't quite have the taste or jolt of the more familiar illegal brew, an opinion that city officials concurred with. Reports from chemists working under Dr. Herman N. Bundesen, president of the City Board of Health, revealed that veteran Prohibition-era beer drinkers, unhappy with the taste and strength of the legal beer, were probably correct in their criticisms. Even comparative analysis of recently seized home brew indicated that home brewers were surpassing the 3.2 percent alcohol limit.

Doctor Robert Wahl, head of the Wahl Institute, explained that his laboratory was in the process of checking the new beer for taste, effervescence, and clarity. Because of the higher alcoholic content that is normally found in darker beers such as a *Kulmbacher* or *Muenchener*, Wahl advised that Americans would have to be content with the pale or *Pilsner* type beers. He noted that research was being conducted at the Institute to develop a dark, flavorful beer that would be under the legal alcoholic content of 3.2 percent by weight, 4 percent by volume. In developing such a beer, Wahl mentioned how important it was for the beer to have what the Germans call *süffigkeit*. A beer has sueffig-keit, explained Wahl, "when you can drink it all afternoon and still not have enough."

Less filling, taste great?

Wahl later reported that his tests had indicated that the new beer was indeed disappointing. Out of ten beers analyzed in his laboratory, Wahl deemed only three to be of good quality.[22]

His assessment of the new beer was immediately challenged by local braumeisters. Brewers William Faude of Schoenhofen and Charles Ell-man of Atlas proclaimed their beer better than pre-Prohibition beer. "Prohibition taught us how to make beer," Ellman argued. "When you are selling a beverage for its taste only, and not for a kick, you must strive for perfection. It's hard to make a drink out of nothing, but the brewers did it!" Looking back at the fact that most of the near beer that left the Chicago breweries was eventually needled with alcohol, Ellman's argument fell short of local reality.

Federal Chemist John W. Fonner, in making his analysis of possible violators of the 3.2 percent limit, found that none of the beers he tested exceeded the legal limit for alcoholic content; on the contrary, most were well under it. Fonner speculated that some of the brewers might have been overly cautious in brewing the new beer, some of which tested at a low of 2.48 percent. Fred D. L. Squires, research secretary for the American Business Men's Prohibition Foundation, agreed with Fonner's analysis of the new beer. "We had forty investigators out [testing] with ebullimeters," said Squires. His findings concluded that the new beer was "a mere froth, running as low as 2.6 per cent alcohol by weight."

A more probable cause as to why the tested beer failed to meet the maximum legal alcoholic content was the fact that the beer now available had been brewed under the old Prohibition formula for near beer. This opinion made more sense. Why brew a full-bodied rich beer with choice ingredients only to have it de-alcoholized? This would explain how the brewers had hundreds of thousands of cases of beer ready for sale in such a short period of time. After all old-time local brewers had been stating for decades that their beer required two months for lagering purposes. Despite the loud protests of local brewers, Chicagoans were getting a weakened version of the kind of beer they had drunk before Prohibition. City brewers continued to insist that their beer was up to government standards, but weekend arrests for drunkenness indicated otherwise. Police records showed only sixty-three persons were charged with drunkenness on Saturday night in Chicago. This was about one-third of the normal arrest figures during a typical Prohibition-era weekend.[23]

ECONOMIC SUCCESS

August A. Busch's prediction of a greatly increased cash flow to the coffers of the federal government proved true. For the first day of nationwide beer sales, it was estimated that the federal tax for beer would bring in $7,500,000 to the United States Treasury. The federal government, anxious to grab its share of this new source of revenue, had placed a $1,000 a year federal license fee on each brewery and a $5 excise tax on every barrel of beer that left the breweries for delivery.

In just forty-eight hours, $25 million had been pumped into various beer-related trades as diverse as bottling manufacturers to the sawdust wholesalers whose product lay strewn on the floors of saloons. In Chicago early estimates placed the retail sale of beer at close to $4 million. Even the nonbeer related State Street department stores enjoyed a sales boon as store owners recorded the greatest spending spree since the stock market collapse and the beginning of the depression. Downtown hotels were forced to turn away potential guests as rooms were booked as quickly as they became available. Nonetheless, revelers from out of town and the far reaches of the city continued to migrate to the Loop for the beer drinkathon.

Chicago and Springfield, still arguing about who would handle licensing of the brewing industry in Illinois and Chicago, looked at these tax and revenue numbers and decided that they too wanted their fair share of this new cash cow. In the meantime, both brewers and retailers enjoyed the local tax and license lull, harvesting a profit far in excess of what would eventually be realized when the city and the state governments started to take their share.[24]

The Morning After, 1933

Only a dictator for the breweries
can meet the problem.
—*Eliot Ness describing the problem of former
bootleggers entering the Chicago beer trade*

THE MOB AND THE LEGAL BREWERIES

The anticipation of legal 3.2 percent beer was having an effect on Chicago bootleggers and their operations. Speakeasy owners were cutting back orders of needle beer and wildcat brew, hoping to be left with little or no syndicate beer by April 7. Chicago bootleggers, reacting to this new threat of competition, tried to compensate for the fall off of orders by bringing down the price of their beer to a record low of $25 a barrel. To further entice saloon keepers to continue to order their beer, syndicate prices started to tumble on bonded Canadian whiskey from $95 to $65 a case. The price of alcohol used for gin blending fell from $27.50 to $17 for a five-gallon tin. Even with bootleggers giving these deep discounts to local speakeasies in order to keep sales steady, owners and managers of Chicago's thousands of watering holes continued to squeeze out whatever profit they could from the illegal brew, refusing to pass the price cuts on to their customers. A glass of bootleg beer was still going for 15 cents a glass, 25 cents for a stein, normal prices when beer was selling for $55 a barrel.[1]

The money-losing situation of syndicate beer makers started to take a more desperate turn, bringing back the mob intimidation tactics of earlier years. Days before legal beer became available in the city, the business manager for the Brewery Drivers' Union and the secretary of the Brewers' and Malsters' Union complained to State Attorney Courtney that hoodlums were not only trying to take over their organizations but also were even trying to organize their own unions. In spite of a report that Al Capone, now at the federal penitentiary at Atlanta, had ordered his mob to "lay off the beer and stick to the red and white" (whisky and gin), local mobsters were making their moves into the legitimate beer trade. The *Chicago Tribune* reported that bootlegger "Red" Bolten was making plans to continue brewing wildcat beer and force it upon West Side retailers. Quite the beer connoisseur, Bolten claimed that the legitimate brewers could not exceed his brew in taste and quality. The paper went on to note that Capone's old gang still had control of an unnamed Chicago brewery (the Manhattan Brewing Company, first acquired by Johnny Torrio back in 1919). The *Chicago Herald and Examiner* claimed that Joe Fusco, described as the "present chief of the Capone outfit," had brought in an old-time brewer as a figurehead operator for some of the breweries they still controlled. Fusco had worked for Capone since 1923 as a bootleg beer truck driver, later graduating to a trusted mob lieutenant position handling beer accounts. With all the reports, rumors, and innuendoes surrounding old bootleggers and the reestablishment of the legitimate brewing industry, one thing was certain—the Chicago bootleggers syndicate would not leave the profitable brewing industry without a fight.

As days passed Courtney received additional information that hoodlum beer drummers were posing as brewery agents throughout the city and forcing sales of beer on terrified retailers. For bootleggers convicted of Prohibition violations and unable to secure a federal brewing permit, the distribution of legal beer seemed to hold lucrative possibilities. Approaching representatives of legal breweries, hoodlum beer drummers tried to convince the owners that they could secure retail accounts for their legal brew. These accounts would chiefly consist of their old bootleg beer accounts. A Milwaukee brewery was reported to have been courted by Chicago hoods with a list of saloons that would buy the brewery's beer if a deal for exclusive distribution rights could be made between the Milwaukee concern and the mobsters. A manager for the Chicago branch of Anheuser-Busch recounted that he also had been approached with a distribution offer by syndicate beer reps.

Federal Agent Eliot Ness, still working in the Chicago Prohibition Unit, held the opinion that if a brewery made an agreement with agents of a bootleg syndicate, the hoodlums might come back to the brewer at a later date and threaten to turn over their retailers to a rival brewery. In this manner the syndicate could demand an even larger cut of the brewer's profits. If any participating brewer did complain to authorities, the mobsters would probably hide behind their political connections. With competition expected to be strong after April 7, the temptation for the legitimate brewers to join forces with the old bootlegger gangs would be there. After all Chicago brewers and bootleggers had profitably tippled from the same barrel of greed and corruption for the last thirteen years.[2]

PROTECTING THE LEGAL BREWERIES

Courtney acted at once to keep the legal brewing industry free of hoodlum influence. Days before New Beer's Eve, the state's attorney called together a conference of all the licensed Chicago brewers to his office to discuss a plan of action. "We will drive the gangsters out if they attempt to enter this new legitimate industry," he assured the brewers but included a warning to them that he would pull their licenses if he thought there was any indication that the mobsters had somehow muscled into their businesses. But the hoodlum beer syndicates were not taking "no" for an answer. In the next few days, retailers reported bomb threats and other strongarm tactics by hoods as the pressures from ex-bootleggers continued.

E. C. Yellowley, who was now in charge of federal brewery permits in the city, said that his office was scrutinizing every application for a brewing permit to weed out anyone with a bootlegging or criminal background. In addition to the permit request, Yellowley warned that applicants would have to submit to character and financial scrutiny from his investigators, a subjective procedure. "We'll investigate them from top to bottom," he declared. Several applications had already been rejected by his office because of obvious hoodlum control. But Agent Ness and others pointed out that hoodlums might bypass the application process for a federal brewing permit and install men of good reputation to act as fronts for their mob controlled breweries, a tactic that was used extensively during Prohibition. Yellowley agreed with Ness's statement, admitting that there was no effective way to ensure that licensed breweries were not indirectly under the control of mob elements. He noted that federal regulations did not require his department to look into stock ownership of a brewery, a legal way to gain brewery control. This legal technicality would soon be exploited by the mob.

Three days later, the *Chicago Tribune* reported that Yellowley had issued a permanent brewing permit for the Gambrinus Brewery to a nephew of Judge Joseph Sabath and Congressman A. J. Sabath. The congressman had been a leading proponent of Roosevelt's plan to grant amnesty to Prohibition violators charged with making beer at or below the 3.2 percent alcohol level, a plan that was later dismissed as being impractical. Prohibition Administrator Malachy Harney, who investigated the application for the permit, admitted that Terry Druggan of the old Druggan and Lake bootlegging syndicate still had a possible claim on the brewery building. His current incarceration in Leavenworth for tax evasion, however, left his existing ownership of the title clouded. Nonetheless the permit was issued by Yellowley's office. Rumors also circulated that bootlegger Joe Saltis had tried to buy a Chicago brewery with $100,000 cash and $200,000 in notes, purportedly financed with the cooperation of saloon keepers from his old beer territory. "Only a dictator for the breweries can meet the problem," declared Ness as similar reports filtered in to his office.[3]

As the legal day for beer drew closer, State's Attorney Courtney and Agent Yellowley disclosed that Leonard Boltz, a reputed bootlegger, had secured corporate charters from the Illinois secretary of state for twelve brewing companies that had allowed their articles of corporation to dissolve. With his new company charters, Boltz was incorporating new firms under the names of Schoenhofen Brewing Company, Seipps Brewing Company, Miller Brewing Company, and nine other names, similar in name to defunct or existing breweries whose corporate charters had run out during Prohibition. Using this legal subterfuge, authorities were worried that Boltz and his gang might confuse retailers into believing that they were dealing with legitimate breweries.[4]

Less than twenty-four hours after the sale of legal beer resumed in Chicago, a bomb placed near their bottling department rocked the Prima Company at 325 Blackhawk Street. Although no one was injured by the blast, the explosion blew an iron door off its hinges and toward an empty stainless steel tank used to temporarily store alcohol during the de-alcoholization of beer. Damage to the plant was estimated at $1,500. Brewery officials claimed that the bombing was probably the work of a disgruntled customer who had requested a small order of beer for immediate delivery at 12:01 A.M. but had been forced to wait while the larger orders were filled first, a highly unlikely scenario.

"We have had no threats nor any trouble with hoodlums or others," a Prima spokesman said. In spite of the claims of the brewery owners, police brought in Jerry Donovan, an official of the newly organized beer drivers union, for questioning about the bombing.

A day later Chicago police fought off an attempted hijacking of a truck containing 250 cases of legal beer. After a car chase and moving gun battle, the hijackers escaped, but the beer was recovered. It was starting to seem just like the old Capone days in Chicago again.[5]

JOE FUSCO

For Joe Fusco, the resumption of 3.2 percent beer meant even more business opportunities than during Prohibition. Fusco, who had taken over the day-to-day beer operations for Capone, was now working for Frank Nitti in the same capacity. In 1931, the Chicago Crime Commission had listed Fusco as Public Enemy Number 1, further disclosing that he was considered "the beer boss of the Capone Syndicate." Even before acquiring this dubious distinction, Fusco was already well known by the Chicago Police Department.

On the night of July 13, 1931, a well-intentioned Chicago police sergeant, John T. Coughlin, had seized a truckload of Capone beer. Coughlin parked the truck in the back alley behind the building and assembled a police guard to watch over it. Fusco was incensed with the seizure, especially since he knew that the Capone gang was current on its regular weekly payoffs to the downtown police. With a federal court order for his arrest on a prior beer sales indictment still unserved, Fusco nonetheless stormed into police headquarters and demanded the return of the truck. Federal agents, newspaper beat reporters, and photographers gathered nearby as the situation started to become an embarrassment to the police.

"How would it look if we let you walk out of here and drive away with that truckload of beer?" a perplexed officer asked the mobster.

"You should have thought of that before you drove it into the alley," Fusco growled back. Dennis Cooney, Capone's vice chief for the First Ward, was summoned to the station to mediate the situation. With a clear sense of reality to all involved, Cooney threatened to make every cop in the district live on their small salaries for the next month if they didn't release the truck, something most of them hadn't done for years. In a face-saving compromise, Fusco was refused the return of the truck and asked to leave. Later during the night, the truck was accommodatingly *stolen* and driven back to his warehouse. While all this negotiating was going on, nobody bothered to bring up Joe Fusco's federal beer indictment.[6]

With the resumption of legal brewing operations in Chicago, Fusco now controlled the territory from 35th Street on the South Side, to 61st Street. As Frank Nitti's beer baron, he also held control over other Capone-sanctioned operatives. In and around the Loop, Harry Cusack and "Hymie" Levine controlled the retail outlets. From 12th Street to 29th ruled Sammy Cusack, brother of Harry. Jack Heinan ruled the territory from 29th to 35th Streets, and Danny Stanton held watch from 61st Street to the south city limits.

When necessary, threats and intimidation were used against those saloon keepers who tried to remain independent of the mob beer drummers. A show of force was seldom required, however. The syndicate was offering one week's worth of credit if a saloon keeper took on their beer. The legitimate breweries were demanding immediate payment upon delivery. For many saloon keepers, their choice of distributor was an easy one.[7]

LEGAL BEER SHORTAGE

Only a few short days after New Beer's Eve in Chicago, most of the legal beer was gone. Officials at Atlas Brewing Company reported that they still had fifty thousand barrels of young green beer on hand in the aging tanks and were seventy-two hours behind on orders. They vowed, however, that "not a bottle of green beer will leave this plant." At the Prima Company, employees couldn't keep up with orders in the bottling department. "The place is like a madhouse," said an employee, "but [we] are doing our level best." Irving Solomon, plant manager at the Schoenhofen Brewing Company, claimed to have back orders of two hundred thousand cases and two hundred railroad cars of beer. Out-of-town breweries such as Anheuser-Busch, Inc., also acknowledged a beer shortage at their depot in Chicago.

By the end of April, Blatz Brewing Company of Milwaukee felt obliged to take out a quarter-page ad in the *Chicago Tribune* saluting President Roosevelt and pledging to him and all their customers that "no beer is to be released until it is *Fully-Aged*," trying to quell mounting complaints that beer was being sold before completing the lagering period.

As beer shortages continued to be reported throughout the city, hopped and unhopped malt extract ads started to run again in the papers, suddenly resurrecting the dying home brew trade. Ever since the announcement that beer would be legally available in Chicago on April 7, the malt shops had been frantically selling off their highly discounted inventories as interest in home brewing waned. With the slowdown in beer production and the unavailability of fully aged beer, malt shops were busy again.[8]

LICENSING OF THE BREWING INDUSTRY

By early April, neither the City of Chicago nor Springfield had reached agreement on beer licensing requirements. Newly elected Mayor Kelly held the opinion that if the state was to license retail outlets wanting to sell beer, the fee should be low enough for independent retailers such as neighborhood grocery stores and drug stores to afford. Beer, he reasoned, was simply a sideline for these businesses and would only be purchased for home consumption. To place an oppressive beer license fee on them might force them to drop beer as part of their normal store inventory and place the exclusive sale of beer back into the waiting arms of saloon keepers, something that most city officials said they were trying to avoid.

Along with Kelly's observations was a strong recommendation to the City Council to force breweries in and out of Chicago to print the alcoholic strength and bottling date on the label of their products, Kelly's idea of Budweiser's contemporary "born on" date. In addition, the mayor wanted bottle manufacturers to produce bottles with raised lettering on them and for breweries to burn their brand name onto the wooden barrels before they left the plant. By adding these steps to the manufacturing process, Kelly hoped to end any chance of Chicagoans purchasing green beer and, more important, eliminate the real possibility that bootleggers might attempt to bottle their own wildcat beer for distribution.[9]

Days before the Chicago City Council acted on Mayor Kelly's recommendations, the Springfield legislature reached agreement on state licensing requirements for the sale of beer. The bill imposed a state tax of 2 cents per gallon on beer, a $50 state license fee on all beer retailers, and limited the amount of local license fees to $200, except in Chicago which could determine its own fee, a concession to home rule advocates. In addition, beer could not be sold "on-premise" unless food was sold or offered for sale.

On April 26, the City Council passed two amendments to the city beer licensing ordinance. The first ruling decreed that all retail beer outlets, rather than just saloons, would be liable for taxation. This $150 license fee, which had already been imposed on on-premise sites, would now be required of all carry-out locations. The fee would be prorated to July 1, when the new licensing period would begin.

Edward J. Kaindl, Chicago City collector, seemed happy with the new arrangement. He had recently reported to the subcommittee on licensing fees that Chicago had already received $570,000 in retailers' fees since beer had become legal. If the $150 fee was retained for the rest of 1933, he projected that an additional $900,000 would flow to city coffers.

The second council amendment compelled brewers to have their company names blown in bottles and labels printed with the alcoholic content and dates of manufacture and bottling. It passed unanimously, forty-seven to zero. Brewers were given just ten days to comply.[10]

THE BREWERS REACT

The bottling and labeling requirements immediately came under fire from local and out-of-town brewers. "The amendment is unnecessary and ridiculous," said H. F. Ernst, owner of the Prima Brewery. Ernst claimed that the amendment would mean the disposal of bottles already in inventory and would place a further burden on overworked bottle manufacturers who were also trying to keep up with demand. Countering this argument, Kelly replied that the brewers could just as easily etch existing bottles with the company and brand name using an acid-etching procedure.

Ernst went on to challenge the need of the amendment. "The consumer is assured right now that any bottle carrying the label of a given brewer contains the beer of that brewer. Federal inspectors see to that." As for the possibility of a brewer bottling green beer, Ernst felt the offenders, if there were any, should definitely be punished, but not the entire brewing industry. Depot managers for some of the out-of-state breweries threatened to pull out of the Chicago market if the ordinance was upheld in court, a bit of puffery in such a lucrative retail market.[11]

The euphoric fizz of early April was starting to go flat for Chicago brewers. On top of threats from bootleggers trying to muscle in on their businesses, the brewers saw federal, state, and local taxation as destroying any chance for a reasonable profit. A $1,000 federal licensing fee, a $5 per barrel federal revenue stamp, a $50 state license, and a 2-cent per gallon tax, coupled with a 3 percent retail state tax, and Chicago's well-intentioned but restrictive bottling requirements, swept away almost all hope that Chicagoans might ever again enjoy a nostalgic, pre-Prohibition priced, nickel glass of beer. Things couldn't have appeared worse for the newly resurrected brewing industry when Democratic Representative Benjamin E. Adamowski of Chicago jumped up on the House floor in Springfield and questioned why the brewers were "charging $17 a barrel for beer they can afford to sell for $8."[12]

GOOD-BYE NICKEL BEER

For a group of politicians that stood to reap so much from the anticipated benefits of the brewing industry, in terms of increased local employment and additional revenue for federal, state, and city treasuries, some local legislators appeared ready to kill this new golden calf—and a golden calf it was. From April 7 until June 1, the Chicago district reaped approximate earnings of $1,667,229 from federal beer stamp taxes, reported Gregory T. Van Meter, collector of Internal Revenue. Chicago had received a total of $570,00 from retail beer license fees, brewers' licenses, and wholesalers' licenses. Projections placed the federal share of yearly earnings from Chicago's brewing industry at around $10 million.[13]

Instigated by Representative Adamowski's demands to have the brewers explain their pricing structure, a House legislative committee began hearings at Chicago's City Hall. On the first day of testimony, not one of the seventeen subpoenaed local brewers appeared with their company records, as ordered by the committee. Things seemed to be going from bad to worse for the brewers when the legislators began to chastise John P. Hart of Aurora, counsel for the Illinois Brewers

Association, who had also been requested to appear. Hart had angered the committee members by publicly claiming that legislators were trying to make political hay by holding the inquiry, a charge that probably had merit. "Most of them," Hart had earlier commented to the press, "are from the poorer districts, where five cent beer might be made a hot political issue."

Because of the swiftness of relegalization and the heavy demand for product, the brewers were brewing and bottling beer as quickly as possible. The variables of new taxes, expansion of the plants, and costs of production were making it difficult for them to come up with reliable cost figures for their beers. Any preliminary numbers would have to be based on what it had cost to make near beer, giving an inaccurate production cost analysis of real beer. Hart refused to be intimidated by the rebuke from the committee for his comments and affirmed his earlier statement.

As Representative Albert Mancin began shouting at Hart for his failure to answer Mancin's questions to his satisfaction, Senator Frank "Bull" McDermott, owner of a small Bridgeport brewery, strode into the proceedings and was requested to take the stand. A portion of the questioning went as follows;

> MANCIN: How long have you been in business, Senator? You own a brewery, don't you?
>
> McDERMOTT: I've owned one for 16 years.
>
> MANCIN: (smiling) I suppose you've lost a lot of money?
>
> McDERMOTT: Half the legislature knows I've lost money. The mayor [former Mayor Dever who had shut down the local breweries in 1923] of this city certainly knew it. The brewing business is an up and down business. I've taken it on the chin for years."
>
> MANCIN: What do you charge for a barrel of beer?
>
> McDERMOTT: Thirteen dollars.
>
> MANCIN: Well, you're making money now, aren't you?
>
> McDERMOTT: Sure I am. But so were your friends making money when they were charging $55 a barrel [the old speakeasy price].
>
> MANCIN: So were your friends making money at that price.
>
> McDERMOTT: I don't doubt it.[14]

Mancin next turned his attention on John G. Weisbach, attorney for the local brewers. "Do you realize the breweries are in contempt?" Weisbach agreed with Mancin that they were but pointed out the difficulty in making an accurate assessment of current costs. "By ___, we'll get it or you'll stop manufacturing beer!" Mancin threatened.

With the conclusion of the threats and verbal jousting, Representative Gary Noonan diplomatically announced that representatives of Prima, the United States, Atlas, Monarch, and Schoenhofen breweries had agreed to allow independent auditors to inspect their company books and would pay any fees incurred. The feisty McDermott agreed to follow the lead of the other breweries and also open up his books for inspection. Everyone seemed to be appeased with the compromise.[15]

Not to be outdone by state representatives, a Chicago City Council subcommittee, drafting a new city regulatory ordinance for beer sales, also questioned Senator McDermott in a meeting in late June. McDermott had appeared to protest the committee's proposed $1,000 retail licensing fee plus an additional fee of $25 for every brewery, distributor, and jobber delivery truck. The new city licensing period was to begin on July 1. McDermott initially tried to appeal to the committee's sense of fair play. With a straight face, the senator claimed that Chicago brewers had made no money in the last fourteen years, a claim that any local politician knew was not entirely true. Alderman Mathias "Paddy" Bauler, whom no one in Chicago could ever accuse of being a saint, jumped on McDermott's weak argument of poverty. McDermott, however, was ready for Bauler and assumed the same adversarial approach he had taken at the House inquiry.

> **BAULER:** You're charging $17 a barrel for beer, aren't you?
> **McDERMOTT:** Say, you got $55 a barrel, so you needn't holler.
> **BAULER:** Don't say that unless you can prove it.
> **McDERMOTT:** You even got $60 a barrel.

McDermott defiantly walked out of the room after rattling Bauler. George H. Kiefer of the United States Brewing Company then jumped into the fray and protested the proposed $1,000 licensing fee for retailers. T. J. Doyle, a representative of the Atlas Brewing Company, explained to the committee that under the new proposal, anyone who was a distributor and jobber would have to pay a double fee.[16]

Some members of the City Council soon realized the dilemma a $1,000 beer licensing fee would create for the small, independent retailer. Mayor Kelly acknowledged the real possibility that the unaffordability of a high-licensing fee might mean a return to the old tied-house saloon and its prior monopoly on retail beer sales, and hinted of a compromise. On July 11, the City Council voted to increase the beer license to $300, rather than $1,000, for all retail on and off-site premises, but knocked down a provision to merge beer retail licenses with other licenses such as for food dispensing and amusement. Separate licenses would now be required for restaurants serving beer, cabarets with food, beer and entertainment sites, and even saloons, which were now required by state regulations to sell food with drink.

When he heard of the City Council's actions, George Patris, the president of the Restaurateurs of Illinois, took note of the new licensing fees and somberly declared the nickel glass of beer dead in Chicago.[17]

ILLINOIS READIES
ITS VOTE FOR REPEAL

As required by Congress, Illinois was busying itself in late April 1933 in preparation for a state election and convention to act on the Twenty-first Amendment, hopefully to repeal the disastrous Eighteenth Amendment. After Congress had refused the state's request for a special cash grant to fund state elections for repeal, Illinois decided to incorporate a June judicial election with the repeal election, combining the expenses of two separate elections. Downstate democrats, however, worried that incorporating the judicial election and the vote for repeal might bring about a backlash from local dry advocates and hurt the chances of some of their Democratic judges running for reelection. As a result of this political concern, the Illinois State Senate, led by these wary Democratic forces, unbelievably voted to postpone the election for repeal until April 1934.

Republicans had a field day with the Senate vote, expressing disbelief that the same party that had been swept into the Oval Office on a platform of repeal, the party of "democratic beer," was now voting to delay the state ratification of repeal. "Evidently," sneered Martin R. Carlson of Moline, "you Democrats don't care to repeal the 18th Amendment."[18]

Colonel Ira L. Reeves of Chicago, commander of the anti-Prohibition organization called the Crusaders, and a pro-repeal lobbyist, thought he saw a darker explanation for the actions of the Democrats. "Naturally they [the brewers] want to prolong their present monopoly as long as possible, and apparently they are lining up the downstate dry legislators to accomplish that purpose." Reeves went on to suggest that brewers had made a pact with prohibitionists. Reeves singled out the boisterous State Senator Frank McDermott with his brewery in Bridgeport. How could McDermott go back to his Stockyards constituency and tell them he voted to defer repeal until next year, Reeves wanted to know?

The logic of Reeves's argument seemed solid. Other repeal advocates affirmed his contention. Since years before Prohibition, brewers and distillers had maintained an adversarial relationship. Their divisiveness was one blatant reason that later prohibitionist efforts had so been so successful. Commenting on the charge that brewers wanted to continue a monopoly on the drink trade, Captain W. W. Bayley, Chicago chief of the Association Against the 18th Amendment said, "It would not be surprising to have proof show up that such is the situation now." It was too much for editors of the trade magazine, *The Brewer and Malster and Beverageur*, who demanded an apology from Reeves. "It is unthinkable that they [the brewers] would ally themselves with the bootleggers and gangsters and the fanatics of the Anti-Saloon League."[19]

Days later, with pressure from all sides and a chance to rethink their positions, the Democrats capitulated. The Illinois Senate voted to restore June 5, 1933, as the day for the election of delegates to the State Repeal Convention. Additional pressures from Governor Henry Horner and various lobbyists groups, including the Women's Organization for National Prohibition Reform, had persuaded the Senate to wisely reverse their ill-advised prior decision. Without protest, the Illinois House of Representatives concurred with the Senate's actions.[20]

ILLINOIS'S REPEAL ELECTION

On April 28, 1933, at 1:43 A.M., Governor Horner signed the House bill ordering the Illinois Prohibition Repeal Convention to assemble on July 10. The haste in passing the bill was to allow the longest amount of time possible to secure the thirty-five thousand signatures needed to place the names of delegates on nominating petitions. In a show of unity, Democratic and Republican Party leaders agreed to split equally the slate of fifty delegates, but only after a unification proposal pushed by Democratic leaders.

With the required nominating petitions finally signed, Chicago precinct workers started to flood their wards with sample ballots. Mayor Kelly asked the people of Chicago to support the vote for repeal. "I urge that all citizens of our great city support the President and his administration in his efforts to bring back prosperity and eliminate the evils which Prohibition has cast into our midst. This can best be done by voting for the Repeal candidates." Perhaps as a further inducement to the electorate to get out and vote, Kelly overruled an earlier opinion by Leon Hornstein, first assistant to Chicago Corporation Counsel William H. Sexton, that the sale of beer on election day would be illegal. Hornstein claimed that the state legislature had forgotten to repeal the pre-Prohibition election law requiring saloons to be closed during elections. Kelly disagreed, Sexton demurred and the saloons of Chicago were allowed to stay open on Election Day.[21]

ELECTION DAY

On the morning of June 5, expectations were high for the repeal of the Eighteenth Amendment. With chances for thunderstorms forecast throughout Monday, a voter turnout for a Chicago judicial election would normally have been predicted to be low. Historically, this pattern of a small voter turnout was in Chicago, and still is, typical for such an election. But this was no simple judicial election. With reports coming in from ward headquarters throughout the city, the Cook County Democratic Organization was predicting an unprecedented turnout of seven hundred ten thousand votes. Nonetheless, ward heelers continued to canvass heavily the city during the day. As a further enticement to get constituents out to vote, local Democratic leaders pragmatically stressed the household economics of repeal. As part of their door-to-door strategy, it was pointed out by Democratic party officials and ward heelers alike that unless the Eighteenth Amendment was repealed, $6 to $10 out of every $100 earned in a weekly paycheck would revert back to the federal government in new taxes.

Repeal meant beer, booze, and no new taxes—one hell of a "read my lips" argument that any tax-paying voter could understand.

Democratic Party leader Patrick A. Nash wasted no words in his final communiqué to Chicago voters before the polls opened. "Support President Roosevelt. Repeal the 18th Amendment. Elect judicial leaders. Vote the Repeal ticket straight. Vote the Democratic judicial ticket straight."

Republican County Chairman William H. Weber was not quite as direct or forceful in his party's approval of repeal. "Vote the Republican judicial ticket straight and destroy the receivership ring," taking a final shot at the Democrats. Although the parties shared an equal amount of delegates for the repeal of the Eighteenth Amendment, Weber's statement conservatively avoided the paramount issue of repeal. The national Republican Party's endorsement and enforcement of Prohibition and the local organization's lukewarm embrace of repeal were noted by beer-drinking Chicagoans. From post-Prohibition on, the Democratic Party, the party of democratic beer and repeal, has held sway in Chicago.[22]

ELECTION RESULTS

The tally of votes was no surprise. Not only was the vote for Repeal in Chicago overwhelming, but also it was a vote of approximately 11 to 1 in favor of it. In Committeeman Moe Rosenberg's 24th Ward on the West Side of the city, reports showed that Repealists had voted yes at an astounding ratio of 76 to 1. Not surprisingly, a Republican precinct captain complained that in one precinct of Rosenberg's ward, 200 votes had been stuffed into a ballot box when that many voters had not even registered in the precinct. Rosenberg, recently indicted by a federal grand jury for income tax invasion, scoffed at the report. In Bridgeport, voters followed the dictates of native son County Treasurer Joe McDonough and voted 40 to 1 for repeal.[23]

The next day, the editorial page of the *Chicago Tribune* declared national prohibition officially dead in Illinois and expressed hope that the remaining dry states would soon follow Illinois's lead. "A law which made the drinking of a glass of beer a crime was unenforceable" said the paper. As evidence of the state citizenry's overwhelming rebuff of Prohibition, a total of 883,000 voters turned out to for approval of the Twenty-first Amendment to the Constitution, more than 560,000 votes for repeal coming from Chicago. All that was left was the state convention.[24]

THE REPEAL CONVENTION

On July 10, Governor Horner opened the convention and officially signaled the beginning of the end of national prohibition in Illinois. "The eighteenth amendment is doomed. Let us pray that with it will go the political cowardice that made it possible." At noon, Democratic state leader Patrick A. Nash presented the resolution to ratify repeal of the Eighteenth Amendment at the state repeal convention. In just fifty-four minutes, the fifty bipartisan delegates went through the necessary procedural motions and unanimously voted to ratify the Twenty-first Amendment, nullifying the Eighteenth. The Prairie Schooner, Illinois, now became the tenth state to moor at the wet dock of repeal.[25]

PART IV

Post-Prohibition

⅓ 15 ⅓

The Prewar Years, 1933–1940

How would your old lady look in black?
—*Frank Nitti, beer distributor*

EARLY PROBLEMS

By late September 1933, twenty-three breweries were up and running in Chicago. Logistically, it appeared to have been an easy rebirth for the local industry, especially for those breweries that had operated under federal permit, producing near beer during national prohibition. For the breweries that had been idle during all, or part, of Prohibition, the capital outlay for rehabbing the equipment and the plants was formidable. Despite considerable rehab and expansion expenses for the plants, the constraints of being closely regulated, thoroughly taxed, and under constant scrutiny from politicians and prohibitionists, the strong initial demand for beer created a time of unrestrained prosperity for many of the local breweries. But for the smaller, undercapitalized breweries, the next few years would become a challenge as the euphoria of high demand for their products leveled off.[1]

Problems started to arise as soon as the cooler months of 1933 rolled in, coinciding with local overproduction. In a rush to keep sales high in the face of the coming relegalization of the liquor industry and the planned openings of more breweries in the area, some brewers began releasing green beer into the local market to keep pace with strong demand. But as demand inevitably tapered and sales started to level off, breweries that had inadvertently overproduced now found themselves with the opposite problem of too much aged beer on hand, some actually going sour in the storage tanks.

Undercapacity changed to overcapacity. Prices started to tumble further since inventories were high. With distributors demanding barrels of beer for as low as $10 and the brewers desperate to unload their excess product, earnings were low and profits absent. Even the return of warm weather the next spring failed to bring hope to some undercapitalized brewers. For the financially sound and well-managed breweries, the average net profit per barrel was now estimated at around $1. The industry average was much less, some breweries showing as little as 25 cents net profit per barrel.[2]

THE SHIPPING BREWERS

Chicago brewers, most without the deep pockets of the national shipping brewers, could only watch as St. Louis and Milwaukee out-advertised them in the local press. The bigger, more financially sound Chicago breweries, such as Schoenhofen-Edelweiss and the United States Brewing Company, believing the need to develop local brand loyalty and, most important, stronger demand, began using the services of local ad agencies to help them accomplish this goal. Though a new and seemingly effective method in selling product, the use of ad agencies nonetheless added an additional drain on the operating expenses of the larger, more secure local breweries.[3]

Salesmen from out-of-town breweries also reinstituted the old turn-of-the-century practice of giving inducements to taverns in the forms of free signage and bar fixtures. Some offered up to two free barrels of beer if bar owners would take on their product. Reports of salesmen once again reverting to the use of "spendings" to secure new accounts were becoming increasingly common. The trade publications sought to address these problems, pointing out that these practices not only ran contrary to Illinois Department of Finance Regulations, but also the recently instituted Code of Fair Competition for the Alcoholic Beverage Industry. This brewing code was intended to foster the noble but naive concept of industry self-regulation, dealing with the issues of pricing, labeling, and wholesale practices and, in a strong sense, leveling the playing field for the small and midsized breweries.[4]

BRAND LOYALTY

Justifying these predatory marketing practices, one brewery executive from a large shipping brewery saw the local brewers, and not the shippers, as having the sales advantage. "If he [the small brewer] can build up a local pride in his product and a local appreciation of the economic value of the business to his locality, we can never sell our products in a more substantial way than he can." But the problems of developing and nurturing brand loyalty were formidable. For almost fourteen years, Chicagoans had been drinking needle and wildcat brew. There had been no favorite brands or full-page ads extolling the virtues of locally brewed "Torrio's Nut Brown Ale" or "Capone's Best Lager Beer." To the Prohibition-era Chicagoan, beer was simply beer.

Blatz of Milwaukee saw this lack of brand loyalty by the beer-drinking consumer and started a newspaper campaign in the late summer of 1933 with half-page ads in Chicago papers for their premium-priced Old Heidelberg beer. Featuring recommendations from the managers of the hometown Bismarck and Widermere hotels, the Blatz ads undermined the concept of whatever developing local brand loyalty might be occurring in the Chicago market by using testimonies from Chicago personalities extolling the virtues of their products. Blatz's Old Heidelberg Inn, the largest restaurant at the 1933 World Fair with a seating capacity of four thousand, became the headquarters of thirsty Chicagoans and visiting out-of-town guests as they enjoyed the sights and sounds of the fairgrounds.

W-G-N radio broadcast six days a week from the Inn, offering the swing sounds of Ernie Kratziner's Orchestra and W-G-N's Herr Louie, interspersed with plenty of commercials for Old Heidelberg. Local brewers were becoming increasingly worried with the tactics of out-of-town competition as sales declined. Circling the wagons, nineteen Chicago area brewers organized the Chicago District Brewers Association, formed to present a united front opposing the mercenary practices of the out-of-town breweries.[5]

Mob Influences Continue

The 1933 World Fair had been a boon for the Chicago economy and the local mob. Most of the saloons that enveloped the approaches to the fair from Roosevelt Road to 23rd Street were being supplied by syndicate-controlled breweries. Those saloon owners who refused mob overtures or defiantly switched beer brands often found their businesses on the receiving end of a pipe bomb. On the fair grounds, the syndicate also had a big piece of the hot dog and hamburger, popcorn and soda concessions. Mobster Charlie Fischetti probably wasn't exaggerating when he said "We got the whole place sewed up."

But the fair would one day come to an end. Plans had to be made for the future. Frank Nitti, now heading up Capone's gang, saw the takeover of the bartender and restaurant unions as the key to the future success of the mob-owned and controlled local breweries. At a Capone-syndicate meeting in the fall of 1933, Nitti laid down his plans for the continued success of the organization. "The bartenders' union is our biggest lever. After we get national control we will have every bartender in the country pushing our brands of beer and liquor."

Union Takeovers

Nitti's plan for domination began with the local bartenders' union. At the time, George B. McLane, a former speakeasy owner and union thug, was running Local 278, the Chicago Bartenders and Beverage Dispensers Union (AFL). In the spring of 1935, McLane received a telephone call from a Nitti emissary requesting his presence at the La Salle Hotel. When he arrived, Nitti bypassed any social niceties and demanded point blank that McLane install one of his men in as a union officer. When the union boss refused, Nitti threatened him. "You put our man in or you will get shot in the head," challenged Nitti.

Weeks later, McLane was again summoned by Nitti to the Capri Restaurant, located on North Clark, just across the street from City Hall and the County Building. At this second meeting were mob chieftains Joe Fusco, Charles Fischetti, Louis Campagna, Paul Ricca, and Nitti. Nitti once again demanded that McLane put a syndicate man on the union board as an officer. When McLane told Nitti that the union executive board would never accept such a move, Nitti said, "Give me the names of any board members who oppose. We'll take care of them." Almost as an afterthought, the mobster then asked McLane, "How would your old lady look in black?"

Still refusing to follow Nitti's order to relinquish control of the union, McLane was once again summoned before the mobster in July 1935. With a final warning of death to him and the members of his union board, the union executive board reluctantly agreed to install Louis Romano. During Prohibition, Romano had been a Capone bodyguard.

One of Romano's first acts was to see that all the syndicate-controlled taverns joined McLane's union.

LOU GREENBERG

The next meeting of McLane and Nitti was facilitated by Alex "Lou" Greenberg. Greenberg had acted as business manger of the Manhattan Brewery since the early years of national prohibition when Johnny Torrio had taken over the brewery. Torrio eventually brought in Hymie Weiss and Dion O'Banion as partners in the operation. Greenberg had taken over control of the brewery after the deaths of both gangsters. Although Greenberg had installed Arthur C. Lueder, Republican candidate for mayor in 1923 and former Chicago postmaster as the company president in early 1933, he still controlled the brewery.

Back in 1933, when Lueder had accepted the position of company president of the brewery, he was asked by reporters of any personal knowledge of the past owners of the Manhattan Brewery. Lueder deadpanned that he understood that gangsters had formerly owned the brewery but that "they were all dead." Lueder later ran successfully for the office of state auditor in 1940. His loyalty as president of the South Side brewery was rewarded with a $20,000 campaign contribution from Greenberg.[6]

At this latest meeting of McLane and Nitti, with Greenberg present, Nitti instructed McLane that all the city bartenders were to push Manhattan Brewery products, including Manhattan and Great Lakes draft beer and Badger and Cream Top bottled beer. On the spirits ticket was Gold Seal Liquor and Capitol Wine and Liquor Company products, owned by Joe Fusco, and Fort Dearborn whisky, the syndicate's own house brand. McLane questioned the effectiveness of this forceful tactic, especially since the national brands such as Budweiser, Miller High Life, and Schlitz were making such a strong drive for control of the Chicago market. "Tell those bartenders that if they don't push our stuff they will get their legs broken," threatened Nitti, deflecting McLane's objections.

Greenberg's Manhatten Brewery was suffering the same financial pressures of almost all of Chicago's post-Prohibition breweries. Making a profit selling legal beer was proving more difficult for Greenberg than the good old days of intimidating saloon keepers to buy product or leaving pipe bomb calling cards when they didn't. In desperation, the brewery started a price war in Chicago that brought operations back to profitability, backed by a return to the aggressive "marketing" by the Manhatten's sales representatives—but more was needed to keep sales up.

Throughout the meeting, Greenberg remained silent but his presence and influence were overwhelming. His years of experience in the brewing, restaurant, and finance businesses had helped guide the local crime syndicate to successfully invest their unreported profits from bootlegging, vice, gambling, and extortion into the legitimate tax reportable assets of hotels, restaurants, laundries, and unions.

The hapless McLane was eventually pushed out as president of the Bartenders Local 278 when Romano took over control of the union in 1935. To complete Nitti's plan of local union domination, Romano organized and led a food and beverage joint council consisting of fifteen union locals, most relating to bartenders, waiters, hotel clerks, cooks and other similar restaurant and service trades. McLane later testified that the joint council collected a tax of 10 cents per member a month from the thirty thousand members of the fifteen unions.

With the Chicagoland unions under his control, Nitti made ready for the takeover of the AFL bartenders' international, a move that later failed.[7]

Repeal

At 4:31 P.M., December 5, 1933, repeal took effect in Chicago with the ratification by Utah of the Twenty-first Amendment. The "Noble Experiment" had lasted 13 years, 10 months, 19 days, 17 hours, and 32 1/2 minutes. President Roosevelt officially proclaimed an end to national prohibition and urged all Americans to confine their purchases of alcoholic beverages to licensed dealers. The president also issued a special plea to state officials not to allow the return of the saloon. A check of the City Collector's Office, however, indicated that close to 7,000 liquor dealers were now ready to serve the 3,500,000 residents of Chicago, averaging one saloon for every 500 Chicagoans. It was about the same number of saloons that had operated in Chicago before the onset of national prohibition.

With the last layer of national prohibition peeled away, the festivities in Chicago to celebrate its end could only be described as "sedate." Although bars at hotels such as the Congress or the Sherman House could claim hundreds of cases of champagne, wine, and ardent spirits sold, only twenty-seven people were arrested in the city for drunkeness.[8]

Two distinctions, however, now separated the old pre-Prohibition saloons from the watering holes of post-repeal. Passed in late November 1933, the Chicago City Council banned the use of the word "saloon" in any establishment sign or ad. In an attempt to civilize the new "tavern" environment, standing at the bar was now prohibited, leading to the use of stools at the bar. The pre-Prohibition practice of brewers paying for liquor licenses and distributing free signage were also addressed in the new city liquor license application. Now a tavern owner could not accept signage worth more than $100 nor credit or money advances from breweries beyond that normally occurring in a retail operation.[9]

STRONG BEER RETURNS

There was some initial confusion as to whether liquor could actually be legally sold until the restriction of the 3.2 percent beer law was modified. Attorney General Otto Kerner clarified this concern by stating, "The 3.2 statute was purely a licensing device to provide revenue for the state, and has nothing to do with the sale of liquor or other beverages of more than 3.2 percent after Repeal. It was more or less an emergency measure to meet the needs which arose when beer was legalized." With that opinion by Kerner, the local breweries announced that ales, stouts, and porters as strong as 4 and 5 percent would be placed on sale, though 3.2 percent beer would still be available.

Beer doctor Max Henius questioned the knee-jerk reaction by some brewers to increase the alcoholic content of beers in direct competition of distilled spirits. In an address to the U.S. Brewers' Association in 1934, Henius asked, "Why, then, undermine the position [that beer is a drink of moderation] by exploiting the higher alcohol content of the heavier beers?" Beer expert Robert Wahl saw the production of higher strength beer as an unfortunate result of market demand, noting that as far as some opportunistic brewers were concerned "the public is going to get what it wants."[10]

The brewing industry was worried with the reintroduction of ardent spirits. As a result repeal was not looked upon by the malt trade as favorably as one might think. An entire generation of drinking Chicagoans had grown up with bathtub gin and "Halsted Street Scotch." In many instances, the more portable, stronger, and readily available booze had been mixed with soda pop or other sweet confections to smooth out the rough taste of the alcohol. Cocktails had changed the tastes of many. With the resumption of legal brewing in April 1933, brewers briefly held a legally monopolized drink market for almost eight months that would soon fade away. During that short time, beer formulas were being adjusted, many beers made lighter and sweeter in an attempt to win over those drinkers who favored the sweeter drinks of Prohibition, especially the new exploitable market of women. As a result of this change in taste, most beer now contained rice and corn to lighten the body of the beer, almost 3.5 pounds of sugar per barrel, and just a "kiss of the hops." Beer became a light, bubbly drink, quite different in taste from the richer pre-Prohibition brew.

December 5, 1933, dropped the exclusiveness that the brewers had temporarily held with the drinking public, once again pitting distillers against brewers. To some brewers, stronger beer with an alcoholic kick, and sweeter, lighter tasting beers were just additional weapons in the battle with distillers for new customers. While Chicagoans had to settle for limited quantities of whisky, domestic and imported wines, and liquors during the early days of repeal, local brewers flooded the market with stronger beers and sweeter reformulated brews.[11]

PACKAGED BEER

Tainted by the stigma of pre-Prohibition corruption and contemporary newspaper reports of mob involvement in Chicago taverns, underage drinking, and solicitation, bottled beer offered the more sedate beer drinker an alternative to draft beer and the associated evils of the tavern, thus weakening draft sales. An emphasis by the brewing industry to focus on the enjoyment of beer in the home and at social events also helped foster a widening shift in beer consumption from draft to packaged beer.

In 1935, the American Can Company introduced the so-called "Keglined" can. This nonreturnable container offered a number of advantages over breakable deposit bottles. The cost of a canning line, however, was more than many of the smaller breweries could afford. A conical-shaped can offered an alternative for those breweries with bottling lines; the coned cans could also be run through the same lines. In addition to the newly introduced flat and coned cans, stubby-shaped, nonreturnable bottles called "steinies" were introduced. For those brewers who had settled on the traditional production of draft beer after repeal, the continuing shift to drinking at home and the introduction of new containers now made the purchase of a bottling or canning line imperative.

The Birk Brothers Brewing Company and the Hoerber Brewing Company were some of the first local breweries to abandon all draft production and switch to bottles and draft. The Best Brewing Company was chosen by the American Can Company for the installation of an experimental canning line. After feeling the effects of the aggressive advertising campaigns of Anheuser-Busch and other invading nationals, Best Brewery president, Jerome Hasterlik, dropped his dwindling tavern accounts. Pleased with the performance of the experimental canning line, he seized upon the idea of providing canned beer to the A&P, Kroger, and National food stores and the house brand, Hillman's Export Beer, to local Hillman's stores. The operation became so successful that the brewery would eventually provide private labels to the Katz drug store chain in Missouri and the California-based Safeway Foods. Alex Greenberg's Manhattan Brewery, with an infusion of mob money, was also one of the first Chicago breweries to put in a canning line. By 1938, the brewery laid claim to being second in canned beer production in the United States, surpassed only by the Pabst Brewing Company of Milwaukee.[12] It did much of the canning for breweries on the South Side.

POSTREPEAL FATALITIES

Without the benefit of the unreported, nontaxable income of Prohibition-era sales and once-guaranteed accounts from mob beer drummers, the Gambrinus Company, Incorporated, and the Frank McDermott Brewing Company passed into Chicago brewery history. Bankruptcy, later followed by a federal indictment of bootlegger Terry Druggan and four brewery officials, sealed the fate of the Gambrinus.

A grand jury alleged that Druggan's interest in the brewery had been concealed when an application for a federal license had been made. The Kiley Brewing Company of Marion, Indiana, took over the location of the defunct Gambrinus Brewery and incorporated the Patrick Henry Brewing Company. The new owners appeared to have had big plans for turning the location into a regional production and distribution point, even introducing a richer tasting all-malt beer to compete with European imports. By 1939, however, they ceased brewery operations in Chicago.[13]

The McDermott Brewery was reorganized in early 1937 and renamed the Beverly Brewing Company. The reorganization efforts, however, were to no avail, and the brewery closed in late 1937.[14]

The problems of the Prima Company were symptomatic of many of the weaker Chicago breweries after repeal. During the last five years of Prohibition, the brewery reported earning more than $200,000 a year. As with the other Chicago breweries that manufactured legal near beer and dealt with the shady underside of operations during the dry era, there was no real competition from other breweries. Even the most mismanaged brewery made money during this period. Whether poorly made or of the finest quality, virtually all of the near beer produced locally rolled into the guaranteed accounts of the city speakeasies as needle beer, the breweries operating under the control or influence of Chicago bootleggers.

During the first year of Repeal, the Prima earned $340,000, not unexpected with the initial strong demand by thirsty Chicagoans. After the heyday of 1933, however, the brewery started claiming a steady loss of income, culminating with a disastrous loss of $155,953.43 during the first nine months of 1936 and the entering of a petition by management to reorganize with the U.S. District Court. Forced to borrow $200,000 each from Harris Trust & Savings Bank and the First National Bank and Trust Company, the brewery later petitioned the federal court that the ousting of the Ernst family that had controlled the brewery after repeal, and the replacing of the brewing family by a bank-appointed manager—at the insistence of the Harris and the First National—had caused an additional loss to the brewery of close to $600,000.[15] After a court ruling in favor of the Ernst family, an appeal by the Harris and First National banks reversed the ruling in favor of the banks. The Supreme Court reaffirmed the ruling, noting that the brewery had been losing money long before the banks had become involved in the plant operations.

In February 1938, a federal judge ordered the acceptance of a meager bid of $145,000 by the management of the South Side Westminster Brewery for the assets of the Prima Company, including its trade names. A few months later, the Westminster Brewing Company filed an amendment to its charter and changed its name to the Prima Brewing Company. It appears unlikely, however, that the small brewery on South Union Avenue, located just a block away from the Manhattan Brewing Company, had the means to make a successful bid on the assets of the Prima Company. Later canning arrangements between the newly named Prima Company and the Manhattan seems to indicate more than a simple show of cooperation. More than likely, the assets of Prima were bought by the mob-controlled management of the Manhattan Brewing Company, indicating that the Westminster Brewing Company was probably also owned or controlled by the management of the Manhattan.[16]

A suit alleging mismanagement and neglect by the widow of Otto Kubin, former president of the Atlas Brewing Company who died in 1929, revealed the financial woes of another famous Chicago brewery. Spurred on by the filing of a bankruptcy petition by the brewery, Kubin's wife charged that the Chicago Title and Trust Company had failed to sell the Kubin estate's holdings of company stock at a time when it would have brought a profitable return to the heirs of the estate, in spite of the title company knowing that the existing brewery equipment was old and needed rehabilitation, and that any expansion of the plant would have been costly. The suit further noted that the price of Atlas stock was $28 per share during the giddy heydays of 1933. At the time of the widow's suit in early 1938, Atlas stock was selling for only 50 to 70 cents a share, a loss to the estate in excess of $1 million.[17]

In late 1940, the trade journal, *Modern Brewery*, reported that "interests associated with the Manhattan Brewing Company" had gained control of a sizable portion of the outstanding stock of the financially crippled Atlas Brewery. It would be safe to conclude that the new masters of Frank Nitti's organization now controlled at least four Chicago breweries.[18]

The War Years and Beyond, 1941–1968

*Lack of fair play, commercial bribery
. . . and the dumping of beer on
local markets at less than cost.*
*—John E. O' Neill of the Small Brewers
Committee describing problems faced by
the small brewer in the post-war era*

LOCAL ADVERTISING

In the months before the U.S. entrance into World War II with the Japanese attack on Pearl Harbor, the use of local print and radio media by Chicago's breweries became unprecedented. Extensive use of tavern window displays, newspaper ads, billboards, and local radio broadcasts brought home the idea that Chicagoans should be enjoying locally brewed beer. Atlas Brewing Company was one of the first breweries to tie in the consumption of their products with the survivalist theme of local brand loyalty starting with a "Be a Chicago Booster, Consume Chicago Beers" campaign. Its hometown appeal to Chicagoland beer drinkers was soon joined by a similar advertising strategy from the Monarch Brewing Company. Ads for Monarch Beer in local papers regularly ended with an imploring reminder for customers to "Be loyal to your own community" in an effort to deflect the growing popularity in Chicago of Milwaukee and St. Louis brands. Birk Brewing Company beer coasters carried the logo of their Trophy Beer on one side of the cardboard coasters and the message "Drink Illinois Made Beer, Create Employment Here" on the other side.

Some Chicago breweries focused their sales campaigns on the more elite taste of a small segment of niche beer drinkers, emphasizing the super-premium quality of their products and developing a contemporary advertising theme used for some of today's higher priced super-premium beer—beer snobbery. The Schoenhofen-Edelweiss Company used this elitist marketing approach, flooding community papers with an extensive ad campaign enticing beer drinkers to pick up a discriminating, but higher priced Edelweiss Beer, "A Case of Good Judgement."

The Atlantic Brewing Company used a demographically diverse newspaper campaign to undercut the average price of beer throughout Chicagoland, offering a normally priced 52 cent package of one quart of beer, one 12-ounce throw away steinie, and one export bottle of their Tavern Ale for only 25 cents. Initial consumer reaction was so strong that the brewery was forced to withdraw the ads in the *Chicago Tribune,* the *Cicero Life,* and the *Chicago Defender* after only three days. As a result of the huge demand for this limited 1 million bottle promotion package, the brewery successfully increased its distribution almost 100 percent in Chicagoland liquor stores and added hundreds of grocery, drug store, and tavern accounts to its local distribution network.

Discounting of product, however, would become a problem for Chicago beers as profit margins narrowed further in the next few years. Early post-Prohibition beer marketing campaigns in Chicago offering discounted prices seemed to prove the most effective in stimulating sales. It was a sales tactic that would later backfire. Given a choice between spending money for advertising or applying the less costly approach of price reductions, most local breweries took the discounted product approach. In time, the local beers often became trade footballs, bouncing from one price level to another, unable to compete against the prestige of the higher priced national brands. It's a beer pricing truism that exists even today: Significantly lower the price of your product and customers will reject any future attempt to bring the price back up to its higher priced former level.[1]

EARLY EFFECTS OF THE WAR

With the Japanese attack on Pearl Harbor and U.S treaty obligations to its allies in Europe, the war brought a two-sided front, and with it the need for conservation of food stuffs and raw materials at home. Nervous brewers nationwide kept a wary eye on Washington, willing to accept grain restrictions and any other reasonable sacrifices that might be asked of the industry, but ready to challenge any potential attempts by prohibitionists to implement a moratorium on brewing operations. The painful lessons of grain rationing during World War I and its backdoor use by drys to institute national prohibition had not been forgotten by the brewing industry.

A defense tax increase of $1 per barrel of beer, now at the $6 federal level, was quietly accepted by the industry, but added a further strain on dwindling profits. A trade study in 1940 of cost and profit breakdowns for small (under 100,000 barrels), medium (100,000 to 300,000 barrels), and large breweries (over 300,000) proved once again that quantity production reduced costs. The study, exclusive of taxes, calculated the cost of production for the small breweries at $9.65 per barrel, $7.61 for the medium-sized breweries, and $7.18 for the large breweries. Adding the new $6 barrel tax to these cost figures dramatically demonstrated the problem of economic survival faced by local smaller-sized breweries.[2]

Brewers' fears of the creeping influence of prohibitionist ideas and a possible return to the restricting years of the First World War and beyond were highlighted locally when the Chicago City Council voted to prohibit women from standing at bars, forcing them to sit at tables. Challenged by Mayor Kelley, the Council later rescinded the ordinance, allowing women to once again take their place at the bar, but only with a male escort.[3]

The Peter Fox Brewing Company

A popular Chicago brewery that seemed to defy all the problems and ensuing challenges that the local industry as a whole experienced after the relegalization of beer in Chicago was the Peter Fox Brewing Company. After acquiring the old Hoffmann Brothers Brewery on West Monroe Avenue, reportedly "from Al Capone," and issuing $500,000 in common stock, the nine Fox brothers began brewing operations in July 1933. Originally involved in a wholesale meat operation on Fulton Avenue, they entered the brewing business with a financial advantage that would be the envy of any start-up operation—no debt or preferred stock. Within a year, they began to pay dividends on outstanding shares of common stock and contemplated further acquisitions.[4]

In early 1942, the Chicago-based brewery bought the Kiley Brewing

Company in Marion, Indiana, a brewery that had entered the Chicago market in the mid-1930s but pulled out around 1939. The Indiana brewery, now known as Fox De Luxe Brewing Company of Indiana, was the third part of the brewery empire that would be owned and operated by the enterprising Fox brothers. Shortly before the Indiana acquisition, the family had also bought a well-equipped brewery in Grand Rapids, Michigan to boost their capacity, bringing up their annual combined total barrelage to 1 million. In 1944, the Peter Fox Breweries ranked thirteenth out of the twenty-five leading breweries in the United States, beating out the sales of Miller Brewing Company of Milwaukee, which ranked sixteenth.

Soon after purchasing the Marion, Indiana brewery, the brothers also entered into oil production in Oklahoma, with a community interest in some of the wells with Standard Oil of Ohio. Because of wartime restrictions, the fifteen or so wells that the company owned were limited to a production of only 200 barrels of oil per well each day. Frank Fox estimated that the wells were capable of producing 1,500 to 2,000 barrels daily when the restrictions were lifted.

The golden touch of the brothers continued throughout the war years when the Chicago headquarters announced a four-for-one split of their common stock in 1944, selling at the time for $95.50 per share. Satisfied shareholders of the brewery's common stock surely agreed with the brewery's famous slogan "Don't say Fox . . . Say Fox DEEE Luxe!"[5]

WAR EFFORTS OF CHICAGO BREWERIES

For local brewers, taking part in community drives to bolster the war effort was not only a demonstration of their loyalty to the cause of peace, but also winning the war became a daily part of operating their breweries. Conservation of fuel and collections of scrap metal, glass, and paper became paramount in the brewers' war efforts, and, if they garnished a little publicity from their collection drives or fundraisers, so much the better.

One of the first local breweries to make use of an equal blending of patriotism and publicity was the Garden City Brewery. With much fanfare, the brewery purchased a two-horse team to make local deliveries. Otto Kudrle, president of the brewery, boasted how reverting back to horse-drawn wagons for beer deliveries would aid in saving fuel for the war effort. Not coincidentally, the horses were named "Prima" and "Tor" after their flagship Primator brand of beer.[6]

On March 31, 1942, the use of tin for the civilian production of beer cans was prohibited. A few months later, civilian steel for crown caps was reduced to 70 percent of 1941 allotments. A quick result of these restrictions was the resurgence in the consumption of draft beer as bottled production drastically slowed. "When you order from the tap—you save a cap" became a familiar saying during the war years. One similarly themed slogan aimed at those who still chose bottled beer was a bit more direct in its wartime message, "Save caps, kill Japs."

Because of the shortage of bottle caps, the industry introduced the steel-conserving but cumbersome, half-gallon "picnic" bottle. The Peter Hand Brewery followed suit in the use of the larger sized bottles but also took the bold step of dating their half-gallon bottles of Meister Brau nonpasteurized draft beer. The use of larger, freshness-dated bottles was certainly a show by brewery management of their war conservation efforts, but also demonstrated a calculated move by the brewery to provide the quicker and much publicized delivery of guaranteed fresh draft beer to retailers and, ultimately, appreciative customers. Buying up huge blocks of time on WGN Radio, the brewery ads heralded the fact that bottled Meister Brau beer was now "Dated draft beer—Guaranteed tap fresh!"

What goes around, comes around. Some sixty odd years later, the industry has once begun a campaign of dating beer for fresh-ness, trumpeting the move as some sort of new approach to product freshness.[7]

Another local wartime effort that received favorable reaction from the public was a paper and cardboard collection organized by the Illinois Brewers Association. With a fleet of five hundred brewery trucks stopping at taverns, restaurants, and hotels throughout the city for the pickup of paper scrap, the successful operation was completed with the handing over of proceeds from the drive to a grateful Mrs. Edward Kelly, wife of the mayor.[8]

Not to be outdone by any competing Chicago breweries, the Peter Fox Brewing Company was duly noted as having set a Red Cross Drive record for contributions by its employees with each employee averaging $13.50 per person.[9]

One of the most ambitious wartime efforts by any Chicago brewery was the "Jobs for G.I. Joe" program, sponsored by the Atlas Brewing Company, in cooperation with the War Manpower Commission's United States Employment Service. This WBBM Radio production featured a live studio audience with a homey mix of entertainment from The King's Jesters, a CBS singing trio; Jimmy Hillard and his orchestra; and a presentation of job-seeking veterans and their stories. Acting as moderator was a young Paul Harvey, himself an ex-soldier. The program was well received by Chicagoans and led to the job placement of many returning veterans, all helped by the politically-connected brewery.[10]

THE CHALLENGES
OF THE POSTWAR YEARS

With peace once again on hand, 550 members of the Small Brewers Committee (SBC) and the allied brewing industries met at the Edgewater Beach Hotel in October 1945 to prepare for the struggles they knew they would soon face. Wartime restrictions on the use of grain, fuel, steel, glass, and other brewing materials had actually offset encroachment by the national breweries on many local markets. As cities rallied during the early and mid-1940s to overcome the enemy and help end the war, the back home efforts of the local breweries during this time were warmly appreciated and remembered by their customers. But with a return to normalcy, smaller breweries prepared for the worst.

NEW REALITIES OF THE SMALL BREWER

The central focus of the SBC meeting was the developing heavy-handed reaction by the big brewers toward the aspirations of the smaller brewers and the nationals' alleged use of unfair advertising and merchandising to increase sales. General Counsel of the organization, John E. O' Neill warned of the dangers that small brewers could face. "Unfair competition, lack of fair play, commercial bribery, subsidization, unfair advertising and the dumping of beer on local markets at less than cost" were described by O' Neill as future problems that the SBC members faced from the larger shipping brewers.

O' Neill's predictions initially seemed overstated, but as the months went on after the war, there was an unmistakable shift in the perception of what the American brewing industry would become, later confirmed by the United States Brewers Foundation. Looking at the future state of the brewing industry in the United States, the organization made public their acknowledgement and seeming acceptance of what many smaller and midsized breweries had feared. "All individuals do not achieve the same stature, mental or physical. That is equally true in business. It is not necessary nor possible for each brewer to be the largest in order to achieve success, but every brewer can be a success-ful brewer if he will. It rests with the individual. Size is not the only hallmark of success."

The fragmented brewing industry, consisting mostly of family run operations, would never be the same, and the smaller brewers knew it. By the early 1950s, the white flag would soon go up for many of them.[11]

A Reprieve

On March 1, 1946, the federal government imposed a 30 percent cut in the use of grains for brewing purposes. With the war over, grain exports to the European theater were desperately needed until a stable agricultural industry could be restored to the war-torn area. The initial result of this grain curtailment when it was announced was a move by U.S. brewers to quickly use up existing stocks of fermentable grains before the March deadline. As a result, national beer produc-tion levels rose by an average of 18.5 percent over 1945's levels though Illinois's production numbers topped off at 23.5 percent. While giants like the Jos. Schlitz Brewing Company tried to make do with the grain restrictions when they went into effect, the nation' smallest breweries were granted an increase in their grain quotas, giving them a slight advantage in keeping their production levels up.

The move to restrict grain to the industry as a whole, however, was challenged by a number of wet politicians when evidence surfaced that exported barley was going to countries that not only were in full beer production, but also had enough excess beer on hand to send to the States. The exportation of Heineken beer to the United States, a product of Holland, was soon banned by the Dutch government after it was revealed that over 8 million pounds of American grain had been shipped to Holland, some of it making its way to the Heineken brewery.

While politicians tried to placate the U.S. brewing industry but still keep grain restrictions in place, the industry turned to the idea of using other fermentables to keep up production. In a meeting of the Master Brewers Association of America in Reading, Pennsylvania in June 1946, Kurt Becker, a respected master brewer and member of Chicago's J. E. Siebel Sons' Company, delivered a speech to the organization's members advocating the widespread use of fermentables that were regarded by the brewing industry as less than regular brewing materials. Rather than watch as beer production levels fell from a lack of grain, Becker proposed the idea of using whey, sweet or white potatoes, and lower grades of brewer's syrup, including molasses and blackstrap.[12]

Though the government grain sanctions ended in 1947, a self-imposed brewers' grain conservation program began on April 15, 1948, that promoted the idea of adding additional adjuncts to American beer. One of the more unusual starches that also gained some industry acceptance was manioca, sometimes known as cassava or arrowroot, derived from a Brazilian tropical plant. Once again, the rich-tasting brews of the turn-of-the-century faded from the legacy of early American beer as government and economic influences reshaped the taste and quality of it.[13]

The Sins of the Past

Business in general, especially during the postwar boom years, was about growth and consolidation. Bigger wasn't necessarily better, but it was becoming a fact of life. In the brewing industry, those early breweries that had had the foresight to export their products in years past had continued to expand their market and their distribution network, had recognized the importance of mass advertising, and were able to accumulate huge fortunes long before the disaster of national prohibition. When the dry years of the twenties and early thirties had shut down the legitimate operations of both big and small breweries, the larger breweries, for the most part, had been fiscally and physically maintained by their farsighted owners.

The Busch family of St. Louis demonstrated a prime example of brewers with vision. Starting with the production of Budweiser Barley

Malt Syrup and Budweiser Yeast during the lean years, and the profitable sales of their corner saloon locations during the early days of national prohibition to the rapidly growing petroleum companies for gas stations, the brewery continued to find ways to stay in business. Further shifting their operations to the manufacturing of glucose, corn sugar, corn oil, and even ice cream, August A. Busch maintained the Busch family fortune during Prohibition for the eventual return of brewing. So sure was he that beer would one day return, he periodically sent his master brewer to Germany to keep abreast of the latest brewing techniques and innovations during the dry years.[14]

From repeal on, several financially strong regional breweries such as the Theo. Hamms Brewing Company of St. Paul, Minnesota; the Falstaff Brewery; Pabst; Schlitz; and others began carefully chosen programs of national expansion, nurtured by their accumulated wealth earned before Prohibition.

On the other hand, most Chicago brewers were now facing the sins of their fathers and grandfathers. Having been content to operate for years in the vast and ever growing Chicago market, few local brewers from the boom years of the 1880s and beyond had made a serious attempt at expansion and the nurturing of future export sales. While Chicago brewers became wealthy during the pre-Prohibition years, visionary out-of-town brewers such as Busch, the Uihleins of Schlitz, and the Hamms of St. Paul became much wealthier, always looking at further expansion and innovation for continued existence.

Local brewmaster Joe Pickett, at one time a man who could easily have qualified for the title "The Hardest Working Man in the Chicago Beer Business" by doing simultaneous duties as brewmaster for three local breweries during the 1940s and 1950s, later acknowledged the fatal shortsightedness of Chicago's brewing industry, especially during the post-Prohibition era. "Many Chicago breweries died of their own weaknesses. Many owners were not interested in perpetuity, just in making as much money as possible while putting very little back into their businesses."[15]

PACT WITH THE DEVIL?

Although a majority of brewers nationwide were probably guilty of some sort of larcenous activities during national prohibition, as Gussie

Busch would later admit, the Chicago brewers had raised violations of the Volstead Act and the Eighteenth Amendment to an art. Content to operate under the protection of Capone, Torrio, or any other assortment of bootleggers of the era, local brewers were eager and willing to share in the illicit, unreported booty that Chicago's mobsters had provided them. Without the artificial market of gangster-provided accounts, maintained by the dual-edged sword of intimidation by mob enforcers and the equally necessary protection that beer drummers provided them from rival gangs, the Chicago brewing industry was being reduced to a handful of small, debt-ridden family businesses. Forced to compete with each other and the bigger, well-funded breweries, flush with cash for new equipment, advertising, and further expansion into the lucrative Chicago market and beyond, the local industry began to crumble.

THE EARLY FIFTIES

A particularly devastating year for Chicago brewers was 1950. After fifty-nine years of operation, the Birk Brothers Brewery closed. Although President Frank Birk's advanced age was given as a major contributing reason for the closing, the North Side brewery, with an annual capacity of two hundred thousand barrels, had reported sales in 1949 of only sixty thousand barrels. The Best Brewing Company, another family owned business of seventy-one years, and the Garden City Brewing Company, also fell victims to the changing business conditions and tastes of Chicago consumers. The Atlas Brewery and its affiliate, the Schoenhofen-Edelweiss Brewery, were gobbled up by Drewry's Ltd., U.S.A., of South Bend in 1951. Prior to its acquisition, the Atlas had been carrying on a desperate struggle of producing old brands from defunct breweries, a move often seen in troubled breweries trying to keep production up after their own house brands have peaked in sales.[16]

TROUBLES AT FOX

Expansionism however, actually led to the demise of a once promising local brewery. A few days before Christmas of 1949, the Peter Fox Brewing Company of Chicago suddenly announced the resignations of J. Raymond Fox, director and master brewer, and Kenneth Fox, who served as advertising manager for the local brewing empire. With his unexplained departure in Chicago still looming, the company soon accepted the additional resignation of J. Raymond Fox as director and head of production for Fox DeLuxe Brewing Companies in Michigan and Indiana. For nervous shareholders watching the unfolding drama at Fox, it would only be a matter of time until the other shoe dropped.[17]

A few months later, the brewery headquarters reported the sale of their Oklahoma City plant, the last plant acquired during their swift expansion phase and located close to their oil drilling operations. The brewery had proven to be a money-losing proposition from the start and had been closed since the fall of 1949. Sold for $90,000, the brewery proved to be a financial misadventure of $267,650. The brewery at Marion, Indiana, fell next in 1951, starting with an asking price of $250,000, later reduced to $150,000. The Indiana brewery had also been closed since late 1949. In December 1951, Vice President Milton Fox announced that the Grand Rapids, Michigan, location would also shut down on December 31. Fox called this latest move an "economy operation" and declined further comment. For all concerned, it was the answer to the mass resignations in 1950.

The local brewery floundered until 1955 when the Chicago plant was finally closed and the entire operation consolidated with the Fox Head Brewery in Waukesha, Wisconsin. Family members still remember the irony of selling to the Wisconsin interests. For years, the family had worked hard to keep the Fox Deluxe name separate from the Fox Head name, "because of apparent Mafia links to Fox Head"[18] The once-thriving Chicago brewery had jumped on the postwar wagon of unbridled expansion but had lost control and come up flat.[19]

LESS FILLING, TASTE GREAT?

In a paradox that still confounds numerous microbreweries in existence today, Chicago consumers during the 1950s were abandoning the shrinking selection of old-time beers with their unique flavors, house character, and filling richness for the blander, lighter tasting beers of the national brands. Those local brewers who initially refused to reformulate their products for the changing taste of beer drinking

Chicagoans were rapidly losing their market, even when the purchasing trends for the less satiating beers of the national breweries reflected repeat and multiple sales. As mass advertising from the nationals relentlessly pounded home the message that their beers were better, image and price became problems for Chicago brewers. "Why should I buy an Edelweiss or a Nectar Ambrosia" must have certainly entered the minds of many local beer drinkers, "when I can enjoy 'The King of Beers' or 'The Beer That Made Milwaukee Famous' for a few pennies more?"

Unable to combat the advertising budgets of the giants, soft local brand loyalties developed. With the resultant poor sales of Chicago-brewed beers, the fall off in sales forced the hands of local brewers to further lower the prices of their products. In order to lower the price of their beer, however, and maintain a reasonable profit margin, they also had to lower the quality of the beer's ingredients and shorten the lagering period. Those smaller breweries that had tried to hold on to the idea of producing richer-tasting beers were now forced to produce cheap versions of their fading, once premium-brewed brews, the cheaper-made beer diplomatically referred to in the brewing industry as "popular-priced." Realizing there might be an additional market in the cheaper beers that the local breweries were beginning to brew, the nationals counteracted the smaller brewers marketing of these budget beers with their own economy versions, backed by their seemingly inexhaustible war chest of advertising dollars.

The price-sensitive sector of local beer drinkers went with the nationals. "Chicago breweries didn't have a chance in a market considered so vital by the big brewing companies," William O' Shea of the Small Brewers Association remarked years later. "The major breweries drew from enormous wealth to heavily advertise their products here and undercut small breweries in Chicago and elsewhere."

Image became everything, and in the eyes of many Chicago beer drinkers, local beers suddenly gained a sometimes justified, negative one. "Unfortunately, most Chicago brands had a 'cheap beer' image, mainly because of the lower retail price and sometimes erratic quality control," noted an executive of a major retail liquor store chain.

Customers and retailers started to react to the cheap price of Chicago beers. With room to carry only a limited amount of beer brands, taverns, restaurants and liquor stores starting dropping the cheaper-priced local brews, unwilling to give up the built-in profit margins that the premium-priced national beers afforded them. Sales slid even further as Chicago breweries now accounted for only 30 percent of the beer supplied to the Chicagoland market during the early 1950s.[20]

DEATH OF LOU GREENBERG

On December 8, 1955, Pearl Greenberg decided to stop at the office of her husband Lou, at the Canadian Ace Brewing Company at 3940 South Union in Bridgeport. She soon left for a quick shopping jaunt in the Loop while her husband finished his business for the day. After finishing her shopping and returning to the brewery, her husband continued to dawdle for another hour or so before finally packing up to return to their suite at the Seneca Hotel, in which Greenberg had an interest. Greenberg had just received word that his planned takeover of the C & J Michel Brewing Company in La Crosse, Wisconsin, had fallen through. Ted Solie, secretary treasurer of the Wisconsin brewery, and a group of investors had decided at the last minute to cancel further negotiations with Greenberg for the finally strapped family brewery due to misgivings regarding "Greenberg's connections with Al Capone and other underworld characters."[21]

After a bumpy post-Prohibition beginning, the mob-backed Greenberg brewery had thrived for years while other Chicago breweries were falling to the wayside. Called before the Senate Kefauver Crime Committee in 1951, Greenberg stated that he "guessed" that he was selling $10 million worth of beer each year. His testimony at the time also revealed his reasoning for changing the long-standing name of the Manhattan Brewery to the Canadian Ace Brewing Company. He explained to the committee that he had made the name change in 1947 "because of Manhattan's bad name," an allusion to its mob connections.[22]

Coming back online as a legal brewery in 1933, the brewery had tried a number of strategies to keep afloat in a competitive market. After a prolonged sales approach of price undercutting of competitors for a number of years while still under the "Manhattan" banner, the brewery eventually moved toward the premium market with the introduction of their "Canadian Type Beer" brand. Although the word "Type" was displayed on the beers' labels, the small-sized font and lighter ink used for the word caused the federal government to eventually pull its approval for the label. With a quick glance at the label, it was feared that customers might mistake the locally brewed product for a higher-priced Canadian import.

While battling with the feds over the ambigous label, the brewery introduced their Canadian Ace brand of beer with the wording "Made in the USA" displayed on the label and profiled it as a higher-priced premium brand.

As part of its eventual metamorphosis from a known mob-controlled Chicago brewery that pumped-out cheap beer, the renamed Canadian Ace Brewery tried to assume an air of respectability.

In late 1955, however, reports indicated that sales at the syndicate-controlled South Side brewery were slipping. In response, the Canadian Ace sales force was making a very visible show of force in its territories, pushing some of the bigger taverns and lounges to take on even more product to boost sales. Complaints from some South Side tavern owners indicated that they were again being muscled by Canadian Ace beer drummers for larger orders. This new sales campaign might have explained Greenberg's unusually long hours during the last few weeks before early December 1955. With Christmas and New Year's Eve approaching, it was one final chance to boost year-end sales.[23]

On their way home, after stopping at a local bakery on 33rd street and Wallace, the Greenbergs decided to eat at the Glass Dome Hickory Pit, a small Bridgeport rib joint on Union Avenue, just minutes from the brewery. Arriving about 6 P.M., the couple remained at the restaurant for about a half-hour and left out the front door toward their car which was parked just a few feet west of the entrance. As Greenberg opened the car door for his wife, two men quickly approached the couple and muttered something to Greenberg as they came up behind him. "No, no . . ." Greenberg almost meekly responded to the men as two shots rang out. Although wounded, the sixty-five-year-old millionaire turned and began giving chase to the two startled men as they ran east across Union. One of the assailants stopped in the middle of the street and fired three more times at the pursuing Greenberg. As the fatally wounded man fell to the street, the gunmen fled down a nearby alley.[24]

There were a number of theories proposed as to who killed Greenberg and why, but the murder still remains a mystery. "This was not a professional gangland killing," said Captain Thomas McLaughlin of the Deering police district. "The M.O. was different. Bullets of .38

caliber were used. Mob slayers mow 'em down with sub-machine guns or heavier weapons," the officer dramatically noted. It certainly, however, couldn't have been robbery since Greenberg was still wearing a $5,000 ring and carrying cash. But the defensive Pearl Greenberg insisted that the slaying must have been the result of a botched robbery attempt. "My husband didn't have an enemy," she said in response as to whether her husband's death had been a result of extortion or perhaps a shady business deal gone sour.

Because the murder involved a mob figure, police rounded up and questioned the usual suspects, including Tony "Big Tuna" Accardo, Jake "Greasy Thumb" Guzik, and mob up-and-coming Gus Alex. All had credible alibis. Greenberg's death was never solved.

Without Greenberg's mob connections and the probable realization by the local crime syndicate that the reign of the national breweries was imminent and overwhelming, the Canadian Ace Brewery folded in 1968, even with its acquisitions of the Prima Brewing Company in 1958 and the Pilsen Brewing Company in 1963. It became quite common during the years before its demise to see Canadian Ace Lager or Ale for sale in cheap plastic bags at eight cans for 88 cents selling at Chicagoland discount stores or drug stores with the ad tag of "8 for 88!" The Canadian Ace death was slow and agonizing as the brewery frantically bought or initiated scores of new labels in a futile effort to keep production figures up.[25]

With the end of Greenberg's legacy and the closing of the Canadian Ace brewery, Meister Brau, Incorporated, became Chicago's only single home-based brewery since the inception of the Haas & Sulzer Brewery in 1833.

MOB INFLUENCES CONTINUE

The investigation of Greenberg's death and later testimony by Gus Alex, a crime syndicate gambling boss and alleged trigger man for the old Capone gang, brought another glimpse into the murky relationship between breweries in Chicago and the old Capone mob.

Called before a Senate rackets committee in the summer of 1958, Alex disclosed to Committee Chief Counsel Robert Kennedy that he had been a "sales representative" for the Chicago branch of the Blatz Brewing Company of Milwaukee from February 1, 1955, to June 20,

1958. His admission came only after the young Kennedy confronted Alex with the mobster's 1956 tax return that listed a $12,000 salary from Blatz for the year. The brewery had inherited Alex in 1955 from a local Blatz distributorship operated by Stanley Stupner.

Stupner, who had once been involved with a Chicago taxi cab union, held a position in the old sales department of Atlas Brewing Company from 1944 to 1952, when the takeover of the local brewery by Drewry's was completed. During the period of Stupner's employment at Atlas, his position was protected by the brewery's president, Louis S. Kanne.

Investigation revealed that Kanne had once been a substantial shareholder in the old Manhattan Brewery with shares he had purchased from the sister of "Hymie" Weiss after the bootlegger had been slain back in the twenties. Kanne later sold his shares of the Manhattan to Lou Greenberg in 1937.

When Stupner left the Atlas Brewery in 1952, he took along Gus Alex to form the local Blatz distributorship. Alex's growing reputation as an understudy of "Greasy Thumb" Jack Guzik and alleged position as the South Side boss of policy gambling and horse booking eventually made the papers, alerting Blatz officials that they had a public relations problem on their hands. His services were eventually terminated by Blatz, leaving Alex without the $1,000 a month salary he had enjoyed for forty-one months.[26]

About the same time that Gus Alex's involvement in the Chicago brewery trade was being uncovered at the Senate hearings, Fulton D. Thorton, president of the Monarch Brewing Company in Chicago, announced the sale of the brewery, equipment, and trademarks to the Joliet, Illinois, based Bohemian Brewing Company. The Joliet brewery, under control of syndicate beer baron, Joe Fusco, since Prohibition days, made public its plan to use the Monarch to expand the marketing area of Bohemian's Van Merritt brand beer.[27]

Eliot Ness's prophecies of twenty years past were still proving true in Chicago.

MONARCH'S AUGSBURGER

In 1958, former bootlegger Joe Fusco took control of the Monarch Brewery, adding to his resume of also owning the Bohemian Brewery in Joliet and the Pacific Brewing Company in California. During his younger years, Fusco also learned the ins-and-outs of beer distribution during Prohibition from his boss, Al Capone. Fusco's sales technique was a simple but effective one, his success secured by the use of a pipe bomb through the front window of neighborhood saloons if the owners foolishly tried to order beer from a rival bootlegger. Needless to say, beer sales for Capone and Fusco soared with such imaginative marketing techniques.

One year after Fusco took over the Monarch, the brewery launched Augsburger beer and attempted to give the brew an air of respectability by labeling it as being brewed by "The House of Augsburg." When the mobbed-up brewery closed in 1967, the label went to the Wisconsin-based Potosi Brewing Company and was brewed there until 1972 when the Joseph Huber Brewery picked it up.

It was at the Monroe, Wisconsin, brewery where the beer was handled as a "craft-brewed" beer, long before the phrase first rolled off the lips of today's beer geeks. Huber took the old formula, tossed it aside, and brewed the golden nectar with a rich grain bill and a generous infusion of "noble" hops.

By 1978, Huber's Augsburger beer was on its way to becoming one of the best-selling super-premium beers in the Chicagoland area. The popularity of the green-bottled beer was helped along by numerous thirty-second radio spots featuring Huber's master brewer, Hans Kessler. For years, the heavily accented German brewer would tongue-and-cheek his way through a series of radio ads pitching his beer, sounding a bit like Arnold Schwarzenegger on a happy drunk.

But in 1987, brewery owner Fred Huber wanted out of the beer business, and he sold the regional brewery to two former Pabst executives. It was a move that Huber soon regretted, especially when the new owners turned around and sold the Augsburger label to Stroh and then started talking about closing the small Monroe brewery.

Feeling betrayed, Huber bought back the brewery in 1989 but was unable to also get the Augsburger label back from Stroh. At the Michigan brewery, the beer slowly started to lose its character, and beer drinkers noticed. By the time Stroh sold out to Pabst and Miller in 1999 and divided its portfolio of various regional brands between the two competing breweries, the Augsburger label was as good as dead. When Pabst stopped production of the once great tasting beer in 2000 to concentrate on its core brands, it looked like the Augie label would be buried like so many other once-popular regional brands before it.

Stevens Point Brewery, another regional brewery in Wisconsin, has stepped into the history of the Augsburger label by securing a licensing agreement with Pabst to brew the beer. Pabst still owns the label and receives a percentage of Augsburger's sales, but "for all intents and purposes," says Stevens Point operating partner Joe Martino, "Augsburger will become a Point brand."

Point master brewer John Zappa now handles the brewing of Augsburger. "We modified the formula to use 100-percent barley malt, hops, water, and yeast," said Zappa. "The result is more of a smooth, flavorful, well balanced lager."[28]

Black Pride Beer

By the late 1960s, the concept and reliance of customer loyalty to any particular local beer brand was a demonstrated myth. Nationals such as Anheuser-Busch, Pabst, and the Jos. Schlitz Brewing Company held sway over the majority of beer sales in Chicago. The sixties, however, were also the beginnings of political strife in the 1968 Democratic Convention and the subsequent Conspiracy Seven trial, the height of the hippy movement, the race riots on the West Side, and the emergence of black nationalism.

Into this mixture stepped forty-seven-year old Edward J. McClellan with an impressive resume that included positions as the urban program director of the National Association for the Advancement of Colored People (NAACP), head of the Human Relations Section of the Chicago Police Department, special consultant to the Community Relations Service of the U.S. Justice Department, former agent for the Army Counter-Intelligence Corps, and Chicago police sergeant. Absent from his credentials, however, were the positions of brewer or beer distributor, but nonetheless, McClellan contracted with the West Bend Lithia Company in West Bend , Wisconsin, to brew Black Pride Beer.

His concept of introducing the beer to black Chicagoans was secondary to the core mission of Black Pride, Incorporated. With a lofty goal of satisfying "the black people's need to achieve economic stature in order to secure the political power that will assure social justice and respect for themselves," McClellan put together an initial funding of seventy-five stockholders at $1,000 per investor and opened up B.P.I.'s "Beer Division" at 1215 East 73rd Street. With the distributorship located in the heart of the South Side, the company targeted the city's approximately 1,200,000 blacks to welcome their brew.

But why use beer as the means to achieve economic growth for the business concept, and ultimately the black community, as the distributorship theoretically would plow profits back into the neighborhoods of the South Side? As trade magazine *Brewers Digest* chronicled in 1969, in what appears to be a possible expanded version of a press release from Black Pride, Inc.

> The answer is simple, according to B.P.I. President McClellan. Surveys available to him revealed that expenditures for alcoholic beverages in the black area are high—higher per capita than in predominantly white areas—and that millions of dollars are spent annually for beer. Those same surveys evidenced that over 70 per cent of the market was held by three large breweries in the country with premium prices predominating. A ready market exists with a pricing structure that is conducive of a reasonable return on investment. At the same time, beer is sold to the retailer in Illinois on a cash basis, thus enabling B.P.I. to generate the greatest productivity from its capital resources. Adding to this is the relatively close shipping point of its product supplier, which results in less of a tie up of funds in product inventory.

At the time, Schlitz beer was widely accepted in Chicago's black community. While billboards for Schlitz used black models in black neighborhoods and advertised their products on black-oriented radio channels, while making racial adjustments for their advertising in Chicago's white community, Black Pride, Inc. took a separatist approach. The lofty description of its business plan, often using the vernacular of the sixties with references to whites as "the man," tried to dispel the notion with customers that the company was not simply a white-owned business, fronted by black flunkies. In reality, McClellan's plan exhibited the same underlying charcteristics of past Chicago breweries hoping for a wave of local brand loyalty, but used the thin veil of the economic plight of blacks to hopefully achieve the same results—sales. The business was doomed from the start.

At one point, McClellan did address the all-important issue of advertising, the life blood of beer sales. "Slick, professionally produced advertising appearing extensively on TV and billboards on behalf of Black Pride beer at this time would only reinforce any suspicion that we might be fronting for white money." He then went on to explain that the key to the company's advertising of Black Pride beer would be, "word-of-mouth."

Black Pride beer was brewed until 1972, the same year that the West Bend Lithia Brewing Company closed. There apparently was no attempt to switch the contract-brewed beer account to another brewery. For all its well-meaning efforts to bring economic growth to Chicago's black neighborhoods, the post-Prohibition business of beer, in black or white neighborhoods of Chicago, now boiled down to a mixture of deep pockets and a flood of mass advertising—especially the use of nationally broadcast television commercials—and established distribution channels.[29]

Meister Brau/Peter Hand, 1965–1978

> If one of the bottles should
> happen to fall . . .
> —*Bus ride ditty*

NEW DIRECTIONS

In early 1965, a group of private investors, led by Purdue University graduate and investment banker James Howard, purchased the Peter Hand Brewery. Howard, as the founder of Growth Capital, Incorporated, and later, Growth International, had found that a diverse investment portfolio of manufacturing and insurance stocks could prove profitable to investors and shareholders. With his successfully proven business philosophy of diversity, Howard began to imprint his past experiences on the conservative traditions of Chicago's dying brewing industry.

The old brewery on North Avenue, originally founded by Peter Hand, a Prussian immigrant and former Civil War veteran, had enjoyed moderate success since its inception in 1891, especially with its popular Meister Brau line. Soon after its purchase, the newly formed company went public with the issuance of 1,200,00 shares of common stock and 500,000 shares of preferred. Howard was eventually named as company president of the newly named Meister Brau, Incorporated.[1]

Following an aggressive program of sales and expansion, M-B soon ranked an impressive twenty-fifth in size nationally, with sales of 899,000 barrels during 1967. Because of management's strong emphasis on mass advertising and continued growth, the company was willing to accept the above average high-end cost of advertising averaging $1.33 a barrel. Having seen so many local breweries fail in the last thirty years, the business-savvy Howard and his fellow investors knew that advertising was the key to increased sales, and most important, continued existence.

The revitalized company placed a high emphasis on the relationship between local sports enthusiasts and beer drinkers, determining that men aged twenty-one to thirty-four made up the majority of both groups, a demographic trait that might seem fairly obvious today, but was fairly new ground during the sixties. During the next few years, the brewery sponsored Blackhawk hockey games and the Chicago Bulls over W-G-N Radio. M-B also held a one-fifth sponsorship of the Chicago White Sox on the old UHF television channels 32 in Chicago and 24 in Milwaukee, a seemingly impenetrable market that the aggressive Meister Brau management was boldly willing to challenge.[2]

DIVERSIFICATION

The years 1967 and 1968 would prove to be fateful years for the brewery as it began to add diversification to its business agenda, a strategy that President Howard had found profitable in his former business role as an investment and finance banker. After buying out Buckeye Brewing in Toledo, Ohio, and their formula for a low-calorie beer in 1967, the Chicago brewery launched Meister Brau Lite, a low-calorie, low-carbohydrate beer that was promoted as having a "nonfilling" quality. The brewery continued its theme of acquiring low-calorie products with its purchase of the O. G. Meyer Candy Company, a Chicago-based manufacturer of sugar-free and regular candies. Rounding out this concept was the inclusion of Jero Black Products, a salad dressing, sauce, and syrup manufacturer, the Mi-Diet Cookie Company, a subsidiary of Mickleberry's Food Products, Incorporated; and the Lite Soap Company of Aurora, Illinois. These purchases were formed into a separate Meister Brau subsidiary known as Lite Food Products, Incorporated.[3]

The brewery also began the Peter Hand Foundation in 1967, an Italian-based agribusiness manufacturer of vitamins and nutritional feed products for livestock that produced vitamins and chemicals for the food, dairy, and drug industries. This purchase was complemented with the additional purchases of Medical Chemicals Corporation of Melrose Park, Illinois, and Lypho-Med, Incorporated, both pharmaceutical operations.[4]

Almost immediately after making these nonbrewing related acquisitions, financial problems for the growing conglomerate began to develop. Despite a sales increase to $37,136,987 in 1967, contrasted with 1966 sales of $35,831,007, President Howard reported a loss of almost $79,000. He described the loss as "nonrecurring," blaming a laundry list of excuses, including start-up cost for the new Meister Brau Lite beer line and the Peter Hand Foundation, plant modernization and expansion costs, depressed prices in the agribusiness sector, and record cold weather throughout their beer marketing area. Efforts in 1968 were reflected in a fall-off in gross sales to $29,173,000 but positive earnings of $234,000.

Once again, the brewery reported an increase in sales for 1969. As in the previous year, sales increased to $39,313,799, but this time earnings were positive at $291,903. Howard also cited nagging drains on M-B's 1969 operations due to continued heavy advertising for their Lite beer, a fall-off in sales from their Buckeye brand and start-up costs for the Lite Food Products, Inc., division. An unaudited financial report of the company later showed that these initial earning figures were inflated. As a result, sales figures were later readjusted to $35,640,000 with earnings pegged at only $93,550.[5] The unedited financial report also expanded on the additional losses coming from the Burgermeister Brewing Corporation plant in San Francisco, the assets of the plant being recently leased by Meister Brau, Inc. Having taken over operations of the West Coast plant in mid-November 1969, M-B attributed the losses from the new brewery operation to normal start-up costs, but the losses at Burgermeister continued into 1970.

As a result of poor earnings, the directors of Meister Brau, Inc., voted to omit the quarterly common stock dividend. More telling than the failure to pay stock dividends, however, was the announcement that Meister Brau was now in the process of refinancing its long-term indebtedness with a $13 million loan. Despite the losses and the multimillion dollar refinancing, Howard seemed encouraged and predicted that subsequent quarters would prove profitable.[6]

GLORY DAYS AT MEISTER BRAU

Even with the initial poor results of its speculative nonbrewing ventures, the company seemed to be on the right track with its expanding brewing operations. In early 1968, Meister Brau, Inc., launched an unprecedented $1 million regional sales campaign that reintroduced the concept of draft beer in bottles and cans. "The Big 1" campaign saturated radio, TV, and Sunday newspaper supplements, "reflecting the acceptance of Meister Brau as number one in taste and the number one takeout beer in the Chicago market," boasted Thierry L. McCormick, vice president for advertising and public relations for Meister Brau's new ad agency, McManus, John & Adams, Incorporated. McCormick also noted that Meister Brau currently enjoyed better than a 19 percent share of the Chicago home consumption market over its nearest competitor's 11 percent share.[7]

Looking to expand their market further, the brewery set up six new distributorships in Indiana, Tennessee, and Wisconsin and took back control of its contracted Lite beer production and distribution in the East from Ballantine & Sons of Newark, New Jersey.

With a reported first quarter loss for 1969 due to a dock strike and later fire at their pharmaceutical plant, and the added burden of additional start-up costs for the expansion of Lite beer into California, sales backlogs were building up for a potentially strong second half performance. The series of losses certainly didn't slow down Meister Brau's continued ad campaigns. Combining their total television ad expenditures for its growing product lines, the brewery spent a total of $215,800 in 1968 for TV ads. It was a drop in the barrel for national giants such as Anheuser-Busch with a bill of $2,495,300 for its television ads and almost $6 million for neighboring Pabst, but M-B's perseverance was showing results, especially in Chicago. Meister Brau's newspaper ad expenditures were almost as great as A-B's at $214,679 and overwhelmed Pabst' newspaper bill of only $47,858. The difference was M-B's total media saturation of the local Chicago market and the profitable results that this blanket coverage gave the company.

Chicagoans had accepted the Meister Brau line as their local beer. Ads in the sports section of the *Chicago Tribune* were aimed at those who enjoyed every conceivable game of competition, accompanied, of course, with a cold beer from M-B. Saturday night TV viewers were enticed for weeks by springtime Meister Brau Bock Beer commercials during the Channel 2 News with anchorman Fahey Flynn and meteorologist P. J. Hoff. Complementing the bock beer ad campaign was a yearly "Bock Is Beautiful" beauty contest, searching for a Bock Queen to hold court over their traditional Bockfest. Consumer reaction was extremely positive to the brewery's perennial Lenten announcement that "Meister Brau Bock Beer is back!" and the aggressive weekly sales pitches for their other brands of popular beers during the rest of the year, including the well-received Meister Brau Lite.

Meister Brau, Incorporated, now ranked last out of the top twenty-five national sales leaders, but in doing so, the little neighborhood brewery had established itself as Chicago's home town favorite *and* a growing national brewer.[8] Continuing its drive to become not only a successful local brewery but also a developing national, Robert E. Ingram, Meister Brau's senior vice president of marketing, announced an expanded national ad campaign, buttressed by a newly organized national sales organization. Greatly encouraged by 1969's sales of over 1 million barrels, the brewery was projecting 1970 sales of more than 1.6 million barrels of beer, a large portion of this increase due to the emerging national acceptance of their Lite beer brand. Ingram went on to predict an astonishing sales target of 2.5 million barrels of beer in 1972, noting that "all our forecasts are on target."

FINANCIAL PROBLEMS CONTINUE

With lingering questions in late 1970 as to Meister Brau's failure to release fully audited returns for 1969, the company was forced to disclose details of its debt restructuring negotiations. M-B's efforts to refinance had delayed the fully audited 1969 financial results as U.S. Steel Finance Corporation, a wholly owned subsidiary of United States Steel Corporation, pored over the company books. Meister Brau's rapid expansion in the brewing industry and its efforts to diversify into profit-draining nonbrewery related businesses had left its assets strong, but the company was unable to maintain positive earnings as beer sales increased yearly. Company losses continued overall.

With the returns for 1969 finally audited and complete, the loan conditions by U.S. Steel Finance were made public. Terms of the new loan agreement indicated just how bad the financial problems at M-B had become and how bad they would continue to be if the Chicago-based brewery failed to win its gamble of increased profits through continued expansion. But this philosophy of nonbrewery related acquisitions, a keystone to the business strategy of Meister Brau Company's

President Howard, had thus far incurred yearly losses and had now forced management to the negotiation table for a hefty cash infusion.

Under the terms of the refinancing agreement, Meister Brau was able to complete certain transactions that were technically prohibited by its old long-term financial agreements. Despite the financial restrictions that M-B had agreed to when securing their past loans, the company had gone on to purchase the Burgermeister plant from the Jos. Schlitz Brewing Company rather than to continue to lease it, and had boldly purchased another candy plant. With the $13 million infusion from U.S. Steel Finance, the Chicago brewery paid $6 million for the Burgermeister plant, $1 million for the candy plant, and used $5,400,000 to repay its original loan holders, ending any possibility of problems with them for exceeding the boundaries of their past loan agreements.[9]

It was, however, a deal with the devil. In return for the cash transfusion, Meister Brau agreed to mortgage its brewery properties, pledged inventories and receivables as collateral, and, not surprisingly, agreed to consult with U.S. Steel Finance before making other acquisitions, a legitimate operating restriction that M-B had also agreed to with its former lenders, but nonetheless chose to ignore. In addition, the brewery was required to pay 4.5 percent interest over prime with principal amortization of $250,000 per quarter beginning in the second year of the three-year loan. The company also agreed to use its best efforts to repay $4 million of the $13 million loan during the first year, either through the selling-off of current assets or with the proceeds of additional financing from other sources. With the new debt restructuring agreement and the possibility that the acquisitions of the last few years might yet prove profitable, M-B continued its day-to-day operations, stubbornly holding on to its financially draining nonbrewery-related assets.[10]

BURGERMEISTER FAILURE

Soon before the bailout agreement went into effect, it became painfully obvious that Meister Brau's most recent acquisitions, including the $6 million Burgermeister plant, would not be the answer to the brewery's growing financial problems, but would only compound them. With reported sales of more than $14 million for the second quarter of 1970, compared with $8,781,107 for the same period of 1969, President and now Chief Executive Officer Howard disclosed an earnings loss of $154,740 for Meister Brau, Inc., totaling $354,899 for the first fiscal half. "Our earnings continue to be adversely affected by recent acquisitions," said Howard, and with an all too familiar refrain, he claimed good things on the horizon. "We believe that the company performance in the second half will result in a profitable 1970 year." Perhaps unwilling to change course in the midst of the not-yet-implemented financial agreement, shareholders reelected Howard and his management team in September 1970.[11]

Howard's enthusiasm proved unwarranted as he once again reported the Meister Brau phenomenon; 1970 sales had unbelievably rocketed past last years sales by almost $21 million to $56,116,502, but the result was an earnings deficit of $2.76 per share. Howard's reaction was not surprising. "Some operations may continue at a loss in 1971; however, we expect total company operations will be profitable."[12]

BEGINNING OF THE END

With one year of operation completed under the new financing agreement, the hard realities of Meister Brau's financial position had become all too obvious. As part of the U.S. Steel financing deal, assets were to be liquidated as needed to meet the obligations of the agreement. In late 1971, Meister Brau, Inc., announced that it had closed the San Francisco Burgermeister plant and had sold the brand name and business to the Theodore Hamm Company, now owned by Heublein, Inc., for an undisclosed amount of cash. Meister Brau still retained physical ownership of the West Coast plant.

Howard had made the trek to San Francisco days earlier to personally announce to brewery employees that the brewery was closing after operating at a loss, despite having regained a production level of 750,000 cases annually. With competition from out-of- state breweries hampering sales and the fact that "Burgie" was a popular-priced beer—the only brand the plant produced—profit margins had become nonexistent. One might question why the validity of relying solely on the production of a single, low-profit brand had not been considered before executing the $6 million purchase that Howard and his board of directors had so eagerly pursued.[13]

With some of the proceeds from the Burgermeister deal, M-B turned around and purchased Better Brands of Illinois, a major beer and liquor wholesaler. The local distributor handled a variety of popular products, including the languishing Miller High Life, popular imports Carlsberg beer and Tanqueray gin, and the latest fad drink, a fruit-flavored malted beverage known as Hop-N-Gator. It appeared to be a step in the right direction for a brewery that had strayed so far from its roots. With this new acquisition, the company hoped that M-B would be able to further its beer distribution efforts throughout the Chicagoland area. Distribution of M-B products, however, was not the problem.[14]

With the good news, however, came the bad. Meister Brau reported a net loss in the spring of 1971 of about $2.1 million on revenue of almost $40 million. This time, there was no hopeful prediction by CEO Howard for a profitable year end. The brewery somberly announced that it was now in the process of disposing of certain assets and busi-ness operations to improve its financial position. At the same time that the board of directors was supposedly liquidating some of the company's assets, the Chicago brewery inexplicably turned around and bought the defunct Warsaw Brewing Company of Warsaw, Illinois, for $86,000, a brewery that had no real value as an asset for a company still trying to make a national impact. Months after its purchase by M-B, the Warsaw brewery still remained closed as Howard and his people belatedly decided that it would be too expensive to put the plant back into operation. With that costly observation, Meister Brau disposed of the Warsaw Brewing Company, taking close to a $46,000 loss for its misadventure. It was the beginning of the end for Chicago's historic brewery and both Howard and his board of directors knew it, or soon would.[15]

IT'S MILLER TIME

On June 28, 1972, the *Chicago Tribune* reported that Miller Brewing Company, a recent acquisition of cigarette manufacturer Phillip Mor-ris, Incorporated, had entered into discussions with Meister Brau, Incorporated, about the possibility of Miller purchasing some or all of Meister Brau's assests. Indirectly connected with M-B through Meister Brau's recent purchase of distributor Better Brands of Illinois, Miller had consistently shown poor sales performance during its postwar years in the Chicagoland market. In addition to poor Chicago sales, a new Fort Worth, Texas, plant for Southern distribution of its flagship brew, Miller High Life, was brewing far below capacity. Even the Miller headquarters brewery in Milwaukee was having problems maintaining a reasonable output. The purchase of a good-selling Chicagoland beer brand would certainly help Miller's under-production plight and hopefully boost its sluggish sales in the Midwest. For the ailing Meister Brau, however, the question would be whether to sell the entire brewery operation, physical plant and all, or maybe one or all of the M-B brand names while retaining the brewery plant.

M-B had already sold off the Burgie label and batch formula and had recently announced the sale of Kanda Corporation, the candy distribution company that the brewery had eagerly purchased just two short years ago, one of the transactions that had precipitated the $13 million loan from U.S. Steel. In spite of management's belated realization that the selling off of its many unrelated brewery operations was now a matter of economic survival, the selling of the soul of Meister Brau, the brewery at 1000 West North Avenue, was still deemed out of the question.

On June 29, 1972, Miller Brewing Company confirmed that it had purchased for cash the trade names of Meister Brau, Meister Brau Lite, and Buckeye beers, and certain assets of Meister Brau, including distributor Better Brands of Illinois which had been recently purchased by M-B. Better Brands was Miller's only conduit to the potentially profitable Chicagoland market. Caught in the middle of Chicago brewery history were three hundred hapless M-B employees.

CEO James Howard had made a prophetic statement in 1967, predicting a place for regional brewers as the smaller city breweries passed on into oblivion. "It's inevitable that the industry should pass from many, purely local operations to fewer more broadly-based operations." Unknowingly, Howard had predicted the final epithet of Chicago's Meister Brau.[16]

BANKRUPTCY

Two weeks after the sale of Meister Brau's brand names to Miller, the beleaguered Chicago brewery filed a petition in Federal Bankruptcy court for voluntary reorganization. CEO Howard optimistically stated that the purpose of filing Chapter 11 was to give the company breathing room in order to propose a rescheduling of debt with the brewery's creditors. Still looking for needed cash, the brewery entered into an agreement with Falstaff Brewing Corporation of St. Louis to sell the San Francisco-based Burgemeister brewery. Falstaff was eager to buy the 20 million case capacity plant to accommodate greatly increased sales of its Falstaff Premium on the West Coast. To ensure a high level of production, Ballantine Ale and Ballantine Beer were also scheduled to be brewed at the plant, avoiding the problems that Meister Brau had incurred with its unforgiving one-brand production philosophy at the West Coast brewery.[17]

In December 1972, while still trying to bail out the debt-ridden brewery, Howard was asked of rumors circulating in brewing and financial circles that he was attempting to acquire the Drewry label from G. Heileman Brewing Company. Once brewed in Chicago by Associated Brewing of Detroit, it would have been a sort of homecoming for a recognized brand label. Tight-lipped, Howard would neither confirm nor deny any negotiating for the Drewry label. "I've talked to quite a few brewers," said Howard, and then seemed to tip his hand. "We could operate it [the Chicago plant] profitably at a forty-percent capacity"—about 400,000 barrels annually.

In spite of an estimated $2,500,000 needed to resume brewing operations, Howard claimed no problems in raising the needed capital. But there was still the little matter of a $1,800,000 payoff to U.S. Steel Finance and more than $6 million in unsecured debt to contend with.

Two months later, on February 9, 1973, Howard was given just five more days by the U.S. District Bankruptcy Court to come up with a workable solution to M-B's financial mess, including the repayment of all outstanding debt. Howard had earlier testified that Meister Brau needed to come up with a low-balled estimate of $750,000 in interim financing in order to start up the brewing of two new brands of beer, Peter Hand Old Chicago and Spartan.

With a $500,000 loan commitment from a Milwaukee-based finance company, the M-B CEO now claimed that he and his board of directors could put the company back in the black by May 1973. Meister Brau's restructuring period was extended. It was the second extension given to Howard by a very understanding bankruptcy referee. This new extension, however, had worried creditors objecting to yet another grace period for the beleaguered brewery.[18]

Days later, the ordeal was over. On February 15, 1973, Meister Brau, Incorporated, was declared bankrupt. With its Buckeye Brewery in Toledo, Ohio; the Jero syrup plant; and the old brewery on North Avenue in Chicago, the assets of Meister Brau, Incorporated, were valued at about $4 million, with a final payment of almost $2 million needed for U.S. Steel Finance and the rest needed to partially satisfy millions of dollars in unsecured debt.

THE PETER HAND BREWERY

In April 1973, the Meister Brau plant was put on the auction block by the Federal Bankruptcy Court. The successful bidders were Fred Huber of the Huber Brewing Company in Monroe, Wisconsin, and Fred Regency, president of a local textile manufacturer. Only one other bidder attempted to beat their high bid of $1,350,000—former Meister Brau CEO James Howard, with an unsuccessful bid of $1,250,000.

A veteran of over twenty years in the beer business, Huber launched an ambitious plan to keep the brewing legacy alive in Chicago. In a local publicity campaign blitz that went on for months, the Wisconsin brewer played hard on the local aspect of the reopened brewery, a tactic that had been seemingly successful for Meister Brau's Chicagoland sales. "People will support a local beer," claimed Huber. "By the end of May, we hope to be in production with our first label, Old Chicago Beer," he predicted.

Estimating a first year run of 250,000 barrels, Huber and marketing director Charles DeLorenzo, a holdover from the old Howard regime, talked of furthering production with new brand lines as sales would hopefully increase. With the proper blend of community pride and aggressive promotion being the key to their success, DeLorenzo went out on a limb with a first year projection of 300,000 barrels and a peaking out at 450,000 barrels. "Chuck may be a little optimistic," conceded Huber. A few months later, however, Huber was taking the same stance. Estimating the Chicago market at around 5 million barrels a year, the brewer gushed dreamily, "If we can grab 10 percent of the trade, we'll be quite happy!"[19]

But times were changing in Chicago and the issues of loyalty and community pride in the choice of local beer had become moot points. As Peter Hand tried to regain a niche segment of Chicago's beer drinkers, the nationals overwhelmingly gained control of the local beer market. The Jos. Schlitz Brewing Company had recently celebrated its dislodging of Anheuser-Busch for the position of number one statewide sales leader, with sales of 1,815,000 barrels in Illinois, or 24.1 percent of the market, with most of the sales coming from Chicago. A-B, with 23.3 percent of the state market, was being hotly pursued by the aggressive G. Heileman of La Crosse, Wisconsin, and Miller Brewing Company, which had risen 9.5 percent in sales since acquiring the Meister Brau and, more important, the Meister Brau Lite label and formula.

Opening up a beer advertising blitz in August 1972, just months after buying the M-B brands, Miller began saturating the Chicago daily papers with full-page ads and multiple thirty-second TV spots during local sportscasts, targeting the old Meister Brau and Meister Brau Lite crowd. With the deep pockets of Phillip Morris and the formula for the old Meister Brau Lite, now known as the new low-calorie, low-carbohydrate Lite beer from Miller, the Milwaukee brewery exploited the same market that M-B had successfully nurtured—young sports enthusiasts. They could now, however, take their advertising efforts to a much higher level; they went totally national, not region by region as Meister Brau had cautiously attempted. "To push a product that held a great deal of appeal for athletic, fitness-conscious people, Miller bought sports. Any sports. By the time Anheuser-Busch went looking for available sports airtime, Miller owned something like 70 percent of network television sports beer advertising," says author Philip Van Munching in his entertaining and informative book, *Beer Blast*.[20]

Lite beer from Miller, son of Meister Brau Lite, soon became *the* beer that made Miller famous. In a bit of ironic beer karma, the renamed Miller Lite is currently the biggest selling brand of beer in the city of Chicago, with a market share of about 23 percent.[21]

With only one city brewery left, the domination of the local beer market by the nationals and the as yet unspoken concession that Chicago would never again be a brewing center, the Chicago chapter of the Master Brewers Association voted unanimously to dissolve its charter. Roger Sieben, a brewmaster at the new Peter Hand Brewery, explained the reasoning behind the dissolution of the local MBA. "Two years ago we had a meeting and said 'Let's really try to have a proper malt and hops session.' Only eight guys showed up." The apathy of the membership was simply a reflection of the attitude of the Chicago beer drinking public as a whole; local brand loyalty was truly dead. In the business of beer, image had become everything—*and still is.*

On September 1, 1978, with sales of less than 100,000 barrels for 1977, and no prospects for a bubbly future, the Peter Hand Brewery closed, ending a 145-year-old brewing legacy in Chicago.

For the next nine years, Chicago would be the exclusive playground of out-of-town brewers.

⚜ PART V ⚜

Aftermath

When You're Out of Schlitz . . .

> You can't have some bean counter
> telling you, "We can't use this kind of
> fermenter because it's labor-intensive;
> you can't have mash-filters." It's amazing
> how fast that killed Schlitz . . .
> —*William Coors, Coors Brewing Company*

A CLEAN SLATE

In contemporary Chicago, the exiting of virtually any local industry to a more hospitable location outside the city's limits or a much-publicized business failure can be cause for civic concern and editorial discourse. Whether the affected workforce consist of thousands or a mere handful of employees, the prestige, history, or political connections behind the business can often instigate public reactions by civic leaders or the editorial pages of the local press.

But when the Peter Hand Brewery rolled out its last barrel of beer in 1978, the reaction in Chicago was quite different. Simply put, there wasn't one, at least not among city officials. Newspaper staff reporters made the obligatory note of the brewery's closing and speculated on how the imposing commercial structure at 1000 West North Avenue might once again be utilized, but local government officials were surprisingly mum about the failure of the last historic Chicago brewery and the end of a significant local industry.

Fred Huber, who had held the dual positions of president of the now-defunct Peter Hand Brewery in Chicago and the Joseph Huber Brewing Company in Monroe, Wisconsin, returned to Monroe to devote himself fulltime to the everyday operations of the successful Huber family brewery. Before he left Chicago, he stayed long enough to witness the dismantling and auctioning off of the plant's brewing equipment and its huge accumulation of Chicago breweriana, some going back almost ninety years. Caught up in the moment, the disappointed brewer was seen actually bidding on items during the auction. "What are you bidding on?" he was asked by one of the liquidators. "It doesn't really matter, does it?" as he mustered for a suitable answer.[1]

His bow to Chicago's heritage as a once important brewing center would be reflected in 1979 in a Commemorative Can Series of Huber beer, honoring the Lill & Diversey, Peter Schoenhofen, John A. Huck, Bartholomae and Roesing, Gottfried, and Michael Brand breweries. The colorful six-packs, filled with a European-styled beer, "reminiscent of those brewed in the last century by the breweries that we're honoring," stirred up interest not only in their unique design, but also, in some quarters, for the distinctive taste of the small-batched beer.[2]

One can only speculate on the reactions, if any, in the board rooms of the national brewers such as Schlitz and Anheuser-Busch to this final page in the long history of brewing in Chicago, but there's a strong suspicion that it was similar to the muted response that was exhibited by the Chicago community in general.

The national brewers had long quit worrying about competition from Chicago's dying brewering industry. As an important brewing center, Chicago had begun its terminal decline on December 5, 1933, the first day of repeal. It's a misconception, perpetuated by the occasional newspaper article that attempts nostalgically to look back at Chicago's once-popular breweries, that national prohibition killed the brewing industry in Chicago. It didn't—repeal did, with its unionism, competition, encroachment by out-of-town shipping breweries, and huge advertising budgets, something the smaller, underfunded local breweries were unprepared for. By the time the mob-influenced Canadian Ace (aka, The Manhattan) Brewery closed its doors in 1968, the memory of the city's brewing history and its industrial significance was already a nostalgic afterthought. The folding of Meister Brau, and then Peter Hand, seemed to finalize the last chapter in Chicago's long brewing history.

BATTLEGROUND CHICAGO

With the retail beer market clear of any lingering obtrusions by local brands, the first tier of national brewers, consisting of the Jos. Schlitz Brewing Company, Anheuser-Busch, Pabst, and the Philip

Morris-owned Miller Brewing Company, began to openly fight for market dominance in Chicago.

The Jos. Schlitz Brewing Company held a unique position in the history of beer and brewing in Chicago. Since the Great Fire of 1871 and the later death of Joseph Schlitz in 1875, Milwaukee's Schlitz beer and its brewing family of Uihleins had ingratiated themselves not only with Chicago's most famous brewing family of Seipps through marriage, but also with the discriminating taste buds of Chicagoland beer drinkers. The response by Schlitz to the void of local suds after the great conflagration, which had wiped out nineteen Chicago breweries, was quick and decisive.

Moving into the Chicago beer market with an abundance of fresh Schlitz beer, the brewery's early sales efforts flooded the Windy City with its golden nectar and left a generations-lasting feeling of good-will by Chicagoans toward the Milwaukee brewery and its flagship brand.

Even the brewery's most popular slogan, "The beer that made Milwaukee famous," was precipitated by the brewery's generosity in shipping beer and drinkable water to Chicago after the fire had destroyed the city's main water pumping station. This gesture was so well received by Chicagoans that the Uihleins capitalized on the attention this act brought their brewery and began using the famous slogan in 1894.[3]

Today, the pre-Prohibition presence of Schlitz and its popularity in Chicago are still reflected by the vestiges of saloons once owned by Schlitz. These remaining dozen or so structures, adorned with the familiar Schlitz logo on the side of each building, can still be found scattered throughout the city.

Chicagoland favorite, Schlitz, had been enjoying the number one spot in Illinois beer sales since 1973 with a 24.1 percent share of the retail market, but had fallen behind Anheuser-Busch in the mid-1950s as number two in national sales. A nationwide bottlers strike at A-B by the Teamsters in 1976, however, gave Schlitz an unexpected opportunity to once again grab hold of the national beer market and further secure its sales lead in Chicago. The strike had left a bad taste in the mouths of thousands of Chicagoland retailers and tavern owners who either ran out of A-B products during the strike or were limited by local distributors to just a few cases per week. With the turmoil at Anheuser-Busch, Schlitz, Miller, Pabst, and the up-and-coming

G. Heileman Brewing Company stepped up production and aggressively began to stock retail shelves and neighborhood tavern coolers with their products to fill the Anheuser-Busch beer void in Chicago.

PROBLEMS AT SCHLITZ

The campaign at the Jos. Schlitz Brewing Company to dislodge Anheuser-Busch as nationwide sales leader was led by Robert Uihlein Jr., representing the fourth-generation of the famous brewing family and, ultimately, the last Uihlein family member to guide the old brewery. Since 1875, when Joseph Schlitz drowned with the sinking of the ship, *S.S. Schiller*, the Uihleins had admirably run the venerable Milwaukee brewery.

Bob Uihlein Jr. had been groomed for leadership at Schlitz since his days as a young man. Following family tradition, Uihlein attended the U.S. Brewers Academy and the Wallerstein Laboratories in New York for specialized training in brewing. Completing studies, he joined Schlitz full time in 1942 in the sales division and was named a general vice president three years later. In due course, Uihlein became vice president in charge of sales, executive vice president in 1959, and in 1961 was named president of the Jos. Schlitz Brewing Company. In 1967, he took on additional duties as board chairman, succeeding Erwin "Ike" Uihlein. Under Bob Uihlein's direction, Schlitz began posting new sales and production records.

By 1973, however, Schlitz began drifting from one managerial crisis to another. Court papers filed by the Securities and Exchange Commission (SEC) in mid-1973 revealed that a compromise had been reached by Schlitz with the newly-empowered Bureau of Alcohol, Tobacco and Firearms (BATF) to stop alleged illegal payments and favors to a number of retailers and restaurants.

The charge of offering "favors" to retailers must have been especially irksome in the eyes of Schlitz management. Schlitz had been giving away promotional materials, including signage, a common practice in the beer trade. The value of the materials dispensed, however, had exceeded the outdated monetary limitations established by the Federal Alcoholic Administration Act on such items after the repeal of Prohibition in late 1933.

Other breweries, including Anheuser-Busch, had also been caught by the BATF in the broad sweep of questionable brewery marketing practices and faced similar charges. In the initial phase of the massive investigation, all but Schlitz begrudgingly paid huge monetary penalties in settlement for their marketing practices. In a meeting in Chicago between the regional BATF and Schlitz's outside counsel, the brewery's legal representative told the BATF regional director that Schlitz would not only *not* pay any fines, but also that the bureau could simply "go to hell." The moment the counsel for Schlitz walked out of the meeting room, the director turned to an assistant in the room and said, "Go make a case against Schlitz."[4] Needless to say, Schlitz went to the top of the BATF hit list. The brewery eventually did reach an agreement with the federal government, but its arrogance drew the attention of the BATF and the SEC for years to come.

The average beer drinker in Chicago probably shrugged his shoulders at the news of the federal charges towards Schlitz, if he noticed at all. After all, whether the local daily news involved "hush-hush" cash payments from crooked contractors or deceptive bankers or charges of illegal marketing practices by breweries to secure business in Chicago, everyone knew that that was the way business was done in "The City That Works." Chicagoans read the business reports, put down their newspapers, and continued to drink and enjoy their Schlitz beer.

REFORMULATION

It was Robert Uihlein's decision to speed up the fermentation process of Schlitz beer in the late 1960s, however, that would eventually end Chicago's love affair with "The beer that made Milwaukee famous," including its very popular seven-ounce bottled Schlitz beer, affectionately known around town as "little Joes." Uihlein switched over the fermentation of its beer from a period of almost two weeks to a shorter cycle of six days in order to get better utilization of the brewery's facilities.[5] Using this approach, Uihlein boasted, Schlitz could achieve a better economy of scale from the company's existing breweries, increase barrelage, and avoid or delay the huge capital investment need for additional plants or equipment. Per barrel savings were estimated at $1 a barrel. With a yearly run of over 20 million barrels, the savings were obvious.

Accelerated batch fermentation, or ABF, is a production theory that had been floating around the brewing community for years. Contrary to the once traditional practice of fermenting lager beer with its unique yeast properties under cool conditions, ABF utilizes a time-temperature process that brings the beer up to a higher temperature in order to speed up the fermentation. To accommodate this quickened brewing cycle, a number of things also need to be considered in the brewing process. Among the choices are a stirred fermentation, semicontinuous processing of the product by blending actively fermenting beer with fresh, unfermented beer to eliminate the lag phase of the fermentation process, and/or changing the composition of the wort. Schlitz chose the latter approach and changed the wort by cutting back on the malted barley used during the mashing process and substituted the grain bill with cheaper adjuncts, including highly fermentable corn syrup.

This accelerated fermentation is followed by a short lagering process that quickly "ages" and conditions the beer before packaging. This also goes against the practice of brewing lager beer under cool temperatures for a longer period of time during the fermentation phase and extending the conditioning and lagering period, once again under cooler temperatures. It was once highly held by lager beer brewers that the traditional lengthier process allowed the beer to develop its characteristic flavor and allowed it to slowly bleed off any off taste usually associated with what's commonly referred to as "green" beer.[6]

The shortened brewing cycle itself seemed to have had no discernable effect on the quality of the beer, but combined with the addition of cheaper fermentables in the wort, it drastically affected the characteristics of Schlitz beer. Schlitz wholesalers began complaining to the Milwaukee brewery about the beer's inconsistent qualities, especially its head retention, a quality anticipated and appreciated by any real beer drinker.

In a 1975 meeting with perturbed nationwide beer distributors, Schlitz representatives acknowledged the foam problem and assured them that it was being corrected. Since late 1974, however, Caris Associated, Incorporated, a Chicago-based Schlitz distributor, had been vehemently complaining to Schlitz personnel "at all levels" that Schlitz was providing them with "poor quality, inconsistent, and unmarketable beer."[7]

In order to correct this deficiency, the brewery, nonetheless kept the ABF process in place and continued to use a cheaper grain bill but also began adding a colloidal foaming agent to the beer to aid head formation and retention. This might have been the end of the problem, but then the brewery also decided to stop the use of papain, a proteolytic enzyme that breaks down and modifies protein molecules from flaking in the beer, a condition precipitated by cooling the beer and commonly known as "chill haze." Schlitz substituted the clearing effects of the papain with the addition of silica gel, which attracts protein molecules and normally aids in clarifying the beer during the filtering or "polishing" process.

The results were disastrous. The combined presence of the foaming agent and the silica gel caused the protein molecules in the beer to abnormally clump, giving the now visible protein a snowflake-like appearance.[8]

In Chicago, once-loyal Schlitz beer drinkers started calling the product "Schitz" beer.

CARIS ASSOCIATED, INCORPORATED

In mid-1971, some of Chicago's leading politicians gathered on the South Side of Chicago for the dedication of a new 70,000 Square-foot Schlitz beer distribution facility. It was a huge, all-inclusive structure of office, meeting, and display material areas, capable of holding over 400,000 cases of beer and 3,600 half-barrels. The new business at Pershing Road and Ashland Avenue was projected to employ ninety people.

The building was the third structure to house the Schlitz distributorship of Caris Associated, Incorporated, since the takeover of the local business by Angelo Geocaris in 1959. The relationship between the Joseph Schlitz Brewing Company and Caris Associated, Inc., had been a profitable one for both parties. In a little over ten years, the growing distributorship had doubled sales of Schlitz products on the South Side of Chicago.

In what today would be a certain political embarrassment for all who attended the opening ceremony, Alderman Ed Burke (14th), Alderwomen Anna Langford (16th), and Alderman Clifford P. Kelly (21st) were joined by John Stroger, then a Cook County Commissioner; Richard J. Martwick Jr., superintendent of Cook County schools, Peter Kotsos, Illinois Liquor Control Commission administrator; and other notable Chicago civic leaders.[9]

Although the political currents of the present administration of Mayor Richard M. Daley would probably swell to *tsunami*-like dimensions if top city officials gathered for a similar event today, political patriarch Mayor Richard J. Daley and his administration had been openly soliciting businesses in the early 1970s to move to the once-barren land where the distributorship was now situated. The area had been left vacant by the closing of the old Chicago Union Stockyards. Daley's dreams were to eliminate the century-old stench of offal and death left by the slaughterhouses with the more agreeable smell of new money. The opening of the Schlitz distributorship was the city's first step in filling the nonperforming land, renamed Donovan Industrial Park, with light industry that could provide the city with a reliable stream of property tax revenues and jobs for local residents.

The presence by young Burke and others to officially open the $1.1 million facility was in condescension to the wishes of the mayor whose own political stronghold of the 11th Ward in Bridgeport encompassed the eastern portion of the vacated stockyards area. No one could dare fault the politicos when they openly shared in the celebratory offerings of the 25 millionth case of Schlitz beer handled by the Geocaris distributorship.[10]

Geocaris Struggles

With the huge investment of a new facility, Angelo Geocaris was in no mood for the stonewalling by Schlitz representatives concerning problems that started to appear in their beer with increasing regularity, soon after the reformulation of the flagship brand. After brewery representatives met with Geocaris in late 1974 to discuss the problems with their beer, it became obvious, by continued complaints of retailers to the local distributor and the later 1975 meeting of Schlitz officials with their nationwide distributors, that little effort was being afforded by Schlitz to alleviate the problem. The brewery did, however, remove the problematic colloidal foaming agent in September 1976.

Loyal Schlitz drinkers found that their beer was again a clean and clear product, but, as had happened a few years earlier, it poured flat or quickly dropped its head. In the meantime, embarrassing reports started to filter out that Schlitz had quietly destroyed 10 million bottles and cans of flaky beer, returned by disgruntled distributors to the Schlitz Tampa Bay and Memphis plants.[11]

For Schlitz Chairman Robert Uihlein Jr., however, the brewery's campaign for national supremacy, which would cruelly turn into the brewery's fateful battle for survival, ended for him in late 1976 when he suddenly passed away from acute leukemia. The reign of the House of Uihlein at the Joseph Schlitz Brewing Company had ended.

Replacing Uihlein would be Eugene B. Peters, at the time, only the second nonfamily member to become president of the brewery in its long history. Peters knew that his ascension to the roles of president and later, CEO, would be a difficult one. "I look at this job as a challenge" he diplomatically noted in an interview in February 1977, and for good reason. In 1973, Roy Satchell had left the company as president after only six weeks, reportedly after battling with Schlitz board members.[12] Of the fifteen-man board, eleven were Uihlein family members.

With Peters at the helm, Schlitz continued to ignore the pleadings by Geocaris and other local distributors of poor quality product until late in 1977. Bill Coors of Coors Brewing Company, opined in an interview in 1999, that the hiring of Peters was a mistake that only compounded the growing problems at Schlitz.

"When Bob died, guess who they put in charge? A bean counter. That's free. You've got to have a bean counter in any company to watch the dollars and cents. But you have to have somebody else that determines policy. You can't have some bean counter telling you 'We can't use this kind of fermenter because it's labor-intensive; you can't have mash-filters.' It's amazing how fast that killed Schlitz."[13]

The question arises why another Uihlein didn't assume the role of CEO of the brewery? Bob Uihlein's sudden death and the placement of Peters as CEO of Schlitz seems to indicate inadequate attention by the board to succession of management, coupled with possible infighting among those family members who might have thought that they were suitable CEO candidates.

Peter's time in the barrel was a short one. In October 1977, board members forced him out, as beer sales continued to decline.[14]

Reaching into a legal bag of tricks, Geocaris once again notified Schlitz of continuing problems with their beer. The distributor cited the wholesaler franchise agreement signed by Caris Associated, Incorporated, and the Jos. Schlitz Brewing Company in March, 1973, in which the two parties agreed to a supplemental schedule, stating

Schlitz's obligation to "conduct all Buyer-Seller relationships in a fair and equitable manner." The agreement, however, also disclaimed any warranty by Schlitz on any beer sold to the Chicago beer distributor. With this caveat in mind, Geocaris's argument focused instead on the claim that Schlitz was abusing its relationship with his distributorship by ignoring its falling sales. This claim was a result of doing little to rectify the poor quality beer that had caused the drop in sales and subsequent loss of profits for Geocaris.

In 1978, Schlitz changed the composition of the beer once more, with indications that the malt bill had been increased. For Schlitz, however, it was too late. Beer drinkers were convinced that the Schlitz brand had become an inferior product. Whether the beer was actually now as good—or better—than that enjoyed in the late 1960s or early 1970s, once-loyal Schlitz drinkers turned their attention to competing brands.

Peter Blum, former archivist for the Stroh Brewing Company, felt that Schlitz's entire approach to winning back customers was a lost one. "Mistake number one was to reduce the malt ratio. Mistake number two was to publicize a more efficient process, when A-B was stressing tradition and parading around draft horses."[15]

For a brewery that had tried for years to maintain a sense of historical continuity with its customers, the second mistake would prove costly.

In Chicago, as the popularity of the Schlitz brand continued to plummet, Old Style beer from the G. Heileman Brewing Company was becoming the new darling of the six-pack crowd, especially after deep discounting by the La Crosse, Wisconsin, based regional brewery.

Schlitz, Part II

A really great tragedy—really, really bad.
—*Schlitz spokesman after a*
failed ad campaign

More Problems for Schlitz

While the Milwaukee brewery battled with its nationwide distributors on one front, the federal government was once again ready to take on Schlitz for alleged bribes and kickbacks, charges more serious than those leveled by the Securities and Exchange Commission back in 1973. In March 1978, reports surfaced in Milwaukee that the Department of Justice was seeking an indictment against Schlitz, charging the brewery with three counts of felony tax fraud, one count of conspiracy to violate the Federal Alcohol Administration Act, and over seven hundred counts of actually violating the act.

Former marketing employees of Schlitz, who had been fired by the brewery after its previous settlement with the BATF, supported this action. Upset that Schlitz management did not share the blame for the business practices that they had been sacked for, the disgruntled former employees gave evidence to a Milwaukee federal grand jury against the Jos. Schlitz Brewing Company.[1]

The violations of the Federal Alcohol Administration Act were especially troublesome because the brewery had agreed four years earlier to halt its illegal inducement activities, but the new allegations suggested that it apparently continued to do so. Court papers identified, among other charges, a cash payment of $265,000 to Carson, Pirie, Scott & Company. The payment was used to sway Carson's with cash "in connection with purchases of Schlitz products for concessions at O'Hare Airport," purportedly at the time, to be the largest draft beer account at a single location in the United States. The indictment included additional allegations that Schlitz had also paid the Chicago

Cubs organization $75,000 to feature their beer at Wrigley Field and had also made payments to the Conrad Hilton Hotel for most favored status in their bars and restaurants. These payments, charged the indictment further, were used to persuade the local businesses to sell only Schlitz beer or to promote Schlitz products more than competing brands.[2]

Smelling blood in the water, the recently closed Peter Hand brewery in Chicago filed a $15 million antitrust suit in mid-September, charging Schlitz with "engaging in illegal bribes, kickbacks and secret rebates over a period of eighteen years." As a result, contended the last operating Chicago brewery, they had lost $5 million in sales and were seeking triple damages. Mimicking the federal charges, the brewery's lawsuit also claimed illegal payments by Schlitz to Carson, Pirie & Scott, the Chicago Cubs organization and "at sports stadia, race tracks . . . and other (local) high-volume outlets."[3]

In a public response to the government charges, D. F. McKeithan Jr., the newest CEO to warm the seat of Schlitz chairman of the board, vowed that "If the company is indicted on these charges, we will have no alternative but to vigorously fight them in court," and denied accusations of Schlitz management having any knowledge of the alleged violations. "While subsequent investigations by both the government and Schlitz's lawyers have demonstrated that these orders [to stop payoffs as per a 1976 agreement for the charges leveled by the federal government in 1973] may not have been followed in some instances by all Schlitz employees, I am convinced that today the company is in total compliance with all state and federal laws."[4]

One might wonder how the alleged payoffs could have been so easily buried in the marketing department's budget without arousing managerial attention. Perhaps also noting the possible implications of such creative accounting methods, Schlitz settled with the government, pleading *nolo contendere* and paid a fine of $750,000.

After the brewery's earlier bravado when the charges initially had become known, the swiftness of the plea seemingly weakened the credibility of management's assertions of having had no prior knowledge of the allegations. Publicly, Schlitz officials argued the necessity of the plea in order to avoid the expense and distraction of management time that protracted litigation would have caused.[5]

The real distraction of management's time was the brewery's plummeting sales.

The Beginning of the End for Schlitz

After the sales figures for 1977 came in, no one could deny that Schlitz was in trouble. Estimates by marketing and business analyst George Lazarus of the *Chicago Tribune* projected a drop in barrelage to 22,200,000 barrels from the 1976 total of 24,162,000. It was the first drop in sales in the last fifteen years for the embattled brewery. With the loss in barrelage confirmed, Schlitz dropped to the number-three national sales position behind the seemingly invincible Anheuser-Busch. The St. Louis-based brewery had made a strong national recovery after the bottlers strike in 1976. In the number-two sales position was Miller Brewing Company, having risen a hefty 32 percent in liquid sold for 1977, much of the rise in barrelage from sales of its Lite beer brand. Schlitz also showed poor bottom line numbers for 1977. Its net income had dropped to $19.8 million from its 1976 showing of $49.9 million, with a sales decline to $937 million from almost $1 billion a year before.

The wheels were starting to come off the Schlitz beer wagon, and as a result, the board members were feeling pressure from stockholders, many of them Uihlein family members. Nonfamily shareholders at the yearly company meeting had reported a very public dispute by Uihlein family members at the annual stockholders' meeting as the falling sales were announced, and accusations of blame were subsequently traded.[6]

McKeithan defended the reduction in earnings for the previous year as simply the reflection of a lower volume of beer having been shipped. As a result of the volume reduction, the brewery also took a $7 million loss in the fourth quarter for the disposition of equipment that had optimistically been purchased earlier for brewery capacity expansion.

During this time, Dan McKiethan's role as Schiltz CEO seems to have been one of compromise between the different factions of Uihlein board members. As a lifelong oilman, McKiethan had no experience in the brewing industry, but his divorced wife was an Uihlein, the daughter of Joseph E. Uihlein Jr., and he was more than familiar with the Uihlein family members of Schlitz management. More important, McKiethan appears to have been willing to invest the time needed to be the company's front man to the public—stockholders, customers, and employees.

Surprisingly, Schlitz stock actually rose $1.38 to $15.50 on the day Schlitz went public with the 1977 earnings numbers. Rumors on Wall Street speculated on a possible merger between R. J. Reynolds Industries and the brewery, a rumor that had been gathering more froth in recent months. It seemed to be a logical fit, considering the successful takeover of Miller by tobacco giant Philip Morris. Schlitz officials admitted that they had had a dialog with Reynolds but that they had also terminated any further discussions of a merger in January of 1978.[7]

The exploratory talks were the first sign that new company president Frank J. Sellinger, CEO McKiethan, and the Schlitz board of directors might actually be wondering what the future would hold for them and the brewery.

Good-bye Gusto

Like an ousted major league baseball manger, tossed aside by the team owner after a dismal season of losses, advertising agencies often take the brunt of a client's attention after a poor-performing fiscal year. The relationship in 1978 between Schlitz and the Chicago-based ad agency, Leo Burnett U.S.A., was no different. After the sales figures for Schlitz came out, Burnett officials knew they had a problem on their hands. The early 1977 numbers had caused Schlitz to hold discussions with other ad agencies, including Foote, Cone & Belding, Grey Advertising, and J. Walter Thompson, Chicago, the ad agency for Schlitz from 1956 until 1961, when Burnett wrestled away the $22 million account from them.

It was the Leo Burnett agency that had introduced the successful "Reach for the Gusto" and "When you're out of Schlitz, you're out of beer" phrases into the American lexicon. The creation of the latter phrase was pure serendipity, put into service after a Burnett official overheard someone in a downtown Chicago bar say it. This little bit of creative plagiarism would become the most successful variation of the Schlitz gusto theme.[8]

With the anticipated 1977 fall in sales, however, the Jos. Schlitz Brewing Company started to act like a drowning man, desperately reaching for the buoyancy of new management, a reformulated beer, and now, a possible new ad agency. Back in 1975, Schlitz had started to grumble to Burnett about the popular gusto ad theme. Eli Wolf, who worked on the gusto campaign in its early years at the Chicago ad agency, recalls the first time Schlitz managers complained about the tone of the ads, specifically the original tag line.

"When the campaign first ran, the theme line was 'Grab for all the gusto you can,'" he recalls. A school teacher out West heard the commercial and wrote an indignant letter to the brewery claiming that the use of the word "grab" set a poor-mannered example for any children who might have heard the commercial. "One complaint from a school teacher and they changed the word 'grab' to 'reach,'" he said with disbelief. With a tinge of drool sarcasm, Wolf "suggested they change it to 'grope.'"[9]

But Miller's new Lite beer was making such a quick and successful jump into the national market that Schlitz now wanted to emulate its rival's marketing approach. The brewery's initial research indicated that the word "gusto" seemed to suggest heaviness, the wrong projection to beer drinkers when Lite beer's success was indicating consumers' changing preferences to a lighter, less-filling brew. At the time, Schlitz was still months away from its introduction of a competing light beer product.

The creative team at Burnett didn't agree with the Schlitz analysis of their gusto theme. Rather than lose the multimillion-dollar account, however, Burnett reluctantly ceased the ad campaign, "but went kicking and screaming all the way," replacing it with the uninspiring tagline "When it's right, you know it."[10]

An executive at rival Miller Brewing was unimpressed with Schlitz's emulation of its Lite beer marketing techniques. "I'm not sure that advertising—whatever Schlitz can produce in sharper promotion—can do a job for that brand," the Miller spokesman prophetically noted. "They've got plenty of other problems"[11]

In the flip-flop management style that Schlitz was now demonstrating with alarming frequency, the brewery did an about-face in late 1977 and once again consulted with the creatives at Burnett. The soft-sell approach for Schlitz was failing, they conceded, as Miller continued to gobble up market share. Now Schlitz had a marketing epiphany, suggesting to Burnett that the gusto concept wasn't so bad after all. Maybe, just maybe, the word "gusto" had become synonymous with the Schlitz brand, an obvious connection that the average Schlitz beer drinker had made sometime earlier. To reestablish this connection,

Burnett was instructed by Schlitz to reawaken the loyalties of former Schlitz drinkers with a hard-hitting variance of the successful gusto campaign.

Somewhere down the line, the concept of "hard-hitting" took a wrong turn.

The "Drink Schlitz or I'll Kill You" Campaign

In September 1977, a group of Leo Burnett's top officials met in their tenth floor conference room in the Prudential Building in Chicago to view four commercials using the resurrected gusto theme. The commercials had been put together quickly, a reaction to Schlitz's insistence on getting something ready as soon as possible. Burnett employees had researched their commercial ideas by taking a simple storyboard with a sketched sequence of the proposed commercials to the Woodfield Mall in nearby Schaumburg, Illinois. Passersby were asked by the Burnett people to look at the storyboards and see if they understood the commercials. Because of the urgency imposed upon the advertising agency by the brewery, the Burnett people wanted to make sure that their initial efforts were on the right track. As a result, they did not ask for the subjects' opinions as to whether they liked the product or its proposed style of presentation. With assurances that the test subjects simply *understood* the concept of the storyboards, the four commercials went into film production.

The commercials varied from one featuring a Muhammad Ali-like boxer with a full entourage to a rugged outdoorsman with his pet mountain lion. In each of the four commercials, an off-camera voice asked the lead characters to give up their Schlitz beer for another brand. The commercials, as Richard Stanwood, at the time Burnett's director of creative services, would later recall, were meant to be "interruptive."[12]

At the screening of the new commercials, the Burnett people watched as the boxer told a disembodied voice that he was going to knock him "down for the count" for even suggesting a switch from the Schlitz label. The outdoorsman in one of the following commercials told his pet mountain lion to calm down after his choice of Schlitz beer was also challenged and snarled back to the animal, "Just a minute, babe. I'll handle this."

The group of fifteen Burnett creatives approved the series of commercials without objection as did Schlitz representatives who viewed the commercials soon after.

The reactions to the commercials once they went public were immediate—people hated them. Burnett officials were appalled at the reaction. Jack Powers, who managed the Schlitz account at Burnett, was stunned by the swift public response to the commercials. "I can assure you that we have no desire to threaten the people of the United States. It [the commercials] was supposed to be fun, tongue-in-cheek stuff."

At Schlitz, the feeling about the unexpected consumer backlash to the series of commercials was much worse. "A really great tragedy—really, really bad," a brewery spokesman admitted.[13]

Ten weeks after the commercials first began to air, Schlitz management ordered them pulled. Soon after, the Leo Burnett ad agency was fired by the Jos. Schlitz Brewing Company. The short-lived run of commercials would go down in advertising history as "The Drink Schlitz or I'll Kill You" ad campaign. As could be expected, the four ads did nothing to improve sales at Schlitz. Second quarter reports in 1978 indicated a 16.5 percent fall off in barrel shipments from the equally dismal 1977 numbers.

In October 1979, with a reported loss of $2.7 million for the first half of the year, the embattled Schlitz brewery finally admitted it was looking for a buyer. Since 1977, Schlitz had been mentioned as having been courted by R. J. Reynolds, Coca-Cola, and General Foods. The three hundred family members who owned about two-thirds of the common stock, however, had continued to bicker among themselves for the last few years about whether or not to sell the brewing business.

The estate plan of the Uihlein family called for giving sons their company shares outright, but to put their daughters' shares into trusts. Twenty years later, there were far more shares in trust than there were in the public market. While the dividends were being paid, there was some return that could justify inaction on the part of shareholders, but if the dividend payments were to be stopped, that would signal the necessity for a sale or merger of the company. In mid-1979, the paternalistic Schlitz board of directors helped the family shareholders make up their minds; they eliminated their dividend payments.

It was time to move on, and the Uihlein family shareholders now knew it. The remaining non-Uihlein shareholders quickly fell into line with family members. (The public market for Schlitz shares was actually created in the 1960s when the widow of an Uihlein wanted to liquidate her shares and the company's management at the time was not willing to "pay up" to what her counsel thought was a reasonable price per share.)

Brewery CEO McKeithan downplayed the move, announcing that the cessation in dividends was "to conserve the cash utilized for dividends for use in the business."[14]

"I think that [the dividend stoppage] was done to encourage recalcitrant family members to be more amenable to an offer," said Emanuel Goldman of Sanford C. Bernstein & Company.[15] An associate of the Uihlein family was more blunt in explaining the board's reasoning for the cessation of the dividend payments. By ending the dividends, any vacillation by shareholders as to the selling or not of the business would have been pointless. "A blood bath was the only way out."[16]

GEOCARIS VERSUS SCHLITZ

After years of poor sales of Schlitz products in Chicago, a revolving door of management changes in Milwaukee, bungled advertising, and continued rumors that the Jos. Schlitz Brewing Company was ripe for a takeover, Angelo Geocaris ended his franchise agreement with Schlitz in September 1981. The disgruntled Chicago distributor soon thereafter filed an arbitration demand with the American Arbitration Association in February 1982 to recover losses due to Schlitz's refusal to act accordingly. This end move came after repeated complaints by Caris, Associated, Inc., to Schlitz brewery representatives of poor quality beer.

The distributor's sudden line-in-the-sand legal action at this particular time and after years of unresponsiveness by Schlitz to his claims of indifference to their buyer-seller relationship seems more than coincidental. In June 1981, workers at the Schlitz Milwaukee plant had gone on strike. The reaction to the work stoppage by the Schlitz board was to close the old and inefficient plant, stopping the fiscal hemorrhaging at the Milwaukee brewery, and pave the way for the best possible price for the entire company by a potential buyer. In a sense, the brewery workers union played into the hands of Schlitz management. As the oldest, but tarnished, gem in the Schlitz crown of breweries, it was also the most costly to operate. The hard-nosed action by Schlitz management to close the old brewery so quickly seemed to ignore any possible repercussions by the Milwaukee brewery worker labor union or unfavorable hometown reactions.

For the people of Milwaukee, the closing of the local brewery was numbing, for some, an affront. Disgruntled Milwaukeeans started calling the hometown beer "Schlitz, the beer that made Milwaukee furious." But even today, the name "Schlitz" is still synonymous with the now Miller-dominated city of Milwaukee.

The cessation of dividend payments to shareholders, a majority of whom were family members, indicated the seriousness of Schlitz management in circling the fiscal wagons of the company. The abrupt action in closing the company's historic brewery and an increasing industry speculation of a takeover, coupled with high activity of Schlitz stock, caused rumors in the brewing industry that something soon might happen at Schlitz.

Geocaris might also have taken notice of the takeover speculation and been trying to avoid any third-party entanglements to his claims of compensation. If so, his fears would have been confirmed a month after he ended his franchise agreement with Schlitz. The G. Heileman Brewing Company of La Crosse, Wisconsin, was trying to buy Schlitz and the Schlitz board of directors and stockholders were ready to sign off on the deal.

In Chicago, Schlitz market share had dramatically dropped from about 40 percent in 1975 to around 13 percent in 1979. The sales decline had deeply affected Caris Associates, Incorporated. From 1976 to late 1981 when Geocaris finally pulled the plug on his franchise agreement with Schlitz, his company's sales of the Schlitz brand had plummeted 83 percent from 4.5 million cases yearly to 750,000.

The eleven other Schlitz distributors in the Chicago area had also experienced similar declining numbers but chose not to instigate legal proceedings towards Schlitz. "If we were to have done something against Schlitz, we should have done a class-action suit, worked together on it," said a longtime Schlitz distributor. "But, Geocaris was a lawyer. We go home and pat our kids on their heads. Lawyers go home and try to figure out how they can sue people."[17] As people who had been in the beer business for years, developing loyalties and friendships in the profitable road of local beer distribution, the majority of Chicago's Schlitz distributors reached a simple consensus, an old-time credo that stopped them from attacking Schlitz while the brewery tried to right itself. "Why bite the hand that feeds you," they asked?[18]

Following a lengthy series of legal arguments as to the arbitrability of Geocaris's claim, arbitration proceedings between Caris and Schlitz began in Minneapolis, Minnesota, but were concluded in Chicago in June 1984. Although the majority of the three-man panel agreed that any award would be judged as to Schlitz's failure "to make any adequate response to the disastrous product problems repeatedly brought to its attention by [Geocaris] and other Chicago wholesalers of Schlitz products—in effect 'stonewalling' the issue for over two and one-half years," they also concluded that Schlitz could not be held liable "for deficient product per se," as had been agreed upon by both parties in the franchise agreement.[19]

During the protracted legal battle, the Joseph Schlitz Brewing Company fell into the hands of the Stroh Brewing Company after the Justice Department thwarted the takeover of Schlitz by G. Heileman. New owner Stroh would challenge the arbitration ruling in the U.S. eighth Circuit Court of Appeals, but in 1986, the court reaffirmed the ruling of the panel of arbitrators that had awarded Geocaris damages of $2,094,665.91 for the years 1976, 1977, and half of 1978.

SCHLITZ TODAY

Ironically, the Schlitz label is now in the hands of the Pabst Brewing Company after the self-imposed closing of the family owned Stroh Brewing Company in 1999. Former Executive Vice President August ("Augie") Uihlein Pabst of the Pabst Brewing had tried to instigate a leveraged buyout of Schlitz back in 1981 after G. Heileman's initial takeover offer, but the weak Pabst offer of cash and high-interest debentures was shrugged off by the Uihlein-dominated Schlitz board of directors.

"I really think we could have pulled it off," argues Pabst to this day, reflecting on what could have been. "The first thing would have been to get rid of our New Jersey plant. The operating costs there were way too high and the plant was so hemmed in that there was no chance for expansion. We could have financially done better by closing the Newark brewery and actually shipping product from our brewery in Peoria, Illinois, to the East Coast.

"The next move would have been to sell Schlitz's [five] can manufacturing plants. Even at fire-sale prices, they would have easily brought in a minimum of $100 million; and then there was the Schlitz pension fund, somewhere around $160 million," and with the added cash in hand, a chance to retire most of the debentures.

One could speculate that the fact that Pabst was also a member of the extended Uihlein family should have added weight to his argument that a Schlitz takeover by the Pabst Brewing Company would have been a more viable alternative than selling out to competitors like Heileman or Stroh, but the Uihlein-dominated board of directors at Schlitz thought otherwise. "Some of the Schlitz board members were good people," said Pabst, "but the others were real leakers."[20]

In the hands of Stroh, the Schlitz label enjoyed a brief resurrection of the old gusto campaign, but Stroh management knew that the battle to bring back the tainted brand would be a difficult one. Peter W. Stroh, president and CEO of the Detroit, Michigan, based brewery was cautiously optimistic in rejuvenating Milwaukee's once most famous beer. "Schlitz sales have shown a long-term decline of more than twenty-five percent a year," Stroh admitted, "but we expect to see a bottoming out before the end of the year, and we're hopeful that sales will begin an upturn by next year."[21]

The Stroh Brewing Company, however, had just come off a down year, with total volume of product falling five hundred thousand barrels. The financial burden of the purchase of Schlitz by Stroh, at a cost of around $495 million, was accentuated with a series of labor problems that year. During the summer of 1982, while Stroh was trying to figure out how to digest the lumbering Schlitz and all its assets, including the Geyser Peak Winery in California, six of Stroh's seven breweries went on strike, summertime being the peak selling season for any brewery.

Although the multiple strikes didn't help Stroh's financial sheet for 1982, the mammoth Schlitz takeover was more burdensome than Stroh was prepared to handle and would haunt the Detroit-based company for years to come. "Physically," says Fil Graff, former editor of the Breweriana Collector *Journal*, "it was Schlitz that swallowed Stroh. The number of people and breweries that came with the deal buried the Stroh folks! [It] may have been Stroh in ownership, but it became a 'Schlitzy' company, and that was the beginning of the end for Stroh."[22]

Bob Bindley, now at Louis Glunz Beer, Incorporated, in Lincolnwood, Illinois, concurs that there was some difficulty in blending personnel from both breweries into one cohesive unit. "There was no problem getting the sales divisions together," recalls Bindley who was at Stroh at the time, "but Schlitz managers pretty much overwhelmed the management divisions at Stroh. There was some tension."[23]

Despite the 1982 losses, Stroh still planned to spend $70 million for advertising in 1983, with an emphasis on the acquired Schlitz brand. Stroh targeted its sales campaign for the "new" Schlitz in the Southeast and Southwest, areas that were fast becoming a major, and very competitive, beer battleground. The selling of Schlitz in the Midwest, where sales had once been at its greatest, was deferred until positive results could be seen in the brewery's southern region sales and marketing campaign. It appeared to be a temporary end run around the Midwest market where the brand had literally left a bad taste in the mouths of once-loyal Schlitz drinkers, avoiding what could have been a disastrous sales campaign from the very beginning.

But after continued problems trying to reestablish the brand with beer drinkers everywhere, the Schlitz label eventually suffered what might be considered years of neglect. A brewer from Stroh, asked about the lack of visibility in Chicago of the once famous Milwaukee label they now owned, admitted in 1991 that "There's virtually no advertising money thrown at the brand," and knew of no future plans to reinvigorate the label.

August Uihlein Pabst, still somewhat embittered by past events, opines that Stroh never really looked to rejuvenating the Schlitz label. "They needed the entry into the national market that Schlitz enjoyed. All Stroh really wanted to do was replace Schlitz beer with their brands."[24]

By the early 1990s, Schlitz sales had fallen to less than .05 percent of the retail beer market in Chicago, buttressing Pabst's argument.[25]

As pathetic as this figure would seem to indicate, the beer has made a surprising reemergence in a number of bars in Chicago in the last few years as a "retro" beer, now ordered by young beer drinkers who were mere babes when the brewery began its decline. A drive through trendy Wicker Park confirms a good number of Schlitz neon signs in the windows of the more progressive bars, but Schlitz beer can also be found on the drink menus of local watering holes as far south as Oak Lawn.

Earle Johnson, owner of the eclectic Quenchers Saloon at Fullerton and Western, finds that the almost-forgotten Schlitz brand serves a dual purpose at his establishment. "Schlitz beer is one of our budget brands but also gets a big call from our younger customers who look at the beer as a retro brand, the beer that their grandfathers drank."[26]

God's Country

We are fighting two very large companies
in the industry and it's important to
build a bigger and better company.
—*Russell Cleary, G. Heileman CEO*

THE LITTLE BREWERY THAT COULD

While the Joseph Schlitz Brewing Company was stumbling through the last troubled years of its proud existence, the La Crosse, Wisconsin, based G. (Gottlieb) Heileman Brewing Company was turning heads in Chicago with the widespread acceptance of its premium-priced Old Style brand. Its president, Russell Cleary, had also caught the attention of a number of smaller, regional breweries throughout the United States in a very effective manner—he bought them.

Founded in 1853 by Gottlieb Heileman, a frustrated brewer who had been unable to reach the status of *Braumeister* in his native Germany, the small brewery was one of scores of remaining regional breweries still in existence after the repeal of national prohibition. In 1957, when Roy E. Kumm was promoted to the role of president of Heileman, the brewery was ranked thirty-ninth among the country's dwindling number of small brewing operations. Its two brands were Old Style and Special Export, a super-premium priced beer that evolved from the Old Style brand in the early 1950s.

Impressed by the far-reaching and methodical business vision of his son-in-law, a young lawyer named Russell G. Cleary, and mixed with a healthy dose of nepotism, Kumm asked Cleary to join Heileman in 1960 as house counsel. In the next few years, the family team would begin to pick up several failing, or near failing, smaller breweries in Wisconsin and Minnesota. Its first major acquisition was in 1967 when it leapt beyond the North Woods to purchase the Weidemann Brewing Company in Newport, Kentucky, for a bargain-priced $5 million. With the wave of troubled regional breweries, at the time almost epidemic, the pickings were many.

Like Schlitz, the G. Heileman Brewing Company, with Cleary now entrenched as president after the death of Kumm in 1971, took advantage of the 1976 nationwide bottlers strike at Anheuser-Busch. The Old Style brand had already been grabbing an increasing portion of the retail market in Chicago before the A-B strike, but during the void left by the labor dispute, Heileman distributors aggressively rolled the beer from "God's Country" into new accounts in local taverns, liquor stores, and supermarkets to fill the empty space left by the A-B strike. "Cleary was smart enough to get in and fill the void," said Walter Baltz, a former Heileman executive, talking about the opportunity created in Chicago by the strike.[1]

Cleary's move to grab a larger piece of the Chicago market was also bolstered by the collapse of a decades-old practice of mutual support by Schlitz and Anheuser-Busch distributors in Chicago. During the sporadic labor problems that occasionally plagued both breweries, a gentleman's handshake between rival Chicago distributors ensured that the retail accounts of the brewery affected by a strike would be covered by the local distributors of their competitor. For instance, if Schlitz had problems, Chicago's A-B distributors would cover their retail accounts and vice-versa. After the strike concluded, the brewery that covered their competitor's accounts would give them back to the one with the settled union problems. Unfortunately for Schlitz and A-B, few tavern owners were willing to allow Schlitz, with their troublesome Milwaukee-brewed beer, to cover their Budweiser taps in Chicago in 1976. Most of these accounts were lost forever by Budweiser when the strike ended.

For G. Heileman, the A-B strike and the troubles with the Schlitz brand in Chicago were pure serendipity. Debbie Perminas, whose parents owned a small neighborhood tavern in Bridgeport during the labor dispute, remembers why her mother took on Old Style in favor of the more popular Budweiser brand. "The Bud driver would come in and tell my mother she could only have two cases for the week. Bud was rationing their beer because of the strike. Two cases. What kind of a living could you make on the profit of two cases of beer?"

It was this question, asked by the owners of hundreds of Chicago neighborhood watering holes, that local Old Style distributors took advantage of. The assault by G. Heileman in Chicago was overwhelming, going bottle by bottle, case by case, tavern by tavern. "The Old Style driver offered discounts and incentives like extra cases of beer. Buy ten cases, get two free—that sort of thing, or he'd give you a free half-barrel just to grab a spot on the tap," recalls Perminas. "My mom tossed the Bud salesman out."[2] To further this kind of campaign, both Old Style salesmen and beer truck drivers were given cash bounties of $50 or more if they brought back the tap handles of a rival brewery.

Some of the means used by Chicago beer truck drivers to push out rival brands, however, were less than subtle. An article in the *Chicago Tribune* described one particularly successful approach used by a driver/helper team in securing new beer accounts in the racially diverse neighborhoods of Chicago: "In the black areas, Old Style was represented as the beer sophisticated beer drinkers [white people] wanted, thus edging out the Schlitzes and Buds. In Bridgeport [a white area], Schlitz and Bud were tagged 'nigger' beer."[3]

Coupled with generous discounting of its Old Style product, the brand controlled 26 percent of the beer market in Chicago by 1978, with the toppled "King of Beers" at 11 percent, and the ailing Schlitz brand at 10 percent and falling.[4]

Discounting did seem to be a big part of Old Style's sudden popularity. "Consumers can be switched to another label, particularly if there's a substantial price differential," noted a manager at a local Armanetti liquor store at the time, and G. Heileman followed the low-price philosophy.[5] A small Foremost Liquors store on 35th and Damen did a phenomenal weekend business of cases of Old Style back in the late 1970s, using aggressive discounting. Every Friday morning, two full refrigerated trailers of Heileman's "double-krausened" beer would be unhitched from tractors and dropped off in the small lot behind the building. By late Sunday afternoon, it was not uncommon for the South Side liquor store to be out of the thousands of discounted cases of Old Style that had been delivered just forty-eight hours earlier.

Cleary's plans of even further expansion became increasingly evident in 1979 when he commented on the state of some troubled rival breweries, the numbers, of which, were growing. "We've got some fairly sick companies in the industry, and it's obvious that more consolidation will take place."[6] With this philosophy in mind, the brewery's president began looking for more distressed labels to complement his portfolio of six major brands—Old Style, Blatz, Rainier, Wiedemann, Schmidt, and the super-premium priced Special Export.

MARKET SEGMENTATION

The concept of market segmentation in the beer industry in the mid-to-late 1970s was not a new one. Virtually every first-and some second-tier breweries followed the marketing pattern of selling different beers at different prices, all complemented with liberal doses of diverse advertising to attract different consumer groups. The biggest brewers such as Anheuser-Busch, with its super-premium-priced Michelob, premium-priced Budweiser, and its cheaper Busch beer or the Schlitz Brewing Company, with its flagship Schlitz brand, its higher priced Erlanger, and its popular-priced Old Milwaukee, used this approach at a national level, where the idea of market and brand segmentation was most prevalent.

Heileman, without a national label or distribution system, nonetheless followed a similar practice at the regional level. To achieve this, they needed an interconnecting but independent network of breweries throughout the United States. For a small brewery like Heileman with its limited assets, the construction of new breweries to achieve this goal would have been cost prohibitive. When contemplating the purchase of Rainier Brewing Company during the mid-1970s in the state of Washington, for instance, Heileman eventually closed the deal for about $8 million. The brewery's estimated costs to build a similar-sized new brewery in the same market were projected to have been at least $50 million.

With this relatively cheap entry into a new market, Heileman also took an approach that few other conglomerate-minded brewers did when expanding their presence—they continued to produce the regional brand favorites. "We don't rush in and tear the sign off the building," said Cleary, explaining his wish to preserve the regional brands of the companies they had taken over. "People resent that. If we had done that at Rainier, for example, it would have been a disaster. Who ever heard of Heileman in Washington?"[7]

In a matter of time, however, Heileman would delicately cross-pollinate the new market with outside brands such as Blatz or Old Style, using the acquired company's distribution systems, supplemented with targeted advertising that appealed to local consumers. In Washington, Rainier was promoted as "Mountain Fresh." Schmidt beer from St. Paul was "The brew that grew with the Great Northwest." In Chicago, Old Style was the beer from "God's Country."

"They use the regionals to gain a foothold," said one industry observer. "Then they start rolling out their high profit brands."[8]

No one could argue that G. Heileman's business plan of acquisition and brand segmentation *wasn't* working, but it was the increasingly familiar charge by rival breweries that Cleary's plan of acquisition was his sole method of success, one critic calling Cleary "a rag picker."[9]

"It's something of a myth to say we do it all by acquisitions," argued Cleary. "In Chicago, it's been all one brand—Old Style."[10] Similar success could also be seen with the Special Export brand in neighboring Milwaukee.

In early 1980, the brewery's board of directors declared a dividend of 20 cents per share for the first quarter, an increase of 54 percent over 1979's first quarter. It was the forty-eighth consecutive year in which "The House of Heileman" had paid a cash dividend to its grateful shareholders. A year earlier, G. Heileman had passed the $500 million mark in sales, and the sales trend continued.[11]

The question soon arose, however, how long this sort of patchwork expansion could continue. "Oh, there are still a few situations out there," said Cleary, confident that his region-by-region march on troubled breweries still had life in it. "Time tends to ripen them; you have to let nature take its course." A short time later, G. Heileman picked up the 400,000-barrel capacity Duncan Brewing Company in Auburndale, Florida, a region that Cleary desperately wanted to conquer.[12]

HEILEMAN GOES NATIONAL

In early 1981, Russell Cleary determined that the nationally known Pabst Brewing Company was ripe for the plucking. The Milwaukee-based brewery had recently announced that it had moved to the number three sales position, displacing the ailing Schlitz. The overture by Heileman for Pabst was a clandestine one, the initial negotiations put together by dissident Pabst board member Irwin L. Jacobs, with encouragement from Cleary.

This takeover would have been Cleary's first bid at a brewery with national stature, and as such, he was willing to pay up to $45 per share for the almost 8.2 million shares of outstanding stock, or around $368 million. The most far-reaching brand that Heileman currently brewed was the earlier acquired Blatz label, with a presence in thirty-five states. The acquisition of Pabst would give G. Heileman 15.5 percent of the U.S. beer market, almost double its current share. The negotiations were tentative as the careful Heileman CEO worked with the dissident members of the Pabst board to come to a possible takeover settlement.

Pabst, however, was having its own problems. Sales had been slipping, and, as a result, the office of president and CEO also seemed to be fitted with a revolving door, mimicking the management problems at Schlitz. A proxy fight and attempted takeover by Jacobs and four seated Pabst board of directors brought attention to how troubled and tentative the leadership situation at Pabst had become. Pabst's ascension to the number three sales position in 1980 had also been revealed to be a bit of chicanery as it was soon discovered that Pabst had actually beat out Schlitz for the number three position by overshipping product to their distributors in the last quarter.

In early July 1981, Heileman abruptly lowered its bid for Pabst to around $24 a share after the announcement by the troubled Milwaukee brewery of another management change. Pabst immediately pulled out of negotiations with Heileman, commenting that the drastically reduced offer was "not even worth considering," but in October, new Pabst president and CEO William F. Smith Jr. reported that his brewery had a net loss of $2,495,000 for the first nine months of 1981.[13]

HEILEMAN AND SCHLITZ

Russ Cleary wasted no time in searching for another acquisition with national stature after the Pabst deal fell through. Heavy trading of Schlitz stock since April, along with a stock year-high price of Heileman shares, seemed to indicate that something might also be in the wind between Heileman and Schlitz, most likely at the same time that the La Crosse brewery had been in negotiations with Pabst. Coupled with the fact that the Schlitz board of directors had met an unprecedented nine times in 1980, the heavy stock trading of Schlitz in the spring of 1981 only added to industry speculation of a possible takeover and merger.

Cleary denied the rumors of a Heileman takeover of Schlitz, as he had done when asked of his intentions during the earlier Pabst negotiations. At Schlitz, however, the shareholders of Schlitz had had enough, especially after dividend payments had ceased. Frank J. Sellinger, the latest individual to assume the hot seat of CEO of Schlitz, played coy with reporters during a meeting on the morning of July 24, 1981, as to the validity of a rumor in Milwaukee that Schlitz and Heileman were holding serious discussions about a possible merger. Admitting that there was a dialog between the two brewing companies, he downplayed the importance of the talks, saying that the discussions were "consistent with (the company's) previously announced policy of exploring all possibilities concerning its business."[14]

Two hours after Sellinger's discussion with reporters in Milwaukee, Cleary reported that Heileman had made a proposal to buy Schlitz for $494 million, or around $17 a share in cash and stock, but emphasized that this move was not an agreement but strictly a proposal.

Industry insiders cheered the possible merger. The Schlitz acquisition would give Heileman a solid number three position in the national sales market behind Anheuser-Busch at number one, and the hard-charging Miller Brewing Company in the number two sales position. It would also double Heileman's market share to around 16 percent, still far below A-B's and Miller's combined market of nearly 50 percent and growing. More important, the merger would give Heileman a national presence.

Cleary was especially interested in the Schlitz beer and can-making operations in the southern part of the country and the huge California market. "They have some excellent production facilities in Tampa, Florida, Winston-Salem, North Carolina, Memphis [Tennessee], Longview, Texas, and in the Los Angeles area," he observed. With the possible merger, Heileman would also pick up the labels for Schlitz, Schlitz Light, the super-premium-priced Erlanger, Old Milwaukee, Old Milwaukee Light, and Schlitz Malt Liquor, and five aluminum plants with a combined capacity of 5 billion cans and lids.[15]

There was one little problem with the breweries combining their operations—they would need Uncle Sam's blessings. Back in 1973, after the acquisition of Associated Breweries, Incorporated, of Detroit, Heileman had agreed to a Justice Department mandate that the La Crosse-based brewery could not pick up another Midwest brewery for ten years without federal approval. This ruling was in deference to a 1968 federal guideline that was brought about to lessen the possibility of a brewing monopoly. This didn't seem to be a problem with a Heileman-Schlitz merger. With A-B controlling 28 percent of the market, and Miller, 21 percent, the merger would still leave the new conglomerate in the shadow of both industry leaders.

To add to G. Heileman's argument that the Justice Department should have no objection to the merger, Schlitz had announced the closing of its Milwaukee brewery, the only Midwest plant of the six nationwide Schlitz facilities. The closing would reduce the overall brewing capacity of Schlitz from 25.6 million to 18.8 million barrels, a significant reduction in capacity, but would also bring about a needed savings for the underutilized nationwide operation which had sold only 14.9 million barrels in 1980. The shutdown seemingly would also lessen any objection by the Justice Department to Heileman picking up another Midwest brewery within the mandated ten-year restriction.[16]

SCHLITZ ACCEPTS

On July 27, 1981, Schlitz agreed in principle to accept the offer from the G. Heileman Brewing Company for $492 million in cash and stock. While Russ Cleary was happy to talk about the merger to anyone who'd listen, family officials at Schlitz declined to comment on the merger. "I can't judge the psychological state of the Uihlein family," said an analyst at Paine Webber Mitchell Hutchins, Incorporated, but there's no doubt that just the thought of the sale of the family owned operation had a profound effect on the brewery clan.

David Uihlein, one of the largest holding Schlitz shareholders and the man who many had assumed would take over as CEO after the death of Robert Uihlein Jr. in 1976, would later comment about the closing of the Milwaukee plant, the first step in the dissolution of the brewing empire, "I wish I could say more than that it's sad," reflecting just a hint of the emotional devastation of the family to the proposed brewery sale.[17]

The consensus in the overall brewing community of the proposed merger, however, was one of balance. By merging an aggressive smaller sized Midwestern brewery with a troubled, but still strong, national giant with a huge presence in the South, industry observers praised the move. "[It] seems like a marriage made in heaven," said beer analyst Robert S. Weinberg. An analyst from the Sanford C. Bernstein & Company in New York was even more enthusiastic about the event.

"It's a super-merger," opined Emmanuel Goldman. "It gives them [Heileman] the geographic balance that they needed."

Weinberg, however, added a caveat to his observation, noting that Heileman's fourteenth acquisition in its long brewing history might be Cleary's last hurrah. "There's not much left for him to pick over for other acquisitions."[18]

PABST, THE SPOILER

In an unexpected merger proposal that that would have industry insiders scratching their heads, Pabst Brewing Company challenged the Schlitz-Heileman merger, just days after Schlitz had agreed in principle to Heileman's proposal. Thomas N. McGowen Jr., who was serving as interim president and CEO of Pabst after a recent management shakeup forced the resignation of Frank C. DeGuire, submitted the maverick brewery's proposal to the Schlitz board of directors on Monday, August 3.

The Pabst proposal raised the eyebrows of more than a few when the brewery offered $200 million in cash and $388 million in debentures, which would have an interest rate of 15.5 percent and could be convertible to Pabst common stock at $27 per share.[19]

A war of words soon escalated between Heileman's Cleary and Pabst CEO, McGowen. "We are proceeding with Schlitz to prepare a definite merger agreement," said Cleary, and then questioned the value of the Pabst counteroffer of $588 million, $94 million more than the Heileman offer.

McGowen countered that Cleary's statements were "patently gratuitous and self-serving," and that the Heileman bid reflected its own self-interest.[20]

What the public didn't realize at the time was Heileman's earlier offer to buy Pabst. As a result of the attempted Pabst takeover, Cleary knew the precarious financial condition not only at Schlitz, but also at Pabst as well. "It is hard to believe that the debentures will trade at par value in view of the recent unprofitable operations of Pabst and Schlitz," he said. In addition, Heileman's CEO suggested that a Pabst takeover of Schlitz would probably be taxable to Schlitz shareholders as a capital gain based on the difference between the cost basis of Schlitz stock and the value of the proposed Pabst debentures. Cleary probably suspected that this subject would definitely draw the attention of the frugally minded members of the Uihlein family who held most of the brewery's stock. Despite the family's long record of philanthropic endeavors, the Uihleins had a nagging reputation for stinginess. "The company hasn't been paying dividends for several years now, and you'd think to hear some of them talk that they'd have to go on food stamps," a family friend had commented.[21]

A Milwaukee brewing industry analyst agreed that a merger between Schlitz and Pabst offered little advantage to either party. "They're talking about combining two entities which have had less than gilt-edged performances in recent years. And there are no indications that either Pabst or Schlitz will be able to improve their operations in the near future."[22]

On October 21, 1981, the entire argument would become moot.

THE JUSTICE DEPARTMENT STEPS IN

As shareholders of Schlitz made ready for a November 13 special meeting in Chicago to vote on the Heileman-Schlitz agreement, the Justice Department chose a startling time to flex its federal authority. In what was the first attempt by the Reagan administration to block a corporate merger, the government agency announced it would fight the merger agreement on the grounds that the combination of the companies might lessen competition in the U.S. brewing industry.

Heileman CEO Cleary immediately lambasted the government's decision to launch an antitrust suit against Heileman and Schlitz. He argued that a reversal of the proposed merger would only strengthen the dominating positions of Anheuser-Busch and Miller, with the anticipation that the two brewing giants might soon approach a combined 60 percent of the beer sales market. "I think this is important to the survivorship of Heileman and Schlitz," said Cleary. "We are fighting two very large companies in the industry and it's important to build a bigger and better company."[23]

Schlitz's D. F. McKeithan put on his best face when he said that "we were pursuing a business combination that would enhance competition in the industry" but the shareholder meeting in Chicago to finalize the deal with Heileman was abruptly canceled, indicating that he realized the futility of opposing the government on the merger.[24]

Beer industry analysts joined in the argument. John Collopy of Robert W. Baird & Company called the antitrust suit "strange, to say the least." Donald W. Rice, of Blunt Ellis & Loewi, Incorporated, commented that the government action was "a little mind-boggling . . . they're one-hundred percent wrong on the competition question. At this point, Schlitz is competition to no one. Putting the companies together would only enhance competition."[25]

A New Approach

It became apparent, however, that if the merger attempt went any further, the Justice Department would follow through with a threatened lawsuit. Publicly, Russell Cleary took the threat of the government's antitrust proceedings with subdued bravado, but not for long. "The Department of Justice approved the sale of Schlitz's largest and newest plant at Syracuse, New York to Anheuser-Busch in February, 1980. It is difficult to understand how the Department could now deny the combination of Heileman in the North and Schlitz in the South that would enable these two companies to effectively compete on a national basis with Anheuser-Busch and Miller," he argued.[26]

The Heileman CEO then tried a humble soft-sell approach, still holding out hope that the government would eventually acknowledge the proposed merger as "pro competitive" and come around to his way of thinking. "The people who are in trouble will have to exit the [brewing] industry," said Cleary, months later in a meeting with investment analysts in Chicago. By going forward with his plans to purchase the smaller and weaker breweries that were falling to the wayside, Cleary hoped to position Heileman as "the one viable solution to [establishing] that third major brewer that has to challenge Anheuser-Busch and Miller." Holding himself and his brewery as the only possible solution to a situation that might become a virtual brewing oligarchy, Cleary invoked that "someone has to lead that second tier group [of breweries] or you'll end up with an auto industry on your hands."[27]

Turning from the merger problems for a moment, the Heileman CEO cited the brewery's continued record of growth in a later speech to the members of the Investment Analysts Society of Chicago. Heileman's earnings for 1981 were $40.2 million on sales of $932 million, or $3.05 per share, buttressing his very public argument that Heileman was indeed the financial remedy to the ailing Schlitz. Included in his presentation was a report from the A. C. Nielson Company, showing that Old Style had achieved a commanding 36 percent of beer sales in Chicago.

Privately, however, Cleary was worried. Walter Baltz, a member of Heileman management at the time, remembered Cleary's reaction when they received notice that the Justice Department was threatening a possible antitrust suit against the Heileman-Schlitz merger. "Walter, I think this does not bode well for the future," recalled Baltz. "I think he had a premonition at that point."

George Smith, treasurer at Heileman, also marked the Justice Department action as the beginning of the end for Cleary and his brewery. "That broke our back," Smith later conceded.[28]

≁ 21 ≁

Heileman Marches On

Now we can all get back to what
we do best and that is sell beer.
—*Russell Cleary after
acquiring parts of Pabst*

HEILEMAN AND PABST, PART II

If Cleary really felt the end was coming, as his associates thought he
did, one wouldn't have known it. In mid-1982, dissident Pabst board
member Irwin Jacobs and his followers announced that they would
tender $24 cash for any and all stock of the Pabst Brewing Company,
the same price that the Pabst board of directors had rejected from G.
Heileman in 1981 as not worth considering. With the continued fiscal
problems at Pabst since then, the offer must now have looked awfully
good to nervous shareholders.

Contingent on the success of the Jacob group takeover, the Pabst
board dissidents publicly announced that G. Heileman would purchase
their Pabst plants in Newark, New Jersey, and Perry, Georgia. Heileman
would also be licensed by Pabst to control all rights to Pabst brands
in the states east of the Mississippi, except Wisconsin, Illinois, and
Indiana—the areas of Pabst highest popularity—and the additional
states of Arkansas, Louisiana, Texas, and Oklahoma, west of the Mississippi, for $135 million.

The deal seemed somewhat awkward and contrived. Why not simply
buy all of the Pabst Brewing Company as Cleary had tried to do in
1981? The Justice Department, however, had once again stepped in to
thwart G. Heileman's dreams of nationwide expansion. "We have not
given up our efforts to persuade the Department that a combination
of Heileman and Pabst in total is pro-competitive," Cleary argued,
taking a page from his earlier Heileman-Schlitz merger proposal

argument, "but we have to protect Heileman from the eventuality that the Department will not permit Heileman to acquire Pabst and instead will stand by and let Pabst become weaker, perhaps beyond being revitalized."[1]

The bastardized proposal and its advantages to the House of Heileman were obvious. If approved by the fed, the Georgia location would give G. Heileman a modern plant and an added presence in the southeast. The New Jersey site was felt by Heileman to offer an extensive distribution network in the northeast where the Wisconsin brewery had a low market share.

For Pabst, the selling-off of the two plants, especially the Newark operation that was considered a white elephant by members of Pabst management, and the relinquishing of rights in various markets, meant a much needed cash infusion, and in effect, would create a smaller and leaner, "new" Pabst Brewing Company, a first step toward its existence today as a "virtual" brewer.

Once again, however, the Department of Justice stepped in to spoil Cleary's plans. Frustrated again, the G. Heileman CEO stated an obvious fact, one that Justice seemingly had to acknowledge. "We are the only strong second tier contender in the brewing industry. Heileman has the demonstrated ability to turn around declining brands and we can only hope that at some point, sensible business arrangements to acquire brands, distribution and capacity, will be approved rather than our having to acquire the wreckage."

As if to back up Cleary's statement, the brewery announced record earnings for the second quarter of 1982, the thirtieth consecutive quarterly sales and earnings increase.[2]

OLYMPIA BEER

In the mid-1970s, Oly Gold, a new low-calorie beer from the Olympia, Washington-based Olympia Brewing Company, started appearing in the Chicago area. It was considered unusual by industry analysts to find a low-calorie beer preceding its original, full-calorie beer into a market, especially a market as huge as Chicago's, but Olympia wanted to take advantage of the new light beer craze. In a few short years, light beer had gone from a zero share to 8 percent of the national market.

Chicago was one market where the appearance of light beer had quickly been accepted by traditional beer drinkers but the movement toward light beer was also seen by industry insiders as cannibalizing the sales of regular beer.

Lite beer from Miller had started this light beer trend and everyone was scrambling to come up with its own equivalent low-calorie/low-carbohydrate beer, often at the expense of their regular brands. With a zero market share in Chicago before the arrival of Oly Gold, the West Coast brewery had nothing to lose and everything to gain with the initial entry of its low-calorie product in Chicago.[3]

In March 1978, regular-brewed Olympia beer finally did make its way to Chicago, courtesy of the brewery's St. Paul, Minnesota, plant, the former home of the Theodore Hamms Brewing Company. Olympia had picked up the regional brewery, cartoon bear and all, in 1975. Olympia's marketing efforts in Chicago were commendable. Months after Olympia's entry into Chicago, the company was busy sponsoring the "World of Blues," a presentation of top blues talent at the first Chicagofest, a community entertainment event that would evolve some years later into the city's annual Taste of Chicago.

Mike Schmidt, the Midwest region manger for Olympia, proudly presented an Oly baseball cap to Mayor Michael Bilandic during opening day ceremonies for Chicagofest and made the best of all the free media publicity he could garner. During the next few years of its rising popularity, Olympia would try hard to imbue its brands with Chicagoans by organizing a yearly "Chicago Sports Hall of Fame." Local beer drinkers were asked to cast their ballots for Chicago sports legend nominees such as White Sox Nellie Fox, Blackhawk Stan Mikita, and Bear Sid Luckman. Members of the Nominating Committee consisted of local media, political, and business illuminaries, including newspaper columnists Irv Kupcinet, Bill Gleason, State Representative Jesse White, and businessman Larry Mages, who owned a chain of Chicagoland sports equipment stores. It was a contrived event, but garnered a healthy dose of local goodwill for the out-of-town brewery.[4]

But by late 1982, Olympia found itself heading in the same direction that scores of regional breweries had since the end of World War II, no longer scrambling for market share but for survival.

The Heileman, Pabst, Olympia Swap-a-Thon

After the G. Heileman Brewing Company opened up a Governmental Affairs Office in Washington, DC, to lobby legislators and regulators, things started to turn around in the episodic battles between government officials and Russell Cleary's dreams of nationwide expansion. In a multistage series of negotiations, mergers, spin-offs, and outright swaps of breweries that quietly began in the late fall of 1982, G. Heileman and Pabst announced at 12:01 A.M., December 23, 1982, that the merger of the two breweries was proceeding. G. Heileman had acquired and retained over 6.5 million shares of Pabst stock. With this stage of the deal complete, Heileman would now control a part of Pabst and, in a step-two move, also pick up a portion of Olympia Brewing Company assets, with the remainder of Olympia going to the "new" Pabst. Pabst had already made a prior tender offer to Olympia on June 1, 1982, picking up 49 percent of Oly's common stock.

This particular part of the swap-a-thon, however, caused a later problem for G. Heileman in mid-1983. The Securities and Exchange Commission sued Heileman, charging the brewery with buying 105,000 common shares of Olympia after Cleary had received advance information on April 19, 1982, from Robert Schmidt, president of Olympia, that Pabst was ready to make a move to acquire his Washington-based brewery. Heileman settled with the SEC and paid a fine of $916,378 but neither admitted nor denied the charge of insider trading.[5]

When this part of the takeover was completed, Heileman would own the Pabst brewing plant at Perry, Georgia; the old Blitz-Weinhard Brewery in Portland, Oregon; and the Olympia-owned Lone Star facility in San Antonio, Texas. With the possession of these breweries, the La Crosse operation would own the following brands: Blatz and its popular-priced brands, Henry Weinhard, Private Reserve, Red White & Blue, Burgermeister, Lone Star, and Buckhorn. Heileman also picked up a quick $30 million in the deal.

With these acquisitions, Heileman now had an overall brewing capacity of 25 million barrels, a bigger presence in the South where they thus far had only 2 percent of the market, and an extraordinarily large group of 2,400 distributors to funnel a wide variety of products to thirsty customers.

The "new" Pabst would continue to brew and sell the P.B.R. brand, Jacob Best Premium Light, the malt liquor Olde English 800, and its Andeker Super Premium, and would pick up the Olympia and Hamms brands. Pabst would also continue to own the Milwaukee plant, the one in Newark it had been trying to unload, Olympia's Washington facility, and Oly's plant in St. Paul, Minnesota—the old Theodore Hamms plant. After the dust cleared, Russell Cleary said of the successful merger, "Now we can all get back to what we do best and that is sell beer."[6]

There was one problem with this realignment of brewing companies, however. Pabst already had a presence in the Midwest market with its Milwaukee plant. The St. Paul plant, picked up from Olympia, was geographically redundant. Pabst had also lost a presence in the South when it gave up its Georgia plant.

In the meantime, Stroh Brewing Company had a problem with its Tampa, Florida, plant. As a stipulation to acquiring Schlitz, Stroh had agreed to a 1982 federal court order to divest itself of a plant in the southeast to win final approval from the federal government.

The solution to the dilemmas faced by Pabst and Stroh was solved in a government-sanctioned agreement by the two brewers to do a straight swap of their problematic plants. In doing so, Pabst regained a southeastern regional presence after losing its Georgia operation. Stroh, in the meantime, had been trucking its flagship product and the acquired Schlitz brands from its Detroit and Memphis breweries into the Twin Cities market at considerable costs. The acquisition of the St. Paul plant took care of this financially draining transportation problem for Stroh and thus began the first round of that perennial question by U.S. beer drinkers—"Which brewery owns what?"[7]

CLEARY'S SOUTHERN CAMPAIGN

After years of battling the windmills of federal regulations, Cleary was one step closer to what he had what he always wanted, a true national presence. The Georgia plant was a real prize. Virgin territory meant the chance to continue G. Heileman's relentless plan of expansion. "When you buy a battleship," said Cleary, "you start a war." Like Sherman did so many years before, Cleary readied his sales force for a cut-and-burn campaign through Georgia and beyond.

Roland Amundson of the Minnesota Beer Wholesalers Association called Cleary's southern strategy, "a real dogfight" for various reasons.[8] Anheuser-Busch had acquired a commanding market share of around 40 percent in the region. Miller was slipping in certain areas but still came in with 27 percent of the area's retail beer market. Even Coors had joined the battle after the family owned brewery finally decided to leave the isolation of its single western market.

As before Cleary's proven sales strategy was simple but direct: Keep the regional favorites, flood the market with a number of acquired brands in Heileman's overflowing portfolio, throw in a couple of popular-priced brands for those beer drinkers who cared more for price than brand, and slowly introduce the premium-priced Old Style to the region. While A-B and Miller went head-to-head with their flagship brands, Heileman would continue to nibble on the toes of the giants with an extensive portfolio of acquired brands.

PROBLEMS EMERGE

Russ Cleary's wide-ranging national balancing act of maintaining small-and middle-sized regional breweries started to show signs of weakening, beginning in November 1984 when the G. Heileman Brewing Company announced that it was dropping its fourteen-year relationship between its Old Style brand and the Chicago office of the ad agency Campbell-Mithun (C-M). The agency had been responsible for the very popular and branded "Pure Brewed in God's Country" campaign. C-M would continue to handle other Heileman brands such as Blatz, Mickey's Malt Liquor, and Special Export, but the Old Style account was to be moved to the Ogilvy & Mather firm in San Francisco, thousands of miles from the brand's core constituency.

John Pedace, the executive vice president of marketing for Heileman, explained away the move by claiming that he simply felt it was time for a change in the handling of Old Style advertising. In Chicago, Old Style was still a strong brand, estimated to control around 30 percent of the local beer retail market. The beer was so popular, in fact, that it was often quipped locally that Old Style was used in Chicago baptisms.

Sales, however, had fallen sharply from a peak estimate of 44 percent of the beer market in 1982. In addition to this downward trend in Chicago, sales were also showing signs of slowing elsewhere.[9]

A little over a week after the announcement by Heileman of the ad agency switch, the brewery hit the local headlines again. C & K Distributors, Incorporated, the largest wholesaler of Old Style beer in Chicago, had filed a lawsuit against the Wisconsin brewery. The suit, filed in U.S. District Court, sought $26 million in punitive damages, alleging that G. Heileman was planning to terminate its wholesaler's agreement with C & K because the local distributor had agreed to also handle Coors beer in Chicago.

Heileman, however, avoided mentioning the Coors deal but instead claimed that the termination notice was actually a result of C & K not properly maintaining their accounts and, as a result, causing a subsequent drop in their sales. Considering the fact that sales of Old Style were dropping in almost all of Heileman's markets, the termination threat had a "shoot the messenger" ring to it. In the suit, C & K argued that "between fiscal years 1973 and 1984, C & K has increased its sales of Heileman products in Chicago from $2.9 million to a peak of $54 million," and claimed itself "the number one beer wholesaler" of the brewery's network of around 2,400 distributors throughout the country.

Also named in the lawsuit were Southwest Beer Distributors, Incorporated, and the Sheridan Beverage Company. C & K alleged that these rival distributors had conspired with Heileman to force out C & K and split their territory with the two competitors.[10]

The brewery backed down on its threat to break the wholesaler's agreement with C & K before the target date of January 1, 1985. Heileman announced in early 1985 that it was going to continue to abide by the agreement as C & K simultaneously agreed to drop its suit. No monies were exchanged, and after both fighting parties went back to their respective corners, the distribution of Old Style in Chicago continued as usual.[11]

Results of G. Heileman's earnings report for the first quarter of 1985 showed why the brewery seemed to be reacting to market conditions since the ad agency shake up in late 1984. For the first quarter of 1985, earnings were down 49 percent from the earnings of the first quarter of the previous year. Sales during the same period were down 6 percent.

Russ Cleary assured shareholders that margins would improve in the next three quarters as price increases and cost control measures kicked in, and blamed the downturn on the cost of launching new products and a further expansion in the Midwest and Northwest regions. But when the numbers for the first half of 1985 came out, earnings were shown to be off a disappointing 12 percent, compared to the first half of 1984.[12]

OLD STYLE LOSES CHICAGO MARKET SHARE

Since its peak in local popularity in 1982, there could be no doubt that by 1985, Old Style beer was steadily losing market share in Chicago. There was no single reason as to why this was happening in the city with a long history of being such a beer-drinking town. Someone once said that there's no accounting for taste, but an argument can be made that during the mid-1970s through the 1980s, the palates of local beer drinkers were changing—evolving, one could even argue.

But why? And how?

One reason the beer market was changing had to do with the evolving collective consciousness of a more worldly and prosperous population—a first sign of globalization. Whether it was a tour of duty in South Vietnam, South Korea, the Philippines, West Germany, England, Spain, Italy, or elsewhere, ex-GIs were returning to the states with remembrances of new taste experiences brought on by their enjoyment of unique foreign cuisine, often washed down with fuller and richer tasting beers than found at their corner tavern.

College programs were being expanded to include a semester or two overseas to broaden the cultural development of American students, also including opportunities to experience new food and drink in the host countries.

Tourists, who were now traveling in record numbers to exotic locales or simply to locations as close as neighboring Canada, Mexico, or any one of the Caribbean countries as airline carrier ticket prices dropped, found themselves confronted with wide selections of crisp Canadian ales, rich Mexican lagers, and even hearty Jamaican stouts.

It was the beginning of a global market, including the beer market.

Brewers and importers had picked up on strong market indicators that there were a growing number of domestic beer drinkers who wanted something different than their everyday beer and would be willing to pay the price for new taste experiences. As a result, the import beer category started taking off. From a total of 27,583,915 gallons of beer brought into the United States in 1970, the figure had risen to an astounding 141,588,868 gallons in 1980, with no signs of leveling off.[13]

The domestic brewing industry came back to challenge the growing import market with a variety of super-premium-priced beers. Schlitz had its Erlanger. Anheuser-Busch, of course, had its Michelob but had also been test marketing the German-brewed Wurzburger beer, brewed by Wurzburger Hofbrau AG but bottled domestically by A-B. Miller was pushing its new Miller Special Reserve. Stroh was expanding the distribution territory for their first ever, super-premium-priced product, Signature beer.

Chicago was especially targeted by the Detroit brewery as a key market for their new higher priced beer. "Chicago," said Kohn Bissell, Stroh vice president for marketing at the time, "is one of the top super premium markets in the nation. This is a cosmopolitan city whose residents can readily identify with our advertising message—'Signature is something different.'"

With the super-premium-priced beers came the higher margins for any retailer who took on these new brews. As was demonstrated in Chicago during the 1940s and 1950s, retailers had dropped cheaply priced Chicago brands for the higher priced and higher margined Milwaukee and St. Louis beers. A growing number of local liquor store, restaurant, and tavern owners of the mid-1980s were once again willing to drop or limit their inventory of lower-margined brews—including the highly-discounted Old Style label—in favor of more profitable beers. Retailers started to limit the size of their orders of Old Style, keeping enough on hand for their steady Old Style customers, but smaller orders indicated that this group was dwindling.

Near the top of this pyramid of local beer drinkers with different or evolving tastes was a very small group of individuals who found satisfaction with the crafted products of small breweries. In 1973, Mike Royko, a columnist, at the time working for the now defunct *Chicago Daily-News*, conducted a taste test that indicated a preference by a sizable audience of local beer drinkers toward beers with character, at the time found only in the beer portfolios of the diminishing number of small regional breweries.

Added to the changing taste pattern of Chicagoland beer drinkers for richer, full-bodied beers was the dichotomy of a growing sector of local beer drinkers who were accepting light beer as their drink of choice. Whether this group consisted of women watching their figures, jocks, or people who figured a low-calorie beer meant they could drink twice as much beer as before, light beer wasn't going away. Its popularity was growing in Chicago by leaps and bounds.

BIRTH OF LIGHT BEER

Popular beer folklore states that the first low-carbohydrate beer was formulated and marketed by New York's Rheingold Brewing Company during the mid-1960s. However, a look through the brewing trade journals of the 1930s and 1940s suggest evidence that American brewers were working with the low-calorie/low-carbohydrate concept at least twenty-five years earlier.

After the end of national prohibition in 1933, brewers began actively courting women as potential beer drinkers. In order to sway women away from the sweet cocktails of the Prohibition era, many American breweries had reformulated their beers from the stronger and richer brews of the pre-Prohibition era and settled for lighter beers with a sweeter taste profile. Some breweries, like the Pilsen Brewing Company in Chicago, even advertised their products as "non-fattening." Pilsen's Yusay brand was actually promoted during the late 1930s and early 1940s with the advertising tag line, "It's The Right Weigh!" Articles in local newspapers during this period often quoted wide-girthed *Braumeisters* who ironically pointed out the low-caloric features of their products, the focus being on female beer drinkers.

Most men at the time probably ignored this information, but they weren't the real targeted audience anyway. With the hoopla that surrounded the return of legal beer, men were accepted as the core market of beer drinkers. Women, a demographic group ignored by brewers before national prohibition, were the new consumer target, now to be courted by American breweries.

Rheingold's Gablinger brand tried to achieve a broader market share with more than just cute advertising, however. They actually "reformulated" their flagship brand in 1967 by adding water to their full-strength beer. No one was fooled by this bit of brewing chicanery, neither women nor an emerging new segment of beer drinkers, health and sports enthusiasts. In short time, the age of sugar-free, low-calorie, and low-carbohydrate food items was upon us, not only in the beer industry but also in the food and soda pop trades.

About the same time that Gablinger was tanking in the retail market with an undrinkable product, beer scientists discovered an enzyme that could convert most of the non fermentable sugars in beer to alcohol. By converting these residual sugars to additional alcohol, the caloric and carbohydrate contents of the beer were lowered. In a final step, the additional alcohol was drawn off, leaving a product that had a fuller taste profile than a noxious beer and water blend.

LITE BEER FROM MILLER

In 1972, the beleaguered Meister Brau, Incorporated, in Chicago sold off most of its beer formulas, trademarks, brands, and labels to the Miller Brewing Company of Milwaukee. Backed by the deep pockets of parent company Philip Morris, Incorporated, and the formula for Meister Brau Lite, the low-calorie/low-carbohydrate beer became known as Lite Beer from Miller.

For a while, the introduction of light beer appeared to be a hard battle in capturing the attention of a sizable number of male beer drinkers. Lite Beer from Miller, and the few other low-calorie/low-carbohydrate beers in the retail beer market, had image problems. Not only was taste an issue, but this new beer style was viewed by hardcore male beer drinkers as wimpy, a women's drink. One industry insider took the argument a step further, actually labeling it as a "fag" beer. But in the emerging era of athletes like Jim Fixx and the success of his running philosophy, a plethora of new health foods, diet sodas, and sugar-free candies, Lite beer started to find an audience.

After a test marketing of Lite Beer from Miller in the blue-collar town of Anderson, Indiana, the beer tested positively. Moved to the national market, the beer continued to test well. There was still, however, the lingering perception that it was a woman's drink—or something worse. Enter the now familiar string of television endorsements by ex-jocks. With the amusing commercials ("Less Filling! Taste Great!") as its first line of assault, Miller began relentlessly pushing Lite beer, buying unprecedented amounts of national TV airtime during sporting events to further the market.

It was only a matter of time before Lite Beer from Miller was perceived by American male beer drinkers as a beer with balls, but with hybrid appeal. It became a man's drink. Health enthusiasts looked at its low-calorie/low-carbohydrate attributes and started to buy. Women liked it because it was promoted as "Less Filling!"

This advance by the light beer segment—currently at around 50 percent of total annual beer sales—even started to effect the taste and richness of regular-brewed beer. Claims Bob Bindley, formerly of the Stroh Brewing Company, "Virtually every brewery has toned down the taste and body of their product line in the last twenty-five years or so in order to approach some of the taste characteristics of light beer."[14]

And there, somewhere in the middle of the changing tastes of Chicagoans, was Heileman's Old Style beer.

What Goes Around, Comes Around

The plight of the Old Style label in Chicago seems to demonstrate a reoccurring phenomenon seen over and over with brands once popular in Chicago. Although one can argue of the apparent blind loyalty of some beer drinkers toward a particular beer brand, unfavorable events or circumstances often appear to trigger a rapid mass exodus by beer drinkers from the once comfortable embrace of the doomed beer.

Looking back over the last fifty years or so, Blatz beer, especially its Old Heidelberg brand, was once a particular favorite in post-World War II Chicago. Today, the Blatz labels are popular-priced (cheap) brands in the Pabst portfolio. Pabst Blue Ribbon was a premium-priced brand that Chicagoans called their own during the post-WWII years. It's now relied upon by neighborhood taverns as an affordable beer that can be sold to tight-fisted pensioners for as little as $1.50 a bottle.

As seen with the Schlitz label, aside from pockets of support in Chicago for the brand as a retro beer, it's become nothing more than another cheap beer, passed on from Stroh to Pabst like an unwanted stepchild.

What middle-aged Chicagoan can't recall the local popularity of Hamm's beer and the slapstick antics of its cartoon bear, once seen in black & white, and later color commercials, between innings of White Sox games during the 1950s and early 1960s?

In the last fifty years, virtually every one of these beers could lay claim to having once been called "Chicago's favorite." Each one of them, however, fell victim to failed advertising campaigns, bungled managerial decisions, competition, price wars, mergers, and a subsequent fall in sales. With the demonstrated rise and fall of these once favorite local brands, with Old Style being the most recent victim in Chicago, it remains to be seen which popular contemporary brands will follow.

"No, Mr. Bond.
I Expect You to Buy!"

"The Chicago market is
a real battleground."
—*Russell Cleary*

CLEARY SELLS HEILEMAN

From late 1985 through most of 1987, G. Heileman's business once again began to show stability, even signs of further growth in the national beer market. The brewery's non brewing operations, which consisted mostly of ten regional baking plants, snack producers, and a precision jet engine parts manufacturer, helped push Heileman sales to record levels. In 1986, second quarter earnings of the Heileman operation reached a new all time record of $20.24 million, an increase of 8 percent over the same quarter in 1985.

Russ Cleary was very pleased with the 1986 numbers and indicated that margins would continue to improve. Accompanying this gratifying news, the board declared a dividend of 13 cents per share, the fifty-fourth consecutive year that Heileman had rewarded its shareholders.[1]

As usual, the La Crosse-based brewery was still out looking for further acquisitions. On December 3, 1986, Cleary announced the purchase of the Champale trademark from Champale, Incorporated, a subsidiary of Iroquois Brands, Limited. "The addition of the Champale Malt Liquors . . . Extra Dry, Pink, Golden and Metbra Non-Alcoholic beer . . . along with the successful cooler lines, including Pineapple Coconut, Strawberry, Citrus and Orange PLUS, the recently introduced Fireside Coolers, are a welcome addition to the Heileman family of specialty beverage products. We intend to reestablish the Champale line on a national basis and will immediately begin the distribution of all Champale products," boasted Cleary.[2]

Without skipping a beat, the brewery moved quickly in 1987 to also pick up labels from the Christian Schmidt Brewing Company. With a payment of $23,530,000, Schmidt's, Schmidt's Light, Rheingold, Knickerbocker, Bavarian, Duquesne, and the Ortlieb brands moved into Heileman's extensive portfolio and in doing so, afforded further penetration in the Eastern United States markets, including Pennsylvania, New York, New Jersey, Ohio, and Connecticut.[3]

Momentarily quieting down critics who felt that Cleary's years of expansion had simply focused on sucking the remaining life out of dying regional breweries, Cleary and a beaming Seattle Mayor Charles Royer dedicated a $12 million expansion of the draft beer department at the Rainier Brewing Company in Washington in August 1987.[4]

But all of these acquisitions and brewery improvements from 1986 through mid-1987 had a feeling of hollowness about them. Russell Cleary's dream of acquiring a national brand had been crushed by the federal government in 1981 with his attempt to merge with the Schlitz Brewing Company. The Pabst deal in 1982/1983 had also been bastardized by government intervention. The newest additions to the Heileman portfolio of regional brands did nothing to help Heileman achieve national status but did enhance the value of the brewery's overall portfolio, something that might catch the eye of a potential suitor.

To support that argument, there was an odd dividend distribution made by Heileman's board of directors in the early part of 1987, right before the latest flurry of acquisitions, that would ring prophetic in the next few months. The board had declared a dividend distribution of one Series A Preferred Stock Purchase Right on each outstanding share of Heileman common stock. Each Right would entitle shareholders to buy one-hundredth share of the Company's Series A preferred stock at an exercise price of $70. The Rights would be exercisable "only if a person or group acquired twenty percent or more of the Heileman common stock or announced a tender of exchange offer that would result in such person or group owning thirty percent or more of the common stock." Heileman would be entitled to redeem the Rights at 5 cents per Right until ten days after a public announcement that a 20 percent position had been acquired.

Said Cleary in issuing the dividend, "The Rights are not being distributed in response to any announced effort to acquire control of the company, but they should help to protect Heileman shareholders from abusive takeover tactics and efforts to deprive them of the long-term value of their investment in Heileman."[5]

But the question surely must have arisen among some shareholders that if no one was making overtures to Heileman for a possible take-over, what was the real purpose of the defensive dividend announcement? Was Cleary making it publicly known that he might possibly want out?

Back in 1980, John Pedace, executive vice president of marketing for the G. Heileman Brewing Company, had made a major policy speech at the Wholesale Beer Association convention in Fort Lauderdale, Florida. His topic was "The A-B-C's of the '80s," a vision of where Heileman was headed in the new decade.

"A" stood for analysis, sermonized Pedace, a truthful inward look at whether management would be willing and able to face the challenges that the new decade would surely bring to the brewing industry. "Get yourself personally prepared for the '80s," he warned his audience, and if the upcoming decade meant a physical, emotional, or financial burden, it might be time to "[get] . . . out of the beer business."

"Now let's take a look at 'B'—belief," continued Pedace. "You've got to face reality. Do you really believe in the beer business and in your future in the beer business? Success begins and ends with believing."[6]

In 1987, Russell Cleary must have gazed long and hard into the Heileman crystal ball, perhaps reflected on Pedace's warnings for the 1980s, looked at a profit-draining predatory pricing battle gone mad and blinked. Heileman CEO Russell Cleary, a man who had put together a brewing empire through regional acquisitions in the short span of seventeen years, knew it was time to go.

"When Busch went back to work after the [1976] strike, they went back in into Chicago," said Heileman's Walter Baltz. "They had very deep pockets and August Busch III kept hammering on us. They just kept pounding and pounding."[7] A-B's weapon to counteract the deep discounting and growing popularity of Heileman's Old Style was to flood the market with its most popular-priced beer, Busch Bavarian. Miller also jumped into the discounting fray with its Milwaukee's Best, both breweries dumping their cheapest products into Chicago, the stronghold of Old Style.

BOND TAKES THE BAIT

There was one sure problem that would ultimately haunt Cleary and his brewery if he went looking for a possible suitor in the U.S. brewing market. Who would, or rather, who could buy his brewing operation? As demonstrated by Heileman's government-thwarted attempt to buy Schlitz in 1981 and the meddling by the feds in the partial buyout by Heileman of Pabst and Olympia in late 1982 and 1983, a possible purchase by Miller, A-B, Pabst, or Coors would certainly have to surmount an antitrust suit by the federal government.

"It doesn't look like one of the other U.S. brewers is going to take a pass at Heileman," an industry insider speculated when it became clear that Russ Cleary wanted out. A rumor that Miller Brewing Company and Heileman had held exploratory talks for a possible merger was dismissed by a source close to Miller. "The feds would turn thumbs down on such a deal because of antitrust."[8]

The answer could only be found by selling the G. Heileman Brewing Company to a foreign entity or breaking up the numerous regional breweries that constituted the House of Heileman and folding them piecemeal into rival brewing operations.

On September 4, 1987, an unsolicited takeover offer by an Australian brewing conglomerate would forever change the composition of Heileman, and ultimately, the face of today's U.S. brewing industry. Originally considered a hostile attempt to gain control of G. Heileman, a $1.01 billion offer by Amber Acquisitions Corporation, a subsidiary of Bond Holdings Corporation of Australia, had a reactive effect on the price of Heileman stock. The unsolicited offer of $38 per share pushed the value of Heileman stock to $42.12 per share by the time the gavel came down on Wall Street on the day of the initial offer. Cleary advised Heileman shareholders to sit tight.[9]

As further indications that Cleary's recent acquisitions and the dividend safeguards that had clicked in during the early part of 1987 had been nothing more than moves to enhance the value of the brewing company and ready it for a takeover, Cleary had also tipped Wisconsin Governor Tommy Thompson that G. Heileman would be on the market.

On September 17, the Wisconsin State Legislature met in a special session and quickly passed two bills that were designed to prevent hostile takeovers and stunt the possibility of the predatory company selling off brewing assets for a period of three years and to only allow a takeover of a Wisconsin-based business with the approval of the targeted company's board of directors.

Stripping Heileman of its brewing interests in order to pay down any leveraged debt or to satisfy investors looking for a quick return on investment could mean job cuts. Being a political creature, Thompson didn't want the headache of possible job losses or layoffs attributed to his office. At the time, Heileman employed about 3,000 people in Wisconsin. Throughout the thirty-one plants that comprised the Heileman empire in the U.S., a nationwide total of 6,300 employees were busy making beer, bread, and snack products, and precision metal parts. "I have received assurances from the Bond organization," said Thompson, "that they do not intend to take action to bust up Heileman, but intend to build Heileman, with the goal of expanding employment and economic activity in Wisconsin."[10]

Cleary was equally concerned on how any takeover of his operation might affect Heileman employees. "We are determined that while fulfilling our responsibility to our shareholders, we will also protect the best interests of all our employees, customers and communities in the state of Wisconsin."[11]

After some delaying tactics and a lawsuit filed by the Bond Corporation in U.S. District Court in Madison, Wisconsin, that challenged the new antitakeover laws passed by the compliant state legislature, Cleary got what he wanted on September 18 when Heileman and the Australian company signed an agreement worth a staggering $1.26 billion to be acquired by Bond Corporation Holdings at a price of $40.75 per share. In addition, Cleary was to remain as chairman and CEO of Heileman and the Pittsburgh Brewing Company, a business the Bond Corporation had bought in 1986 for $28.5 million. Pittsburgh was known for its Iron City beer and had also been contract-brewing a new product called Samuel Adams beer for the Boston Beer Company. Bond also agreed to honor any current labor agreements and all commitments to distributors and vendors.[12]

It seemed like a win-win situation for everybody.

ALAN BOND

Heileman's new boss, Alan Bond, was no stranger to multimillion dollar operations. An avid fine art collector, who had also won the

America's Cup in 1983, the Australian businessman was chairman of Bond Corporation, a publicly-held company based in Perth, Australia, that had interests in media, energy, real estate, and brewing. Bond was the leading brewer in Australia, with a commanding control of 45 percent of the beer market in the land down under. His brewing empire also extended to Great Britain, Japan, parts of Asia, and the Middle East.

Bond's acquisition of Heileman, however, looked shaky from the start, despite the Wisconsin brewery's attractive 1986 sales of $1.33 billion and a net income of $48.3 million. One of the first decisions that the brewery's new management made to shore up the company's numbers was to move its sales and marketing division to Chicago. Said senior executive vice president of marketing and sales, Ian S. Crichton, "Chicago will be a better communications hub for us. It also is our top market for Old Style."[13] Depending on whom you talked to at the time, Old Style still held a market share of somewhere between 25 to 30 percent of the Chicago beer market.

The brewery also decided to boost marketing expenditures by 60 percent to a total of more than $150 million. The question on the lips of industry analysts, however, was where Bond was going to not only come up with the money for the increased advertising budget, but also find the necessary funds to meet an estimated interest and principal payment of $150 million in his first year as owner of G. Heileman.

But Bond was confident that the combination of the Pittsburgh Brewing Company and G. Heileman, now known as Bond Brewing USA, a concentration on boosting export sales to Australia, the Far East, and the United Kingdom and the temporary cessation of dividend payments to shareholders, would help the business prevail. In doing so, the new Bond Brewing USA might be able to seize the number three sales position behind number two Miller and the "King of Beers."

Alan Bond, however, felt that the real key to pushing the Stroh Brewing Company, the current number three sales leader, to number four, was to revert back to Russell Cleary's proven approach of further acquisitions with an emphasis on their portfolio of favorite regional brands. Key areas of marketing concentration would be Chicago with its Old Style brand, Rainier in Seattle, and Schmidt in Minnesota.[14]

CLEARY RESIGNS

Still sitting as CEO of Heileman, but with his influence waning as the people brought in by Bond started to pick up on the nuances of the U.S. beer market and spread their wings, Russell Cleary watched the changes made by his new owners, especially the move of the marketing and sales departments to Chicago. Cleary no longer had to worry about keeping shareholders happy with the perennially expected dividend payments, a position that clearly gave him relief.

"When you're tied to making so many cents per share per quarter, you're much more limited in your ability to investment spend," admitted Cleary as Bond Brewing USA was attempting to bolster its marketing and production expenditures. As to whether these approaches would benefit sales of Old Style, especially in Chicago where sales had been slipping for the last few years, Cleary confessed, "We're in a tough market."[15]

By early 1989, Russ Cleary decided to call it quits. Replacing him would be Alan Bond as chairman of the board at Heileman, with Peter Beckwith on board as deputy chairman. Beckwith would also be responsible for the worldwide operations of the parent operation, Bond Corporation. Murray S. Cutbush, who had headed up the team that had acquired the Pittsburgh Brewing Company back in 1986, was appointed CEO and president of G. Heileman.

"In his eighteen years as president, Russ Cleary led the Company through a remarkable period of growth, aggressive acquisition and transition," acknowledged Alan Bond, "laying a solid foundation which will take us into the future." And a remarkable career it was. During the time that Roy Kumm and later, Cleary, took control of G. Heileman, the brewery had made more than fifty acquisitions. The brewery had grown from the number fifteen to the fourth-ranked brewing operation in the United States, from 1971 to the Bond acquisition. During that time, sales increased from $100 million to more than $1.3 billion. It was an incredible run.[16] Cleary indicated that he would continue to live in the La Crosse, Wisconsin, area while pursuing his business interests.

It was the end of an era in the U. S. brewing industry and, unfortunately, the beginning of a new era that would soon come crashing down.

TROUBLES FOR BOND

While CEO Murray Cutbush was announcing that Heileman's projected first quarter results for 1990 were on track, partially as a result
of modifying the debt structure still bogging down the brewery after
its acquisition in 1987, a court ruling in Australia forced the highly-
leveraged Bond Corporation Holdings into receivership. This move had
come about by the request of bankers in Australia, worried about the
financial stability of the parent company. As part of the result of the
receivership action in Australia, a $50 million interest payment due
on U.S. debentures was halted. The banks had moved against Bond
Corporation and its Australian breweries, claiming that the business
had breached several covenants in a loan agreement.[17]

But while Cutbush was putting a favorable spin on operations and
future financial projections at Heileman, the fact of the matter was
much different. Heileman's brands were continuing to lose market
share, and the brewery was "faced with a highly competitive market
in which they have not been overwhelmingly successful, except in
regional areas like Chicago," said Michael J. Branca, an analyst for
Value Line. Much of this fall-off in business was due to a continuing
pricing battle between Anheuser-Busch, Miller, and Coors. "Heileman cannot compete with a company like Budweiser," continued
Branca,"which is the low-cost producer and has forty-two percent of
the [beer] market."

Marc Cohen, an investment analyst for Sanford C. Bernstein &
Company, publicly brought up a thought that was silently crossing
the minds of people throughout the U.S. brewing and investment
industries. The problems of Bond Corporation, noted Cohen, "raises
the possibility" of a sale of Heileman.[18]

A look at the overall financial condition of the Bond Corporation
made Cohen's observation more than a strong possibility. Total debt
for the Australian business conglomerate was approaching $5.56 bil-
lion. The Heileman deal still had Bond Brewing USA staring at an
additional debt of $850 million from the 1987 acquisition of Heileman.
With beer sales declining, there simply was no way that Bond Brewing
USA could find the necessary funds to stave off future interests payments or necessary marketing dollars to compete against A-B, Miller,
or Coors, nor could it expect financial solace from its embattled parent
company, now doing battle in the Australian court system.[19]

In an attempt to financially stabilize Heileman during the last few years of Bond's ownership, one of the first expenditures that had been cut back was advertising. From its projected commitment in 1987 of an advertising budget of $150 million, marketing expenditures in 1989 had drastically plummeted to $40 million, further halved to $20 million by 1990.[20]

In Old Style's stronghold of Chicago, the results of the advertising cutbacks were becoming obvious. First to go was G. Heileman's sponsorship of the Chicago Marathon, a three-year $4 million commitment that had once saved the event from oblivion.[21] Local retailers also felt the advertising pinch. "You didn't have to read the newspapers to know Old Style was in trouble," said Earle Johnson, owner of the popular Quenchers Saloon. "Point-of-purchase materials started drying up, signs, posters, little things like that. Coasters were virtually impossible to get from the drivers when they filled our weekly orders for Old Style."

"I remember we had a neon Old Style sign in our tavern that was broken," recalls Johnson. "For six months, I kept on asking the Heileman salesman to either fix it or get me a new one and for six months, all I got was the runaround."[22]

Even local media advertising suffered. With a declining market share in Chicago hovering around 20 percent, Heileman hired Jerry Della Femina who was considered a bit of an innovative maverick in the advertising business. With his agency headquartered in Manhattan in New York, Della Femina seemed to be somewhat out of touch with Chicago, its history, and perhaps its demographics. At the 1990 All-Star baseball game held at the Chicago Cub's Wrigley Field, at the time with its outfield walls covered in summer ivy splendor, the ad executive, who was seated in the park's Old Style hospitality suite, turned and commented to a group of fellow executives. "Isn't Comiskey Park wonderful?" he said, referring to the American League park on the South Side of Chicago.[23]

Nothing like knowing your target audience.

In mid-1990, Alan Bond resigned as chairman and director of Bond Corporation Holdings Limited, beginning the first step in the restructuring of the parent company. Already stripped of most of his real estate, media, and natural resource assets by the Australian courts, Bond's departure would also trigger the selling-off of his widespread ownership in the Australian brewing industry.

Beer industry analyst Robert Weinberg of Robert S. Weinberg & Associates summed up the entire Bond takeover.

> The private value of any company is pretty subjective. At the time, we said that Heileman would be a bargain at $300 million, and overpriced at $400 million. Within a month of that, Alan Bond bought it for $1.2 billion. I was amazed. Bank of Boston was the syndicate manager, and they were a reputable bank. I went in shock. I knew I could be wrong by 50%, or even 100%. But I could not be wrong by a factor of three or four. There is no way.
>
> What Bond had probably done was hire a big consulting firm, and then told them to take Heileman's historic growth rate, and reduce it, and present that as a projection. I think the M.B.A.s at the consulting firm did a bang-up industrial engineering study, and presented it to the bank, and the bank said 'this looks good.' The loans were made, and no one thought to examine how that high historic growth was achieved, which was through a constant stream of mergers and acquisitions. Russell Cleary was the genius at that. When he realized that there was no one left to acquire, he found a bigger fool.[24]

G. Heileman Regroups

In January of 1991, Heileman filed to reorganize under federal bankruptcy law, just three short years after Alan Bond had bought the brewery. Under the protection of Chapter 11, Bond's interest in the brewery would be cut to a negligible amount while three groups of creditors, including a coalition of U.S. and Canadian banks, tried to work out a way of retiring almost $800 million of secured and unsecured debt. Most of this debt was incurred when Bond paid the record-breaking $1.26 billion for Heileman.

Said Russ Cleary after the dust settled. "It was that late '80s mentality. They thought they could pay anything—make a wild shot and get it turned around. But with that debt, it was just too difficult to sustain [the company]."[25]

Under fresh leadership, including new CEO Thomas Rattigan, Heileman seemed on the road to a strong recovery, so much so that rumors started to arise that the brewery, now with its headquarters in Rosemont, Illinois, was being courted by new suitors, including Stroh and the Pittsburgh Brewing Company. As part of the financial restructuring agreement, Bond Brewing USA had been dissolved, and the Pittsburgh Brewing Company left as an independent entity. Russell Cleary was said to be part of the Pittsburgh suitors, and perhaps as much for sentimental as well as business reasons, these investors were reported to have the inside track on the Heileman buyout.

So much for Cleary's retirement.

⚜ 23 ⚜

Here We Go Again

"Stroh has the wherewithal to go it
alone and will take the necessary
steps to remain competitive."
—*Lacy Logan, Stroh spokesperson*

HICKS, MUSE TO THE RESCUE

On November 1, 1993, the G. Heileman Brewing Company decided
to accept an offer by Hicks, Muse & Company of $390 million for the
purchase of its financially reorganized brewing operation. Having
dusted itself off from the devastating Alan Bond era, the brewery had
attracted the attention of Hicks, Muse & Company, a Dallas-based
investment firm that had a background in leveraged acquisitions. The
company, under the management services of Turner & Partners, would
join two other Hicks, Muse & Company businesses—Hat Brands,
Inc., makers of Stetson and Resistol hats, and Neodate Services, Inc.
This business was a fulfillment, database, telephone customer service, and direct marketing services organization for the publishing
industry. Neither operation had anything to do with brewing, with
all its peculiarities.

Thomas Rattigan, who was to be replaced as Heileman's chairman
and CEO when the deal was completed, seemed genuinely happy with
the acquisition, despite the fact that he was soon to be out of a job.

"This definitive agreement with one of the top U.S. investment
firms represents the successful culmination of our efforts to properly
position Heileman for continued profitable growth and long term
success," said Rattigan.

Since the successful completion of our financial reorganization in 1991, Heileman has significantly improved its volume
performance versus the industry, has been consistently

profitable, and has successfully met its post-reorganization expense and debt obligations. With the financial and operational support of Hicks, Muse and Turner & Partners, Heileman management will continue to build the value of the company and its strong niche brands for the benefit of our wholesalers, retailers, consumers and employees.[1]

Heileman's new board chairman after the transaction was completed early in 1994 was William J. Turner, head of Turner & Partners, an affiliate of Hicks, Muse & Company. He acknowledged the successful efforts of Rattigan and his managerial team in turning the brewery's dismal financial picture around. "We are very pleased with the trend in business results at Heileman and expect to continue with the basic strategic direction set by Tom Rattigan and his team regarding capital improvement, product line extension, innovative packaging alternatives, advertising concepts, merchandising programs and their focus on continued growth of the company's highest-margin brands."[2]

Turner's comments, however, signaled the death of the poorest performing brands in Heileman's scores of harvested labels, pared down to around 2,200 employees in its offices in La Crosse, Wisconsin, and Rosemont, Illinois. Also to be anticipated were layoffs and/or consolidations at Heileman's five breweries in La Crosse, Baltimore, San Antonio, Seattle, and Portland. Combined total capacity for these five plants was 13.2 million barrels but only 8.3 barrels would be brewed in 1984.[3]

Part of the brewing slack was made up with the contract brewing agreements between the La Crosse plant and the brewing of Samuel Adams beer for the Boston Beer Company and the shifting of some 900,000 barrels of the Pabst brewery production in Milwaukee's old Pabst plant to La Crosse. The entire Pabst production run would later move to La Crosse in late 1996 when the old Milwaukee brewery was closed.

But for the most part, Heileman's sales remained stagnant. On August 18, 1995, the brewery announced that it would run out of cash by September 30.[4] Admitted Thomas O. Hicks, chairman and CEO of Hicks, Muse, Tate & Furst, Incorporated, "Since we acquired Heileman in 1994, we have awaited a rebound of the beer industry and an improvement in Heileman's financial performance, neither of which, for various reasons, has not occurred. Accordingly, we have determined to focus our resources elsewhere."[5]

Analyst Robert Weinberg felt the Hicks, Muse purchase was done for all the wrong reasons and why they bailed from Heileman so quickly. "[Their] only justification for buying Heileman in the early 1990s was that they were buying something for about $300 million that someone in the recent past paid $1.2 billion for. If that was the only justification they had, then that was a bad decision."[6]

THE STROH REGIME

Once again, Heileman found itself becoming involved in another acquisition. This time, however, the brewery that had built its fortunes for decades on the mergers and acquisitions of scores of regional breweries would not reemerge as an independent entity as it had done after the purchase by Bond and the subsequent reorganization efforts by Thomas Rattigan and his team. The Stroh Brewing Company was about to swallow up G. Heileman and absorb it as it had the Joseph Schlitz Brewing Company some fourteen years earlier. "There is no beer called Heileman," Heileman spokesman Roy Winnick conceded. "It's reasonable to assume that the Heileman name will be at least reviewed, if not phased out. That's a decision for Stroh."[7]

After Heileman went into voluntary bankruptcy and Hicks, Muse et al. took a $54 million loss, Stroh retired Heileman's bank debt and assumed all of the brewery's debt, a move that cost Stroh around $300 million. In La Crosse, Wisconsin, there was concern as to whether the hometown brewery would be sold off by Stroh or perhaps closed. "There's been $100 million in improvements in that plant," said Russell Cleary. "There's good water and a dedicated, quality work force. I can't believe they would close that. It would be a mistake."

La Crosse Mayor Patrick Zielke noted that the sale of Heileman to Stroh marked the end of a long era for the House of Heileman in La Crosse, but he was happy that the sale was to a brewing family. "At least it's someone in the brewing business that came in and bought them out instead of somebody who sold long underwear," said Zielke, a reference to Hicks, Muse and their clothing line.[8]

William Henry, the first non-Stroh family member to become CEO at Stroh, made an astounding statement after the merger began. "It took us a long time to put this deal together," said Henry and acknowledged that Stroh had held merger talks with Heileman years earlier, including during the time that Russell Cleary had been Heileman's CEO. After at least six attempts since 1981 to put a deal together with Heileman, claimed Henry, Stroh finally had what it wanted.[9]

When former G. Heileman CEO Russell Cleary, however, was asked for his interpretation of events, his was of a different opinion from that of the CEO of Stroh. "It [the merger of Heileman and Stroh] was something I worked on 15 years ago with Peter Stroh," said Cleary. "Only it was supposed to be Heileman buying Stroh."[10]

Now that Stroh finally had what it wanted, the cost-cutting blood bath at G. Heileman began. First to go was M. L. "Lou" Lowenkron, Heileman's latest CEO, a leftover from the Hicks, Muse reign. Although some of Heileman's marketing executives would be transferred to Stroh's Detroit offices, over 150 staffers were purged from the La Crosse location. In Rosemont, Illinois, around forty staffers were offered full-time or transitional, positions but the Chicago suburban office was up for a lease renewal and would not be renegotiated.[11]

Stroh's CEO Henry, a former accounting executive, next turned his attention to the plethora of distributors they now had in their fold. A total of 577 Heileman distributors had come with the acquisition, adding to Stroh's 339 and another 445 distributors that handled both brands.

While Stroh was trying to figure out what to do with Heileman's assets, another round of price-cutting, instigated by the Miller Brewing Company in an attempt to stimulate its lagging sales of Lite and Miller Genuine Draft products, produced a typical counterreaction by Coors and Anheuser-Busch. Beer prices tumbled again.

Said Mike Brooks, A-B's vice president of sales, "Anheuser-Busch is committed to ensuring the competitive price positioning of all of our products and will meet any discount offered by our competitors," a strategy that had been a credo at the St. Louis-based brewery since the days that founder Adolphus Busch was at the helm.[12]

The latest price war was especially troublesome to the 1,361 distributors now under Stroh's control and beer retailers in general. In terms of Stroh distributors, there were simply too many of them chasing too few dollars, and Henry knew it. During a speech in early September 1996 in Oak Brook, Illinois, before the Associated Beer Distributors of Illinois, Henry compared Stroh's distributorship numbers with that of rivals A-B, Miller, and Coors. Number one A-B had only 790 distributors nationally, Miller was at 685, and Coors with 600. Stroh currently had almost twice as many distributors as any one of its competitors.

With the national beer-pricing war continuing with a vengeance, Stroh's CEO wanted to see higher volume wholesalers covering bigger sales territories. His studies had concluded that 475 of the brewery's distributors were accounting for 80 percent of their sales. With the price war limiting profits to just pennies per case, most of Stroh's distributors were simply spinning their wheels.

Henry also responded to the 150 brands of beer that Stroh now held in its collective portfolio. Of these, at least 20 percent of them represented no more than 1 percent of the brewery's volume. "We'll do some [brand] cutting," acknowledged Henry.[13]

In Chicago, retailers too were feeling the pinch from the price-cutting by the major brewers. "If retailers can't make money on the [beer] product," said Fred Rosen of Sam's Wines & Spirits, "they're not interested in selling it." And with a swipe at the major brewers, Rosen added, "Instead of being the cheapest, they should focus on being the best."[14]

Locally, suitcased-sized 30 packs of Old Style were selling as low as $7.99 as the price war continued.

THE BEGINNING OF THE END

For all the cost-cutting measures imposed by Henry on the new conglomerate, including a complete lack of television advertising in Chicago in 1996 by Stroh for the still-popular Old Style beer, the Detroit-based brewery continued to slide downward financially. For the first quarter of 1996, Stroh production fell by 10 percent while sales of its Heileman products slipped 1 percent to 1.7 million barrels. Almost half of the Old Style production went to beer drinkers in the Chicagoland area.[15]

Lacey Logan, spokesperson for the Stroh Brewing Company, pointed out that the brewery had actually chosen to reduce sales, in large part due to its decision to eliminate the weakest selling brands in its extensive portfolio. The continued discount pricing led by Anheuser-Busch and Miller, however, was causing unavoidable problems for Stroh. "This type of pricing strategy driven by these two large brewers does damage to all [brewers]," Logan complained. "It not only drives margins down, but in the long term, it diminishes brand equity and value."[16]

By 1998, it was clear that Stroh was in trouble. Not only was the brewery struggling with its continuing trend of falling sales and the incessant hammering down of profit margins due to the continuing price wars, but also its debt load, increased substantially by its purchase of Heileman, was squeezing out the meager profits the brewery had actually been making due to its drastic cost-cutting actions.

The ending of an arrangement with Pabst to contract brew a number of their brands in Stroh-owned plants, which accounted for around 15 percent of Stroh's total production, was the final nail in the coffin for Stroh, as Stroh board member William Howenstein conceded.[17] In December 1998, the family owned Stroh Brewing Company announced that it was closing its brewery in Tampa to further cut capacity. In addition, mid level managers at the Detroit headquarters were getting pink slipped.

Although spokeswomen Logan declared that "Stroh has the where-withal to go it alone and [would] take necessary steps to remain competitive," the industry waited for the other shoe to fall.[18]

They didn't have to wait long. On February 8, 1999, William L. Henry announced that the Stroh Brewing Company had signed agreements with Pabst and Miller to sell off its portfolio of brands. Pabst picked up a significant number of brands that had once helped Heileman propel itself to the number three brewing operation in the U.S., including Chicagoland favorites, Old Style and Special Export. Said John Stroh III, a fifth-generation member of the Stroh family and president and CEO of The Stroh Cos., Inc., the parent company of the brewing operation,

> My family and I struggled with this decision. Emotionally, it was an extremely difficult one to make, knowing that it would impact our loyal employees, and recognizing that it would mean the end of our family's centuries-old brewing tradition that had become, in essence, an important part of our identity. Emotions aside, this was not a cavalier financial decision either. Over the years, we have had several opportunities to sell the business, but due to the family's commitment to our brewing heritage, we felt none were

compelling enough to pursue. However, in light of this attractive offer, and the long term competitive outlook of the brewing industry, we concluded that it is the appropriate time to exit the beer business and focus on the family's other ventures.[19]

Terms of the buyout deal were withheld but an industry estimate topped out at around $400 million. In the next few months, and with final approval from the federal government, Miller and Pabst started taking over production of Stroh's beer portfolio.

On May 28, however, Stroh spokesperson Logan made an announcement that would signal the end of 141 years of Heileman products being brewed in La Crosse, Wisconsin. "It is our expectation that the plant will close on July 30."[20] Logan's estimate was off by one week. On August 6, 1999, the last case of Old Style was packaged at the Wisconsin plant.[21]

Beer and Politics in Chicago

"This Bud's a dud."
—*Jesse L. Jackson*

STRANGE BREW

The relationship between beer and Chicago politics has always been an antagonistic one. From the 1855 efforts by Mayor Levi Boone to close lager beer saloons on Sundays to the first National Convention of the Prohibition Party in Chicago in 1871 to the fanatical pursuits of local dry advocates in the years before the liquor trade was shut down in Illinois on July 1, 1919, it seems that every few years, another local group or personality decides to mix beer and politics.

THE KING OF BEERS

In early September 1982, Jesse Jackson, head of the Chicago-based Operation PUSH (People United to Save Humanity) and B. W. Smith, a PUSH representative in Buffalo, New York, simultaneously announced the beginning of a nationwide boycott of Anheuser-Busch products. Smith also served on the National Selective Patronage Council, an organization that purportedly represented fifty African American organizations. In his announcement, Jackson, whose command of facts and figures often seems to change as the situation demands, claimed that African Americans were spending about $800 million yearly on A-B products, yet only one of the brewery's distributors was black owned. He also claimed that blacks made up somewhere between 15 to 22 percent of A-B's customers. If these figures can be believed as reasonably accurate, the number of African American consumers of Busch products in Chicago would have had to figure to be at the low end of Jackson's parameters, perhaps even lower. Despite the best efforts of Anheuser-Busch, their products have never been popular in Chicago's black community.

Continuing his argument of economic entitlement, Jackson also questioned why only 2 percent of A-B's $254 million annual advertising budget was being placed through African American ad agencies. The call for a boycott was instigated by Jackson after Anheuser-Busch management refused to meet the civil rights activist and share information about its business with Jackson and Operation PUSH representatives. "When they have refused to meet," said Jackson, "they have in effect rejected this body of distinguished Americans," and then slipped into one of his trademark Doctor Seuss-like malapropisms. "PUSH and Busch must meet in the marketplace."[1]

When notified of the Chicago minister's call for a national boycott of Anheuser-Busch products, a Busch spokesman rebutted a portion of Jackson's argument, claiming that A-B had three minority-owned distributorships, not one as Jackson claimed, with one more coming online.

The timing of the boycott seemed peculiar. The day before Jackson grabbed national headlines with his challenge to A-B, brewery officials in St. Louis had proudly announced the establishment of a $5 million fund to help finance additional minority ownership of its distributorships. "Our record of commitment," said a Busch representative, "speaks for itself."[2]

NAACP Says "No" to Jackson

Days after the boycott officially began, the seven regional directors of the National Association for the Advancement of Colored People met in New York. After the meeting began, the group felt it necessary to renounce any involvement with Jackson and Operation PUSH's boycott of A-B products. Benjamin Hooks, executive director of the NAACP kept quiet in any condemnation of Jackson and his actions, but allowed the directors to make a public statement concerning the boycott. The tone of their statement indicated an uneasiness by the board with Jackson's actions. "The NAACP does not have a campaign against the Anheuser-Busch Company nor have any of its [1,800] units been authorized to form coalitions with other groups for that purpose," clearly chastising PUSH. To emphasize their displeasure with the possible inference that anyone in the NAACP might have projected a tacit approval of Jackson's boycott, they added a warning, "NAACP units may not join any coalitions to carry out programs without the express approval of the national office."[3]

But in an example of African-American unity, not one of the seven national NAACP regional directors directly mentioned Jackson by name or his Operation PUSH Director Virna Canson, described by local newspaper columnist Vernon Jarrett as " . . . [a] militant NAACP West Coast director." Jarrett noted, however, that Canson did take umbrage with the decision by any *local* black organization to declare a national boycott without canvassing other minority-led organizations for approval. Noting that the power of a national boycott of any product or company can be a powerful one, Canson emphasized that boycotts are "our weapons of last resort, and we must not permit anybody to play with the boycott or the ballot like they are basketballs to be dribbled carelessly."[4] During the national NAACP meeting, Jarrett added, several Chicagoans had questioned why Anheuser-Busch had been singled out for Jackson's declared boycott rather than Schlitz, Miller, Pabst, or G. Heileman. At the time, Heileman's Old Style brand was the number one selling beer in Chicago.

The delegates' questions had validity. A-B had demonstrated a history of contributing to minority programs and subscribing to the policy of affirmative action since 1969. That year, the Congress of Racial Equality had asked their members to support a boycott of Anheuser-Busch products, alleging that minorities accounted for less than 3 percent of A-B's 5000 employees. Busch officials moved quickly to stem any problems with the black community and soon adopted a company affirmative action program, bringing up its minority hiring to 18 percent of its employees, estimated in 1982 to be around 14,000.

With its new hiring policies in place, the brewery also began a minority-purchasing plan that was putting millions of dollars into black advertising agencies and banks. A-B had also been counted on for years for its sponsorship of the United Negro College Fund's annual telethon. The fact that the St. Louis brewery had just announced the establishment of a $5 million fund to help finance additional minority ownership of its distributorships, one day before Jackson's call for a boycott, only added to the confusion by NAACP delegates.

William Douthit, president of the Urban League of Metropolitan St. Louis, was as perplexed about the calling of the boycott as the Chicago delegates at the NAACP meeting. "Anheuser-Busch is the last company in this country that I would want to see pressured on behalf of the black community. Busch has done hundreds of things for the black community on its own, without any push from anyone."[5]

Another fact that Jackson conveniently chose to ignore in justifying the boycott was that A-B was one of the few large American corporations with two African American vice presidents. One of these men, Wayan Smith III, a Busch vice president and a member of the board of directors, and Jackson had actually established a cordial relationship while informal discussions between A-B management and Jackson of an "economic covenant" had been going on, starting about a year before the boycott. Smith had even spoken at Operation PUSH headquarters in Chicago as a guest speaker for the group's national convention in July of 1982.

So it was a surprise when press director Frank Watkins, a spokesman for Jackson, elaborated on why Jackson had actually called for the A-B boycott. Aside from Jackson's claim that management was refusing to sit down with him to discuss economic parity, Watkins declared that A-B had launched an attack against Jackson, Operation PUSH and the civil rights movement. "The reason [for the boycott] was that they [A-B] attacked us. So we had to, you know, respond to defend our integrity and our organization, and in the final analysis, the civil rights movement itself."

When Smith heard Watkins's explanation, he denied any attacks by A-B management on Jackson and argued that he could "document several meetings with Jackson and written invitations to Jackson seeking his cooperation."[6]

JACKSON LAWSUIT

NAACP leaders and Douthit weren't the only ones to express their displeasure with the boycott and Jackson. As the boycott dragged along, both sides taking potshots at each other, the St. Louis Sentinel and the St. Louis Argus, both African American newspapers, entered the fray. Both papers focused their wrath, not on A-B but rather on Jesse Jackson. The Sentinel personally attacked Jackson, calling him "self-serving" and alleged that he "badgers and intimidates" black business leaders into joining the economic arm of PUSH. The paper went on to claim that Jackson had demanded $500 each from black businessmen to support his A-B boycott.[7]

As a result of the newspapers' allegations, Jackson filed a $3 million lawsuit against the more vocal *St. Louis Sentinel* both on his own and Operation PUSH's behalf. But after the *Sentinel*, with approval from the court, moved to force Jackson to open the financial books of PUSH to prove the *Sentinel*'s contentions, Jackson suddenly dropped the lawsuit.

It's interesting to note that it took Jackson's forced disclosure in 2001 of a love child and charges of payments to his mistress before he made the financial books of Operation PUSH and related organizational records available, nineteen years after the *Sentinel* had tried to force him to do so.[8]

THE BOYCOTT DRAGS ON

During the twelve months in which the boycott lingered on, both sides increased their vocal attacks toward each other, with Jackson often instigating each new campaign. At first, A-B took a muted response approach to Jackson's laundry list of complaints, hoping the boycott would loose momentum. But after the *Chicago Tribune* printed an in-depth explanation by Jackson that attempted to answer the same three lingering questions that had dogged his boycott from the beginning— Why Busch? Why Busch first? Why PUSH alone?—Anheuser-Busch started to step up its response to Jackson's charges.

A-B board member Wayan Smith III became the brewery's point man in the war of words, answering Jackson's growing list of charges. These had now been broadened by Jackson to include allegations of a lack by A-B to institute "reciprocal trade with the black community . . . refusing to share basic information that other companies have shared with us," complaints that the brewery's public-relations firm, Fleishman Hillard, had launched "a national discrediting campaign" against the Chicago activist and Operation PUSH and demands by Jackson to meet personally with brewery board chairman and president, August A. ("Three Sticks") Busch III.[9]

At a press conference held at Anheuser-Busch offices at 4841 South California on Chicago's South Side, Smith finally lashed out at the boycott, calling it "ill-founded." After listing A-B's long list of contributions to minority groups, the brewery board member admitted that "we do not understand the boycott ourselves."[10]

Jackson's boycott took on a darker façade when PUSH officials started alluding that A-B Chairman Busch was to black economic development what former Birmingham, Alabama, police commissioner Eugene "Bull" Conner was to the early civil rights movement. The thought of equating brewery CEO Busch with the man who had directed police dog and water cannon attacks against civil rights protesters in the 1960s was over the top, and Wayan Smith III responded forcefully. He called the PUSH boycott "morally indefensible, intellectually dishonest and factually in error." Smith also claimed that the brewery's sales figures were indicating that the boycott was not succeeding.[11] But somehow, someway, Jackson got his hands on internal A-B documents that showed that despite record sales, the boycott was effective, especially in Chicago's African American community. Playing into Jackson's hands, Anheuser-Busch representatives admitted that the reports were authentic.

For a while, the boycott and the continuing battle between Smith and Jackson seemed to take on a comical tone. During the boycott, Jackson would take his entourage to various A-B plants throughout the country. Because of Jackson's need for publicity, Smith would be tipped off in advance as to where Jackson was headed. In each city, Jackson would arrive at the local A-B brewery and demand to speak with plant officials. Officials would willingly comply and grant Jackson access to the brewery but would then escort Jackson to a quiet office where Smith would be patiently waiting. Thwarted by Smith's checkmate, Jackson would leave the brewery to the awaiting crowd of media, cameras ready. As local black leaders stood with Jackson, he would ceremoniously pop open a can of Budweiser, pour the contents on the ground, and declare that "Bud's a dud!" This little example of guerrilla theater would be played out a number of times in different cities.

Seven months after the boycott began, A-B representatives announced that their former Chicago South Side company headquarters location would now be the headquarters of the Hometown Distributing Company, A-B's fourth black-owned distributorship, but first in Chicago. The business would also be the first wholesaler to come online since A-B's establishment of a $5 million fund to help finance additional minority ownership of its distributorships.

Although a fourth black-owned beer distributorship had already been planned before the boycott had been announced, a Jackson aide took advantage of the news, calling it "further evidence that the boycott is working effectively."[12]

THE BOYCOTT ENDS

As the boycott continued, with Jackson still demanding to negotiate with Chairman Busch but finding Smith thwarting his actions at every turn, Busch finally contacted Washington attorney Edward Bennett Williams and asked him to intercede with the stalemated negotiations. Jackson agreed to meet with Williams in a Washington hotel. In a short time, it became apparent that some sort of agreement between Jackson and the brewery was imminent. Whatever the end result of a year's worth of battles would be, both sides were sensitive to saving face.

After representatives and attorneys for PUSH and A-B got together for a final round of negotiations, Williams, CEO Busch, and Jackson met alone for a little over an hour. After the meeting, August Busch III announced an agreement. "We are determined to strengthen our partnership with the minority community. We are determined to continue to increase our proper and fair role as a responsible company, responsive to community needs."

The agreement included:

Making $23 million in purchases from minority suppliers, an increase of $5 million from 1982.

Awarding $10 million in construction contracts to minority-owned companies, double the 1982 figure.

Depositing $14 million in minority banks, a $4 million increase over 1982.

Increasing advertising with minority-owned media to $8 million, four times the 1982 figure.

Doubling a $5 million special fund set up by the brewery to help increase the number of black distributorships.[13]

It appeared to be a clear victory for Jackson, but on some points he seems to have come up short. Jackson never got a signed agreement to these proposed commitments by Anheuser-Busch. He also lost a major element of his demands to have a joint committee of PUSH and Busch officials oversee the agreement. Jackson acquiesced to the brewery's demand that A-B officials alone would be responsible for monitoring the progress of the unsigned agreement.[14]

ANHEUSER-BUSCH AND JACKSON TODAY

Sixteen years later, Anheuser-Busch officials announced that two of Jackson's sons were going to purchase the River North Distributing Investment Capital Corporation, A-B's most lucrative beer distributorship in Chicago. Yusef Jackson, an attorney for the Chicago law firm, Mayer Brown & Platt, and his brother Jonathan Jackson, would be joined by Donald Niestrom Jr., a veteran of the Chicago beer trade.

The story of how the Jacksons and Anheuser-Busch came into such a relationship was elaborated on by Yusef during a number of newspaper interviews. At a Los Angeles, California, dinner party hosted by billionaire supermarket tycoon Ron Burkle in 1996, Jackson and brewer scion August Busch IV struck up a conversation. "We had a lot of common themes in our lives," recalled Yusef and as the conversation progressed, "We started talking about doing business," related Jackson.[15] Young Jackson had been brought along to the party by his father, Jesse, who was the featured speaker at the Burkle affair. After the gathering, young Busch mentioned to Burkle that he had enjoyed his conversation with Yusef and questioned Burkle whether the younger Jackson was "someone we should work with?"[16]

The question may have been more than rhetorical. Back in Chicago problems had been brewing at A-B's River North distributorship. For a number of years, the local company had been guided by J. C. Alvarez, a Hispanic woman, and Donald Niestrom Sr., a white Chicagoan with years of experience in the beer business. It was reported to be an unfortunate mix of leadership at the North Side distributorship as the partnership failed to gel. Along with the clash of personalities exhibited by the two, allegations of fiscal irregularities and racial discrimination at the distributorship surfaced.

With threats looming by some black employees to picket the business, charging that blacks were being ignored for promotions, A-B knew it had a potential problem on its hands, especially after employees threatened to bring in the NAACP, the Equal Employment

Opportunity Commission, and, finally, Jesse Jackson and his Rainbow/
PUSH organization.

Before the problems could peak, however, Anheuser-Busch sent a
team of brewery officials and auditors to investigate the complaints
at the River North distributorship, eventually replacing Alvarez and
Niestrom with a temporary general manager. As the disputes and
accusations faded at the distributorship, August Busch IV and Yusef
Jackson were putting the finishing touches on the purchase of the
River North location by Yusef, his brother Johnathan, and Donald
Niestrom Jr., son of the recently deposed Donald Niestrom Sr.

Although neither brother had any experience in the beer trade,
Yusef claimed to have studied the beverage industry in college. Despite
their beer trade inexperience, Bank America, under the auspices of
the Charlotte, North Carolina, based Nations Bank, gave the brothers
a $6.7 million loan to help complete the purchase of the assets, equip-
ment, and warehouse on Goose Island. If that was the price for the
entire operation, as critics wondered, it was an awfully good one. In
1991, Anheuser-Busch had spent $10.5 million, including an incentive
of $2.6 million from the City of Chicago, to purchase the land and
build the 79,000 square-foot warehouse.

Neither the Jackson brothers nor A-B would comment on the price
or particulars of the deal. Said Yusef when pressed for more information on the purchase, "We negotiated a straightforward deal and paid
a competitive price for the company along with its property."[17]

The business is indeed a gainful one. With a territory that extends
from Lake Michigan, west to Harlem Avenue, north to Irving Park,
and south to Roosevelt Road, the distributorship is estimated to sell
$30 to $40 million worth of Anheuser-Busch products yearly.[18]

WHAT GOES AROUND, COMES
AROUND . . . OR DOES IT?

Ironically, perhaps, the Jackson brothers initially refused to answer
questions by the local press as to how many of the one hundred or so
drivers and sales representatives they now employ are minorities—the
same sort of question that their father had demanded of Anheuser-
Busch years ago.

A statement by Yusef Jackson in his position as company president only deepened criticism of the Jacksons' hypocrisy. "River North Sales and Services is . . . a private business. All of our actions in acquiring and operating this business have been ethical and proper. As for your questions, much of the information involved is either proprietary or personal. Our choice is to keep it private."[19]

Anheuser-Busch, in answering a related query by the *Chicago Sun-Times* as to how many A-B distributorships are currently owned by minorities, responded that it has "several minority owners" but refused to say how many. This certainly would indicate a different tone by the brewery than in 1982 when they were countering Jesse Jackson's accusations of low minority ownership with an exact count of three black-owned distributorships, with one more on the way.[20]

In March 2001, patriarch Jesse L. Jackson was attempting to quell a growing plethora of questions about his finances. This was a result of the revelation of a federally financed $763,000 no-bid contract from the state of Illinois awarded to PUSH and a payment of $35,00 from one of Jackson's organizations coupled with a monthly payment of $3,000 to Karin Stanford, a former employee with whom Jackson had fathered a child. As part of his damage-control campaign, Jackson was willing to sit for a two-hour interview by *Sun-Times* reporters and members of the paper's editorial board. A part of the interview follows:

> **SUN-TIMES:** Did you have any role with your sons getting the beer distributorship?
>
> **JACKSON:** If Bush is qualified to run the country, they are qualified to run a beer distributorship. At some point those guys met August [Busch IV] and they started doing business. I know nothing about it, really. I don't know how they did that. Their business is private and apart from what I'm doing. They paid all the right dues and exercised the right discipline to become business people and political leaders. I respect that, and I want all other people to respect that, too. I can take my hits. I will take them. But they should not be profiled or otherwise suggestions dropped that they are less than able to do what they do. That is very insulting to me.
>
> Very insulting.[21]

In perhaps the same reposturing vein as his father, River North CEO Yusef Jackson later decided to be a bit more candid with the press about the racial makeup of the distributorship's personnel. Jackson claims that the 100 man workforce now consisted of 53 percent white, 27 percent black, 19 percent Hispanic and 1 percent Asian. Jackson adds that one-half of the firm's sales force is composed of women.[22]

As seen earlier, Bud products haven't been favored by Chicago beer drinkers since the early 1970s. Locally, Schlitz wrestled the number-one sales position from A-B in 1973, Old Style had its strong run during the late 1970s and 1980s, keeping A-B at bay, and Miller products have dominated local beer sales since the overwhelming acceptance of its Lite beer. Some beer authorities have speculated that A-B's lack of favor in Chicago might be due to the brewer's history of union problems, turning off the taste buds of Chicago's working-class beer drinkers. But in how many white, working-class neighborhood bars did the Jackson/A-B ownership question play out over and over again after the 1983 Jackson/A-B agreement? The purchase by Jackson's sons of one of the largest A-B beer distributorships in Chicago and the lingering questions by the local media as to how this occurred has added to the Jackson family/A-B controversy.

Could the Jackson family's relationship to Anheuser-Busch hold some responsibility for A-B's lagging sales here, especially in the white, working-class neighborhoods of Chicago? A-B's sales might be lagging in Chicago but for the Jacksons, at least, Bud is certainly not a dud.

G. Heileman's PowerMaster

In June of 1991, while a reorganized G. Heileman was trying to get back on its financial feet after the exiting of the Alan Bond regime, the brewery announced the creation of a new malt liquor called PowerMaster. This new brew would be added to its collection of other high octane brews, including its best-seller, Colt 45. PowerMaster would have an alcoholic content of about 5.5 to 6 percent, depending on the legal restrictions of some western states. "Upper strength malt liquors, those with a higher alcohol content, are growing," said a brewery spokesman.[23]

Some industry observers, however, weren't too sure about bringing one more malt liquor into the beer market, especially with the growing waves of neo-prohibitionism and push for moderation in the consumption of alcoholic beverages in general. "It's a gutsy move on Heileman's part," said an industry observer, "but I'm not sure they can pull it off."[24]

One could also see Heileman's logic in introducing yet another malt liquor. The malt liquor market had shown increases of 300,000 barrels in each of the last two years to 6.1 million barrels in 1990. In an otherwise stagnant market and in a rebuilding phase, Heileman was willing to bring out PowerMaster and pit it against the Stroh brewery's Schlitz Malt Liquor, A-B's King Cobra, and Miller's Magnum.

About the same time that PowerMaster was making its debut in Chicagoland, Reverends George Clements and the *bete noire* of the Chicago Roman Catholic Archdiocese, Father Michael Pfleger, showed up at Heileman's La Crosse, Wisconsin, offices and demanded to speak with the brewery's president, Thomas Rattigan. The priests contended that the new PowerMaster with its high alcohol kick was being targeted at black communities.

When the duo was informed that Rattigan was out of town and that no other member of the brewery's management team was willing to meet with them, they refused to leave the company offices. Company officials called the police who promptly arrested the clerics for trespassing.

In the courtroom of La Crosse Municipal Court of Judge Robert Joanis, the two were released on $85 signature bonds and admonished by the judge that any future protests could land them in jail. He also ordered that they return to La Crosse on August 22 to answer the trespassing charges. In typical defiant fashion, the priests vowed that they would return to the brewery and continue their fight against the marketing and selling of the new PowerMaster product.[25]

THE FED STOPS POWERMASTER

Clements and Pfleger, however, represented just a small part of a national campaign to usurp the placement by Heileman of PowerMaster in the retail market. Various black leaders, Surgeon General Antonia Novello, and representatives of antidrinking groups had already caught the attention of Washington bureaucrats, and in doing so, stirred the Bureau of Alcohol Tobacco and Firearms into action.

In early July, BATF representatives descended on La Crosse, and in a two-hour meeting, informed Heileman officials that they were pulling approval of the PowerMaster label, a necessary step in getting the product to market. Citing laws established by the Federal Alcohol Administration Act of 1935, the BATF claimed that were invoking a passage in the act that forbade the labeling or advertising of beer as being "strong, full strength, extra strength or high test," all words that could be construed as an indication of high alcoholic content.

After the U. S. brewing industry had lost its eight-month exclusive right to manufacture 3.2 percent beer with the repeal of Prohibition on December 5, 1933, many breweries came out with lines of what were commonly referred to as "headache beers," malted beverages with a high-alcohol content. These beers were brewed in an attempt to blunt a possible loss of market share to distilled spirits manufacturers. After claiming since the nineteenth century that beer was a "drink of moderation," the move by brewers to manufacture and advertise high-alcohol products seemed a bit hypocritical. But still gun shy that the federal government could giveth and taketh away the right to brew beer again, the U. S. brewing industry grudgingly accepted the labeling restrictions.

Following a very wide interpretation of these post-Prohibition guidelines, the BATF claimed that the word "Power" violated federal law. Heileman was allowed to sell its existing stock of PowerMaster for the next four months but would have to stop any advertising of the product.[26]

In a statement by G. Heileman after the BATF's decision, the brewery acknowledged the financial burden that continued litigation over the issue would entail. In the midst of reorganization, the brewery decided to take their medicine and move on.

When pressed by reporters as to how the PowerMaster label could have been approved by the BATF and then suddenly pulled after lobbying by antidrink proponents, Dan Black, deputy director of the bureau and associate director of compliance operations at the BATF explained away the inconsistency. "With upwards of 80,000 labels a year . . . sometimes these things happened."[27]

St. Sabina's Pastor Pfleger was overjoyed by the BATF ruling. "When we are spiritually strong, there's no problem we cannot overcome. We have a serious alcohol problem in the [African American] community, and this means that something worse won't be added to it," said Pfleger, who then added, "Big business better watch out if it's doing wrong."[28]

ST. IDES

A scant month after Fathers Pfleger and Clements were savoring their victory, another local antidrink group, calling itself the Citywide Coalition against Alcohol Billboards, loaded up a bus full of protestors and headed to Heileman's offices in suburban Rosemont, Illinois, to protest another malt liquor brewed by Heileman called St. Ides.

The group, led by Paul Kelly, director of alcohol and drug prevention at the Bobby Wright Health Center on South Kedzie Avenue, claimed that the La Crosse brewery had no limits in the production of its beer, especially its higher alcohol products, a rather vague argument. "Anything is permissible as long as it is for dollars," said Kelly. "The advertising, it's tied to gangs and sexual promiscuity. If gangs and promiscuity are not major agendas that have to be addressed in the African American community, there are none. They are taking dollars. We are taking lives."[29]

At the time, St. Ides was gaining popularity in the black community, especially after rap and movie star Ice Cube was making commercials for the beer. In one commercial aired on African American oriented television programs, Ice Cube rapped some of the more compelling reasons for buying St. Ides.

"Get your girl in the mood quicker," sang Ice Cube, "and get your jimmy thicker with St. Ides malt liquor."[30] After the beer was highlighted in the movie, *Boyz N the Hood*, sales really took off.

There was one little thing wrong with Heileman's involvement with this malt liquor. It wasn't their product, though they did contract brew the beer for the McKenzie Corporation out of San Francisco, California. Meeting with the group of protestors, Hubert A. Nelson, Heileman's marketing director, told them they were making a mistake in targeting Heileman.

"We have nothing to do with the product," said Nelson. "We brew the product under a special contract. We are like Maytag to Sears. We owned PowerMaster. We took total responsibility for that. We will not take responsibility for St. Ides. So if you want to protest, I guess you can call them."[31]

⊰ 25 ⊱

New Casualties, New Beginnings

The easiest way to amass a small
fortune in the micro brewing
industry is to start with a big one.
—*Jim Koch, Boston Beer Company*

HISTORICAL PRECEDENCE

If you understand the reasons why the old Chicago brewing industry
collapsed so many years ago, it becomes a bit mind-boggling to find
that the hard lessons of past failures in the local industry have had,
nonetheless, no appreciable influence on the recent decisions of a
number of would-be brewers to try their hands at brewing. There are
six historical reasons why the former brewing industry collapsed in
Chicago. They are:

Non portability of product
Poor quality products
Little (or no) advertising effort
Poor distribution
Underfunded operations
No brand loyalty

NON PORTABILITY OF PRODUCT/ POOR DISTRIBUTION

By the early 1900s, the bottling of beer in Chicago was an established
and growing practice. Bottled beer gave the consumer a choice of
where, when, and how often he could enjoy his libations. This containerizing practice had an immediate effect on saloons that served
draft-only products and many of the smaller and midsized brewing

operations that provided the kegged beer to these retail operations. Local lager beer saloons starting closing throughout the city as breweries with bottling facilities bypassed the neighborhood watering holes and started selling their beer directly to households.

Bottling machinery was then, and still is, an expensive investment for any brewery. One hundred years ago, a handful of local breweries that could not afford this costly bottling equipment, farmed out their draft products to the scores of independent bottling operations that had sprung up throughout the city. These bottling enterprises also containerized soda pop and mineral and seltzer waters for the nonalcoholic drink industry.

The use of independent bottling shops was only a temporary fix as brewing and bottling costs increased. Once again, the smaller local breweries had to come to terms with the growing popularity of bottled beer. Between 1910 and 1918, twelve small to midsized breweries that could not, or would not, add a bottling line to their operation closed in Chicago as bottled beer continued to gain a wider acceptance.

When the initial yoke of national prohibition was lifted in Illinois on April 7, 1933, a handful of small-sized, often underfunded operations jumped into the local brewing industry, trying to take advantage of the unbridled euphoria surrounding the return of real beer. Once again, breweries such as the Gambrinus Brewing Company tried to get into the Chicago market with draft-only products. Served only in finer restaurants, nightclubs, and hotel bars, Gambrinus products would eventually contend with not only the portability of bottled beer but also with the newest industry effort after 1935 of containerizing beer in cans. Financially unable or simply unwilling to put in a bottling line, weak, draft-only sales forced the brewery to close in 1936.

PAVICHEVICH BREWING COMPANY

If ever a contemporary brewery was destined to fail in the Chicago market, the Elmhurst, Illinois, based brewery would have to be found on the top of the list. Putting together seed money of $500,000, owner Ken Pavichevich found himself a professional brewer to help develop a unique flagship brand of lager beer. After a public stock offering in May 1988 of $1.5 million and establishing a $750,000 line of credit with the Gary-Wheaton Bank, former Chicago policeman, model, and oil executive Pavichevich built a 9,600-square-foot brewery. It was a beautiful, state-of-the-art 40,000-barrel brewery, built at an estimated cost of $2.2 million. Pavichevich spared no expense in bringing the brewery on-line. He did, however, fail to immediately put in a bottling line, a move that would haunt the brewery until the day it closed.[1]

An article in the late 1980s in a brewing trade journal explained the owner's early sales strategy. Using Chicago as the epicenter, Pavichevich planned on selling his beer as a draft-only product in a fifty-mile radius of the Windy City. Articles in local newspapers in early 1989 confirmed his draft-only plan. In its first year of production, the brewery would serve a mere 120 accounts. In order to operate at full capacity, the brewery would have needed to sell each outlet about 334 barrels a year, or almost one 31-gallon barrel per day.[2]

Each draft account was given sets of gold-rimmed tulip glasses and paper stem collars with the brand name of "Baderbrau" predominately featured on both items. Tavern and restaurant owners were instructed on the proper pouring technique of the excellent tasting beer, a dramatic exercise that required patience on the part of the waiting beer drinker.

Drinkers who were looking for a richer, thicker brew, found Baderbrau to be an exceptional beer. The problem, however, in getting sales to equal the annual capacity of the brewery, was due, in large part, to a lack of portability of the product. After enjoying a beer or two at one of the limited restaurants and taverns that carried the beer, the customer had no opportunity to bring home more of the beer for later enjoyment, putting a limit on sales. In terms of sales, it doesn't take a beer consultant to realize that two beers enjoyed at a bar do not equal the same return on investment that a six-pack (or more) of beer bought for home consumption provides.

The opening sales campaign of exclusively using draft beer to introduce product is, however, a sales and marketing tactic that even the big breweries have used for decades. Get the new beer on local draft lines, create a buzz about the product accompanied with frequent tasting events (especially if you're a craft brewer), throw in some effective advertising followed by having your sales force relentlessly push the product, test the reaction of the market to the new beer, and build up demand—then bottle the product.

For Baderbrau, however, there were two problems with this all-draft approach. The combination of limiting potential consumption with an exclusively all-draft product, mixed with costly newspaper and radio advertising, put an immediate fiscal strain on the new brewery. Added to this approach was the apparent reasoning by Pavichevich not to follow through with the final act of bottling the product, a follow-up move that would have increased distribution and overall sales.

Liquor stores are not in the habit of storing obscure or slow-selling draft products in their inventory so any chance of finding a keg of Baderbrau at your favorite liquor store was extremely remote. With a bottled product, chances would have been considerably better that the same liquor store that failed to carry Baderbrau beer in kegs might at least have had Baderbrau six-packs on its shelves.

Unable to find a distributor for their product, Pavichevich started to personally deliver barrelled beer to some of his retail outlets using a single truck or his own car. But by mid-1989, he was starting to back-track from his all-draft plan and mentioned to a local reporter that his brewery would eventually be bottling Baderbrau products "despite certain misgivings."[3] What those misgivings were are unknown, but by the time the Elmhurst brewery put in a top-of-the-line Krones bottling machine, Pavichevich was reporting a net loss of $444,957 for the six months ended on July 1, 1990.

POOR QUALITY PRODUCTS

In the early history of beer and brewing in Chicago, there were only two things necessary to bring together beer drinker with *any* brand of beer—freshness and availability. Poor quality beer was the bane of the early brewer. Stories of breweries making bad beer were common reading in the early brewing trade journals and local newspapers of the 1870s and 1880s. Practices in production that are routinely accepted in the brewing trade today, such as the sterilization of brewing equipment, using pure yeast cultures, and practicing overall quality control from fermentation until kegging or bottling of the product and beyond, were virtually non existent 150 years ago. It's enough to make one wonder how the industry as a whole could have survived these early years of hit-or-miss brewing.

As demonstrated by the fall of the Jos. Schlitz Brewing Company, a drop-off in the quality of a beer brand, or perhaps more important, the perception by your customers of a fall-off in the quality of a beer brand, can end the reign of even the biggest of breweries.

THE CHICAGO BREWING COMPANY

In June 1990, the Chicago Brewing Company opened as the only commercial bottling brewery in the Windy City since the demise of the Peter Hand Brewing Company in 1978. The brewery was a huge one, over 12,000 square feet, and located in the former site of an old pickle factory, just east of the Kennedy Expressway. Even with extensive modifications to accommodate the brewing equipment, the layout was a rambling one. One local beer writer claimed that the brewing equipment and accessories totaled around $3 million.[4] Ray Daniels, director of Craft Beer Marketing for the Colorado-based Brewers Association, however, recalls the brewery's equipment somewhat differently. "[It] . . . was like those of many other small brewers of the time, a patchwork of old and used equipment."[5]

At one point, the rakes in the 40-barrel lauter tun in the brewery, used to drain the sweet mixture of wort from the spent malted barley, did not work and hadn't for some time. These rakes were supposed to level off the mash. This equipment failure set up a number of possible problems, including slow and stuck runoffs of the fermentable wort, the possibility of losing the whole mash, poor extraction of fermentables from the malted barley, and, as a result, greater than necessary malt costs to make up for poor extraction.

The brewery's bottling line was another problem. For some time, the amount of adhesive used to glue the bottle and neck labels to the 12-ounce glass containers couldn't be adjusted to the proper setting. Bottles were coming off the line with either excessive amounts of glue smeared across the front of crooked bottle labels or with labels simply adhered to the bottles with hot water as the bottling line operator overcompensated for the abundance of adhesive used to hold the labels in place by turning off the glue setting. Customers would pull a bottle of their flagship brand, Legacy Lager, from a six-pack and watch as the neck or bottle labels fell off. With only seconds to catch the eye of a beer drinker faced with scores of different beer brands on liquor store shelves, the amateurish packing of Legacy Lager left customers moving on to a competing beer.

The amount of beer that was streamed into the bottles from the secondhand filling line was also a problem, sometimes leading to underfilled bottles referred to in the brewing industry as "shorties." These bottles would be pulled from the line and sometimes sold at discounted prices to Chicago policemen who would come around to the brewery on a regular basis looking for a bargain.

The problems on the outside of the beer could not compare to what was going on inside the bottle. According to observations by Daniels while he worked at the Chicago Brewing Company, contamination of product was a real problem, a result of the poor layout of the brewery. "The grain storage and grinding were part of the same big open room as the fermentation operations and bottling line—a pretty big problem from a contamination point of view [as grain dust could settle on the beer]. Not surprisingly, they had some terribly infected beers at times."[6]

Steve Hamburg, a former president of the Chicago Beer Society, a local beer appreciation group, also remembers problems with CBC's bottled products. "I used to recommend to friends that they just stick to their draft products because there was too much variability between six-packs. On one occasion, a friend and I did a series of taste tests with six bottles from the same six-pack. Three bottles were gushers."[7]

Randy Mosher, author and beer style instructor at the Chicago-based Siebel Institute of Technology, comes right to the point with why the Chicago Brewing Company, in his opinion, had its share of problems. "Bad brewery layout, a result of not enough money, made for a lot of bad beer," he says.[8]

If the beers at the CBC had a propensity for bacterial infection, one might imagine that some sort of quality control testing of their products would have been instituted. "Generally, problematic infections in a brewery are at very low levels and are first detected by growing the culprits up on an agar plate," explains Daniels. "When I was at Siebel, they told us that a microscope was useless as a Q.C. [Quality Control] tool. If you could see bacteria with a microscope, the beer or wort in question was grossly infected and beyond salvage. Yet while I was at the Chicago Brewing Company, they had beer in the fermenter that was so loaded with lactic acid bacteria that they were clearly identifiable under the microscope."[9]

The standard practice at any brewery after running into a situation like this would have been to dump the infected batch of beer, break down the brewing equipment, and sanitize everything involved in the brewing process. Daniels, however, claims that while he was at the CBC, brewery personnel did the unthinkable. "My recollection is that the number of bacteria visible under the scope equaled the number of yeast [cells]. I don't recall what they did with the beer, but I'm fairly certain that it was not discarded. What I do remember is that they repitched the yeast after performing an acid wash [to cleanse the yeast], a procedure that had no chance of eliminating the bacteria."

"Now, having said all that," Daniels concedes, "these guys managed to make some good beer from time to time."[10]

Little or No Advertising Efforts

In a historical context, the advertising of beer is a relatively new concept. Of course, the transcending simplicity of brewery drummers passing out brewery and brand trade cards to saloon owners during the 1870s to the quirkiness of Miller's "Dick" commercials in the late 1990s might make one wonder if the concept has been evolving or regressing.

By the 1860s, with Chicago situated as the largest railroad hub in the Midwest, out-of-town breweries found that they could economically compete with the numerous breweries in and about Chicago. The Great Chicago Fire of 1871 and the loss of nineteen local breweries further opened up Chicago to the overtures of the Milwaukee and St. Louis breweries, adding to the growing competition in Chicago's own industry. This flooding of the market with both local and out-of-state beers now made advertising a viable and necessary approach in hopes of winning the pocketbooks and stomachs of Chicago beer drinkers.

From simple brewery trade cards evolved outdoor advertising, newspaper ads, and some of the most prized modern-day breweriana, color lithographs, beer trays, and embossed glasses. But by 1910, newspapers were the principal, low-cost method for breweries to get their message out to the public that their beer was the best.

With the return of beer in 1933, the smaller Chicago breweries tried to match the advertising efforts of the out-of-town breweries but soon found themselves outspent by their competitors at an alarming rate.

They eventually dropped the cash-draining effects of massive advertising campaigns and reverted to the discounting of their products to win back Chicagoland customers.

It was the beginning of the end for hometown brand loyalty as the undeniable influence of mass advertising on beer drinkers would prove king.

ADVERTISING AND
DISTRIBUTION PROBLEMS

Today, beer advertising has become a Frankenstein monster. Chicago print, television, radio, sports sponsorship, even neighborhood and church festivals have been touched by the hundreds of millions of beer advertising dollars funneled through local ad agencies such as Leo Burnett, Young & Rubican, Foote, Cone & Belding, and Chicagoland beer distributors.

And there, right smack in the middle of the hundreds of millions of dollars spent yearly for beer ads and brewery-sponsored events, are microbreweries, tiny islands of would-be entrepreneurs surrounded by a sea of deep-pocketed corporate giants, looking for their own niche market of loyal customers. It might seem like an impossible task, but with the success of a growing number of small-sized breweries throughout the United States, the question arises, Why can't small Chicago area breweries emulate the sometimes spectacular achievements of a growing number of out-of-state craft breweries to win the support of local beer drinkers?

Mass advertising works for well-financed national breweries, but for virtually any small local brewery, large-scale advertising of their products is a fiscal impossibility. Beer advertising requires a huge budget and scores of advertising creative teams to develop a viable campaign and is better left to the national breweries. Consistent, imaginative, and affordable marketing of products, however, is a practice that any size brewery can reasonably exercise.

"Trying to advertise a small product in a big market like [Chicago]," says Randy Mosher, "just doesn't make sense. Marketing and promotions can be done for less," he concedes, "but ain't nothin' free."[11]

Owners of the Chicago Brewing Company probably would have

agreed with Mosher's assessment that the selling of beer "comes down to marketing."[12] The CBC's primary focus of their early marketing efforts appears to have been to garner low-cost but high-profile public attention by making a connection between the legacy of the old Chicago brewing industry and their own contemporary brewing efforts.

With ambitious initial plans of opening not only a commercial brewery but also a restaurant and pub on North Sheffield, the owners took the easiest way of making a connection to the old brewing industry. One might call it "The Chicago Way," by claiming that the future pub's bar was once owned by Al Capone and that the brewery had bought the bar, once stored in a garage in Cicero, a former Capone-run Chicago suburb.[13]

After looking at the floundering results of the Sieben's and Tap & Growler brew pubs, the owners retrenched from the pub/restaurant/brewery concept and settled on a commercial bottling brewery site on North Besly, retaining the concept of attaching the brewery's existence to the nostalgia of the old local brewing industry. In short time, their flagship brand, appropriately named Legacy Lager, was born, followed in due time by Legacy Red Ale, Heartland Weiss, and Big Shoulders Porter.

The owners continued to hammer home their part in the continuing history of Chicago's breweries by arranging beer tastings at organizations such as the Chicago Historical Society and ensured that every newspaper reporter who wrote about the North Side brewery understood a thing or two about the local beer industry's long and colorful heritage and CBC's part in it. Their approach was cheap guerrilla marketing with a seemingly understandable theme that bridged the old with the new.

When the brewery failed to develop a hometown following with this one-legged approach, the owners tried to leapfrog into other markets outside Chicago. Recalls Ray Daniels,

> One of the biggest problems [CBC] had was that they never developed a following in Chicago—never built the home-market buzz that is needed to carry a brand beyond its home base. Instead, they shipped beer anywhere and everywhere that they could to try to build volume and cash flow. I remember being told at one point that they had just

shipped a container of beer to California. But there was no
support of any kind for it out there—no ads, no promotional
dollars, no visits by brewery personnel. It went out there, got
sold and that was the end of it; there were no repeat orders.
All that does is trash a market for you forever.[14]

The Chicago Brewing Company's product exportation to out-of-state
markets also caused repercussions in their home market. Jerry Glunz,
formerly part of local distributor Louis Glunz Beer, Incorporated,
recalled CBC's self-inflicted problems with the local distribution of
the brewery's products. "We'd get a retailer to set aside space on their
store's floor for a fifty-case display of CBC's beer, but when our truck
showed up to pick up the product from the brewery, they'd be short.
It wound up that they'd shipped most of the beer out for an order to
a different state."

Glunz felt there was a real demand in Chicago for CBC's beer but
found it difficult to fill open orders with their products. "I thought they
brewed a good product but they couldn't satisfy our retailers, always
coming up short on orders," something difficult to understand with
a 30,000 barrel system. "It was like they didn't have a plan," added
Glunz.[15]

The Pavichevich brewery took a much different approach to marketing their beer in Chicago. The Elmhurst, Illinois, brewery attempted
to immediately establish its Baderbrau brand as a high-end, super-
premium-priced product with mainstream appeal. To accomplish
this, owner Ken Pavichevich distanced his product from the emerging
microbrew industry's portfolio of ales, stouts, and quirky, less known
types of beers, and began referring to his lager product as a "boutique
beer." To that end, his draft beer started showing up in high-end establishments like the 21 East Hotel, the North Shore Hilton, and trendy
Chicago places like Shaw's Crab House, Café Ba-Ba-Reeba, and Oprah
Winfrey's Eccentric Restaurant.

The aggressive marketing efforts of the brewery garnered some free
publicity in local newspapers. Little bits and blurbs starting showing
up in print about Baderbrau beer. One mention in the local press
noted a request by President George Herbert Walker Bush's advance
men for a case of Baderbrau on one of the president's visits to Chicago.
Not to be outdone by the president, Illinois Governor Jim Thompson
made a small stink about Bush's present and was immediately sent

four cases of the creamy-headed beer by Pavichevich. Of course, this presentation of Baderbrau to "Big Jim" was also reported the next day in Chicago newspapers.

Soon after, the brewery's press kits included a notation about the president's fondness for the Elmhurst-brewed beer, an additional claim that Baderbrau was being served at official functions by the consul general of the German Consulate in Chicago, and an endorsement by noted beer author Michael Jackson. It was cheap guerrilla marketing at its best.

But it was the Elmhurst brewery's claims of the beer as being a "nutritional product" that started to wear thin and skirted dangerously close to violating Bureau of Alcohol, Tobacco and Firearms regulations.[16] Part of the brewery's press-kit material also consisted of a nutritional analysis sheet of Baderbrau, including a breakdown of how much of a person's daily caloric and vitamin requirements could be met with one liter of their beer.

In BATF Part §7.54 *Prohibited Statements for Malted Beverages*, under Section e, *Curative and Therapeutic Claims*, the bureau's regulation states

> Advertisements shall not contain any statement, design, representation, pictorial representation, or device representing that the use of malt beverages has curative or therapeutic effects if such statement is untrue in any particular or tends to create a misleading impression.[17]

The nutritional analysis sheet might have been argued as a valid informational tool, as other breweries have also taken this approach, but a handwritten letter from a cancer victim written to the brewery, which accompanied the press kit, pushed dangerously close to violating Section e.

In the letter, the ailing customer proclaimed that Baderbrau was not only "thirst quenching," but that the beer also "seemed to have hidden medicinal benefits."[18]

Like the Chicago Brewing Company, the Pavichevich brewery also tried to jump from the fiercely competitive Chicagoland market to the West Coast. In the spring of 1991, the brewery targeted the Oakland, California, area for its Baderbrau products with talk of later expanding to Portland, Seattle, and Denver.[19]

Finally in 1993, Pavichevich enlisted the help of the Pacific Beverage Marketing Group, with a staff of only five, to get his beer distributed in about twenty states. The marketing group was backed by the distribution muscle of Chicago-based Paterno Imports. It was an odd fit, however, since Paterno's speciality was the distribution of fine wines.[20]

Pavichevich also entered into an agreement with two owners of a Chicago advertising firm called Leap Partnership to develop an extensive marketing plan for the struggling brewery. In return for 100,000 shares of Baderbrau stock and seats on the Elmhurst brewery's board of directors, R. Steven Lutterbach and Frederich Smith allegedly promised Pavichevich that they "would use all efforts" to arrange for the Miller Brewing Company to use the Chicagoland brewery as a "test facility" for new products.[21]

It might have been a deal with the devil for some craft brewers, consorting with a larger national brewery, but the idea of using his brewery as a "pilot brewery" for the testing and launching of craft-styled Miller products was surely tempting for Pavichevich and would have ended his chronic problems of brewing under capacity and a lack of advertising and marketing money. Most important, implementation of the agreement would have given him the all-important distribution of product not only in the Chicagoland area but also possibly throughout the country.

A long two years after the agreement was to have gone into effect, however, Pavichevich filed suit in the Cook County Circuit Court, claiming that Lutterbach and Smith had pulled out of the agreement a scant two months after having promised to help the frustrated brewery owner.

According to the suit, Pavichevich charged that the two advertising firm owners "abruptly resigned" from the brewery's board without following through on their promised services.[22]

A year later, bruised and beaten by its own managerial inadequacies, the brewery would enter Chapter 11 protection but soon found itself up for auction as nervous creditors called in their loans.

Said Ken Pavichevich as the brewery went under and entered another chapter in the long and disappointing history of the Chicago brewing industry, "We were five years too early in tapping the microbrew popularity in Chicago."[23]

And a few million dollars short.

UNDERFUNDED OPERATIONS

This category of brewery problems inevitably becomes the burden of almost every brewery that has come and gone in the Chicagoland area. Throughout the existence of the old Chicago brewing industry, the cash flow of any brewing operation could be dried up by any number of events.

Destruction by fire was a particularly troublesome occurrence that often wiped out the fortunes of small, uninsured local breweries. Competition, price wars, and the need to implement the many technological changes that rapidly developed in the late 1880s also had its crippling effects on the continued successful operations of local breweries.

An atmosphere of financial setbacks also occurred in the Chicago brewing industry after Prohibition. Successful businessmen, with no experience in the brewing industry, jumped blindly into the trade as euphoric beer drinkers welcomed back the return of legal beer. It appeared at the time that even inexperienced businessmen operating any-sized brewery were assured of windfall profits. But as consumption patterns leveled off and overhead increased, investors found themselves bought out or forced to close by better funded competitors.

Chicago architect Daniel Burnham once said, "Make no small plans." What he should have added to this familiar adage might have been something that today's wannabe small brewery owner needs to repeat to himself like a daily mantra "if, and only if, I have the big bucks to follow through on my dreams."

During the earliest stages of the microbrewing craze, beer magazines and newspapers were resplendent with stories of home brewers who had won a national brewing award for "Best Pale Ale" or "Best Pilsener," using the freshest ingredients and latest innovations in home brewing equipment and techniques. Buttressed with these quaint awards plus the limited knowledge gained after two weeks at brewing schools that were suddenly attracting public attention as the microbrewing phenomena blossomed, scores of basement brewers were patching together stainless steel equipment from defunct dairy operations in Wisconsin for their cottage beer operations.

For the better-heeled entrepreneurs with similar dreams of turning out the next Anchor Steam or Sierra Nevada ale, liberal financing terms from the vendors of state-of-the-art brewing systems were all that were needed to start calling themselves Braumeisters. Almost overnight, brewery consultants also started popping up, offering their "expertise" for these start-up operations. The chants of "turn-key operation" from these sales people/consultants often had a soothing Lorelei-like effect on would-be brewery owners. "Just sign here," the equipment vendors said, and many brewing entrepreneurs did. It all seemed oh-so-easy.

It was only after the beer didn't come out as expected or distributors wanted nothing to do with unknown, unadvertised beers, or that retailers simply refused to give up profitable tap handles to beers their customers never heard of, that the harsh reality of owning a brewery in a very competitive market started to take hold. By that time, the money had run out.

Although some battle-scarred, but hardened microbrewery owners have endured the market dynamics that have led to the high attrition rate of small-sized brewing operations, there are still wishful dreamers who continue to think that the mere entry into the industry guarantees success.

Says one local brewery owner who's seen his shares of ups and downs in trying maintain a presence in the Chicago beer market; "I have a brewer friend at a brewpub who can't believe they lose money because it's so cheap to make beer, but he only factors ingredients into the equation, leaving out utilities, salaries, rent [and] debt service on the equipment," a recipe for disaster.[24]

PAVICHEVICH BREWING

With $500,000 of seed money, a $750,000 line of credit with the Gary-Wheaton Bank, and $1.5 million from a public stock offering, Ken Pavichevich seemed poised to grab a part of the huge Chicagoland beer market. Jim Koch from the Boston Beer Company, however, took one look at the Elmhurst, Illinois, operation in 1990 and gave his epitaph for the local brewery, "He [Pavichevich] could take away all my customers in Chicago and still go bankrupt in two years."[25]

Koch made this pronouncement based on a study of the financial status of the local brewery and his educated claim of knowing the start-up costs, overhead, and distribution figures of his competitor. "He started too big," argued Koch further. "The biggest way to amass a small fortune is to start with a big one. With microbrewing, you need to build up patiently. And the problem with a multimillion dollar setup is that there is a lot of pressure to grow."

The Sam Adams brewer was in the right church with his prediction, but in the wrong pew. When the Elmhurst brewery failed, it wasn't in 1992, but in 1997. Pavichevich was left holding a called-in $1.25 million note from the U.S. Bank of Pittsburgh and over $1 million in unsecured loans.[26]

CHICAGO BREWING COMPANY

After all the problems noted earlier with CBC's operation, the final straw was the one that all breweries with fatal problems ultimately face—they run out of money. Soon after the Pavichevich Brewing Company filed for Chapter 11 protection, the Chicago Brewing Company put their brewery equipment and beer brands up for auction. Back in September 1996, they too had filed for protection under Chapter 11, and they began a voluntary financial restructuring. CBC officials hoped that this reprieve might give them time not only to pay down debt but also to find some "white knights" to help with a cash infusion.

At the time of the restructuring, CBC President Steve Dinehart seemed optimistic about getting the brewery back on track. "New money will come in," he hopefully noted, "and our customers will have a greater selection and depth." But at the same time, Dinehart acknowledged some of the difficulties his brewery had been facing, and would continue to face, in Chicago. "[Chicago] is a residual market for everyone," he complained. "As a result, you have to deal with every beer in the U.S., and they all [the breweries and their local representatives] give stuff away like crazy," something an underfunded operation simply can't afford.[27]

Months later, and with all restructuring avenues exhausted, it was also over for the Chicago Brewing Company. With a growing debt of $2.5 million and a 1996 production run of only 5,000 barrels in a brewery with a 30,000-barrel capacity, the brewery went up for auction.[28]

NO BRAND LOYALTY

It was often a complaint from old-time Chicagoland brewers, especially in the post repeal years, that local beer drinkers had little hometown loyalty to the numerous beers that were still being produced in Chicago up through the 1970s. Not garnering sufficient local loyalty, however, was often self-inflicted. But as has been seen in the last twenty-years or so, a strong sense of loyalty for the national brands has developed among traditional beer drinkers,.

In Chicago, you can be a "Bud Man," an "MGD girl," or pound back cans of the "Silver Bullet." Although once a hometown favorite, Old Style has lost much of its luster; however, there are still lingering pockets of neighborhoods in Chicago where the beer from "God's Country" is still popular. As noted earlier, a handful of young local beer drinkers are even asking for Schlitz at their favorite watering holes, remembering the brand as "Grandpa's beer."

You never, however, see this sort of blind loyalty to brands with craft beer drinkers. No one from this group can ever be heard proclaiming "I'm a Goose Island man and a Cub's fan!"

Why? As Greg Hall from the Goose Island brewery has opined during some of his complimentary beer tastings, a lack of hometown loyalty helped ruin the old Chicago brewing industry and, unless fought with various contemporary methods of marketing and advertising, might also cripple today's Chicagoland breweries.

But is a lack of loyalty for local beers a big reason why Chicago's earliest microbreweries failed?

Jim Ebel, co-owner, of Two Brothers Brewing Company, Warrenville, IL, doesn't think so:

> Well, I don't think it is "the" reason for brewery failures, although I'd agree with the Halls that loyalty here is probably the worst out of any region in the country.
>
> This may be tangential, but I think the reason so many breweries have closed is usually based upon many internal reasons, not external. By this I mean quality control problems, poor financial planning, etc. and much of this was a direct result of people getting in the business that had no right being there.
>
> This isn't confined to Chicago by any means. I think when the boom hit everyone saw dollar signs, but a lot of people didn't take the time to really figure out what running a brewery is about, or how much it really costs."[29]

Randy Mosher, author of *Radical Brewing*, agrees that brand loyalty for craft-brewed beers is illusive:

> The "drink local" strategy hasn't worked for 150 years but I hardly ever talk to a craft brewer who thinks he can't count on it.
>
> [But] it is arrogant to assume that local people will support you simply because you are local. This is a transaction—you have to deliver to people something of value before they will repurchase, establish a relationship. This includes not only the liquid, but the story that is wrapped around it.[30]

LeRoy Howard, former partner at Three Floyds Brewing Company, Munster, IN, thinks there are a number of inherent causes for the lack of loyalty toward hometown beers:

> The specialty beer industry has opened up Pandora's Box. Now the consumers know there are a bunch of different styles and want to try them.
>
> Looking across the specialty beer market (domestic craft-brewed beer and specialty imports) as it has spread across the country, I would say that the consumer is not inherently brand loyal, but is category loyal. Meaning, they will more likely drink a specialty beer over a standard domestic like Bud, Miller, Coors or an import like Corona, Heineken, or Molson.
>
> In making their choice for a specialty beer, they will feel free to experiment. But let's look at this as a matter of degrees. I think most of our consumers have a brand or brewery (or two or three) they really like and more often than not will look for those brands (Goose, Sierra, Three Floyds). But if they want to explore something new, they look to other breweries, other styles, and to other brewing cultures (Belgian, German, etc.).
>
> What to do if your local brewery isn't brewing a rich Oatmeal Stout? You find someone who does.
>
> Looking for a sour, tart lambic? Look to European or domestic brewers producing it.

This is based on a specific dynamic, which is the basis of our industry. We have this specialty beer market because consumers got tired of the same old thing being offered and went out looking for something new and different. Some of these adventurers ended up building their own breweries and starting their own brands.

But a company can only produce and market so many brands. So by definition, their consumers will go out looking at other brands and styles. To expect this consumer to stay loyal to only one brand and not move around and try styles that brewery isn't even producing doesn't make sense.

We do get a local benefit in this industry, but it is no way as strong as it was historically perceived to be. I say perceived, because when consumers had no choice, they drank the local brew. Once choice was offered, they began looking around and trying other brands.

And if [we] are talking about the sort of brand loyalty that Anheuser-Busch, Miller, and Coors enjoy, well you have to buy that sort of loyalty. Even the big guys wouldn't have that sort of loyalty if they didn't spend millions on advertising and other promotional efforts.[31]

Steve Hamburg, beer consultant and local freelance writer, attributes the problems of poor products and advertising efforts by small local breweries as stalling any notion of local beer brand loyalty:

I don't think you can blame the failure of [the] Chicago Brewing Company on a lack of loyalty by Chicago drinkers. The infamous "curse" here has, at its roots, a more fundamental flaw—poorly conceived and operated businesses, often with no real passion for beer.

Part of the reason more Chicagoans don't drink local craft beer is that most of the local breweries have done a poor job promoting themselves.

Another, more fundamental reason, is that their beers just aren't good or unique enough.[32]

Goose Island

Seventeen years after Fred Huber pulled the plug on the Peter Hand Brewery, the Goose Island Brewery opened as a true brewing and bottling operation at 1800 West Fulton Avenue. From all appearances, owner John Hall and his brewmaster son Greg have seemingly tapped the code as to what makes a small Chicago brewery successful in a local market swimming in brands from brewing giants such as Anheuser-Busch, SABMiller, the newly merged Molson Coors, the vaporous but persistent Pabst Brewing Company—with no physical plants but a nostalgic portfolio of faded brands contract-brewed by others—and monstrous conglomerates such as Interbrew.

Recalling the original assumptions of why the Chicago brewing industry collapsed, a look at how this solitary brewery has taken on the biggest brands and the fickle tastes of Chicago beer drinkers and survives and thrives is warranted.

In 1986, Goose Island owner John Hall was flipping through a magazine while waiting to board his flight. An article about microbrewed beers caught his eye and eventually led to him to leave his position of twenty-one years with Container Corporation of America and establish a brewpub on North Clybourn in Lincoln Park rather than open a bottling brewery. "I had a vision of bottling and distributing beer, but I didn't think the market was ready at that time. I thought it was more realistic to open a brewpub and start small," says Hall. His vision proved prophetic.[33]

With numerous failed local examples of how not to operate a brewpub in Chicago, Hall patiently established the branding of his establishment, and most important, its line-up of small-batched beers. In 1995, John and his son Greg took the next carefully measured step and opened the Goose Island Fulton Street Brewery at 1800 West Fulton. They managed to push the brewery from its status as a start-up microbrewery (up to 15,000 barrels produced per annum) to its reclassification as a regional brewery (15,000 to 2 million barrels) in its first calender year of operation, a distinction that neither the Chicago Brewing Company nor the Pavichevich Brewing Company could achieve in their short years of existence. "Distribution is a good part of our success—and of course, good quality beers," notes Hall. "The variety of beers we now have kind of covers the spectrum," figures Hall, "but there are enough beers in our portfolio to keep beer drinkers interested and develop loyalty to our products. That's important. How much choice do you really get from Anheuser-Busch, for instance?"[34]

With a brewing capacity of 1.6 million cases, the Halls concentrate on what they do best—brew beer—and leave the sales, marketing, and distribution of their beers to United States Beverage LLC of Stamford, Connecticut. Distribution of their beers is carefully monitored. Greg Hall, who heads up the Fulton Street brewing team, explains the brewery's guarded philosophy of shipping beers to distant markets just to make a sale. "We know our limits on distribution [currently in twelve states] and know the boundaries of how far we can ship while maintaining the freshness," says the brewer.

Along with some contract-brewing for independent parties and the bottling of their Orange Cream Soda and Root Beer, the Goose Island Beer Company (now consisting of the Clybourn brewpub, another pub on North Clark Street, and the bottling brewery on Fulton) has managed to achieve what other Chicago breweries tried so hard to do in a span of more than 170 years but failed—build a loyal following of Chicagoland beer drinkers while successfully expanding their market beyond the confines of the Windy City.

"We aim to be Chicago's hometown beer," says John Hall.

Brewing Legacies

PART OF MY fascination with the history of beer and brewing in Chicago is the occasional discovery of an old brewery structure to add to the portfolio for my bus tours of the city's oldest breweries. Typically an old building or two, they are usually devoid of the structural companions that made up a pre-Prohibition brewery complex. At times, all that's left is a single entity, unceremoniously housing a dog grooming business, a Starbucks, a condominium, or in the most extreme case, an empty lot. *Chicagoland Breweries & Saloons Tours* has been been bringing these buildings to the attention of interested groups since 1999. But each year or so, a building disappears. In 1999, it was the Birk Brothers Brewery, the White Eagle in 2003, and in 2005, the William Pfeiffer and the Henn & Gabler (aka the McDermott Brewery) breweries. A recent drive-by of the Brand Brewery on Elston indicates one more historical structure awaiting its demise as a demolition crew chips away at the north end of the complex. I look at this push toward "progress" as an affront to the efforts and memories of some of Chicago's most neglected architects.

Chicago's predominance as a center for brewery architecture is well documented in the brewing trade journals of the 1870s and beyond. Centrally located in the Midwest, with an unfolding architectural school of new building design evident during this period, Chicago enjoyed a strategic advantage over East Coast architects, including established Old World brewery developers.

From the designs of local architects Frederick Wolf, Frederick Baumann, Louis Lehle, August Maritzen, Wilhelm Griesser, and others arose a proliferation of ornate but equally functional breweries built in Chicago and throughout the United States. The team of Wolf and Lehle is probably recognized as the most notable Chicago partnership in local brewery architecture. Their influence and design were also greatly utilized by the Jos. Schlitz Brewing Company of neighboring

Milwaukee and other breweries as far away as the Philippines. Many of the architectural drawings of these buildings can now be found at the Chicago Historical Society.

What catches the eye of even the untrained observer of local brewery design is the use by these architects and industrial engineers of the rounded arch style that can still be seen in the relics of the Schoenhofen Brewery office building on South Canal. In a study of architecturally styled contrast, the reconditioned Schoenhofen warehouse and powerhouse stands immediately east of the original Schoenhofen Brewery office structure. The reconditioned warehouse building exhibits a prairie-style of industrial design once favored by local architect Richard Schmidt during the early 1900s and stands as testimony to the evolving styles of a succeeding generation of brewery architects.

Some interesting side-bars concerning the Schoenhofen Brewery office building:

1. It's been reported a number of times in various publications that the building once served as a Jewish meeting hall, evidenced by the Star of David, immediately underneath the dates "1860 A.D. 1886" and above the front entrance The hexagram, however, was used extensively in the old brewing trade as a sign or symbol of the brewers' trade. Its medieval origins appear to go back as far as 1397 to brewing guilds in Southern Germany.
2. Below the "brewers' logo" is a patch of new bricks that were used to fill-in a hole where the terra cotta bust of Peter Schoenhofen once was exhibited somewhat prior to early 1985. The piece has never shown up in local breweriana auctions or on eBay.

Later-built brewery structures are almost devoid of ornate style and maintain a functional industrial look, a reflection of the changing economic conditions of the local brewing industry after 1900. As dictated by the evolving philosophy of the Chicago School of Architecture, form now followed function.

What these ornate brick buildings from the late 1870s to the turn of the century all shared in common was the central concept of natural gravity flow in the brewing operation. By the mid-1880s, the enormous brewing kettles were often stabilized with the interlacing support and structural features of the towers themselves. This dependent support technique probably explains why almost all of the brew house towers of the remaining old brewery structures still found throughout the city today have been removed; without the interlocking combination of kettles, which were resold or melted down for scrap when the firms closed, the existing walls of the towers would have soon collapsed.

SCHLITZ TIED-HOUSES

Schlitz and its old tied-houses are local curiosities with examples that can still be found throughout the Chicagoland area. This English-influenced practice of selling one—and only one—brand of beer through a retail outlet in return for the brewery paying all the saloon keeper's licensing fees and surety bonds, literally and legally tied a saloon to the brewery. The still-standing saloon buildings exhibit a deliberate similarity in design and function, although there are some exceptions. Two of the most beautifully maintained Schlitz buildings can be found at the Southport Lanes & Billiards at 3325 North Southport Avenue and Schuba's at 3159 North Southport, both within walking distance of each other. The Southport Lanes location is particularly interesting with its two interior murals of wood nymphs dancing through a Teutonic forest, one scene stretched across the top of the backbar, the other over the original four-lane, hand-set bowling alleys. Other locations of Schlitz tied-houses are on Belmont and Leavitt, Belmont and Damen, Armitage and Oakley, Armitage, just west of Damen, 21st and Rockwell, 35th and Western, 69th and Morgan, and 94th and Ewing.

BREWERY RELICS

A surprising number of old breweries can still be found throughout the city. Unfortunately, almost all of them have been deprived of their traditional towers. Nonetheless, a few of these relics still exhibit a majestic presence.

North Side Breweries

1. **BARTHOLOMAE & LEICHT BREWING COMPANY**—Sedgwick and Huron. In its final existence, it became part of the Milwaukee

and Chicago Breweries, Company, Ltd. conglomerate, aka the United States Brewing Company. The rounded arches and red brick make it a distinctive structure in the neighborhood.

In a real sense, it was the direct successor of the John A. Huck Brewery, the first brewery in Chicago to brew lager beer. Andrew E. Leicht had been the assistant superintendent of Huck's brewery. Both he and Philip Bartholomae had developed an interest in buying Huck's brewery, but after the fire of 1871 destroyed it, the partners commissioned the building of the Bartholomae & Leicht Brewing Company in 1873. The brewery had an annual capacity of 80,000 barrels. It closed in 1911. The last standing remnant of the brewery now houses a number of condos and small businesses. Beautiful.

2. **BRAND BREWING COMPANY**—2530 Elston Avenue. Another member of the old United States Brewing Company investment syndicate. Built in 1899 by brothers Virgil M. and Armin W., it's often mistakenly identified as the Michael Brand Brewing Company, built across the street by their father in 1878. Closed in 1935 and destroyed by fire sometime after 1955.

Its original capacity was 100,000 barrels annually. Designed by the Fred Wolf Company. The building is still in good shape but with an ugly, out of place structure added on to the front of the brewery at a later date. There's evidence, however, that it has a date with the wrecker's ball.

3. **MICHAEL BRAND BREWERY**—2525 Elston. There's some confusion with this brewery, once owned by Michael Brand, and the Brand Brewery across the street, owned by his sons. What's left of the brewery is now occupied by a restaurant equipment supplier. It was absorbed into the United Breweries syndicate in 1890. One of its most famous beer brands was Rheingold, later picked up by an East Coast brewery. Closed in 1955.

3. **THE HOME BREWERY**—2654–2670 West Elston, just north of the Brand Brewery. An unremarkable structure built in 1910 and closed in 1920, it reflects the economic reality of breweries built at this time in Chicago; function ruled over ornate and expensive

design. The designers of this brewery, unfortunately, took this concept to the extreme. A stone's throw away from Brand's Brewery, with an unremarkable presence.

4. **BEST BREWING COMPANY**—1301–1329 Fletcher Street. Originally built in 1885 as the Klockgeter & Company and renamed in 1890–1891 as the Best Brewing Company, the structure has been painstakingly preserved. It's now a condo complex, appropriately named "The Brewery." A brewery with a 150,000 barrel annual capacity, it closed in 1961. Best remembered as the brewery that provided canned beer to local grocery store chains, including A&P and National, and local Hillman's stores. A definite "must see" on your tour.

5. **CITY BREWERY COMPANY**—Rice (one block north of Chicago Avenue) and Hoyne. Part of the City of Chicago Brewing and Malting Company and later the Chicago Consolidated Brewing and Malting Company. At one time owned by local politician F. J. Dewes and known as the F. J. Dewes Brewery Company, some of the original complex is still scattered throughout the neighborhood although the brew house has been leveled. Closed in 1906, the original ice and refrigeration plant was in operation until recently—and looks like it will be demolished—while a larger building across from the old ice house has been turned into condos. Sprawling and industrial in design, it's worth a look.

6. **WEST SIDE BREWERY**—916 North Paulina. At one time owned by the Conrad Seipp Brewing Company, it became another element of the City of Chicago Consolidated Brewing and Malting Company brewing syndicate during the 1890s. At the turn of the century, the brewery covered almost the entire frontage of the 900 block of North Paulina. All that's now left is a single structure, minus its tower and top floors but still conspicuous at the south end of the block. Recently gutted and rehabbed as lofts, some of the Italianate architectural features remain visible. Had an annual capacity of 150,000 barrels. Decapitated and amputated of its neighboring structures, there's not much to look at now but it's nice to know that the remaining part of the plant still serves a useful function.

7. **NORTHWESTERN**—2270–2332 Clybourn. As indicated by the sprawling address, this brewery was a good-sized complex with a brewing capacity of 150,000 barrels annually. Built in 1888, it sat on the former site of the Nickerson Distillery. Merged into the United Breweries Company in 1898 and closed in 1921 after dabbling in the production of non alcohol malt tonic. All that's left is a single small building at 2274 Clybourn.

8. **PETER HAND**—Sheffield and Concord Place. The brewery proper was located nearby at 1000 West North Avenue. Across the street from the main structure was a garage, adorned with glazed terracotta logos from the brewery. In 1997, the garage met the same fate as the destroyed brewery. Soon thereafter, however, a new Cost Plus (now World Market) building was erected on the garage site, but amazingly, the architectural design included the saved logo pieces of a hand grabbing the letter "P." If you look up at the corners of the contemporary building, you'll see a resurrected part of Chicago's old brewery history.

South Side Breweries

9. **CARL CORPER BREWING COMPANY**—4160 South Union Avenue. Although the brewery is long gone, the barren site holds a bit of Chicago brewing industry significance. In early 1904, after being arrested for operating a brewery without a license and faced with bankruptcy and personal ruin, brewer Corper put a gun to his head and performed the fatal "Dutch Act" in the brewery office. The brewery was later known as the Westminster Brewing Company after national prohibition, and soon after as the Prima Brewing Company. It's safe to say that it was once a part of the Frank Nitti-controlled Manhattan Brewery combine.

On Union Avenue, just a bit north of a railroad viaduct stands a red brick wall, part of the original brewery. The south end of the wall still exhibits the classic rounded arches with the adjoining north part of the building that typified turn-of-the-century warehouse structure.

10. **MUTUAL BREWING COMPANY**—22nd & Spaulding Ave. Built in 1907, its owners openly continued to brew beer until 1924, five

years after the Illinois State Search & Seizure Act and Prohibition were in full force. With a Greek-influenced pediment over the old entrance and a battered cornerstone which still gives testimony to its opening day dedication, it's representative of a mix of pseudo-classical and industrial design. The cornerstone, however, does raise the interesting question as to whether it's a time capsule, possibly containing company papers or brewery memorabilia of interest.

11. **HOERBER BREWERY**—The brewery, once at 1617–1929 West 21st Place, is gone. Head west, however, and turn north on Paulina and you'll find the original brewery stable with a terra-cotta horse head still guarding the former entrance.

12. **PETER SCHOENHOFEN BREWING COMPANY**—18th & Canalport. Originally the Gottfried & Schoenhofen Brewery, the old red brick structure is everything a brewery hunter would want in a brewery building. Over the front entrance are the dates 1860 A.D.-1886. The year 1860 represents the original founding date of the G & S concern, originally located on 12th & Jefferson, but the significance of the end date of 1886 is unknown. The structure was built in 1867 and might represent the oldest existing brick structure in Chicago.

    Also note the star symbol representing the art of the brewer; it is not the Star of David, though claims have been made that King David was once a brewer.

    The reconditioned warehouse/powerhouse to the east of the original structure was built during the first few boom years of the early 1900s. Behind the building are three 1600-foot deep artesian wells, now capped. Additional structures of the brewery complex can be found scattered throughout the neighborhood, including what was once the old Stark's Warehouse structure on 16th and Canal, giving evidence of the huge size of the original nineteen-building brewery complex. Evidence can be seen of refurbishing on a number of the easily recognizable brewery buildings. Absolutely the most impressive and beautiful brewery ruins in Chicago.

13. **STEGE BREWERY**—Although the brewery at 15th and Ashland is long gone, one of its tied-houses still stands at 24th and Western on

the northeast corner. Look on the side of the building and you'll see the brewery's concrete relief logo.

14. **INDEPENDENT BREWING ASSOCIATION**—821–825 West Blackhawk at Halsted. This brewery was built by local investors, in answer to the growing infiltration of British investors into the Chicago brewing industry before the turn of the century. The brewery was operated during the early years of national prohibition as the Primalt Products Company and after Repeal as the Prima Company. The plant had an annual capacity of 150,000 barrels. A goodly number of the sprawling brewery buildings have been nicely restored and are now being used as office buildings. The complex easily rivals the Schoenhofen Brewery in elegance. A worthy stop on your brewery tour.

Guided bus tours for groups of 35 or more can be arranged. More information can be found at http://www.chicagoland beerhistory.com or contacting Bob Skilnik at 1-815-557-4608.

Glossary

G means German language.

ALE—lightly carbonated malted beverage produced from the top fermenting yeast, *saccharomyces cerevisiae*. Ferments out in 5 to 7 days. A precursor to lager beer.

BARREL HOUSE—a low class saloon. Customers usually stood around full barrels of inventory, using the containers as a bar.

BAUDELOT (G)—used to cool the boiling unfermented wort before pitching the yeast. Usually consist of a series of horizontal tubes, assembled into vertical stands. Replaced the inefficient coolship for the receiving of hot wort.

BIER GARTENS (G)—in Chicago, usually was an outdoor beer drinking area, heavily attended by German families on Sundays. More often than not, the original bier gartens were found in picnic groves or adjacent to a brewery.

BLIND PIGS—any unlicensed saloon or tavern

BLUE LAW—prohibits dancing, sports and drinking on Sundays; of puritanical derivation.

BRAUMEISTER (G)—literally, a brewing master. The highest level in the brewing trade.

COMFORT STATION—a public toilet or restroom

CONCERT SALOONS—turn of the century saloon that offered music and entertainment. Prostitution was not uncommon at these establishments.

COOPER—a person who makes or repairs barrels.

COPPER—the metal container in which the wort and hops are boiled. Originally made from copper. Contemporary vessels are usually stainless steel.

DIVE—a cheap, disreputable saloon.

DRINK OF MODERATION—beer. Originated by beer advocates during the late 1800s to distinguish the gentle effects of a moderate amount of beer consumption from the stronger effects of hard alcohol. The expression is still used in the brewing industry today.

DRUMMER—traveling beer salesman. During national prohibition, its use meant an agent of a bootlegger, who used intimidation and force when necessary to make a sale.

DRY—antidrink advocate.

EBULLIMETER—device used to measure alcoholic content.

FAMILY ENTRANCE—side entrance of a saloon. Properly escorted women would be brought into the saloon through this entrance. The almost instinctive habit of husbands escorting their wives through the side entrance of Chicago taverns would prevail through the 1950s.

FREE LUNCH—evolving from a complimentary heated oyster with every beer, the free lunch would later become a spread of meats, vegetables, and breads, washed down with a nickel glass of beer.

GOLDEN GATE—an original keg tapping device. Virtually obsolete today.

GOVERNMENT TUNNEL—restricted use tunnel that led from the beer storage tanks to the bottling department.

GREEN BEER—unfermented or partially fermented beer, not ready for consumption.

HOME RULE—the administration of the affairs of a precinct, ward, city, county, or state by the citizens who live in it.

HOP-JACK—straining device used to remove hops from the wort.

KILN—a single, double, or triple floor structure that removes moisture from the malt. The color of the malt depends on the length and intensity of the kilning process.

KRAEUSEN (G)—the introduction of young fermenting beer to beer that has achieved fermentation. The process creates a secondary fermentation which makes for carbonation and a completely fermented product.

LAGER BIER (G)—beer produced from the use of the bottom fermenting yeast, *saccharomyces uvarum*. Usually ferments out in 7 to 14 days and is stored (lagered) in a cool environment for an extended period of time for a final fermentation and rounding out of flavor.

LOCAL OPTION—often used by prohibitionists, it allows constituents in any precinct, ward, city, or county to petition for the elimination of the serving of alcohol in any given area. Enforced through referendum.

MALT—barley that has been steeped in warm water to initiate growth. After removal from the water, it is transferred to a compartment with a perforated floor through which warm humidified air is passed. After germination, the malt is transferred to the kiln for the final operation.

MASH—a mixture of water and ground malt from which are derived the necessary sugars for fermentation.

NATIVIST—a person who favors an American-born individual over immigrants.

NEEDLE BEER—near beer, usually injected with alcohol through the bung of the barrel.

PASTEURIZATION—the heating of beer to a temperature of 140°F for a predetermined period of time. Used to ensure microbiological stability of beer.

PICNIC BOTTLE—half-gallon bottle used during the World War II period.

PITCHING—the introduction of yeast to raw, unfermented beer.

PLACING THE BEER—establishing a beer account at a retail location.

PORTER—a type of ale, brownish or ruby in color and sweet in taste.

PROHIBITION—the forbidding by law of the manufacture, sale, or consumption of alcohol. National prohibition.

ON-PREMISE—the consumption of a drink at a bar or saloon.

RACKING—removing beer from a barrel or other device, usually for bottling.

RATSKELLER (G)—beer tasting room, usually located in the lower level of the brewery.

SCHWIMMERS (G)—tear drop or conical shaped metal containers for holding blocks of cooling ice. The containers were placed into the hot wort and allowed to "swim" on the surface of the wort.

SET-UPS—soda pop or seltzer used as an accompaniment to liquor. A "wash."

SHIPPING BREWERS—refers to any brewery that exports beer outside of their local market.

SMALL BEER—low alcohol beer.

SPENDINGS—an allocated amount of money used by beer salesmen to entice saloon customers to try their product with free drinks.

STEINIE—stubby sized, throw-away twelve-ounce bottle.

STERNEWIRTH (G)—free beer dispensed to brewery workers, often in lieu of higher pay.

TEETOTALER—a person who drinks no alcohol.

TIED-HOUSE—a saloon owned or controlled by a brewery.

WET—one who favors the use and manufacture of alcohol.

WILDCAT BREWERY—an unlicensed, clandestine brewery.

WORT—raw, unfermented beer.

Brand Slogans

IN THE COMPETITIVE years following repeal, advertising was the key element in distinguishing one brand of local beer from another. Slogans could be repeated in everything from radio and the scarce television commercials to print ads on billboards or packaging. The following list of brand slogans, container tags, and coaster slogans range from the obscure to the sometimes laughable. But in these short sentences is the genesis of today's beer advertising.

AMBROSIA BREWING COMPANY

Nectar Ambrosia
Premium Beer

"Properly Brewed, Aged, and Mellowed"
"For Particular People"

ATLANTIC BREWING COMPANY

Riviera Special Dark
Barbaross Beer
Tavern Pale Ale

"The Kind Dad Use to Drink"
"Premium Beer Brewed with Exactness"
"Sure It's Different . . . It's Brewed for Me"
"The Beer for a Good Head"

ATLAS BREWING COMPANY

Atlas Praeger

"Atlas Praeger, Got It? Atlas Praeger, Get It!"
"America's Most Imitated Beer!"
"Always Better Never Bitter!"
"Bitter Free"
"Best Beer in Town"

Bull Dog Malt Liquor	*"Robust Character, Mellow Smoothness"*
G*E*S Premium Beer	*"Yours for Better Living"*
Muenchener	*"For Particular People"*
Premium 9.0.5. Beer	*"Properly Aged in the Brewery Cellars"*

BEST BREWING COMPANY

Malt Marrow	*"The Family Treat That Can't Be Beat"*
Hapsburg	*"Made Best by Best"*

BIRK BREWING COMPANY

T·A·P Beer	*"Just Like Old Times"*
Trophy Beer	*"Taste How Good Good Beer Can Be!"*

DREWRY'S BREWERY

Genuine Bock Beer	*"A Famous Name since 1877"*
Drewry's Malt Liquor/Stout	*"A Man's Drink"*
Tropical Extra Fine Ale	*"Taste Tells"*

GARDEN CITY BREWERY

Old Brew Beer	*"Chicago's Best by Test"*
	"Wow! That's the Beer"
	"Above Par in Every Way!"

KEELEY BREWERY

Keeley Beer and Ale	*"Taste Just Right"*

MANHATTAN (CANADIAN ACE) BREWERY

KC's Best	*"Mellowed And Balanced"*
Lubeck Premium Beer	*"Old World Import Flavor"*
Black Dallas Beer	*"Brewed from the Finest Ingredients for Real Beer Lovers"*

McAvoy Brewing Company

Malt Marrow	*"Beats 'Em All"*
Alpha	*"A Distinctive Beverage"*

Meister Brau, Incorporated

Meister Brau Lite	*"Non-Filling"*
Meister Brau Beer	*"The Master Brew"*
	"The Custom Brew"
	"Gives you more of what you drink beer for"
	"You can't serve a finer glass of beer!"
	"The Beer"

Monarch Brewing Company/Van Merritt

Bullfrog Beer	*"Our Old Famous Brand"*
Monarch Beer	*"Brewed Better . . . To Taste Better"*
	"Let Your Taste Decide"
	"Fun for the money!"
Monarch Encore	*"The Mark of Perfection in Beer"*
Van Merritt	*"C'Mon Man . . . Have a Van"*

Peter Fox Brewing Company

Fox De Luxe Beer	*"Don't Say Fox . . . Say Fox Deee Luxe!"*
	"The Beer of Balanced Flavor"
	"Vitamins B and C in Every Drop"
	"For Finer Flavor—Finer Beer"
Patrick Henry Malt Liquor	*"Velvet Smooth"*

Peter Hand Brewing Company

Peter Hand's Reserve	*"Sets a New Standard of Excellence for Both the New World and the Old"*
	"There's So Much in Reserve for You!"
	"The Remarkable American Beer with the Continental Character"

PILSEN BREWING COMPANY

Yusay Pisen Beer

"Often Imitated but Never Duplicated"
"It's the Right Weigh"
(Advertised as a dietetically nonfatten-
ing drink)

PRIMA/BISMARCK BREWING COMPANY

Prima Beer

"The folks at home are thirsty too—Take
some Prima Home with You!"

Prima Three Star

"Say Prima Please and It Sure Will"

SCHOENHOFEN-EDELWEISS BREWERY

Edelweiss

"A Case of Good Judgement"

Centennial Beer

"Our Finest Beer in 100 Years"

UNITED STATES BREWING COMPANY

Gold Crown

"The Talk of the Town"

Loewen Brau

"The perfect Dark Beer"

Rheingold

"Not a common name. Not a common
beer . . ."
"Extra Pale like a Liquid Gold. It's
always the Favorite where Beer
is sold"
"Its popularity sweeps the country"

Chicago Club

"A real New Brew that's Flavored right,
we're sure you'll Like it, try it tonite!"

WHITE EAGLE BREWING COMPANY

Chevalier

"For Your Health's Sake"

Appendix of Chicago Breweries

THE ALPHANUMERIC LISTINGS of Chicago breweries are arranged in the following manner;

1. The first listing next to each numeric or alphanumeric entry gives the name of the brewery, the original address and the founding and ending date of the brewery.
2. Listings for any brewery entry will change to an alphanumeric entry when the one of the following events occur in the history of the brewery;
   a) name change as a result of incorporation, merger, or purchase by another
   b) party or brewing concern
   c) address change due to renaming or renumbering of street
   d) address change to a physical move to another location
   e) a gap in production due to Prohibition, fire, or other natural disaster, or bankruptcy

1 Albrecht & Finkler (Home Brewery)	1709 Lincoln Ave.	1901–1902
2 American Brewing Company	922 N. Ashland Ave.	1890–1901
3 Augsberg Brewing Company	3024 W. 30th St.	1934–1934
4 Adam Baierle	34–38 N. Market	1863–1869
5 Banner Brewing Company	1088–1092 Wilcox Ave.	1896–1897
6a Bartholomae & Leicht (Eagle Brewery)	684–706 Sedgwick St.	1873–1877
6b Bartholomae & Leicht Brewing Co.		1877–1889
6c Bartholomae & Leicht Brewing Co. (United States Brewing Co.)		1889–1890

6d Bartholomae & Leicht Brewing Co. (Milwaukee and Chicago Breweries Co., Ltd.) (aka United States Brewing Company)		1890–1911
7 John Behringer	157 Orchard near Willow	1861–1869
8a Bemis & Rindge		1862–1864
8b Downer, Bemis & Company	23rd & Kankakee	1864–1866
8c Downer, Bemis & Company	23rd & S. Park Ave.	1866–1869
8d Downer & Bemis Brewing Co.		1869–1882
8e Bemis & McAvoy Brewing Co.		1882–1887
8f McAvoy Brewing Co. (merged with Wacker & Birk)	91 S. Park Ave.	1887–1889
8g McAvoy Brewing Co. (Chicago Breweries, Ltd.)		1889–1920
8h McAvoy Company (Wacker & Birk Brewing & Malting Co.)		1920–?
9a Berliner Weiss Beer Brewery, Ferdinand Harke	82 Willow, Rear	1874–1875
9b Berliner Weiss Beer Brewery, August Harke		1875–1876
10a Matthias Best	Indiana Ave. near 12th & The Lake	1858–1863
10b Killian or Christian Schott	Indiana Ave. near N. Halleck	1863–1865
10c Martin Best	721 Indiana Ave.	1865–1866
11a M. Best	Foot of 14th St.	1852–1854
11b Conrad Seipp		1854–1855
11c Conrad Seipp	Foot of 27th St.	1855–1858
11d Conrad Seipp & Co. (aka Conrad Seipp)	Lakeshore near Northern, Rio Grande, Hardin Pl.	1858–1860
11e Seipp & Lehmann		1860–1872
11f Conrad Seipp	Lakeshore foot of 27th St.	1872–1876

11g Conrad Seipp Brewing Co.   1876–1890
(merged with West Side
Brewery Co.)

11h Conrad Seipp Brewing Co.   1890–1933
(City of Chicago Consolidated
Brewing & Malting Co., Ltd.)

12a Binz & LaParle   Cottage Grove,   1866–1868
between 27th &
28th Sts.

12b F. Binz Brewery   1868–1878
(aka Michael Keeley Brewery)   1876–1878

12c Keeley Brewing Co.   1878–1920

12d Keeley Brewing Co.   516 E. 28th St.   1933–1953

13a Blattner & Seidenschwanz   Hinsdale St. between   c1850–1857
(aka Blattner & Co.)   Rush & Pine Sts.

13b Seidenschwanz & Wacker   1857–1858

13c Wacker & Seidenschwanz   N. Franklin near   1858–1865
(aka Wacker & Co.)   Green Bay,
Asylum Place,
Dyer & Sophia

13d Frederick Wacker   848 N. Franklin St.,   1865–1867
later Webster Ave.

13e F. Wacker   1867–1872

13g Wacker & Birk Brewing &   Des Plaines &   1882–1889
Malting Co.   Indiana Sts.
(merged with McAvoy
Brewing Co)

13h Wacker & Birk Brewing & Malting 516 E. 28th St.   1889–1918
Co. (Chicago Breweries Ltd.)

14a Bohemian Brewing Co. of Chicago 680–706 Blue Island 1891–1896
Ave.

14b Atlas Brewing Co.   1896–1920
(aka Atlas Brewing Co. of   1896–1902
Chicago)

14c Atlas Beverage Co.   1920–1929

14d Atlas Brewing Co.   1944–1951
(affiliated with Schoenhofen-
Edelweiss)

14e Atlas Brewing Co. (branch of Drewry's Ltd., South Bend, IN)		1951–1962
15 William Bohn	651 37th St.	1893–1993
16a Brand Brewing Co.	1251 Elston Ave.	1899–1909
16b Brand Brewing Co. (aka Producer's Brewing Co.)	2530 Elston Ave.	1901–1922 1916–1920
16c Brand Co. (aka Prima Products Co.) (aka Royal Brewing Co.)		1932–1935 1932 1934
17a Brand & Hummel Brewing Co.	Ave. L & 100th St.	1880–1887
17b South Chicago Brewing Co.		1887–1895
17c South Chicago Brewing Co.	Ave. N & 100th St.	1895–1897
17d South Chicago Brewing Co. (aka United Breweries Co., aka South Chicago Brewery)		1897–1922
18a Michael Brand	Elston Ave. near W. Fullerton	1871–1879
18b Michael Brand & Co.	Elston Ave. near Snow St.	1878–1879
18c The Michael Brand Brewing Co.		1886–1889
18d Unites States Brewing Co. of Chicago (aka Michael Brand Brewing Co.) (Milwaukee and Chicago Breweries, Ltd.)		1890–1927 1890–1915 1890–1927
18e United States Brewing Co.		1932–1955
19a Brewer & Hofmann Brewing Co.	41–55 S. Green St.	1886–1902
19b George J. Cooke		1905–1910
19c George J. Cooke Co.	14–30 N. Green St.	1910–1922
20a Brisach & Hessemer	Oak St. near Green Bay	1858–1859
20b Joseph Brisach	Foot of Oak St.	1859–1860
21 Broadway Brewing Co.	5245 Broadway	1934–1934
22a Bucher & Hiller	Green Bay Rd.	1858–1866
22b George Hiller	9104 N. Clark & Green Bay Rd. & Wolcott	1866–1868
23a George Burroughs		c1850

23b Frederick Burroughs	144 W. Lake near Union	c1854–1862
24a Valentin Busch	31 Cedar St. near Green Bay & Wolcott	1851–1858
24b Busch & Brand		1858–1873
24c Busch & Brand Brewing Co.		1873–1879
25a Calumet Brewing Co. (aka Calumet Brewery)	10555–10557 Torrence Ave.	1901–1909
25b Calumet Brewing & Malting Co.	Torrence & 106th St.	1909–1911
25c Bessemer Brewing Co.		1911–1913
26a James Carney	39–63 S. Water St.	1840–1855
26b John O' Neill		1855–1860
27 Castle Brewery Co.	E. Chicago Ave. & River St.	1896–1896
28 Chicago Ale & Malt Co.	S. Water & Clark	1861–1867
29a Chicago Brewing Co.	64–80 W. North St.	1888–1898
29b Chicago Brewing Co. (United Breweries Co.)		1898–1909
29c Chicago Brewery (United Breweries Co.)	1269 W. North	1909–1919
30a Chicago Union Brewing Co. (aka Union Brewing Co.) (aka Patrick O' Neill)	27th St. & Johnson	1867–1885
30b Cooke & Stenson		1885–1887
30c Cooke Brewing Co.	Brewery Ave. & 521 E. 27th St.	1887–1910
31a Citizens Brewing Co.	Archer Ave. & Main Sts.	1893–1898
31b Citizens Brewing Co. (United Breweries Co.) (aka Citizens' Brewery)	Archer Ave. & Throop St.	1898–1920
31c Bismarck Brewing Co. (aka Hunter's Brewery Inc.)	2738–2762 S. Archer	1933–1941 1940–1941
31d Prima-Bismarck Brewing Co.		1941–1951
32a Columbus Brewing Co.	297 Cornell & Noble	1902–1910
32b Lutz Brewing Co.		1910–1910
32c Atlantic Brewing Co.	1401 Cornell & Noble	1910–1912
33a Corper & Nockin	101–109 Webster Ave.	1886–1891

33b	Birk Bros. Brewing Co.		1891–1909
33c	Birk Bros. Brewing Co.	1315–1325 Webster Ave.	1901–1923
33d	Birk Bros. Brewing Co.	2117 N. Ward at Webster	1933–1936
33e	Birk Bros. Brewing Co.	2117 N. Wayne St.	1936–1950
34a	Carl Corper Brewing & Malting Co.	39th & S. Union	1893–1898
34b	Carl Corper Brewing & Malting Co. (United Breweries Co.)		1898–1900
34c	Carl Corper Brewing Co.	41st & Union	1903–1904
34d	Globe Brewing Co.		1904–1910
34e	Brand Brewing Co., No. 2	4057 S. Union	1910–1913
35	Matthew Cziner	18 Canalport Ave.	1874–1875
36a	Francis J. Dewes	764 W. Chicago	1882–1885
36b	F.J. Dewes Brewery Co.		1885–1890
36c	F.J. Dewes Brewery Co. (City of Chicago Brewing and Malting Co.)		1890–1898
36d	City Brewery Co. (Chicago Consolidated Brewing and Malting Co.)		1898–1906
	(aka Malt Sinew Co.)		1901–1906
37a	Arah P. Dickinson	Cass & Michigan	1858–1859
37b	Dickinson & Bemis	Cass & Kinzie	1859–1860
37c	Arah P. Dickinson (aka North Star Brewery)		1860–1864
38	Thomas Donovan	Pine & Pearson Sts.	c1860
39	Downer, Bemis & Co. (Ale & Porter Brewery)	16th St. at The Lake	1860–1864
40a	Morgan Doyle	423 Wolcott	1863–1864
40b	Doyle & Brother	State St.	1864–1866
40c	Doyle & Brother (aka Doyle & Co.)	423 N. State St.	1866–1878 / 1874–1875
40d	John Devereaux		1878–1879
41a	Eagle Brewing Co.	1469–1479 N. Western Ave.	1901–1909
41b	Eagle Brewing Co.	2608–2631 N. Western Ave.	1909–1927

42 Simon Eichenseher	Larrabee between	1858–1866
(aka Eichenseher & Screiber)	Willow & Center	1863
43a Endlich & Saladin	164–168 Archer Ave.	1858–1860
43b William Saladin		1860–1870
43c Matheus Gottfried		1870–1882
43d Gottfried Brewing Co.	2249 Archer	1882–1924
44a Ernst Bros. Brewing Co.	47–67 Larrabee St.	1884–1889
44b Ernst Bros. Brewery		1889–1890
(Milwaukee and Chicago		
Breweries)		
(aka United States Brewing Co.)		
45 Erickson & Berquist	123 S. Edgwick	1874–1875
46 Julius Fachenbach	449 W. Fullerton	1898–1902
47a Ernst Fecker, Jr	863–869 Dudley St.	1894–1895
(ale & porter brewery)		
47b Geo. J. Stadler Brewing Co.	863–869 Winchester Ave.	1895–1899
47c Stenson Brewing Co.		1899–1903
47d Stenson Brewing Co	1748 N. Winchester	1909–1923
47e Stenson Brewing Co.		1933–1943
48a The Fecker Brewing Co.	871–875 Dudley St.	1890–1895
(lager brewery)		
48b The Fecker Brewing Co.	871–875 Winchester	1895–1898
48c The Fecker Brewing Co.		1898–1901
(United Breweries Co.)		
49 F.C. Feigel	721 Indiana Ave.	1875–1876
50 August Fischer	20 S. Des Plaines Ave.	1888–1888
51 William Fleming	Hinsdale St. near Green Bay Rd.	1858–1876
52a William Fleming & Co.	Wolcott near Church	1861–1863
52b Excelsior Brewery, William Fleming	110 Grand Haven	1863–1869
(aka Fleming & Conway)		1863–1864
53a Fortune & Co.	62 Oakwood	1864–1865
53b Schmidt & Katz		1865–1866
53c Schmidt, Katz & Leverns		1866–1867
53d Schmidt, Katz & Co.		1867–1869
54a Fortune Bros.	138–144 W. Van Buren	1857–1881
54b Fortune Brothers Brewing Co.	225 Des Plaines	1881–1920
54c Fortune Bros. Brewing Co.	725 W. Van Buren	1936–1948

55a	E. Funk & Co.	144–146 Willow St.	1874–1877
55b	Ernst Funk		1877–1884
55c	Ernst Funk	50 Clyde St.	1884–1891
55d	Ernst Funk	50 Osgood St.	1891–1909
55e	Ernst Funk	1921 Osgood St.	1909–1911
56a	Gambrinus Brewing Co.	1525–1547 Fillmore	1900–1909
56b	Gambrinus Brewing Co.	3032–3058 Fillmore	1909–1922
56c	Gambrinus Brewing Co.		1933–1935
56d	Gambrinus Co., Inc.		1935–1936
56e	Patrick Henry Brewing Co., Inc.		1936–1939
57	Garden City Brewing Co.	868 Hoyne	1890–1890
58a	Garden City Brewing Co.	21st Pl. & S. Albany	1901–1902
58b	Garden City Brewery		1902–1925
58c	Garden City Brewery	2111–2123 S. Albany	1933–1951
59	Jacob Gauch	Indiana St. between Pine & St. Clair	c1845
60	Joseph Geeman	Clybourn near Larrabee	1862–1865
61a	Gillen, Schmidt & Co.	404–416 E. 25th St.	1878–1880
61b	Henry F. Gehring (aka Bavarian Brewing Co.)		1880–1884
61c	Bavarian Brewing Co. (aka O' Donnell & Duer)		1884–1891
61d	Cantwell & Ryan Eagle Brewing Co.		1891–1893
61e	Cantwell Eagle Brewing Co.		1893–1897
62	Goose Island Beer Company	1800 W. Fulton	1995–
63a	Gottfried & Schoenhofen	178 W. 12th St.	1860–1864
63b	Gottfried & Schoenhofen	34–50 Sewar St., 18th & Canalport	1864–1867
63c	Peter Schoenhofen		1867–1879
63d	Peter Schoenhofen Brewing Co. (merged with National Brewing)		1879–1925
64	Gutsch Brothers	160–169 W. Lake St.	1859–1865
65	Haas & Powell	27–31 W. Madison	1870–1871
66a	Haas & Sulzer Brewery		1833–c1836
66b	William Haas & Co.	Pine & Chicago Ave.	c1836–1841
66c	Lill & Diversey		
	(aka The Chicago Brewery)		1841–1871
	(aka Lill's Chicago Brewery)		1867–1869

67a Peter Hand Brewery Co.	37–59 Sheffield Ave.	1891–1909
(aka Peter Hand Brewing Co.)		1891–1891
66b Peter Hand Brewery Co.	1612–1632 Sheffield Ave.	1909–1920
66c Peter Hand Brewery Co.		1933–1967
66d Meister Brau, Inc.	1000 W. North Ave.	1967–1972
(aka Warsaw Brewing Co.)		1971–1972
66e Peter Hand Brewing Co.		1973–1978
67 Thomas G. Hanson	28 Chicago Ave.	1862–1867
68 Healy & Regitz	129–131 Fullerton Ave.	1887–1888
69a Henn & Gabler Brewing Co.	35th & Ullman St.	1892–1895
69b Henn & Gabler Brewing Co.	34th & Court St.	1895–1898
69c Henn & Gabler Brewery		1898–1901
(North Western Brewery)		
(United Breweries Co.)		
69d Northwestern Brewery Co. No. 2		1901–1908
(United Breweries Co.)		
(aka Henn & Gabler Brewery)		
70 Matthew Hitz	Green Bay & Cedar	1855–1862
71a Jos. Hladovec Brewing Co.	1090–1118 W. 21st St.	1890–1892
71b Monarch Brewing Co.		1892–1898
71c Monarch Brewing Co.		1898–1904
(aka Monarch Brewery)		1898–1909
(United Breweries)		
71d Monarch Brewery	2419–2443 W. 21st St.	1909–1922
71e Monarch Beverage Co.		1923–1932
71f Monarch Brewing Co., Inc.		1932–1936
71g Monarch Brewing Co.		1936–1958
71h Van Merritt Brewing Co.		1958–1967
(aka Bohemian Brewing Co.)		1958–1967
(aka House of Augsburg)		1959–1967
(aka Monarch Brewing Co.)		1958–1967
72a John L. Hoerber	216–224 W. 12th St.	1864–1882
72b Bartholomay & Burgweger Brewing Co		1882–1887
72c William Ruehl Brewing Co.		1887–1898
72d William Ruehl Brewing Co.		1898–1907
(aka Ruehl Brewery)		
(United Breweries Co.)		

73a John L. Hoerber	186 Griswold St.	1858–1864
73b Hoerber & Gastriech		1864–1865
73c John L. Hoerber		1865–1865
73d Michael Sieben	186–188 Pacific Ave.	1865–1876
74a John L. Hoerber	646–662 Hinam	1882–1885
74b John L. Hoerber Brewing Co.	646–662 W. 21st Pl.	1885–1909
74c John L. Hoerber Brewing Co.	1617–1629 W. 21st Pl.	1909–1927
74d The Hoerber Brewing Co.		1934–1941
75a Hofmann Bros. Brewing Co.	107 W. Monroe	1896–1909
75b Hofmann Bros. Brewing Co.	2606–2626 W. Monroe	1909–1925
75c Peter Fox Brewing Co.		1933–1955
76 Home Brewery	2654–2670 Elston Ave.	1910–1920
77 Home Brewing Co.	1294 W. 61st St.	1895–1895
78 Home Weiss Beer Brewery (aka Home Brewery)	2702 N. 40th St.	1913–1916
79a Huck & Schneider	Chicago Ave. & Division	1847–1855
79b John A. Huck (Eagle Brewery)	Wolcott near Division	1855–1860
79c Huck's Chicago Brewing Co.		1860–1869
79d John A. Huck Brewing Co.	445–449 N. State	1869–1871
80a Illinois Brewing & Malting Co.	38th & S. Centre Ave.	1901–1910
80b White Eagle Brewing Co.	3735 S. Centre Ave.	1910–1913
80c White Eagle Brewing Co.	3735–3757 S. Racine Ave.	1913–1925
80d Mid-West Products Co.		1926–1932
80e White Eagle Brewing Co.		1933–1950
81a Independent Brewing Association (aka Prima Tonic Co.)	585–612 N. Halsted	1901–1909 1905–1907
81b Independent Brewing Association	1440–1472 N. Halsted	1909–1915
81c Independent Brewing Association	821–825 Blackhawk	1915–1920
81d Primalt Products Co.		1920–1925
81e The Prima Co. (merged with Bismarck Brewing Co.)		1933–1938
82a Joseph Jerusalem	Foot of Elm St.	1868–1871
82b Joseph Jerusalem	357–365 Rush St.	1872–1887
82c Ulrike Jerusalem	562–564 N. Halsted	1888–1891

82d Gustav Eberlein		1891–1903
82e Ulrike Eberlein		1903–1908
(aka Eberlein Weiss Beer Brewery)		1904–1908
83a Joseph Junk	3700–3710 S. Halsted	1883–1887
83b Magdalena Junk		1887–1904
(aka Junk's Brewery)		1890–1892
83c Jos. Junk Brewing Co.		1904–1909
83d South Side Brewing Co.		1909–1921
83e South Side Ice & Beverage Co.		1922–1926
83f South Side Brewing Co		1934–1937
(aka Frederick Bros. Brewing Co.)		1934–1937
83g Ambrosia Brewing Co.		1937–1959
(aka Frederick Bros. Brewing Co.)		1937–1941
83h Atlantic Brewing Co., plant 2	827 W. 37th Pl.	1959–1965
84 Henry Kassens	Hyde Park	1884–1884
85 George Keller		1867–1869
86a Kerber & Stege	583 N. Clark	1864–1866
86b Herman Spanknebel		1866–1867
86c Edward Stege		1867–1868
87a Klockgeter & Co.	1317 Fletcher	1885–1886
87b Kagebein & Folstaff		1886–1889
(Lakeview Brewery)		
87c Alvin Greiner		1889–1891
87d Best Brewing Co. of Chicago		1891–1915
(aka Best Brewing Co.)		
87e Best Brewing Co. of Chicago	1301–1329 Fletcher	1915–1928
87f Best Brewing Co. of Chicago		1932–1950
(aka Best Brewing Co.)		1933–1934
(aka National Brewing Co.)		1933–1935
87g Best Brewing Corp.		1950–1961
(aka Malt Marrow Brewing Co.)		
88 William Knight	Hubbard between Lincoln & Roby	1861–1863
89 Koch & Poggensee	455–457 W. North	1905–1906
90a Koch & Reyber	Hyde Park	1888–?
90b Louis Wagner		?–1891
91 Koller Brewing Co., Inc.	39th & Racine	1933–1953
92 A.G. Kurth	1049 N. Oakley Ave.	1888–1888
92a Louis Lamm	941–943 N. Western	1897–1891

92b	Germania Brewing Co.		1898–1899
92c	Germania Brewing Co.	588 N. California	1899–1900
93	Ludwick & Co.	31 Green Bay Rd.	1858–1863
94a	Charles B. Mader	347 Milwaukee Ave.	1884–1888
94b	Mader & Bartelme		1888–1890
94c	Charles B. Mader		1890–1893
94d	C.B. Mader & Co.		1893–1895
94e	Siegler & Schiemann Brewing Co.		1895–1897
94f	Imperial Brewing & Bottling Co.		1897–1898
94g	Globe Brewing Co.		1898–1901
94h	Charles B. Mader		1901–1902
94i	Chicago Consolidated Bottling Co.		1902–1904
94j	Koch & Poggensee		1904–1907
95a	Manhattan Brewing Co.	3901 S. Emerald Ave.	1893–1933
	(aka Malt Maid Products Co.)		1923–1932
	(aka Malt Maid Co.)		1923–1932
	(aka Fort Dearborn Products Co.)		1925
95b	Manhattan Brewing Co.	3900–3950 S. Union	1933–1947
95c	Canadian Ace Brewing Co.		1947–1968
	(aka Ace Brewing Co.)		1958–1962
	(aka Ace Hi Brewing Co.)		1958–1962
	(aka Allied Brewing Co.)		1954–1957
	(aka Berlin Brewing Co.)		1964–1965
	(aka Bismarck Brewing Co.)		1963–1968
	(aka Cold Brau Brewing Co.)		?
	(aka Crest Brewing Co.)		1961–1964
	(aka Empire Brewing Co.)		1959–1963
	(aka Essex Brewing Co.)		1957–1961
	(aka Essex Brewing, Ltd.)		1957–1961
	(aka Gipps Brewing Co.)		1956–1963
	(aka Gold Brau Brewing Co.)		1958–1968
	(aka Hapsburg Brewing Co.)		1964–1967
	(aka Jester Brewing Co.)		1953–1957
	(aka Kings Brewing Co.)		1959–1962
	(aka Koening Brau Brewing Co.)		1955–1967
	(aka Kol Brewing Co.)		
	(aka Leisy Brewing Co.)		1960–1964
	(aka Lubeck Brewing Co.)		1960–1964

(aka Malt Maroow Brewing Co.)		
(aka 9–0–5 Brewing Co.)		1962–1965
(aka Old Missouri Brewing Co.)		
(aka Old Vienna Brewing Co.)		1962–1964
(aka Pilsen Brewing Co.)		1962–1968
(aka Prima Brewing Co.)		1955–1964
(aka Prima-Bismarck Brewing Co.)		1956–1960
(aka Royal Brewing Co.)		1964–1966
(aka Schultz Brewing Co.)		
(aka Star Union Brewing Co.)		1963–1968
(aka Superior Brewing Co.)		1963–1965
(aka Tudor Brewing Co.)		
(aka United States Brewing Co.)		
(aka Westminster Brewing Co.)		1958–1962
(aka Westminster Brewery, Ltd.)		1958–1962
(aka Windsor Brewing Co.)		1956–1960
96 MacDonald Brewery	1300–1308 McKinley Ave.	1935–1935
97 Frank McDermott Brewing Co.	3435–3441 S. Racine	1925–1937
(aka Beverly Brewing Co.)		1937
(aka Hunters Brewery, Inc.)		1934
(aka Frank McDermott)		
98 Metropolitan Weiss Beer Brewing Co.	3802 S. Armour Ave.	1898–1898
99a Mette & Vogt	471 E. 26th St.	1888–1889
99b John Vogt	467–473 26th St.	1889–1892
99c Vogt & Sweeney		1892–1895
(aka Vogt & Sweeney Brewing Co.)		1892–1895
99d Mullen Brewing Co,		1895–1904
(aka James J. Mullen)		1895
100a George Metz	401–403 Wolcott	c1850–1869
(aka Union Brewery)		
(aka George Metz & Killian Schott)		1862–1863
(aka Metz & Brand)		1863–1864
100b Metz & Steges	401–403 N. State	1869–1875
(aka Union Brewery)		
100c George Metz, Jr.		1875–1877

101a Miller & Son	State St. between Goethe & Division	1863–1870
101b Seipp & Lehmann		1870–1871
102a H.B. Miller & Son	Wolcott & Grand Haven Strip	1865–1865
102b H.B. Miller & Son	420–440 N. State St.	1866–1868
103 John B. Miller	Larrabee between North & Blackhawk	1859–1862
104 Timothy Mitchell	Hyde Park	1862–1864
105 Moser Bros.	62–64 Hulburt	1866–1868
106a Mueller Bros.	1131–1137 Fulton	1887–1890
106b The Star Brewery Co.		1890–1897
(aka Star Brewery)		
(aka The Star Brewery of Chicago)		1896–1898
106c The Star Brewery		1898–1902
(branch of United Breweries Co.)		
(aka Star Brewery of Chicago)		1898–1900
107a Mueller Brothers	28 S. Des Plaines	1884–1888
107b Mueller Bros. Brewing Co.		1888–1890
108a A.&G.H. Mueller (aka Mueller Bros.)	152 W. Randolph	1859–1862
108b Mueller Bros.	308 W. Madison	1862–1865
109a Simon Munger	212 W. Chicago Ave.	1888–?
109b Henry P. Caldwell		?–1891
110a John Nangle	Lydia between Union & Halsted	1861–1864
110b John Nangle	154 N. Rueben	1864–1868
111a National Brewing Co.	846–860 W. 18th St.	c1889–1909
(aka National Malt Tonic Co.)		1900–1909
111b National Brewing Co.,	1900–1910 W. 18th St.	1900–1910
111c Schoenhofen Co.,		1925–1933
(aka National Brewing Co.)		1925–1933
(aka National Malt Tonic Co.)		1925–1928
111d Schoenhofen Edelweiss Co.	1900–1956 W. 18th St.	1933–1944
111e Schoenhofen Edelweiss Co.		1944–1951
(affiliated with Atlas Brewing Co.)		
111f Schoenhofen Edelweiss Co.		1951–1966
(branch of Drewery's, Ltd., South Bend, IN)		

(aka Atlas Brewing Co.)		1951–1966
(aka Barbarossa Brewing Co.)		1959–1966
(aka Drewery's Ltd., USA)		1962–1966
(aka Great Lakes Brewing Co.)		1957–1964
(aka 9-0-5 Brewing Co.)		1960–1962
(aka Prost Brewing Co.)		1961–1965
(aka Trophy Brewing Co.)		1960–1964
111g Schoenhofen Edelweiss Co.,		1966–1971
(branch of Associated Brewing		
Co., Detroit, MI)		
(aka Associated Brewing Co.)		1970–1971
(aka B.B. Brewing Co.)		1966–1971
(aka Drewery's Ltd., USA)		1966–1971
112a Mutual Brewing Co.	3324 W. 22nd St.	1907–1924
(aka The New Brewery)		1907
112b Mutual Ice & Beverage Co.	22nd & Troy	1933–1933
113 Non-Alcoholic Beer Co.	54 Clybourne Ave.	1893–1893
114a North Western Brewing Co.	781–831 Clybourne Ave.	1888–1898
114b North Western Brewing Co.,	1898–1909	
(United Breweries Co.)		
(aka North Western Brewery)		
114c North Western Brewery,	2270–2332 Clybourn Ave.	1909–1921
(aka North Western)		1918–1921
115a O' Donnell & Duer	3937 S. Wallace	1892–1904
(aka Bavarian Brewing Co.)		
115b Muller Brewing Co.		1904–1917
115c National Brewing Co.		1917–1918
116a Chas. F. Ogren	W. Division & Wood Sts.	1886–1888
116b Chas F. Ogren	625–629 Shober St.	1888–1892
116c Chas. F. Ogren Brewing Co.		1892–1895
116d Chas. F. Ogren Brewing Co.	625–629 N. Irving Ave.	1895–1909
(aka Ogren Brewing)		1908
(aka Charles F. Ogren & Co.)		1898–1909
116e Charles F. Ogren	1222–1228 N. Irving Ave.	1909–1913
(aka Ogren Brewing Co.)		
117 Old Abbey Brewery Corp.	4539–4541 Armitage Ave.	1936–1941

118a John O' Neill Brewery	Cedar St.	?–1860
118b Dickinson & Bemis		1860–1862
119 John Parker	115–117 Dearborn	c1854–1856
(Garden City Brewery)		
120a William Pfeifer	499 Milwaukee Ave.	1888–1891
120b William Pfeifer	339–347 Leavitt St.	1892–1909
(aka Berlin Weiss Beer Co.)		1892–1905
(aka William Pfeifer Weiss Beer Co.)		1892–1905
(aka Pfiefer's Berlin Weiss Beer Co.)		1905–1909
121c William Pfeifer	718–742 N. Leavitt St.	1909–1918
(aka Pfiefer's Berlin Weiss Beer Co.)		
121d Superior Brewing Co.		1933–1941
(aka Hunter's Brewery, Inc.)		c1936
122a John Pforr	147–149 Fullerton Ave.	1888–1892
122b Catherine Pforr		1892–1895
122c Catherine Pforr	74 Perry St.	1895–1897
(aka John Pforr)		
122d John Pforr,		
(aka Catherine Pforr)		1898–1900
(aka Catherine Pforr Estate)		1901–1903
(aka J. Pforr & Co.)		1903–1904
(aka Pforr Weiss Beer Brewery)		1904–1908
122e Edw. J. Birk & Bro.	2341 Perry St.	1910–1912
123a Phoenix Brewing Co.	53–63 W. Division St.	1896–1898
123b Phoenix Brewing Co.		1898–1901
(United Breweries Co.)		
124a Pilsen Brewing Co.	368 W. 26th St.	1903–1909
124b Pilsen Brewing Co.	3043–3065 W. 26th St.	1909–1920
124c Pilsen Brewery Co.		1933–1962
(aka Pilsen Products Co.)		1933–1936
125a Pohl Bros.	27–35 Cooper St.	1881–1882
125b Pohl & Henry		1882–1884
125c Paul Pohl		1884–1905
125d Paul Pohl Brewing Co.	2335–2344 Cooper St.	1905–1913
125e Tabor Brewing Co.		1913–1915

125f North American Brewing Co.		1915–1932
(aka Bosworth Products Co.)		1927–1932
125g Bosworth Products Co.	2336 Bosworth Ave.	1932–1933
125h Atlantic Brewing Co.,	1545–1549 W. Fullerton	1933–1965
(aka Champagne Velvet		1960–1965
Brewing Co.)		1960–1965
(aka C.V. Brewing Co.)		1960–1964
(aka Excell Brewing Co.)		
(aka Red Top Brewing Co.)		
(aka Savoy Brewing Co.)		
(aka Tuxedo Brewing Co.)		
126 Quist & Carlson	895 Sheffield Ave.	1908–1908
127a Jacob Rehm & Co.	333–337 W. 12th St	1865–1866
127b Rehm & Bartholomae		1866–1868
127c Bartholomae & Co.		1868–1873
127d Bartholomae & Roesing		1873–1888
127e Bartholamae & Roesing Brewing &		1888–1890
Malting Co.		
127f Bartholomae & Roesing Brewing &		1890–1909
Malting Co.,		
(Milwaukee and Chicago Brew-		
eries Co., Ltd.),		
(aka United States Brewing Co.)		
127g Bartholomae & Roesing Brewing &	908–920 W. 12th St.	1890–1909
Malting Co.		
(Milwaukee and Chicago		
Breweries Co., Ltd.)		
128 Joseph Reidelberger	Green Bay Rd. near Franklin	1864–1865
129 Reiser & Portmann	223 Michigan St.	1859–1860
130 Riverside Brewing Co.	4511 S. Kedzie	1938–1938
131a Henry F.L. Rodemeyer	368–370 Ohio St.	1858–1859
131b Schock, Devry & Co.		1859–1860
132a Charles Rooth	336 S. State St.	1859–1860
132b Thies & Bouland		1860–1862
133a Ruehl Bros. Brewing Co.	2646 Harvard St.	1901–1915
133b Ruehl Bros. Brewing Co.	2630–2660 Arthing- ton St.	1915–1925
133c Roosevelt Brewing Co.		1933–1938

134a J.S. Saberton	Wolcott & Church	1854–1857	
(aka Saberon Brewery)			
(aka Truman Downer)			
(aka North Star Brewery)		1854–1857	
(aka J. A. Irvin)		1855	
(aka Isaac Irvin)		1856	
134b Arah P. Dickinson,		1857–1858	
(North Star Brewery)			
(aka Dickinson & Downer,			
North Star Brewery)			
134c James McDonald		1859–1860	
134d J. S. Saberton		1861–1864	
135a J. J. Sands (Columbia Brewery)	Pearson & Pine Sts.	1855–1863	
135b Sand's Ale Brewing Co.		1863–1871	
(Columbia Brewery aka Hiram			
Wheeler & Sons)			
136a Scanlon & Prinderville	251 Kinzie	1862–1864	
136b John Scanlon		1864–1867	
137 Scheffel & Co.	18–20 Hawthorne Ave.	1891–1899	
138 Schmidt & Bender	509–511 Larrabee	1866–1870	
139 Schoenhofen Edelweiss	2132–2146 S. Laflin	1954–1962	
(branch of Drewry's)			
140 Fred. Seibt	785 N. Halsted	1882–1884	
141a Michael Sieben	172–180 Clybourn	1896–1898	
141b Michael Sieben		1898–1905	
(United Breweries Co.,			
aka Sieben Brewery)			
142a Michael Sieben	335–345 Larrabee	1876–1895	
142b Excelsior Brewing Co.		1895–1898	
142c M. Sieben's Brewery	1454–1478 Larrabee	1911–1914	
142d Sieben's Brewery Co.		1914–1920	
142e Mid-City Brewery Co.		1920–1924	
(aka The George Frank Brewery)			
142f Sieben's Brewery Co.		1933–1967	
143a Siebert & Schmidt	22 N. Clark	1860–1864	
(aka Siebert & Co.)			
143b Siebert & Schmidt	Assylum Pl. near	1864–1866	
	N. Clark &		
	Green Bay Rd.		

143c K. G. Schmidt	9–35 Grant Pl.	1866–1871
143d Schmidt & Glade		1871–1882
143e K. G. Schmidt Brewing Co.		1882–1890
143f K. G. Schmidt Brewing Co., (Milwaukee and Chicago Breweries Co., Ltd.) (aka United States Brewing Co.)		1890–1909
143g K. G. Schmidt Brewing Co.	415–445 Grant Pl.	1909–1917
144 Siebert & Woelffer	32–38 Chicago Ave.	1866–1868
145a The Standard Brewery	12th & S. Campbell	1892–1920
145b The Standard Products Co.		1920–1923
146a Edward R. Stege	15th & S. Ashland Ave.	1890–1905
146b Edward R. Stege Brewery	1508 S. Ashland Ave.	1905–1923
147 John Stutz	245 Cottage Grove Ave.	1865–1867
148a N.P. Svenson	18 Huron	1866–1867
148b Henderson & Vedell		1867–1868
149 Ernst Tosetti Brewing Co.	Wright, Butler & 40th Sts.	1886–1915
150a Adolph Wagner	70–72 Clyde	1886–1887
150b Katherine Wagner		1897–1898
150c Robert Seyer		1890–1890
150d Columbia Weiss Beer Brewing Co.	70–72 Osgood St.	1893–1896
150e Martin J. Schnitzins (Columbia Weiss Beer Brewery)		1896–1905
151 E.A. Wagner & Co.	80 Willow St.	1882–1882
152 Louis Wagner	567 96th St.	1895–1897
153 Ludwig Wagner	942 N. Clark	1867–1883
154a Frank Walther Brewing Co. (aka Frank Walther)	402–416 Paulina	1878–1881
154b East Side Brewery Co. (aka West Side Brewery)		1881–1890
154c West Side Brewery Co., (City of Chicago Consolidated Brewing)	916 N. Paulina	1890–1919
(aka The Malt Sinew Co.)		1907
155a Westminster Brewing Co.	4160–4182 S. Union	1935–1938

155b Prima Brewing Co.   1938–1941
       (Prima Co.)
       (aka Old Missouri Sales Co.)

156a White Eagle Brewing Co.   18th St. &   1900–1909
                                          S. Ashland Ave.
156b White Eagle Brewing Co.   1703 S. Ashland   1909–1910

Bibliography

Background Materials

Ahern, M. L. *The Political History of Chicago*. Chicago, IL: Donohue & Henneberry, 1886.

Allsop, Kenneth. *The Bootleggers and Their Era*. Garden City, NY: Doubleday, 1961.

Anderson, Will. *The Beer Book, an Illustrated Guide to American Breweriana*. Princeton, NJ: The Pyne Press, 1976.

Andreas, A. T. *History of Chicago*. Volumes 1–3, New York, NY: Arno Press, 1975.

——. *History Of Cook County Illinois*. Chicago: A. T. Andreas, 1884.

Asbury, Herbert. *Gem of the Prairie*. DeKalb, IL: Northern Illinois University Press, 1986 (reprint).

Bergreen, Laurence. *Capone the Man and the Era*. New York, NY: Simon & Schuster, 1994.

Broderick, Harold M., editor. *The Practical Brewer, A Manual for the Brewing Industry*. Madison, WI: Master Brewers Association of the Americas, 9th Printing, 1991.

Calkins, Raymond. *Substitutes for the Saloon*. New York: Houghton Mifflin Company, 2nd edition, 1919.

Chicago Blue Book of Selected Names of Chicago and Suburban Towns. Chicago: The Chicago Directory Company, 1893–1915.

Duis, Perry R. *The Saloon: Public Drinking in Chicago and Boston, 1880–1920*. Urbana: University of Illinois Press, 1983

Flinn, John J. *History of the Chicago Police*. Chicago, Illinois, under the auspices of the Police Book Fund, 1887.

Farr, Finis. *Chicago, a Personal History of America's Most American City*. New Rochelle, NY: Arlington House, 1973.

Guyer, I. D. *History of Chicago; Its Commercial and Manufacturing Interests and Industry.* Chicago: Church, Goodwin & Cushing, 1862.

Harrison, Carter H. *Carter H. Harrison.* Chicago: Ralph Fletcher Seymour, Publisher, 1944.

———. *Stormy Years.* New York: Bobbs-Merrill Company, 1935.

Hernon, Peter, and Ganey. *Under The Influence the Unathorized Story of the Anheuser-Busch Dynasty.* New York: Simon & Schuster, 1991.

Hofmeister, Rudolph. *The Germans of Chicago.* Champaign, IL: Stipes Publishing, 1976.

Keil, Harmut. *German Workers' Culture in the United States 1850 to 1920.* Washington and London: Smithsonian Institution Press, 1988.

Keil, Harmut, and Jentz, John B., editors. *German Workers in Industrial Chicago, 1850–1910: A Comparative Perspective.* DeKalb: Northern Illinois University Press, 1983.

Kobler, John. *Capone, the Life and World of Al Capone.* New York: Putnam, 1971.

Kogan, Herman, and Cromie. *The Great Fire, Chicago, 1871.* New York: G. P. Putnam's Sons, 1971.

Landesco, John. *Organized Crime in Chicago.* Chicago and London: The University of Chicago Press, 1929.

Leonard, William. *The Lill Story in the History of Chicago.* Chicago: Lill Coal & Oil Company pamphlet, 1958.

Lowe, David. *Lost Chicago.* Boston: Houghton Mifflin Company, 1975.

Lyle, John H. *The Dry And Lawless Years.* Englewood Cliffs, NJ: Prentice-Hall, 1960.

Mezzrow, Mezz, and Wolfe, Bernard. *Really The Blues.* Garden City, NY: Doubleday, 1972.

Moses, John, and Kirkland. *History of Chicago.* Chicago: Munsell & Company, 1895.

Murray, George. *The Legacy of Al Capone.* New York: G. P. Putnam's Sons, 1975.

Ness, Eliot. *The Untouchables.* New York: Julian Messner, 1966.

Pegram, Thomas R. *Battling Demon Rum: The Struggle for a Dry America, 1800–1933.* Chicago: Ivan R. Dee, 1998.

Peterson, Virgil W. *Barbarians In Our Midst.* Boston: Little, Brown Books, 1952.

Pierce, Bessie Louise. *A History Of Chicago*. Volumes 1–2, London: Alfred A. Knopf, 1940.

Schmidt, John R. *"The Mayor Who Cleaned Up Chicago" A Political Biography Of William E. Dever*. DeKalb: Northern Illinois Press, 1989.

Seeger, Eugen. *Chicago, The Wonder City*. Chicago: 1893.

Sheahan, James W. and Upton, George P. *The Great Conflagrations, Chicago*. Chicago: Union Publishing, 1871.

Sullivan, Edward D. *Rattling the Cup on Chicago Crime*. New York: The Vanguard Press, 1929.

Wendt, Lloyd, and Hogan. *Lords of the Levee*. Cornwall, NY: Cornwall Press, 1943.

Wilson, Samuel Paynter. *"Chicago" and Its Cess-pools of Infamy*. Chicago: 3rd ed., 1910.

Magazine Articles

Allen-Taylor, J. Douglas. "Liquid Trouble," *MetroActive*, Boulevards New Media, Inc., July 24–30, 1997.

Angle, Paul. "Michael Diversey & Beer in Chicago." *Chicago History, the Magazine of the Chicago Historical Society* (Spring 1969).

Appel, Susan K. "Chicago and the Rise of Brewery Architecture." *Chicago History, The Magazine of the Chicago Historical Society*, Vol. 24, No. 1. Spring, 1995.

Johnson, William Oscar. "Sports and Suds." *Sports Illustrated*, August 8, 1988.

Renner, Wilson. "A Perfect Ferment: Chicago, The Know-Nothings, and the Riot for Lager Beer," *Chicago History, the Magazine of the Chicago Historical Society*, Vol. 5, no. 3. Summer, 1976.

"The Saloon Question in Chicago." New York, American Association of Economic Studies, *Economist*, Vol. 2, no. 2, MacMillan Company, 1897.

"Twelve Pack Newsletter," Minnesota Beer Wholesalers. Unknown.

Zelek, Eugene F. Jr., *"Legal Aspects of Sensory Analysis,"* Food Technology, November 1990.

BREWERY TRADE JOURNALS

American Brewers Review, Chicago, Henius, Max and Wahl, Robert
The Brewer and Malster and Beverageur, Chicago, Eugene A. Sittig
& Sons
The Brewers Digest, Chicago, Siebel Publishing Company
The Brewers' Journal, Chicago, Gibson Publishing Company
Brewery Age, Chicago, Brewery Age Publishing Company
Modern Brewery, New York, Modern Brewery, Incorporated
Modern Brewery Age, Chicago, Brewery Age Publishers
The Western Brewer, Chicago, J. Wing/H.S. Rich & Company

BREWERY RELATED PUBLICATIONS

Arnold, John P. *Origins and History of Beer and Brewing.* Chicago:
Alumni Association of the Wahl-Henius Institute of Fermentol-
ogy, 1911.
A Handbook of Facts and Figures. New York: United Brewers Industrial
Foundation, 1937.
American Breweriana Journal, Pueblo Co., American Breweriana
Association, Incorporated.
Baderbrau Tips, Pavichevich Brewing Company.
Baron, Stanley Wade. *Brewed in America, a History of Beer and Ale
in the United States.* New York: Arno Press, 1962.
Bull, Donald, Friedrich, Manfred, and Gottschalk. Bullworks, *Ameri-
can Breweries,* Trumbull, CT: Bullworks, 1984.
Cochran, Thomas Childs. *The Pabst Brewing Company.* Westport, CT:
Greenwood Press, 1975.
Henius, Max and Arnold. *History of the Brewing Industry and Brewing
Science in America.* Chicago: Privately printed, 1933.
One Hundred Years of Brewing. Chicago & New York: H. S. Rich,
1903.
Pospychala, Phil, and McFarland. *The Great Chicago Beer Cans.* Lib-
ertyville, IL: Silver Fox Productions, 1970.
Schlueter, Herman. *The Brewing Industry and the Brewery Workers'
Movement in America.* Cincinnati, OH: International Union of
United Brewery Workers, 1919.

Tenth Anniversary Reunion of Chicago. Westport, CT: Blakely Printing Company, 1901.

The Breweriana Collector. Detroit, MI: Journal of the National Association Breweriana Advertising. Summer, 1991.

The First Fifty Years of the Pilsen Brewing Company 1903–1953. Chicago: Pilsen Brewing Company Pamphlet, 1953.

United States Brewers' Association. *Brewery Production Figures,* 1941.

Van Munching, Philip. *Beer Blast.* New York: Random House, 1997.

COLLECTIONS, ARCHIVES, DIARIES

Application for City Retailer's License Alcoholic Liquor, City of Chicago, Form C Z 502-Corporate Form.

Archives of Lake View City, Chicago, IL, Saloon Applications, Northeastern University, 1872–1889.

Charles Schaffner Collection, Chicago, IL, Agreement and Lease, Box 321, 1902–1917, Chicago Historical Society.

Chicago City Council Proceedings Files, Springfield, IL, Illinois State Archives, 1833–1871.

Manuscript Collection of William B. Ogden, William B., Letter Book, Chicago Historical Society.

John Herbert Weiss Papers [manuscript], 1 volume, 1900–1904, Chicago Historical Society.

Inaugural Addresses of the Mayors of Chicago, 1840–1995, edited by Shah, Tiwana, O' Brien, Ellen, and Benedict, Lyle, Chicago, IL, Chicago Public Library, Municipal Reference Collection, 1998.

Indictment of Capone, District Court of the United States of America for the Northern District of Illinois, Eastern Division, June Term, 1931.

Journal of the Proceedings of the City Council of the City of Chicago, Chicago, IL, Chicago Public Library, Municipal Reference Collection, 1933–1934.

List of Licensed Saloons in the City of Chicago, Chicago, July 1, 1908, Chicago Public Library, Municipal Reference Collection.

A Memoir of Edward G. Uihlein, translated by Rosina L. Lippi and Jill D. Carlisle, 1917, 1 Box, Chicago Historical Society.

Records of the Alien Property Administration, Schoenhofen Family, National Archives, Trust Files, 2752, 2662, 3436, 4922.

Record of the Seventh Brewers' Congress, U.S. Brewers' Association, 1867.

Report of the Special Investigating Committee of the City Council, Chicago, IL, Chicago Public Library, Municipal Reference Collection, March 7, 1904.

Stroh Container Co. v. Delphi Industries, Inc. 783 F. 2d 743 (8th Cir. 1986) Stroh Container Company Formerly Known As Jos. Schlitz Brewing Company.

Taft Papers, Library of Congress.

Testimony of Prohibition Agents John Showalter and Andrew Hermanson, United States of America, Northern District of Illinois, Eastern Division, State of Illinois, County of Cook, May 20, 1924.

United States Brewers Foundation, Seventh Annual Meeting, 1946.

United States of America v. Stenson Brewing Company, Number 6721, District Court of the U.S. Northern District of Illinois, Eastern Division.

NEWSPAPERS, ARTICLES

Beloit Daily News
Chicago American
Chicago Daily Democrat
Chicago Daily News
Chicago Herald
Chicago Herald and Examiner
Chicago Journal
Chicagoland Brew News
Chicago Record-Herald
Chicago Sun-Times
Chicago Times
Chicago Tribune
Crain's Detroit Business
La Crosse Tribune
Milwaukee Daily News
Milwaukee Sentinel
Nation's Restaurant News

New York Times
Oakland Tribune
Press Publications
St. Louis Globe

Notes

CHAPTER 1

1. A. T. Andreas, *History of Chicago*, Vol. I (New York: Arno Press reprint, 1975), p. 116.
2. A. T. Andreas, *History of Cook County Illinois* (Chicago: A. T. Andreas, 1884), pp. 129–131. This information was provided to Andreas in a letter written to him by Charles Butler in 1881.
3. *Ibid.*
4. *Ibid.*
5. David Lowe,. *Lost Chicago* (Boston, MA: Houghton Mifflin Company, 1975), p. 16; Finis Farr, *Chicago, A Personal History of America's Most American City* (New Rochelle, NY: Arlington House, 1973), pp. 38–39.
6. There is some dispute as to whether the brewery was established in 1833 or 1836. If, however, Sultzer and Haas did indeed purchase the land for the brewery directly from Ogden, it would have been after 1835 when Ogden arrived in Chicago to check on the family land holdings. I have used 1833 as the year of their arrival since the subsequent events of the brewery changing hands so often in the late 1830s makes 1836 little sense as the first year of operation. The land for the brewery was most likely sold to Haas and Sultzer by Charles Butler.
7. I. D. Guyer, *History of Chicago: Its Commercial and Manufacturing Interests and Industry* (Chicago: Church, Goodwin & Cushing, 1862), p. 40; A. T. Andreas, *op. cit.*, p. 564; *Chicago Sun-Times*, August 16, 1953.
8. Stanley W. Baron, *Brewed in America. A History of Beer and Ale in the United States* (New York: Arno Press, 1972), p. 164. Finis claims that Butler was still in control of the property at this time.
9. *One Hundred Years of Brewing* (Chicago and New York: H. S.Rich, 1903), p. 86.
10. Baron, *op. cit.*, p. 164; *Chicago Sun-Times*, August 16, 1953.
11. Rudolph Hofmeister, *The Germans of Chicago* (Champaign, IL: Stipes Publishing Company, 1976), p. 134.
12. Manuscript Collection of William B. Ogden, William B. Ogden Letter Book, Ogden to A. Logan, October 12, 1839, Chicago Historical Society.

13. *Ibid.*, Ogden to J.A. Hoes, November 13, 1840.
14. *Ibid.*, Ogden to Townsend, July 15, 1839.
15. E-mail to the author from Valerie Turness, February 5, 1999. According to Ms. Turness, a descendant of Diversey, the correct spelling of the brewer's last name is actually "DIVERSY." The added "e" seems to be a result of his own inconsistency of signature.
16. *One Hundred Years of Brewing, op.cit*, p. 202; Andreas, *op. cit.*, p. 331.
17. William Leonard, *The Lill Story in the History of Chicago* (Chicago: Lill Coal & Oil Co., 1958), pp. 7–8.
18. Hofmeister, *op. cit.*, pp. 100–101.
19. *Chicago Sun-Times*, October 31, 1997.
20. Donald Bull, Manfred Friedrich, and Robert Gottschalk, *American Breweries* (Trumbull, CT: Bullworks), 1984, pp. 57–68.
21. *One Hundred Years Of Brewing, op. cit.*, p. 232.
22. *Ibid.*, p. 232. Perry Duis, in *The Saloon: Public Drinking in Chicago and Boston, 1880–1920*, claims that Valentin Busch and Michael Brand were responsible for bringing lager yeast to Chicago in 1854. According to *One Hundred Years of Brewing*, Busch began an ale brewery in Chicago in 1851. In 1853, Busch took on Brand as a partner in their Blue Island location and their branch in Chicago. The same source of reference, however, states that that brewers John A. Huck and his partner, John Schneider, founded the first lager brewery in Chicago in 1847. By 1854, lager beer in Chicago had already become the preferred drink of German Americans. According to the *Milwaukee Sentinel* of September 12, 1854, because of the hot summer of the same year, Chicago ran out of this unique style of beer, prompting Milwaukee brewers to export their surplus stock to thirsty Chicagoans. Timewise, it would seem highly unlikely that Busch and Brand could have introduced lager beer to Chicagoans and gained widespread acceptance for their product in a period of just months.
23. "The Desplaines Hall Workers Club Picnics in Ogden's Grove," *Der Westen* (July 22, 1896), pp. 206–8.
24. *One Hundred Years of Brewing, op. cit.*, p. 329.
25. Andreas, *op. cit.*, pp. 575–76.
26. *Milwaukee Sentinel*, September 12, 1854.
27. Bull, Friedrich, and Gottschalk, *op. cit.*, pp. 57–68; Andreas, *op. cit.*, p. 370.

CHAPTER 2

1. Bessie Louise Pierce, *A History of Chicago*, Volume 2 (London: Alfred A. Knopf, 1940), pp. 13, 17.
2. *German Workers in Industrial Chicago, 1850–1910: A Comparative Perspective*, Harmut Keil and John B. Jentz, editors (DeKalb: Northern Illinois University Press, 1983), p. 23.

3. *One Hundred Years of Brewing*, pp. 207–53. Philadelphia brewer John Wagner is attributed with brewing the first lager beer in the United States.

4. Eugen Seeger, *Chicago, The Wonder City* (Chicago: 1893), p. 109.

5. Richard Wilson Renner. "In a Perfect Ferment: Chicago, the Know-Nothings, and the Riot for Lager Beer," *Chicago History, Magazine of the Chicago Historical Society*, vol. 5, no. 3 (1976): pp. 161–63.

6. *Inaugural Addresses of the Mayors of Chicago, 1840–1995, Inaugural Address of Mayor Levi Boone, March 13, 1855*, Shah Tiwana, Ellen O' Brien, and Lyle Benedict, editors, Municipal Reference Collection, Chicago Public Library, 1998, pp. 5–6.

7. *Chicago City Council Proceedings File, 1833–1871*, Illinois State Archives, File numbers 0073 A, 0093 A, March 26, 1855; 0149 A, April 2, 1855; 0150 A, April 4, 1855; 0220 A, April 16, 1855.

8. *Chicago Daily Democrat*, January 26, 1849, June 26, 1850, January 21, 1854.

9. Renner, *op. cit.*, p. 165.

10. Virgil W. Peterson. *Barbarians in Our Midst* (Atlantic, Little, Brown Books, 1952), p. 21; *Chicago City Council Proceedings File, 1833–1871*, Boston, File number 1133 A, September 10, 1855.

CHAPTER 3

1. Stanley W. Baron, *Brewed in America. A History of Beer and Ale in the United States* (New York: Arno Press, 1962), pp. 213–214; Gerald Carlson, *The Social History of Bourbon* (Lexington: University Press of Kentucky, 1963), p. 95.

2. Donald Bull, Manfred Friedrich, and Robert Gottschalk, *American Breweries* (Trumbull: Bullworks, 1984), pp. 59–67.

3. Bessie Louise Pierce, *A History of Chicago*, Volume II (London: Alfred A. Knopf, 1940), p. 89.

4. *John H. Weiss Papers* [manuscript], with a biography of Conrad Seipp, 1900–1904, one volume, Chicago Historical Society, *One Hundred Years Of Brewing* (Chicago: H. S. Rich, 1903), p. 422.

5. *One Hundred Years of Brewing, op. cit.*, pp. 321–22.

6. *Ibid.*, p. 416.

7. *Ibid.*, p. 422; A. T. Andreas. *History of Cook County Illinois* (Chicago: A. T. Andreas, 1884), figure for 1870, p. 370.

8. *Chicago City Council Proceedings Files, 1833–1871*, file number 1451 A, April 27, 1867.

9. *Chicago Tribune*, November 6, 1867; March 1, 14, and 17, 1868; and January 26, 1869. The brewery was also known as the Patrick O' Neill Brewery.

10. Lloyd Wendt and Herman Kogan, *Give the Lady What She Wants*, a book on the one hundred-year history of Marshall Field & Company, as quoted in William Leonard, p. 9.

11. *A Memoir of Edward G. Uihlein*, translated by Rosina L. Lippi and Jill D. Carlisle, 1917, one box, Chicago Historical Society.

12. James W. Sheahan and George P. Upton. *The Great Conflagration, Chicago* (Chicago: Union Publishing, 1872), p. 141.

13. Herman Kogan and Robert Cromie, *The Great Fire, Chicago 1871* (New York: G. P. Putnam's Sons), p. 109.

14. *One Hundred Years of Brewing, op. cit.*, p. 322.

15. Uihlein, *op. cit.*, p. 9.

16. I. D. Guyer, *History of Chicago: Its Commercial and Manufacturing Interests and Industry* (Chicago: Church, Goodwin & Cushing, 1862), pp. 42–43.

17. *One Hundred Years of Brewing, op. cit.*, p. 322.

18. John Arnold and Max Henius, *History of the Brewing Industry and Brewing Science in America* (Chicago: privately printed, 1933), p. 95. Lehle had been employed by Wolf as early as 1874. See Appel, Susan K., "Chicago and the Rise of Brewery Architecture," *Chicago History, Magazine of the Chicago Historical Society* 24 (spring 1995): 10.

19. Thomas Childs Cochran, *The Pabst Brewing Company* (Westport: Greenwood Press, 1975), pp. 107–110.

20. *Tenth Anniversary Reunion of Chicago* (Westport: Blakely Printing Co., 1901), p. 19; *The Brewers Digest* (April 1947).

21. Cochran, *op. cit.*, pp. 126–27.

22. *One Hundred Years of Brewing, op. cit.*, pp. 588–93.

23. Arnold and Henius, *op. cit.*, pp. 106–107.

24. H. Allen Brooks, *The Prairie School.* (New York: W. W. Norton Co., Inc., 1976) attributes his work to Garden who worked for Schmidt and later became his partner. See pp. 53–55. Schmidt also designed a mansion for Peter Schoenhofen's son-in-law, Joseph Theurer, in 1896. The building was sold to chewing gum magnate, William Wrigley Jr. in 1911, and is now referred to as the Wrigley Mansion. Other Chicago buildings of note built by the firm of Schmidt, Garden, and Martin are the Montgomery Ward Catalog House on the Chicago River, the Humbolt Park Boathouse, and the Michael Reese Hospital. Adolph Cudell was also noted for the design of brewer Conrad Seipp's family home on South Michigan Avenue and his palatial Black Point summer home on Geneva Lake, Wisconsin. He also built an ornate residence on West Wrightwood for brewer F. J. Dewes.

25. For a more detailed discussion of Chicago brewery architecture, see Appel, "Chicago and the Rise of Brewery Architecture," *Chicago History, Magazine of the Chicago Historical Society,* 24 (spring 1995), pp. 4–19.

26. Pierce, *op. cit.*, Vol. II, p. 89.

27. *Ibid.*, Vol. III, p. 153.

28. *Record of the Seventh Brewers' Congress*, U.S. Brewers' Association, Incorporated, 1867, p. 10.

CHAPTER 4

1. *Chicago Tribune*, January 1, 1880.
2. Donald Bull, Manfred Friedrich, Robert Gottschalk, *American Breweries* (Trubull, CT: Bullworks, 1984), pp. 57–68.
3. *One Hundred Years of Brewing*, pp. 488–95.
4. *Ibid.*, p. 488.
5. *Ibid.*, p. 492.
6. *Ibid.*, p. 495.
7. "Budweiser" was derived from the name of the town of Budejovice, in Bohemia. Early brewers argued that the name could be freely used to describe a particular style of beer, as the pilsner beer style is associated with the city of Pilsen.
8. *Chicago Tribune*, January 1, 1880; *Western Brewer* (June 1884). The *Western Brewer* uses a figure of 375,549 barrels of beer produced in Chicago in 1879.
9. *Chicago Tribune*, January 1, 1880.
10. Thomas C. Cochran, *The Pabst Brewing Company* (Westport, CT: Greenwood Press, 1975), p. 172.
11. Perry R. Duis, *The Saloon: Public Drinking in Chicago and Boston, 1980–1920* (Urbana: University of Illinois Press, 1983), p. 19.
12. Bessie Louise Pierce, *A History of Chicago*, Volume II (London: Alfred A. Knopf, 1940), p. 153; *The Chicago Blue Book of Selected Names of Chicago and Suburban Towns* (Chicago: Chicago Directory Company, 1893–1915).
13. A. T. Andreas, *History of Chicago* (New York: Arno Press, 1975), pp. 355–56.
14. Carter H. Harrison, *Carter H. Harrison* (Chicago, IL: Ralph Fletcher Seymour, 1944), pp. 113–14.
15. Rudolph Hofmeister, *The Germans in Chicago* (Champaign, IL: Stipes Publishing, 1976), pp. 119, 137.
16. Hofmeister, *op. cit.*, p. 106; John Moses and Joseph Kirland, *History of Chicago* (Chicago: Munsell & Co., 1895), pp. 133, 226, 253.
17. John J. Flinn, *History of the Chicago Police* (Chicago, IL: Under the Auspices of the Police Book Fund, 1887), p. 138; *Chicago Tribune*, April 25–26, May 28, 29, 1873.
18. Flinn, *op. cit.*, pp. 142–143.
19. *Ibid.*, p. 145; *Chicago Tribune*, May 28–29, 1873; Ahern, *op. cit.*, pp. 34–37.
20. Flinn, *op. cit.*, pp. 137–146; Herbert Asbury, *Gem of the Prairie* (DeKalb: Northern Illinois University Press, 1986), pp. 144–145; *Inaugural Address of the Mayors of Chicago, 1840–1995, Inaugural Address of Mayor Harvey Doolittle Colvin, December 1, 1873*, p. 5.
21. Duis, *op. cit.*, pp. 175–78, 234.

CHAPTER 5

1. Herman Schlueter, *The Brewery Industry and the Brewery Workers' Movement in America* (Cincinnati, Ohio: International Union of United Brewery Workers, 1910), pp. 256, 258.
2. *Ibid.*, pp. 94, 262–63.
3. *Western Brewer*, August 1877; John J. Flinn, *History of the Chicago Police* (Chicago: Under the Auspices of the Police Book Fund, 1987), p. 196.
4. Schlueter, *op. cit.*, p. 129.
5. *Western Brewer* (May 1886); *Chicago Tribune*, April 13, 1888.
6. *Chicago Tribune*, April 13, 1888.
7. *Western Brewer* (April 1888); *Chicago Tribune*, April 13, 1888.
8. *Chicago Tribune*, April 14–25, 1888.
9. Schlueter, *op. cit.*, pp. 167–170.
10. *Ibid.*, p. 167.
11. Alfred Kolb, *Als Arbeiter in Amerika. Unter deutsch-americanishen GrossStadt-Proletariern*, 5th ed. (Berlin: Siegismund, 1909), pp. 74–79.

CHAPTER 6

1. John E. George, "The Saloon Question in Chicago," *Economic Studies* 2 (1897): p. 69.
2. *Ibid.*, p. 69.
3. *Chicago Tribune*, March 4, 1891.
4. The early use of the name Budweiser was not exclusive to Anheuser-Busch. Philip Van Munching, *Beer Blast* (New York: Times Business, Random House, 1997), p. 16, claims that even Miller and Schlitz both used the name at one time. DuBois Brewing of DuBois, Pennsylvania, continued to brew DuBois Budweiser until 1970 when the Pennsylvania Supreme Court ordered them to stop.
5. George, *op. cit.*, p. 70.
6. Donald Bull, Manfred Friedrich, and Robert Gottschalk, *American Breweries* (Trumbull, CT: Bullworks, 1984), pp. 57–68.
7. George, *op. cit.*, p. 68.
8. *Western Brewer* (June–September 1892).
9. *Western Brewer* (December 1891); *The First Fifty Years of the Pilsen Brewing Company, 1903–1953* (Chicago: Company pamphlet, 1953); Perry Duis, *The Saloon: Public Drinking in Chicago and Boston, 1880–1920* (Urbana: University of Illinois Press, 1983), p. 38.
10. George, *op. cit.*, pp. 71–72.
11. *Western Brewer* (September 1890).
12. George, *op. cit.*, p. 72.
13. *Western Brewer* (March–May 1892); *Chicago Herald American*, April 3, 1894.

14. *Milwaukee Daily News*, July 12, 1890.
15. *Ibid.*
16. George, *op. cit.*, p. 73; Duis, *op. cit.*, pp. 41–42.
17. Perry Duis, *The Saloon: Public Drinking in Chicago and Boston, 1880–1920* (Urbana: University of Illinois Press, 1983), pp. 41–42.
18. *Chicago Herald and Examiner*, December 28, 1937; "Gambler Box Iv Th' Yards," *Chicago History* 5 (winter, 1976–77): 213–21.
19. Duis, *op. cit.*, p. 38.
20. *Western Brewer* (November 1893).
21. *Western Brewer* (September 1895).
22. *One Hundred Years of Brewing* (Chicago, IL: H. S. Rich, 1903), p. 505.
23. *Western Brewer* (June 1892).
24. *Western Brewer* (May 1894).
25. *Chicago Herald American*, April 3, 1894.
26. *Chicago Herald American*, April 10, 1894; Bull, Friedich, and Gottschalk, *op. cit.*, p. 60.
27. Bull, Friedrich, and Gottschalk, *op. cit.*, p. 9.
28. Duis, *op. cit.*, p. 39.

CHAPTER 7

1. Thomas Childs Cochran, *The Pabst Brewing Company* (Westport, CT: Greenwood Press, 1975), pp. 139–42.
2. Perry R. Duis, *The Saloon: Public Drinking in Chicago and Boston* (Urbana: University of Illinois Press, 1983, pp. 22–28, 82–83.
3. John E. George, "The Saloon Question in Chicago," *Economic Studies* 2 (1897): p. 76; and Bessie Louise Pierce, *A History of Chicago*, Volume III (London: Alfred A. Knopf, 1957), p. 151.
4. *Archives of Lakeview City, 1872–1889*, 7/0015/08–11, Chicago, IL, Northeastern University.
5. *Charles Schaffner Collection*, Agreement and Lease, Box 321, Chicago Historical Society.
6. *Chicago Times*, August 5, 1877; Duis, *op. cit.*, p. 83.
7. *Chicago Herald*, April 3, 1894.
8. *Charles Schaffner Collection*, *op. cit.*
9. *A Memoir of Edward G. Uihlein*, translated by Rosina L. Lippi and Jill D. Carlisle, Chicago Historical Society, 1917.
10. Royal L. Melendy, "The Saloon in Chicago," *American Journal of Sociology* 6 (1900–1901): 296.
11. *Ibid.*, p. 297.
12. Herbert Asbury, *Gem of the Prairie* (DeKalb: Northern Illinois University Press, 1986), pp. 271–75; Duis, *op. cit.*, pp. 94–95.
13. Samuel Paynter Wilson, *"Chicago" and Its Cess-pools of Infamy* (Chicago, IL: 1910), pp. 199–200.

14. *Chicago Herald*, April 1,1894.
15. Hartmut Keil, *German Workers' Culture in the United States 1850 to 1920* (Washington, DC, and London: Smithsonian Institution Press, 1988), pp. 48, 305; Melendy, *op. cit.*, pp. 304–05.
16. Duis, *op. cit.*, p. 66.
17. For the account of the mayor's meeting with the brewers and his estimate of their political power, see Carter H. Harrison, *Stormy Years. The Autobiography of Carter H. Harrison* (Indianapolis, IN: Bobbs-Merrill Company, 1935), pp. 340–41.
18. George, *op. cit.*, pp. 83, 88.

CHAPTER 8

1. John Herbert Weiss Papers [manuscript], One Volume, Chicago, IL, 1900–1904, Chicago Historical Society.
2. *Western Brewer* (July 1900).
3. *Ibid.*
4. *Western Brewer* (April 1901 and October 1902).
5. *Ibid.* (May 1900 and February, March 1901).
6. *Ibid.* (June 1901).
7. John Herbert Weiss Papers, *op. cit.*
8. *Ibid.*, March 9, 1901.
9. *Western Brewer* (January 1903 and May 1903); *American Brewers' Review* (September 1903).
10. *American Brewers' Review* (September, October 1903, and November 1905).
11. *Ibid.* (July 1903).
12. *Ibid.* (April 1904).

CHAPTER 9

1. Thomas R. Pegram, *Bottling Demon Rum: The Struggle for a Dry America, 1800–1933* (Chicago: Ivan R. Dee, 1998), pp. 113–21.
2. *American Brewers' Review* (March 1903).
3. *Report of the Special Investigating Committee of the City Council*, Chicago, March 7, 1904.
4. *American Brewers' Review* (January 1906).
5. *Ibid,* (August 1907).
6. Perry R. Duis, *The Saloon: Public Drinking in Chicago and Boston, 1880–1920* (Urbana: University of Illinois Press, 1983), pp. 181–83; Finley Peter Dunne, *Dissertations by Mr. Dooley* (New York: Harper & Brothers Publishers,

1906), p. 312. Martin Dooley, the Sage of Archy Road, began appearing in the *Chicago Post* in 1893. The columns proved wildly popular, both in Chicago and in national newspapers. A number of books contain Dooley's columns on peace, war, and life in general.

7. *Western Brewer* (November 1905).

8. *American Brewers' Review* (December 1905).

9. *Chicago Record-Herald*, February 3–28, 1906; *Chicago Tribune*, May 6, 1906.

10. Duis, *op. cit.*, p. 259; *American Brewers' Review* (September 1906).

11. Duis, *op. cit.*, pp. 259–260.

12. *American Brewers' Review* (February 1906); Pegram, *op. cit.*, p. 97.

13. *Western Brewer* (May 1907).

14. *American Brewers' Review* (June 1907).

15. Finis Farr, *Chicago: A Personal History of America's Most American City* (New Rochelle, NY: Arlington House, 1973), p. 308.

16. *Western Brewer* (December 1907).

17. *Chicago Tribune*, September 27, 1908.

18. *List of Licensed Saloons in the City Of Chicago*, Chicago, July 1, 1908; *Chicago, Illinois Crime Statistics 1860–1920*, Illinois State Archives.

19. *Western Brewer* (February and April 1910).

20. *Ibid.* (March 1910).

21. *Ibid.*

22. H. C. Stunts to William Taft, September 5, 1911, Taft Papers, Library of Congress.

23. J. Wilson to William Taft, October 21, 1911, Taft Papers, Library of Congress.

24. Duis, *op. cit.*, p. 292.

25. *Western Brewer* (May 1910).

26. Duis, *op. cit.*, p. 298.

27. Donald Bull, Manfred Friedrich, and Robert Gottschalk, *American Breweries* (Trumbull, CT: Bullworks, 1984), pp. 57–68.

28. *Chicago Tribune*, October 5, 1915; *Chicago Daily News*, October 5, 1915.

29. *Chicago Tribune*, October 5, 1915.

30. *Ibid.*

31. *Chicago Daily News*, October 5, 1915.

32. *Chicago Tribune*, October 6, 1915; *Chicago Daily News*, October 4, 1915.

33. *Chicago Tribune*, October 5–10, 1915; *Chicago Daily News*, October 6, 9, 11, 1915.

34. *Chicago Tribune*, October 9, 1915; *Chicago Daily News*, October 9, 1915.

35. *Chicago Daily News*, October 6, 1915.

36. *Chicago Tribune*, October 8, 1915; *Chicago Daily News*, October 8, 1915.

37. *Chicago Tribune*, November 8, 1915; *Chicago Daily News*, November 8, 1915.

38. *Western Brewer* (September 1917).

CHAPTER 10

1. Stanley W. Baron, *Brewed in America: A History of Beer and Ale in the United States* (New York: Arno Press, 1962), pp. 302–4; *Chicago Tribune,* August 11, 1917.

2. Baron, *op. cit.,* p. 304; *Chicago Tribune,* December 18, 1917.

3. Baron, *op. cit.,* p. 303.

4. *Brewers' Journal* (December 1918); *Chicago Tribune,* November 30, December 1, 1918.

5. As quoted in David Lowe, *Lost Chicago* (Boston, MA: Houghton Mifflin Company, 1975), p. 201.

6. *Brewers' Journal* (November 1918, April 1919).

7. *Records of the Alien Property Administration,* Schoenhofen Family, National Archives, Trust Files, 2752, 2662, 3436, 49022. For a comment on how this same situation affected the Busch family of St. Louis, see Peter Hernon and Terry Ganey. *Under the Influence, the Unauthorized Story of the Anheuser-Busch Dynasty* (New York: Simon & Schuster, 1991), p. 94, 102–3; Rudolph Hofmeister *The Germans of Chicago* (Champaign, IL: Stipes Publishing, 1976), p. 71, 74.

8. *American Beer History as Traced through the Song Sheet Music of Tin Pan Alley,* American Breweriana Journal, May-June 2003 (American Breweriana Association, Inc., Pueblo, CO), pp. 22–23. After disappearing from the Chicago area in the early 1960s and going through a raft of ownerships, the brand has returned to Chicago as a nostalgic treat, now manufactured by Chicago's Clover Club Bottling, Inc. The bottling company also contracts with the landmark Berghoff restaurant and local Goose Island Brewery to make their root beer products.

9. *Chicago Daily News,* January 9, 14, 1919.

10. *Chicago Daily News,* January, 1919; *Chicago Tribune,* May 1, 1919; *Brewers' Journal,* (December 1918)

11. *Chicago Daily News,* June, 1919.

12. *Western Brewer* 52, no. 4 (April 1919)

13. *Chicago Tribune,* April 2, 1919.

14. *Ibid.,* April 3, 1919.

15. *Brewers' Journal* (May 1919)

16. *Ibid.* (May 1919)

17. *Chicago Tribune,* June 29, 1919.

18. *Ibid.,* April 3, 1919.

19. *Ibid.,* June 30, 1919.

20. *Chicago Daily News,* June 28, 1919.

21. *Ibid.,* June 28, 1919.

22. *Chicago Tribune,* June 30, 1919; *Chicago Daily News,* June 30, 1919.

23. *Chicago Tribune,* July 4, 1919.

24. *Ibid.,* July 1, 1919.

25. *Ibid.,* July 1, 1919; *Chicago Daily News,* July 1, 1919.

26. *Chicago Tribune*, July 2, 1919; *Chicago Daily News*, July 1, 1919.
27. *United States of America v. Stenson Brewing Company*, Number 6721, District Court of the U.S. Northern District of Illinois, Eastern Division; *Chicago Tribune*, July 4, 1919; *Brewers' Journal* (August 1919).
28. *Chicago Tribune*, July 4–5, 1919; *Chicago Daily News*, July 7, 1919.
29. *Chicago Tribune*, July 4, 1919; *Chicago Daily News*, July 8, 1919.

CHAPTER 11

1. *Brewers' Journal*, October, 1919.
2. *Chicago Daily News*, September 11, 1923.
3. *Ibid.*, November 17, 1924; *Chicago Tribune*, November 18, 1924; John H. Lyle., *The Dry and Lawless Years* (Englewood Cliffs, NJ: Prentice-Hall, Inc., 1960), p. 84; John Landesco. *Organized Crime in Chicago* (Chicago and London: University of Chicago Press, 1929) p. 97.
4. *Western Brewer* (September 1919, October 1919).
5. Herbert Asbury, *Gem of the Prairie* (DeKalb: Northern Illinois University Press, 1986), pp. 326–7; *Chicago Daily News*, September 11, 1923; Landesco, *op. cit.*, p. 87.
6. *Chicago Daily News*, September 12–13, 1923.
7. *Ibid.*, September 13, 1923.
8. *Ibid.*, September 15, 1923.
9. *Ibid.*, September 21, 28, 1923.
10. *Ibid.*, September 29, 1923.
11. *Chicago Tribune*, October 8, 1923.
12. *Ibid.*, October 3, 1923.
13. *Ibid.*, October 8, 1923; *Chicago Tribune*, September 23, 1923.
14. *Chicago Journal*, November 3, 1923; *Chicago Herald and Examiner*, September 23, 26, 29, 1923; *Chicago Daily News*, November 8, 1923.
15. City of Chicago Council Proceedings, December 12, 1923.
16. *New York Times*, November 18, 1923.
17. Testimony of prohibition agents John Showalter and Andrew Hermanson, May 20, 1924, United States of America, Northern District of Illinois, Eastern Division, State of llinois, County of Cook; *Chicago Herald Examiner*, May 20,1924.
18. *Chicago Daily News*, November 19, 1924.
19. Asbury, *op. cit.*, pp. 345–7.
20. *Ibid.*, pp. 348–9, *Chicago Herald Examiner*, May 20, 1924.
21. *Chicago Herald Examiner*, May 19, 1924.
22. *Ibid.*, May 22, 1924.
23. *Chicago Tribune*, November 18, 1924.
24. *Chicago Daily News*, November 17, 1924.
25. Mezz Mezzrow and Bernard Wolfe, *Really the Blues* (Garden City, NY: Doubleday, 1972), pp. 52–53; Peter Hernon and Terry Ganey *Under the*

Influence: The Unauthorized Story of the Anheuser-Busch Dynasty (New York: Simon & Schuster, 1991), p. 155.

26. Laurence Bergreen, *Capone the Man and the Era* (New York: Simon & Schuster, 1994), pp. 134–5.
27. *Ibid.*, pp. 141, 143–5.
28. *Ibid.*, pp. 146–7, 564–6.

CHAPTER 12

1. Peter Hernon and Terry Ganey, *Under the Influeuce: The Unauthorized Story of the Anheuser-Busch Dynasty* (New York: Simon & Schuster, 1991), pp. 131–2.
2. *Malt Age* "The Archer Case" (Chicago, IL: Malt Age Publishing Co., January 1927), p. 17.
3. *Malt Age* (Chicago, IL: Malt Age Publishing Co., February 1927), pp. 7–8.
4. Kenneth Allsop, *The Bootleggers and Their Era* (Garden City, NY: Doubleday, 1961), p. 125.
5. Laurence Bergreen, *Capone: The Man and the Era* (New York: Simon & Schuster, 1994), p. 181.
6. Interview with Ed Chensky, March 4, 1998, Riverside, Illinois.
7. John Kobler, *Capone: The Life and World of Al Capone* (New York: Putnam & Sons, 1971), p. 111; John H. Lyle, *The Dry and Lawless Years* (Englewood Cliffs, NJ: Prentice-Hall, Inc., 1960), p. 16; Edward D. Sullivan, *Rattling the Cup on Chicago Crime* (New York: Vanguard Press, 1929), p. 149. Kobler reports that Collins was offered $10,000 per month. Lyle claims the bribe was $1,000 per day. Sullivan writes that Dever was offered $100,000 for his cooperation during the "Beer Wars."
8. Allsop, *op. cit.*, p. 211; *Chicago Tribune*, February 17, 1931.
9. John R. Schmidt, *"The Mayor Who Cleaned Up Chicago" A Political Biography of William E. Dever* (DeKalb: Northern Illinois University Press, 1989), pp. 163–6, 169.
10. *Chicago Herald and Examiner*, April 13, 1927; *Chicago Post*, April 7, 1927.
11. *Chicago Tribune*, February 17, 1931.
12. Allsop, *op. cit.*, p. 209.
13. Eliot Ness, *The Untouchables* (New York: Julian Messner, 1966). Most of the account of Ness and his raids is taken from chapters 6 through 19. *Chicago Tribune*, June 13, 1930; *New York Times*, June 18, 1931.
14. Bergreen, *op. cit.*, p. 433.
15. Eliot Ness to George E. Q. Johnson, March 26, 1932, as quoted in Bergreen, *op. cit.*, p. 411.
16. Eliot Ness, *op. cit.*, pp. 200–209.
17. *Indictment of Capone*, June Term, 1931, District Court of the United States of America for the Northern District of Illinois, Eastern Division.

CHAPTER 13

1. *St. Louis Globe-Democrat*, July 20, 1931; *Modern Brewery Age* (January 1933) *Chicago American*, February 9, 1933.
2. *Chicago American*, February 16, 1933.
3. *Chicago Herald Examiner*, January 8, 12, 14, 16, 24, 1933; *Chicago American*, February 15, 1933.
4. *Chicago Tribune*, February 21, 24 March 2, 22, 24, 25, 1933; *Chicago Herald and Examiner*, March 13, 25, 1933; *Chicago Daily News*, April 6, 1933.
5. *Chicago Tribune*, March 19, 22, 1933; *Chicago Herald and Examiner*, March 19, 24, 1933.
6. *Chicago Tribune*, March 17, 24, 30, 1933; *Chicago Daily News*, April 6, 1933; *Chicago Herald and Examiner*, March 14, 16, 23, 1933; *Brewer and Malster and Beverageur* (March 1933); *Western Brewer* (April 1933); George Murray, *The Legacy of Al Capone* (New York: G. P. Putnam's Sons, 1975), p. 238.
7. *Chicago Herald and Examiner*, April 4, 1933.
8. *Chicago Tribune*, March 28, 1933.
9. *Chicago Tribune*, April 2, 1933; *Chicago Herald and Examiner*, April 2, 1933.
10. *Chicago Tribune*, April 2–3, 5, 1933; *Chicago Herald and Examiner*, April 2–3, 1933.
11. *Chicago Tribune*, April 2, 1933; Peter Herman and Terry Ganey, *Under the Influence: The Unauthorized Story of the Anheuser-Busch Dynasty* (New York: Simon & Schuster, 1991), p. 153.
12. *Chicago Tribune*, April 5, 1933; *Chicago Daily News*, April 6, 1933.
13. *Chicago Tribune*, April 6, 1933.
14. *Chicago Tribune*, March 22, 30, April 6–8, 1933; *Modern Brewery Age*, April 15, 1933; *Chicago Herald and Examiner*, March 20, 1933.
15. *Chicago Tribune*, March 30, April 6, 1933.
16. *Chicago Tribune*, April 7, 1933; *Chicago Daily News*, April 7, 1933; *Chicago Herald and Examiner*, April 4, 1933; *Brewery Age* (April 1933).
17. *Chicago Tribune*, April 7, 1933; *Chicago Herald and Examiner*; April 7, 1933; *Brewery Age* (April 1933).
18. *Chicago Tribune*, April 7–8, 1933; *Chicago Herald And Examiner*, March 28, 1933; *Nation's Restaurant News* (February 1996) p. 31; *American Breweriana Journal* (August 1996) p. 7.
19. *Chicago Herald and Examiner*, April 7, 1933.
20. *Ibid.*, April 7, 8, 1933; *Chicago Daily News*, April 7, 1933
21. *Chicago Tribune*, March 23, April 8, 1933; *Chicago Herald and Examiner*, April 7, 1933.
22. *Chicago Tribune*, January 2, April 9, 11, 1933.
23. *Chicago Tribune*, April 8, 10–11, 1933; *Chicago Herald and Examiner*, March 15, 25–27, 1933.
24. *Chicago Tribune*, April 8–9, 1933; *Chicago Herald and Examiner*; March 27, April 8, 1933.

CHAPTER 14

1. *Chicago Tribune*, March 19–21, April 11, 1933; *Chicago Herald and Examiner*, March 25, 1933.

2. *Chicago Tribune*, March 29, April 11, 1933; *Chicago Herald and Examiner*, March 20, 31, 1933.

3. *Chicago Daily News*, April 6, 1933; *Brewery Age* (April 1933); *Chicago Tribune*, March 3, April 3, 11, 1933; *Chicago Herald and Examiner*, April 4, 1933.

4. *Chicago Herald and Examiner*, April 3–4, 6, 1933.

5. *Ibid.*, April 8–9, 1933.

6. George Murray, *The Legacy of Al Capone* (New York: G. P. Putnam's Sons, 1975), pp. 201–2.

7. *Chicago Herald and Examiner*, April 10, 1933.

8. *Chicago Tribune*, April 11, 30, May 5, 1933; *Chicago Herald and Examiner*, March 20, April 14, 1933.

9. *Chicago Tribune*, April 25, 27–28, 1933.

10. *Ibid.*, April 20, 27, June 16, 1933; *Brewery Age* (April 1933); *Journal of the Proceedings of the City Council of the City of Chicago 1933–1934*, Amendment to Article VIII, Chapter 62 of the revised city code, Section 1, 3143-H, p. 92.

11. *Chicago Tribune*, April 28, 1933; *Chicago and Herald Examiner*, March 26, 1933; *Chicago Daily News*, April 29, 1933.

12. *Chicago Tribune*, April 20, 1933.

13. *Ibid.*, June 10, 19, 1933.

14. *Ibid.*, June 6, 1933.

15. *Ibid.*, June 5–6, 1933; *Chicago Daily News*, June 5, 1933; John Landesco, *Organized Crime in Chicago* (Chicago and London: University of Chicago Press, 1929), pp. 240–41, states that McDermott had been indicted for violations of the Volstead Act but the particulars of his arrest were never recorded in the Chicago Police Department's Identification Bureau, a typical action during Prohibition. This absence of arrest information usually occurred during the early years of national prohibition if the case was dismissed or reduced to a small fine.

16. *Chicago Tribune*, June 6, 1933.

17. *Ibid.*, July 12, 1933.

18. *Ibid.*, April 20, 1933.

19. *Ibid.*, April 22, 1933; *Brewer and Maltster and Beverageur* (March 1933).

20. *Chicago Tribune*, April 26, 1933.

21. *Ibid.*, April 26, and June 2, 5, 1933; *Chicago Daily News*, April 29, June 3, 1933.

22. *Chicago Tribune*, June 5, 1933.

23. *Ibid.*, June 7–8, 1933; *Chicago Daily News*, June 5, 1933.

24. *Chicago Tribune*, June 7–8, 1933.

25. *Ibid.*, July, 10–11, 1933; *Chicago Daily News*, July 11, 1933.

CHAPTER 15

1. Donald Bull, Manfred Friedrich, and Robert Gottschalk, *American Breweries* (Trumbull, CT: Bullworks, 1984), pp. 58–67; *Modern Brewery*, September 15, 1933.
2. *Brewery Age* (November 1933, December 1934).
3. *Ibid.* (December 1934); *Modern Brewery*, April, August, 1933.
4. Stanley Baron, *Brewed in America: A History of Beer and Ale in the United States* (New York: Arno Press, 1962), pp. 325–26.
5. *Brewery Age* (July, November 1933); *Modern Brewery* (November 1933); *Chicago Tribune*, September 6, 14, 1933.
6. *Chicago Herald Examiner*, July 23, 1933; Ovid Demaris, *Captive City* (New York: Lyle Stuart, Inc., 1969), p. 224.
7. The account of Nitti's activities is based on George Murray, *The Legacy of Al Capone* (New York: G. P. Putnam's Sons, 1975), pp. 181–94.
8. *Chicago Tribune*, July 6, 1997.
9. *Chicago Herald Examiner*, December 1, 1933; *A Handbook of Facts and Figures*, New York, 1937, United Brewers Industrial Foundation; *Journal of the Proceedings of the City Council, 1933–1934*, Article VIII A, 3143-N, 3143-R, p. 1126; *Application for City Retailer's License Alcoholic Liquor*, Form C Z 502-Corporate Form.
10. *Chicago Tribune*, December 12, 1933.
11. *A Handbook of Facts and Figures*, 1937.
12. Baron, *op. cit.*, pp. 327–28; *Brewery Age* (March 1937); *The Breweriana Collector*, Journal of the National Association Breweriana Advertising, 74 (summer 1991) p 10; Phil Pospychala and Joe McFarland, *The Great Chicago Beer Cans* (Libertyville, IL: Silver Fox Productions, 1979), p. 23.
13. *Brewery Age* (May 1938); *Chicago Tribune*, August 10, 1939; Bull, *op. cit.*, p. 61.
14. *Brewery Age* (April 1937; May 1937; June 1937).
15. *Ibid.* (April 1937).
16. *Ibid.* (February 1938; April 1938); Pospychala and McFarland, *op. cit.*, pp. 64, 73.
17. *Brewery Age* (March 1938).
18. *Modern Brewery Age*, (October 1940).

CHAPTER 16

1. *Brewers Digest* (March and April 1941).
2. *United States Brewers' Association*, Brewery Production Cost Figures, 1941.
3. *Brewers Digest* (June 1941; April and December 1942); *Modern Brewery Age* (July 1940).
4. Letter from Willaim Fox II, February, 3, 1999. Bill, son of Kenneth Fox who

served as advertising manager for the firm, remembers his mother claiming the Capone connection.

5. *Western Brewer* (July 1933); *Brewery Age* (September 1934); *Brewers Digest* (September 1943; June, August, and October 1944).

6. *Brewers Digest* (April 1942).

7. *Ibid.* (October 1942).

8. *Ibid.* (February 1944).

9. *Ibid.* (April, 1944).

10. *Ibid.* (December 1944).

11. *Ibid.* (October 1945); *United States Brewers Foundation*, Seventh Annual Meeting, 1946, p. 21.

12. *Modern Brewery Age*, (October 1946).

13. *Ibid.* (August, 1946).

14. Peter Hernon and Terry Ganey, *Under the Influence: The Unauthorized Story of the Anheuser-Busch Dynasty* (New York: Simon & Schuster, 1991), pp. 132–34, 152.

15. *Chicago Tribune*, April 24, 1977.

16. *Modern Brewery Age* (September and November 1950); Donald Bull, Manfred Friedrich, and Robert Gottschalk, *American Breweries* (Trumbull, CT: Bullworks, 1984), pp. 58, 65.

17. *Modern Brewery Age* (January 1950); *Brewers Journal* (February 1950).

18. Letter from Fox, William, February 11, 1999.

19. *Modern Brewery Age* (March 1950; August, October, December 1951; July, August, December 1955).

20. *Chicago Tribune*, April 24, 1977, *Brewers Journal* (April 1950).

21. Letter from Dan Solie, April 2, 2003. Interestingly, the original brewer for the C & J Michel Brewery was Gottlieb Heileman, founder of the G. Heileman Brewing Company.

22. *Chicago Tribune*, December 9–10, 1955.

23. *Chicago American*, December 9, 1955; *Chicago Tribune*, December 11, 1955.

24. *Chicago Tribune*, December 10–11, 1955; *Chicago American*, December 9–10, 1955.

25. Phil Pospychala and Joe McFarland, *The Great Chicago Beer Cans* (Libertyville, IL: Silver Fox Productions, 1970), pp. 23–32; *Chicago Tribune*, April 24, 1977.

26. *Chicago Tribune* and *Chicago American*, August 1, 1958.

27. *Brewers Journal* (September 1958).

28. Telephone interview with master brewer John Zappa, October 7, 2003.

29. A detailed account of Black Pride Beer can be found in the December 1969 issue of *Brewers Digest*.

CHAPTER 17

1. *Brewers Digest* (January 1968).
2. *Ibid.* (February 1968; July 1968; November 1968). Also see William Oscar Johnson, "Sports and Suds," *Sports Illustrated*, August 8, 1988.
3. *Brewers Digest* (May 1968; March 1969); *Modern Brewery Age* (July 2000). The *M.B.A.* article claims that the first batch of Meister Brau Lite was brewed at Buckeye's Toledo, Ohio, plant; Philip Van Munching, *Beer Blast* (New York: Random House, 1997), p. 31.
4. *Brewers Digest* (November 1969).
5. *Brewers Digest* (March 1969; August 1970); *Modern Brewery Age*, August 3, 1970.
6. *Chicago Tribune*, March 9, 1968; *Brewers Digest* (May 1968); *Modern Brewery Age*, August 3, 1970.
7. *Brewers Digest* (June 1968). The nearest competitor was probably Anheuser-Busch.
8. *Ibid.* (March 1969; June 1969); *Modern Brewery Age*, March, 1969, August, 1969.
9. *Brewers Digest* (August 1970).
10. *Ibid.*
11. *Ibid.* (October 1970).
12. *Ibid.* (May 1971); *Modern Brewery Age*, April 4, 1971.
13. *Brewers Digest* (January 1972).
14. *Ibid.*, (February 1972; March 1972).
15. *Ibid.* (April 1972).
16. *Chicago Tribune*, June 28, 30, July 11, 1972; *Brewers Digest* (August 1972).
17. *Brewers Digest* (August 1972); *Chicago Tribune*, July 12, 1972.
18. *Chicago Tribune*, December 22, 1972, February 7, 10, 1973.
19. *Ibid.* April 14, 19, July 3, 1973.
20. Van Munching, *op. cit.*, p. 64.
21. *Chicago Tribune*, April 30, 1974, November 30, 1997, March 7, 1998; *Brewers Digest* (September 1972).

CHAPTER 18

1. *Chicago Tribune*, February 27, 28, 1979.
2. *Brewers Digest* (April 1979).
3. *Chicago Tribune*, August 27, 1981.
4. Philip Van Munching, *Beer Blast* (New York: Random House, 1997), p. 46.
5. Dan Baum, *Citizen Coors* (New York: HarperCollins Publishers Inc. 2000), p. 145.
6. Harold M. Broderick, editor, *The Practical Brewer* (Madison, WI: Master Brewer's Association of the Americas, 1977), pp. 167–68.

7. *Stroh Container Co. v. Delphi Industries, Inc. 783 F. 2d 743 (8th Cir. 1986) Stroh Container Company Formerly Known as Jos. Schlitz Brewing Company.*

8. Eugene F. Zelek, Jr., "Legal Aspects of Sensory Analysis," *Food Technology* (November 1990).

9. *Brewers Digest* (July 1971).

10. *Ibid.*

11. Baum, op. cit., p. 145.

12. *Chicago Tribune,* February 27, 1977.

13. *Modern Brewery Age,* September 13, 1999.

14. *Chicago Tribune,* November 4, 1977.

15. E-mail, May 25, 2001.

CHAPTER 19

1. Van Munching, *op. cit.,* p. 46.

2. *Chicago Tribune,* March 16, April 8, 1977.

3. *Brewers Digest* (October 1978).

4. *Ibid.,* (April 1978).

5. *Ibid.,* (December 1978).

6. *Chicago Tribune,* November 4, 1977, January 24, 1978.

7. *Ibid,* October 13, 1977, February 3, 1978; *Brewers Digest* (June 1978).

8. *Chicago Tribune,* August 9, 1978.

9. Interview, November 21, 2000.

10. *Chicago Tribune,* January 6, 1978.

11. *Ibid.,* June 6, 1978.

12. *Ibid.,* August 9, 1978.

13. *Ibid.,* August 9, 1978.

14. *Brewers Digest* (September 1979).

15. *Chicago Tribune,* October 14, 1979.

16. Not for attribution.

17. Not for attribution.

18. Not for attribution.

19. *Stroh Container Co. v. Delphi Industries, Inc. 783 F. 2d 743 (8th Circuit 1986) Stroh Container Company Formerly Known as Jos. Schlitz Brewing Company.*

20. Interview, June 6, 2001.

21. *Chicago Tribune,* April 4, 1983.

22. E-mail, January 31, 2001.

23. Interview, May 8, 2001.

24. Interview, June 6, 2001.

25. Zelek Jr., *op. cit.,* p. 168.

26. Interview, May 8, 2001.

CHAPTER 20

1. *La Crosse Tribune*, August 6, 1999.
2. Interview, November 4, 2000.
3. *Chicago Tribune*, June 18, 1980.
4. *Ibid.*, November 15, 1978; June 18, 1980.
5. *Ibid.*, January 1, 1978.
6. *Ibid.*, September 1, 1979.
7. *Ibid.*, November 15, 1978.
8. *Ibid.*, November 15, 1978.
9. *Ibid.*, August 2, 1981.
10. *Ibid.*, November 15, 1978.
11. *Brewers Digest* (March 1980; November 1979).
12. *Chicago Tribune*, November 15, 1978; *Brewers Digest*, (July 1980).
13. *Chicago Tribune*, July 3, 1981, February 25, 1982; *Brewers Digest*, (November 1981).
14. *Chicago Tribune*, July 25, 1981.
15. *Ibid.*, July 28, 1981; *Brewers Digest*, September, 1981.
16. *Ibid.*, August 1, 1981.
17. *Ibid.*, July 25, 1981; August 27, 1981.
18. *Ibid.*, August 2, 1981.
19. *Ibid.*, August 5, 1981.
20. *Ibid.*, August 6, 1981.
21. *Ibid.*, August 27, 1981.
22. *Ibid.*, August 6, 1981.
23. *Chicago Tribune*, August 24, 1981.
24. *Brewers Digest* (November 1981).
25. *Chicago Tribune*, October 22, 1981.
26. *Brewers Digest* (November 1981).
27. *Chicago Tribune*, February 19, 1982.
28. *La Crosse Tribune*, February 22, 1999.

CHAPTER 21

1. *Brewers Digest* (July 1982).
2. *Ibid.*, (August 1982).
3. *Chicago Tribune*, February 16, June 19, 1978.
4. *Brewers Digest* (September 1978, October 1980).
5. *Chicago Tribune*, June 30, 1983.
6. *Brewers Digest* (January 1983).
7. *Ibid.*, June, 1983.
8. As quoted in *Twelve Pack Newsletter*, Minnesota Beer Wholesalers Association, *Brewers Digest* (June 1983).

9. *Chicago Tribune*, November 6, 1984, October 13, 1987.
10. *Ibid.*, November 17, 1984.
11. *Brewers Digest* (February 1985).
12. *Ibid.*, (August 1985).
13. *Ibid.*, (April 1982).
14. Interview, May 8, 2001.

CHAPTER 22

1. *Brewers Digest* (August 1986).
2. *Ibid.*, (December 1986).
3. *Ibid.*, (April, June 1987).
4. *Ibid.*, (September 1987).
5. *Ibid.*, (February 1987).
6. *Ibid.*, May, 1980.
7. *La Crosse Tribune*, February 22, 1999.
8. *Chicago Tribune*, September 5, 1987.
9. *Ibid.*, September 5, 1987.
10. *Ibid.*, September 22, 1987.
11. *Ibid.*, September 22, 1987.
12. *Brewers Digest* (October 1987) 8; *Chicago Tribune*, September 5, 1987.
13. *Chicago Tribune*, January 29, 1988.
14. *Ibid.*, September 29, 1988.
15. *Chicago Tribune*, February 22, 1988.
16. *Brewers Digest* (February 1989).
17. *Chicago Tribune*, December 30, 1989, January 3, 1990.
18. *Ibid.*, December 30, 1989.
19. *Ibid.*, December 30, 1989, January 3, 1990.
20. *Ibid.*, January 25, 1991.
21. *Ibid.*, June 2, 1991.
22. Interview, May 8, 2001.
23. *Chicago Tribune*, June 2, 1999.
24. *Modern Brewery Age* (March 2001).
25. *La Crosse Tribune*, March 1, 1996.

CHAPTER 23

1. *Brewers Digest* (December 1993). *Chicago Tribune*, November 1–2, 1993.
2. *Brewers Digest* (December 1993) 11.
3. *Chicago Tribune*, August 9, 1995, November 3, 1996.
4. *Ibid.*, August 22, 1995.
5. *Brewers Digest* (April 1996).
6. *Modern Brewery Age*, March, 2001.

7. *La Crosse Tribune*, March 1, 1996.
8. *Ibid.*, March 1, 1996.
9. *Chicago Tribune*, September 11, 1996.
10. *La Crosse Tribune*, March 1, 1996.
11. *Chicago Tribune*, July 2, 1996.
12. *Ibid.*, September 11, 1996; June 12, 1997.
13. *Ibid.*, September 11, 1996.
14. *Ibid.*, June 12, 1997.
15. *Ibid.*, March 19, 1997.
16. *Ibid.*, January 31, 1999.
17. *Crain's Detroit Business* (February 1999).
18. *Chicago Tribune*, January 31, 1999.
19. *Brewers Digest* (January 1999).
20. *Beloit Daily News*, May 29, 1999.
21. *Chicago Tribune*, August 9, 1999.

CHAPTER 24

1. *Chicago Tribune*, September 5, 1982.
2. *Ibid.*, September 5, 1982.
3. *Chicago Tribune*, September 26, 1982.
4. *Ibid.*, September 26, 1982.
5. *Chicago Tribune*, October 5, 1982.
6. *Ibid.*, September 26, 1982.
7. *Ibid.*, September 13, 1983; *Chicago Sun-Times*, February 4, 2001.
8. *Ibid.*, September 13, 1983, March 6, 2001.
9. *Ibid.*, October 5, December 30, 1982, September 9, 1983.
10. *Ibid.*, January 11, 1983.
11. *Ibid.*, September 13, 1983.
12. *Ibid.*, August 11, 1983.
13. *Ibid.*, September 9, 1983.
14. I have to make a personal observation as to the reaction at the time by some Chicagoans to the agreement between Jackson and his organization, Operation PUSH, and the Anheuser-Busch Brewing Company. Shortly after the agreement between PUSH and A-B went public, I was sitting in a bar near Midway Airport on Chicago's Southwest Side, sucking on a very sour Heineken. A beer driver for G. Heileman came in for a delivery and turned to a couple of patrons sitting at the bar and enjoying their Budweisers.

"What are you drinking that nigger beer for?" the driver barked to the two Budweiser drinkers. "Don't you know that Jesse Jackson sits on the board of directors at Bud?"

After about five minutes of everyone in the bar arguing back and forth as to whether Jackson really sat on the board of directors at Anheuser-Busch, or perhaps even owned a part of A-B or one of its distributorships, the Old

Style driver left, having stirred the pot, but the heated Jackson "discussion" went on for the next hour.

15. *Chicago Tribune*, November 17, 1998, April 8, 2001.
16. *Ibid.*, April 8, 2001.
17. *Chicago Sun-Times*, February 4, 2001.
18. *Ibid.*, February 4, 2001; *Chicago Tribune*, November 17, 1998.
19. *Chicago Sun-Times*, February 4, 2001.
20. *Ibid.*, February 4, 2001.
21. *Ibid.*, March 8, 2001.
22. *Chicago Tribune*, April 8, 2001.
23. *Ibid.*, June 17, 1991.
24. *Ibid.*, June 17, 1991.
25. *Ibid.*, June 27, 1991.
26. *Ibid.*, July 4, 1991.
27. *Ibid.*, July 4, 1991.
28. *Ibid.*, July 4, 1991.
29. *Chicago Tribune*, August 8, 1991.
30. J. Douglas Allen-Taylor, "Liquid Trouble," *MetroActive*: Boulevards New Media, Inc., July 24–30, 1997.
31. *Chicago Tribune*, August 22, 1991.

CHAPTER 25

1. *Chicago Sun-Times*, March 15, 1989; *Modern Brewery Age* (September 1989).
2. *Modern Brewery Age* (September 1989).
3. *Chicago Tribune*, July 13, 1989.
4. *Chicagoland Brew News* (December/January 1998).
5. E-mail, March 15, 2001.
6. *Ibid.*
7. E-mail, February 23, 2001.
8. E-mail, February 22, 2001.
9. E-mail, March 15, 2001.
10. *Ibid.*
11. E-mail, February 22, 2001.
12. *Chicago Tribune*, February 1, 1995.
13. *Ibid.*, June 27, 1988.
14. E-mail, March 15, 2001.
15. Interview, May 8, 2001.
16. *Baderbrau Tips*, Pavichevich Brewing Company.
17. http://www.atf.treas.gov/regulations/27cfr7.pdf.
18. Not for attribution.
19. *Oakland Tribune*, May 1, 1991.
20. *Modern Brewery Age* (July 1991, May 1993).

21. *Chicago Tribune*, January 15, 1996.
22. *Ibid.*
23. *Ibid.*, April 30, 1997.
24. Not for attribution.
25. *Press Publications*, date unknown.
26. *Chicago Tribune*, June 27, 1997.
27. *Chicago Sun-Times*, November 21, 1996.
28. *Chicago Tribune*, June 11, 20, 1997.
29. E-mail, July 23, 2001.
30. E-mail, February 22, 2001.
31. *Ibid.*
32. E-mail, February 23, 2001.
33. http://www.gooseisland.com/beers/brewery.html.
34. Telephone interview, October 31, 2005.

Index

T

U